Sectarian War

Pakistan's Sunni–Shia Violence and
its Links to the Middle East

Sectarian War

Pakistan's Sunni–Shia Violence and
its Links to the Middle East

KHALED AHMED

OXFORD
UNIVERSITY PRESS

OXFORD
UNIVERSITY PRESS

Great Clarendon Street, Oxford OX2 6DP

Oxford University Press is a department of the University of Oxford.
It furthers the University's objective of excellence in research, scholarship,
and education by publishing worldwide in

Oxford New York

Auckland Cape Town Dar es Salaam Hong Kong Karachi
Kuala Lumpur Madrid Melbourne Mexico City Nairobi
New Delhi Shanghai Taipei Toronto

With offices in

Argentina Austria Brazil Chile Czech Republic France Greece
Guatemala Hungary Italy Japan Poland Portugal Singapore
South Korea Switzerland Turkey Ukraine Vietnam

Oxford is a registered trademark of Oxford University Press
in the UK and in certain other countries

ISBN 978-0-19-547956-0

Typeset in Adobe Garamond Pro
Printed in Pakistan by
Kagzi Printers, Karachi.
Published by
Ameena Saiyid, Oxford University Press
No. 38, Sector 15, Korangi Industrial Area, P.O. Box 8214,
Karachi-74900, Pakistan.

To Najam, who 'sent' me to the Woodrow Wilson Center, to Maryam-Eman and Taimur, who gave me emotional sustenance, and to my mother, who gave me her word that she won't die before my return, and kept it.

Contents

Acknowledgements

Sectarian War was written during a nine-month stay at the Woodrow Wilson Center in Washington D.C. in 2006. I cannot forget the inspiration provided to my work by people who managed the Center and the scholars who worked there. I will always remember President and Director of the Center, Lee H. Hamilton, a member of the bipartisan group that had published its *Iraq Study Group Report* that year. Listening to him often during lunch, I was convinced that if there were more people like him in the United States, the world would be a better place.

A very protective Robert M. Hathaway, Director, Asia Program, at the Center, 'micro-edited' the manuscript and guided me in correcting the mistakes I was making and encouraged me to persist in the line of inquiry I had embraced. Ambassador William Milam, who writes a column in the *Daily Times*, self-effacing when it came to discussing his work, produced the most useful insights in conversations we had as he kindly helped me get along in Washington. Another Pakistan and India 'hand' Dennis Kux was similarly helpful in getting me to 'cope' with the social side of D.C.

Outside the Center, I will always fondly carry with me the memory of the late Khalid Hasan, correspondent of the *Daily Times* in Washington, who lent me a thousand dollars upon my arrival to help me get myself a place to live. There was Shuja Nawaz whose classic study of the Pakistan Army helped my work, apart from his hospitality and inimitable kind-heartedness. Visits with my learned World Bank cousin Shahid Javed Burki and other World Bank friends, Khalid Ikram—the son of the famous Pakistani historian S.M. Ikram—and Ijaz Nabi, now teaching at LUMS in Lahore, are precious memories of my stay in Washington.

Sincere gratitude is in order for three great academics in the United States: Ayesha Jalal, Vali Raza Nasr and Yitzhak Nakash, the last named having kindly accepted to preside over the presentation of the first draft of this book.

I will always be beholden to Murtaza Solangi of VOA (Voice of America), chief of Pakistan Radio in 2009, because without him and Khalid Hasan I could not have tackled the logistics of my departure from D.C. for home. And I cannot forget the good time I spent in the various restaurants of D.C. together with Sadi Mirza, the most widely read engineer I have known.

Last but not least, I am grateful to the Trustees and Advisory Council of the Fellowship Fund for Pakistan committee in Karachi, headed in 2006 by Mr Ishrat Hussain, Governor, State Bank of Pakistan who accepted the plan of this book and allowed me the stipend that made my stay in the US possible.

Introduction

You talk about God a lot, and you make me feel guilty
by using that word. You better watch out!
That word will poison you, if you use it
to have power over me.
                    – Rumi, *A Man and a Woman Arguing*[1]

Tens of thousands of lives have been lost in Pakistan's sectarian war in the last two decades of the twentieth century. And the mayhem continues into the twenty-first century. A very tolerable level of Sunni–Shia tension was inherited by the country from the British Raj, but the two sects squared off violently only after 1980. Like all internecine conflicts, the war of the sects has been characterised by extreme cruelty. It coincided with the onset of the Islamic Revolution of Imam Khomeini in Iran and the threat its 'export' posed to Saudi Arabia and other Arab states across the Gulf.

Pakistanis invariably blame Saudi Arabia and Iran for the violence since they funded and trained the partisans of this war. They are aware that Pakistan was subjected to someone else's 'relocated' war. Much of the internal dynamic of this war remains hidden from public view. A kind of embarrassment over the phenomenon of Muslim-killing-Muslim has prevented Pakistanis from inquiring frankly into how the two hostile states were able to transplant their conflict in Pakistan.

Sectarian violence has also drawn its strength from the past. The schismatic past was concealed behind two important layers of governance. First, the British Raj was able to almost completely uproot the Sunni–Shia confrontation during its tenure from 1857 to 1947. A refusal to recognise the jurisprudence of *takfir* (apostatisation) and a competent encoding of the Muslim Family Law, separating the two sects, almost buried the conflict that had its seeds in the seventh century.

The Pakistan Movement in India, which resulted in the creation of Pakistan against the wishes of Great Britain and the secularists of India, was spearheaded by the two sects together. The movement carried the promise of a finally successful coexistence and possible integration of the two sects. Early governance in Pakistan was in some ways an extension of the secular impartiality of the British Raj. However, after Independence in 1947, two developments took place that sowed the seeds of sectarianism that were to bear fruit later on.

Pakistan began to look for its identity in the stance its representative political party, the All-India Muslim League, had adopted during its competition with the secular and much larger All-India National Congress. Because of the early military conflict with India in 1947, Pakistan's nationalism began to coalesce positively around Islam and negatively around India. Its textbooks sought their exemplary personalities in historical Muslim 'utopias' and imagined 'golden ages' that highlighted the particularism of Muslim identity instead of its 'liminal' cross-fertilisation with Hinduism at the cultural level.

Pakistani textbooks went back to pre-British Raj days and selected periods of Muslim rule where pluralism was at its lowest, and highlighted instead the separation of Hinduism from Islam. (Liberal Mughal kings who treated the Hindus well also accepted the Shia as Muslims.) Most of this selection turned out to be sectarian. While it set Muslims and Hindus apart, it also emphasised the conflict between Sunni and Shia communities. In the early period of Pakistan's history, ignorance of the schism—or amnesia induced by the British Raj interregnum—allowed this bias to go unnoticed.

During the Saudi–Iranian standoff in 1980, Pakistan was drawn to the Saudi side for a number of reasons. It had a large expatriate labour force stationed in the Arab Middle East, particularly in the region of the Gulf where the Gulf Cooperation Council (GCC) was formed in 1980 to ward off the Iranian threat. Before 9/11, almost 80 per cent of Pakistan's 'foreign remittances' were earned from this region. Saudi Arabia was also the most important ally—

after the United States—in 'frontline' Pakistan's war against the Soviet Union in the 1980s.

Saudi Arabia funded the jihad, it bought Pakistan its first instalment of the forty F-16 warplanes from the United States, it gave Pakistan the seed-money for its Zakat fund which now stands at almost Rs 12 billion annually to be distributed among the poor but which went predominantly to the seminaries during the 1980s. Saudi Arabia allowed Pakistan to buy Saudi oil on 'deferred payment', which meant free oil. The 'Islamization' of Pakistan under the military ruler General Ziaul Haq proceeded under the tutelage of Saudi Arabia.

It is not possible to examine the Saudi–Iranian conflict exclusively in a non-sectarian perspective. The schism was reflected in the Afghan jihad, but after the jihad ended, it was reflected in the ouster, from the first government-in-exile, of mujahideen belonging to the Shia militias. The Afghan mujahideen government was set up in Peshawar in 1989, but, under Saudi pressure, the Shia militias were not given representation in it. The rise of the Taliban in 1996, quickly recognised by Saudi Arabia and Pakistan, was in a way a reversal of Iran at Saudi hands in the final count. The Taliban were recruited from the Deobandi and Wahhabi outfits, which were historically anti-Shia.

In 1986, the Deobandi seminaries of Pakistan and India had issued *fatwas* of apostatisation against the Shia population and thus upheld the manifesto of the Sipah-e-Sahaba, a party formed in 1985 in Pakistan on the basis of its demand that the Shia be declared non-Muslim by the state of Pakistan through an amendment to the Constitution. The state had already set the precedence of apostatising Muslim communities and declaring them non-Muslims under the Second Amendment of 1974.

The anti-Shia *fatwas* were 'managed' through a Deobandi scholar of India, Manzur Numani, who had earlier written a book against Imam Khomeini and Iran. Funded by the Saudi charity Rabita al-Alam al-Islami (World Islamic League), he wrote to the Deobandi seminaries of India and Pakistan, asking them to give their juristic opinion on the Shia faith. In 1986, all of them sent to him *fatwas* declaring the Shia *kafir* or non-Muslim. No attention was paid to the character of the Shia faith in Pakistan, a grave mistake made at the political level.

The Shia of Pakistan had developed as a community tied to the teachings of Najaf. Their religious leaders followed the school of Najaf, which meant non-acceptance of the Iranian brand of faith founded on the concept of *Velayat-e-Faqih* by Imam Khomeini, giving the Shia clergy the right to rule under the divine charisma of the ruling jurist. There was a strong implication in this of the sharing by the ruling jurist of the divinity of the innocent Twelve Imams. The Shia community of Pakistan was not politically aligned to its clergy, it was even less connected with the clerical hierarchy of Iran. The Shia of certain regions of Pakistan began going to Qum instead of Najaf only after the state of Pakistan, under General Zia, decided to collaborate with Saudi Arabia.

Laws promulgated in Pakistan against the apostatisation of the Shia do not contain any provision banning the issuance of *fatwas* as 'private' edicts that violate the sovereignty of the state. The state is reluctant to bring the controversy of the apostatising *fatwas* into the courts of law because the courts themselves function under the Sharia and will find it hard to disagree with the *fatwas* as edicts. The state rightly refuses to recognise the Shia as a separate community and has not given them a separate status in the census, meaning that the state does not 'officially' discriminate on the basis of sect.[2]

It is generally agreed that the Shia are 15 to 20 per cent of the total population, with significant concentrations in Quetta in Balochistan, Kurram Agency in the tribal areas, and Gilgit in the Northern Areas (now Gilgit-Baltistan). If the Northern Areas is given the status of a separate province, it will be a Shia-majority province. Pakistan is second only to Iran in respect of the number of Shias living in it.

THE STATE AND THE IDEA OF 'SEPARATE' IDENTITIES

Violence against the Shia is related to the question of identity. Pakistan began by positing only two permissible identities in the state: the Muslim and the non-Muslim. It wanted the two classifications 'separated' before promising them full rights of citizenship under the Constitution. The idea of 'separating' Muslims and non-Muslims was planted in the Pakistani mind by two separately accepted doctrines, one secular and the other religious. The Muslim League had put forward its demand for a 'separation' based on religion in India. It asked the British Raj to give Muslims representation separately from the non-Muslims. This was in opposition to the secular Congress that claimed to represent the entire population, Hindu and non-Hindu.

Muslim support to the Muslim League stance grew in the midst of communal tensions in India on the eve of Independence. The British administration in India had allowed Muslims separate representation through Communal Awards since 1909. The idea of 'separate electorates' was thus born, demanded by the Muslims and rejected by the secular Congress which relied on the principle of representation embodied in joint electorates, implying that there was just one nation in India.[3] The Muslim League claimed that there were two nations and moved gradually towards the demand for a separate state as communal violence gathered strength in India.

After 1947, the Muslim League did not abandon its two-nation doctrine and insisted on embodying it in the new state to demonstrate that its pre-1947 demand was right. When Pakistan's first prime minister, Liaquat Ali Khan, unfurled the Pakistani flag in front of the Constituent Assembly on 11 August 1947, he proudly indicated the white patch on it as representing the non-Muslim minorities.[4] The flag was the old all-green Muslim League flag modified to contain the white band for the minorities. The prime minister insisted that the flag actually promised the minorities the rights that the Congress in India was not willing to give.

The Muslim League also recommended separate electorates in the Constitution that had yet to be passed, ignoring the fact that in India separate electorates were demanded by Muslims as a minority, but in Pakistan it was imposing separate electorates on the non-Muslims as a majority.[5] This separation contained the seeds of a later polemic about who should be put in the green section of the flag and who should be consigned to the smaller white section. It developed that there were strong historical impulses in the Muslim community to refuse Muslim identity to certain Muslim sects.

The secular view supporting 'separation' and the religious view mandating 'separation' seem to exist in parallel in the history of Pakistan. It is impossible to accept that the non-clerical but rightwing Muslim League leaders who ruled Pakistan after 1947 were unaware that an Islamic state living under the Sharia will never allow non-Muslims a status equal to the Muslims. Their 'separation' envisaged equality, but the clerical 'separation' envisaged inequality.

Under Islamic Sharia, non-Muslims live in the state as a *zimmi* (protected) population after paying a special tax called *jizya*. The Muslim League leaders could not have been unaware that many pre-British Muslim kings of India had imposed *jizya* on their non-Muslim subjects; yet they promised the protesting non-Muslim members of the Constituent Assembly that they would be equal citizens and not debarred from important state offices.

On the other hand, the Islamic doctrine clearly excluded non-Muslims from higher offices of the state. The non-Muslim members were even more vehement in their demand in 1949 that the Objectives Resolution foreshadowing the Constitution of Pakistan not be based on the Quran and Sunnah. The 'minorities' did not want to be treated 'separately' and they did not believe the non-clerical leaders of the Muslim League when they assured them of non-discrimination.[6] The non-Muslims were not willing to be placed in the white patch of the Pakistani flag.

It is somewhat surprising to note that even those Muslim members of the Constituent Assembly, who were potentially a minority because of their sect, did not see through the Objectives Resolution. One Ahmedi minister of the government, against whom there was already a campaign of exclusion, actually supported the principle of 'separation' embedded in the Objectives Resolution of 1949. In 1993, when the Shia community realised that they, too, could be lifted from the green section of the national flag and placed in the white patch, they tried their best to oppose the principle of 'insult' (of the Companions of the Prophet) as a yardstick of apostatisation.[7]

The Shia, too, had ignored the entire centuries-old jurisprudence of the Islamic schism and supported the 'principle of separation' at Independence. They even supported the apostatisation of the Ahmedis in 1974 without realising that, once established, the principle of apostatisation, or rendering a Muslim non-Muslim, could be applied to other sects too. The tendency to regard sect as a separate religion was always there but was ignored by its victims.

Had *takfir* or rendering Muslims non-Muslim not been accompanied by mandated inequality and imposed disabilities, the Muslim sects could have accepted the state's process of self-cleansing. But, as shown in the case of the Ahmedis, persecution followed the act of *takfir*. Patterns of state-backed and vigilante persecution after *takfir* follow the patterns of genocide noticed in the tribal warfare in Africa.[8]

The Shia community now realises that if they are apostatised under pressure from the powerful Deobandi seminaries and their state-protected armed militias, they might have to endure the fate of Hindus, Christians, Sikhs and Ahmedis. They also grasp the irony of the fact that the Ahmedis are non-Muslims only in Pakistan and in their passports; the moment they cross into India they become Muslims again. If Pakistan were to apostatise the Shia formally, it would be hard put to prevent them from becoming Muslims again when they visit Iran or Iraq. So involved and subjective is the question of identity in the state of Pakistan.

THE STATE AND NATIONAL IDENTITY

Human identity is moulded by many existential factors. Man acquires his earliest self-identification from his parents. Since the parents derive their identity from the community, the individual grows to accept the identity of the group too.[9] And if he lives in a state, he also responds to the stimuli offered by the state in favour of a 'national' identity. Each individual derives satisfaction from belonging to a group. He obtains validation of the views he holds and the acts he performs from this nexus called *asabiya* by Ibn Khaldun.[10]

The *asabiya* binds one to one's family, to one's tribe and finally to the state. A state is rarely the container of one *asabiya*. Its subjects will either have one main *asabiya* in majority—while the other identities rest in the class of minorities—or it will have more than one big *asabiya* and will need to keep its mandated national identity so abstractly defined that the major identities do not clash. More than one big *asabiya* will otherwise give rise to movements of separatism, throwing open the possibility of the creation of a new state in conflict with the one it has separated from.

Small groups do not wish to be treated as minorities. They wish to lose their identity in the larger group, unless the small group sees benefit in being separate. When is such separation desirable? In India, the Muslim experience indicated fear of discrimination under communal conditions. This fear sprang from the consciousness that for centuries a Muslim 'conqueror minority' had ruled over the majority Hindu population who might now take revenge on them. They perceived governance during the self-government period after 1900 under the British Raj as skewed in favour of the Hindu majority. Objectively, the minority felt threatened when it saw the majority community making efforts to strengthen its religious identity in such a way as to exclude the minorities. Seeking or awarding a separate classification is never beneficial.[11]

The overarching state, which was supposed to protect all identities against the empowerment of a single identity, did not seem equipped to protect them. After 1947, the Muslims began to move towards an emphasis on their Islamic identity and did not discuss too seriously the repercussions such an emphasis will have on the non-Muslims. They quickly forgot that they had demanded separate electorates as a minority in British India but were now mandating separate electorates for the non-Muslims of Pakistan from the position of a majority. The non-Muslims were fearful of being 'separated' as they equated it with 'exclusion'. Pakistan, in fact, did two things wrong: it separated the group identities while it should have merged them; and it merged the regional identities (provinces) while it should have given them autonomy through decentralisation. It mandated 'separate electorates' and formed, under duress, One Unit (one province) called West Pakistan out of four geographic entities.

What the non-Muslims implicitly wanted was a system of multiple identities in Pakistan. It meant that the state should stand aside and allow individual citizens to have whatever identity they wanted. They wanted the state to define citizenship in such a way as to assimilate the smaller identities. If the state became the guardian of multiple identities within its borders it would have allowed as many identities in a single individual as he may have wanted. This would have watered down the group *asabiya* and removed a major cause of aggression from society. The state of Pakistan instead held up a single identity for the 'nation' and sought to include the 'minorities' separately with 'assurances' of equal citizenship that did not appear credible. The non-Muslims saw in it a subliminal message that they could avoid exclusion only if they converted to Islam.

The state's behaviour in East Pakistan remained suspicious because there was a large Hindu population attached to the majority Muslim population through the 'multiple' Bengali identity based on language. From the history of governance in East Pakistan, it becomes apparent that Pakistan's insistence on separate electorates was meant to oust the Hindus from the representative institutions of the state.[12] In the event, the state was not able to eliminate the 'dual' Bengali identity. Later, in Sindh where the Sindhi identity too tended to be multiple on the basis of language, it sought to establish a coercive single identity. Today, Sindhi nationalism in Pakistan is separatist in nature.

Nations are said to be formed after the state is created through programmes of 'nation-building'. In the case of the Muslims of India, however, it is claimed by Pakistan's official nationalism that the Muslim nation was formed first in India in opposition to Hinduism. The Muslims of India collectively 'dreamed' of a homeland where they could practise their religion and live according to it. The All-India Muslim League, therefore, welcomed only Muslims into its fold. Yet it was led by Jinnah, an Ismaili who converted to Shiism, but with firm secular credentials who found Gandhi's frequent reference to religion distasteful when both were members of the Congress.[13]

The non-Muslims of East and West Pakistan accepted that they would live in Pakistan for two reasons. First, was the personality of the Muslim League leadership, which had abstained from expressing its political agenda in Islamic-clerical terms.[14] The non-Muslims, mostly belonging to the lower caste, saw the anti-Jinnah fundamentalist Muslim clergy of India aligned with the Congress whose predominantly upper-class Hindu membership they feared because of its deep-seated acceptance of untouchability. Second, was the claim of 'equality' made by the Muslim League for all castes and creeds based on the 'egalitarian' message of the Quran. The non-Muslims agreed to stay in Muslim Pakistan in the hope that equal citizenship would gradually allow the state to accept multiple identities.

The Shia in Pakistan continued the attitude of indifference towards their faith that they had imbibed during the British Raj. The continuation of the Sunni–Shia merger of identities after 1947 proceeded on the basis of the erasure of the collective Shia memory. This is apparent in the fact that the Shia hadith collections that most offend the Sunnis have remained untranslated from Arabic and Persian. On the other hand, Islamization in Pakistan has been underpinned by a massive publication of Sunni hadith collections in Urdu. Most Shias simply do not know the rituals that differentiate them from the Sunnis. This has happened in spite of the fact that their mosques and graveyards, their *namaz* and their religious festivities have always been different and separate from the Sunnis.

During *ashura* (first ten days of the month of Muharram when the martyrdom of Imam Husayn is mourned) Shia rituals of self-flagellation separated them from the Sunnis, but many Sunnis tolerated this separation because of their Low Church reverence for Imam Ali and his sons, Imam Hasan and Imam Husayn. Compared to each other, the Shia, as opposed to the Sunnis, were seen making more of an effort to move in the direction of Sunni identity. In contrast to the Ismaili Shia community, the Twelver Shia community stepped more readily into the melting pot of identities in Pakistan.

THE STATE AND ITS STRATEGY OF 'EXCLUSION'

When the state mandates a narrow and well-defined identity for its citizens, it tends to exclude some communities. In the case of non-Muslims, a separate classification is made and they are placed there as citizens of lesser status. In the case of sects within Islam, the state of Pakistan has manifested two modes of operation. In the first mode, it uses *takfir* to convert the targeted Muslim sect into a non-Muslim category and clubs it together with self-confessed non-Muslims. It does so 'under great popular pressure' but does not take responsibility for what happens to the identity of the apostatised community after apostatisation. For instance, if the apostatised community finds it hard to accept the label of 'non-Muslim', and thus runs the risk of becoming indeterminate in identity, the state pays no attention to it. It then visits the 'indeterminate' community with punishment through regulations that appear absurd and impossible of observance.[15] This conforms to the theory of the inner and outer dimensions of identity: one is what one is because of one's self-perception; and one is what one is on the basis of how one is perceived by others. It also fits into the theory of rejection of an old identity and seeking a new one.[16] The state excludes certain communities by labelling them.

In the second mode, the state excludes certain communities by re-labelling itself. For instance, under General Zia it intensified the ideology under Sharia in such a manner that the Sunnis became redefined while the Shias became excluded from this redefinition. The enforcement of *zakat* (poor due collected by the state) forced the Shia community to elect a different identity by refusing to pay *zakat* to the state. The process of exclusion has leaned on the intensification of the Sunni identity, a kind of hyper-*asabiya* that took the Sunnis from a Low Church identity to a High Church one.[17] The state may say that it has not apostatised the Shia. It may assert that it will stand firm against the demands of *takfir* being made by the extremist Sunni clergy, but its organised campaign of intensification of the identity of the majority sect has already started the process of exclusion.

Pakistan began to Islamize the state after 1947 and reached a high point of social transformation in the 1980s when Islamization was done in the midst of jihad. The jihad against the Soviet Union and India was a deniable proxy war and required the organisation of militias as surrogates of the Pakistan army. The militias were armed and were embedded in the civil society of Pakistan. The state agreed tacitly to share its internal sovereignty with them as new centres of power. Most of the violence committed against the Shia came from these militias. States that embark upon genocide also rely on the institution of militias.[18] The *takfir* of the Shia was thus indirectly mandated by the state.

The Ahmedi community had no defence after it was excluded in 1974. The Shia community reacted differently to exclusion because its *takfir* was not done by amending the Constitution. It organised itself to face the coercion and violence of the Sunni militias. In this, it was assisted by the neighbouring state of Iran. The Shia began to come out of their 'forgotten' identity and began to 'push back'. The Shia clergy deployed their own militias and began to target-kill the offending Sunni clerics in contrast to the Sunni militias that targeted the Shia at large. This counter-aggression was doomed from the start for a number of reasons.

The Shia community was not able to follow its clergy because it was not 'empowered' by the state the same way as the Sunni clergy was. Shia clerics had been traditionally trained in Najaf and Qum but the Shias had not much knowledge about this tradition. When Ayatollah Khomeini came to power in Iran, they thought 'ayatollah' was a name rather than a title. There was no ayatollah of the Shia in Pakistan. If there was a Hojatul Islam (a lower rank than the ayatollah) in the district of Sahiwal in Punjab, they did not know him. One Pakistani had actually arisen to the rank of Grand Ayatollah at Najaf in Iraq, but the Pakistani Shia did not know him. He too, conscious that the Pakistani Shia community will pay him no regard, never visited Pakistan after leaving for Najaf as a youth.

The support from Iran was actually counterproductive. The Shia student militia that operated for some time in Punjab against the violence of the Sipah-e-Sahaba simply ignited more Deobandi violence. The jihadi militias were not available to the Shia community as the Shia jihad against the Soviet Union was based in Iran and was not allowed to merge with the Sunni militias in Pakistan by Saudi persuasion and Pakistan's growing official hostility. It was an unequal war in which the Shia were defeated. Many Shia citizens with means fled Pakistan never to return. Many Shias were killed simply because they were well known.

The pattern of target-killing by the Shia became rare but when it happened, a very prominent apostatising Sunni cleric was usually killed. Increasingly, the Shia were becoming ghettoised and therefore easy to kill. Regional identities rather than religious identities were given to them to mark them for persecution. The Hazaras of Quetta were killed as Hazaras and the Turis of the Kurram Agency were similarly treated, instead of as Shias. In Gilgit in the Northern Areas, where the Shia formed the local majority, the encounters were more bloody and offered a glimpse of the conflict involving entire communities, as in Iraq.

The Shia stopped marrying into the Sunni community although this pattern of behaviour was more observable among the middle and lower middle classes than in Pakistan's elite. The Shia 'discovered' their identity through the action of the state. A 'discovered' identity is usually accompanied with violence and responds to external stimuli.[19] This is so because the negative aspect of discovery of the self is 'recognition' by others of what one really is. The trauma of 'discovery' comes from a realisation that the identity assumed to have existed in the past is superior to the one that has to be lived. Suddenly it requires a special effort of resistance to be Shia in Pakistan. An opposition thus develops towards the Sunnis—some of them friends—who seem to be having an easier time existing in Pakistan.[20]

Gradually, the Sunni community has become sensitive to names too. In earlier times such Shia names as Naqvi, Jafri and Rizvi aroused no curiosity; now there is a tension in the air the moment the names are mentioned. Even then, one must assert that in Pakistani society names make no difference to most people; however, in certain regions of the country they have become a dangerous give-away. Among the secular Sunnis who seek to give no cause of complaint to the Shia, their Sunni names, like Abu Bakr and Umar—names that the Shia never take—become an embarrassment. The extremist Sunnis have begun to name their sons Muawiyya, the man who contested the caliphate of Ali and whose son Yazid got Imam Husayn martyred. A war of names is on because the history of the great schism is being regurgitated from the pulpit of the Sunni clergy under internal and external stimuli.

IDENTITY, INTIMIDATION AND VIOLENCE

The state may not clearly enunciate it but its 'ideology' will create classifications and affiliations resulting in violence that it may not want. When a community 'discovers' itself under the spur of intended or unintended 'exclusion', it gravitates to its inner core for protection. This 'inner core' identity resides in the narrative of Shiism represented by the clergy that was ignored in the past. A kind of group behaviour takes over, internalising morality and permitting intolerance of opposed identities. Intolerance is based on a group bias drawn from the human capacity of repugnance and hatred. Hatred is a natural phenomenon at the level of the individual. When an individual hates another individual there is always a clear reason for this hatred, usually a reaction to infliction of pain. Once affiliated to a group, an individual may feel hatred without personal cause. When you kill a Shia, there may be nothing that the murdered person may have done to hurt you. The Shia too responded increasingly from the identity of a group. Globalisation of information, bringing news of other communities being subjected to sectarian violence, also played a part in it. The news that Saddam Hussein was systematically persecuting the Shia of Iraq aroused different feelings among the Sunnis and the Shia of Pakistan, causing a 'dichotomy' of response at the national level.

When the sectarian trouble began in consequence of the Islamizing process initiated by General Zia in the 1980s, the press in Pakistan was not free. At the international level, too, there was very little information about the oppressed Shia communities in the Middle East. Because of the lack of freedom of expression in the Arab world, the Lebanese civil war (1975–1990) was not understood as the assertion of the majority Shia population. Even after 1979, when Iran began to come out in defence of the Shia minorities across the Gulf, there was nothing in the Pakistani press that would presage the advent of a Sunni–Shia conflict.

The press in Pakistan began its journey of freedom in 1986 when Prime Minister Mohammad Khan Junejo removed the punitive gag laws from the newspapers. This laid the foundation of a deluge of information on the functioning of the state and the state of religion in Pakistan. There was, however, a sharp dichotomy between the Urdu and the English-language press. The Urdu press understood the sectarian strife better than the English press, but it abstained from offering information and analysis on it for two reasons: because the newspapers were mostly owned by Sunnis affiliated with the Sunni religious parties and ran their newsrooms with the help of a young manpower drawn from the seminaries; and because of the general trend of not discussing sectarian violence out of a 'sense of shame'. On the English side, journalists who came from liberal backgrounds and lived in the secular spaces still existing in the country, lacked knowledge of the schism and did not possess the vocabulary in which to report and analyse sectarian developments.

When the killings intensified in the 1990s, they began to be reported along with bits of information about the groups who were doing the killing. The real information breakthrough came after 9/11 when the Western press and intelligence agencies began to 'reveal' a much deeper level of information based on their cooperation with the Arab intelligence agencies. Sectarian conflict now began to be identified with Saudi Arabia and Iran more clearly.

In the 2000s, revealing of Shia identity was enough to unleash violence from the militias earlier fielded by Pakistan in its deniable wars called jihad. Since the state had willingly surrendered a large measure of internal sovereignty to these militias it found itself incapable of controlling the identity-related violence. Its ideology, after its intensification by General Zia and jihad, inclined many state functionaries to privately challenge the 'religion' of the Shia. At the level of the communities, the big cities went through traumas incidental to the decaying of the state in the face of violence.

Moderate Muslims who previously rose to the defence of the Shia now tacitly chose to take the side of the Sunni killers 'by not protesting'. Intimidation was palpable, especially after a Low Church Sunni community (Barelvis), historically known to tolerate and mix with the Shia, was also subjected to violence in 2006. This intimidation, exercised by the sectarian militias, has resulted in widespread Sunni conversion to sectarianism because of its most important corollary, the Stockholm Syndrome, a security-driven desire to adopt the identity of the tormentor.[21]

The moderate or 'liminal' Sunni has succumbed to intimidation in a variety of ways. Pakistan's sectarian scene needs to be studied much more deeply than it has been so far. On closer clinical scrutiny, it will be discovered that the most significant and powerful role in violence is that of intimidation. Even those who take great risks in defending the Shia community are not free of the Stockholm Syndrome. Pushed to the wall, the Shia community has turned inwards and has refused to join the Sunni moderates in loving their tormentors. But there are ways in which even the Shia have tried to move close to their killers in order to lessen some of their suffering, especially through the device of blaming the United States of America every time Shia deaths are clearly owed to sectarian Sunni action. This has happened despite the fact that their 'discovered' identity is greatly buttressed by the Shia revival in the region, led by Iran.

The Islamic Revolution in Iran has brought to the fore the country's traditional antipathy towards the West in general and the United States in particular. Iranian nationalism has melded with clerical Islam to further intensify this antipathy. The Shia clergy of Pakistan is obligated to follow the Iranian line. This brings them close to the Sunni clergy in Pakistan which regularly issues *fatwas* of death on America because of America's betrayal of the Muslims in the Middle East and its invasion of Afghanistan.

The mainstream Shia party, Tehrik-e-Jafaria, often condemning the Americans after an orgy of Shia-killing by the Sunni militias, joined the clerical alliance, the Muttahida Majlis-e-Amal (MMA), on the eve of the 2002 elections. Starting 2003, the Shia were regularly massacred during their *ashura,* but the Shia party clerics kept blaming the Americans in tune with Grand Ayatollah Sistani in Iraq. This manifestation of the Stockholm Syndrome did not work for the Shia of Pakistan. Shia scholar Hassan Turabi, a member of the MMA council, was killed through a suicide-bomber in 2006 soon after he had spoken at a Sunni clerical rally condemning Israel and the United States for the invasion of Lebanon. Intimidation, the most outstanding element in the Islamic wave of the twenty-first century, has paralysed the moderate Muslim in the Islamic world. Intimidation of the moderate and the 'liminal' has been found to be one of the eight ways to genocide in the case of Rwanda.[22] In Pakistan, this was illustrated by the massacre of the moderate pro-Shia Barelvis in Karachi in 2006.

LOW CHURCH, HIGH CHURCH AND WAHHABISM

Pakistan was the western stretch of the British Raj. The British colonial administration treated it as a bastion of low-growth tribal territory with a level of municipal order that compared badly with the eastern and central reaches of the Raj. Punjab had brackish water and cities had come up along fast-flowing rivers at places where sweet underground water was available. A canal system, unique in the world of the early twentieth century, was introduced and new cities developed along the new irrigation network. The countryside was sparsely populated and was 'settled' by the colonial administration through large feudal holdings distributed among its loyal elites. What is now Pakistan was predominantly Low Church where Islam was practised around the shrines of mystical saints who provided religious guidance through folklore.[23]

The saints, also called Sufis, focused on 'inclusion' and cultural coexistence with potentially conflictual religious and sectarian identities. The more warlike Muslims in the north looked at the 'irenic' or 'conflict-avoiding' approach of the sufi with contempt. The Sufi culture, centred around shrines, sought symbiosis with other religions and was strong in Punjab and Sindh. Almost 90 per cent of Pakistan was dominated by this Low Church cult of the saints. Muslim culture grew out of the common man's desire to live in peace and be entertained in a rough environment where life was difficult.

The territory of the Pushtuns beyond the Indus River was always High Church. The Pushtuns lived under a tribal code that conformed to some of the features of the Islamic Sharia taught in the more settled urban culture close to the old Mughal capital city of Delhi. For instance, the system of *diyat* or 'blood-money' under Sharia is practised under Pushtunwali but remains unknown in the non-Pushtun regions of Pakistan. The Pushtuns of what is today the Frontier Province and Afghanistan were attracted to the strict madrassa-related Islam dominant in the cities of central and western India. They flocked to the city of Deoband in today's

Haryana state to be trained as prayer-leaders and thus absorbed a High Church version of Islam. Committed to the madrassa, they tended to reject mysticism and the shrines of the Sufi saints like all Deobandis of India.

In the fullness of time, this tendency was to bring the Pushtuns close to the Arab Islam that mostly rejects mysticism, and to Wahhabi Islam that is vehemently opposed to the 'hybrid' culture produced by the Sufis. Pakistan, dominated by feudal landlords who frequently traced their lineage to the local saints, promoted the Barelvi version of Islam that accepted mysticism and was centred around the shrines of the great Sufis.[24] When the Pakistan Movement began in India under the leadership of the All-India Muslim League, it found the Muslim High Church of Deoband aligned with the All-India Congress party. Only the Low Church Barelvis were in favour of the Pakistan Movement.

Two developments after 1947 caused the gradual transformation of the state in Pakistan from Low Church to High Church. First was the transfer of the Congress-aligned Deobandi and Ahle Hadith (Wahhabi) seminaries from India to the big cities of Pakistan. For several decades, starting in the second decade of the twentieth century, the Deobandi–Ahle Hadith leaders remained loyal to the Congress because of Gandhi's espousal of the pan-Islamic Khilafat Movement. By the end of the 1930s, Muslim disenchantment with Congress-dominated local governments in Northern India proved that for the Hindu leaders the Khilafat Movement was simply a political stratagem to isolate the Muslim League.

The second development in favour of High Church in Pakistan was the requirement of the new state to legislate according to Islamic law or Sharia. Even though the Muslim League leaders were liberal and secular in their approach, they found the mystically inclined Barelvi shrine ill-equipped to guide the Islamic state. Like most radical religious movements, Deobandism grew in the cities while Barelvism survived in the countryside. The Deobandi seminary was deeply involved in the Shia issue since the eighteenth century and had a tradition of apostatising the Shia. The growth of High Church seminaries in Pakistan after 1947 tended to highlight the sectarian rift in Pakistan's religious circles. The attraction of the High Church to the more austere and anti-sufi Arab Islam further prepared the ground for the sectarian war that was to engulf Pakistan in the 1980s under General Zia's rule.

Pakistan's High Church seminaries opened themselves to a reinforced Arab Islam that took hold after the defeat of Arab nationalism during the Cold War. The process of Islamization of the Arabs happened when Egypt was defeated at the hands of Israel in 1967. The internal struggle between Egypt as the leader of left-leaning pro-Soviet Arab nationalism and fundamentalist pro-America Saudi Arabia was resolved in the latter's favour. The Arabs turned away from socialism and looked to their religious leaders for the rediscovery of solidarity that pan-Arabism had provided in the past.

In the larger picture, it was the rolling back of the Soviet influence and the dominance of the United States in the Middle East that changed the map of political values in the region. An emphasis on religion and its repositories among the clergy led to the 'discovery' of sectarian identities in many parts of the Middle East. Thus in 1980, when jihad in Afghanistan began after the Soviet invasion of the country, the stage was set for the advent of an Arab brand of Islam in Pakistan. Already considerably High Church because of its obligation of legislation according to Islam, the state of Pakistan was ready to absorb a still harder version. With it came an intense wave of violent sectarianism for which Pakistan's civil society was not prepared.

THE FUTURE OF SECTARIAN VIOLENCE IN PAKISTAN

In Pakistan, sectarian violence is not a communitarian phenomenon, except in certain regions where concentrations of Shia settlements have the ability to strike back and settle scores. Unlike Iraq where the two communities are consciously squared off against each other, in Pakistan Shias by and large follow the political parties. There is no Shia 'vote bank' to freeze the democratic process in its evolution. In Iraq a series of elections in 2005 and 2006 have shown that the Shia vote only for Shia candidates. In Pakistan the only example of such a negation of pluralist democracy has happened in the city politics of Sindh where an ethnic 'vote bank' has emerged on a permanent basis, accompanied by violence.[25] In Iraq the Shia have been voting on the advice of the Grand Ayatollah Sistani who has promoted the electoral process with the *arrière-pensée* that the Shia majority in Iraq will emerge as the rulers of the country.

In Pakistan, the Shia participate in the bipartisan system as polarised between the liberal Pakistan People's Party (PPP) and conservative Pakistan Muslim League. Some of the Shia leaders of the PPP at the regional level continue to be visible although the Shia clerics have sought refuge in the Sunni-Deobandi clerical alliance, the Muttahida Majlis-e-Amal (MMA). One reason the urban Shia have stayed away from their clerical leaders is this decision of the Shia clergy to join the MMA. In doing this, they have behaved as if it was an act of despair. They have shown a tendency in the past to align themselves with the liberal PPP like other minorities in Pakistan. In the post-Zia period, however, the PPP was compelled to seek alliances with openly anti-Shia organisations like Sipah-e-Sahaba. This recalled the PPP's desertion of the Ahmedi community in 1974 after leaning on the organisational capacity of the persecuted minority for its electoral campaigns.

Out of all the big cities, Karachi has witnessed some Shia response at the street level to the sectarian activities of the Deobandi seminaries, but by and large even in Karachi the Shia community has stayed away from violence, relying on the Muttahida Qaumi Movement (MQM) and other non-religious parties for their political expression. In Lahore and Rawalpindi, in the province of Punjab, where the biggest Shia seminaries are located (and have been targeted), the Shia have stayed away from their clergy and have not indulged in street violence. Shia 'retaliation' has come from secret Shia militias run by organisations that remain officially banned. One can speculate that once the 'external' causes of sectarian strife are removed or minimised sectarian violence will subside in Pakistan. Since 2004 the violence has become one-sided and Shia retaliation to Deobandi acts of terrorism has only been *in extremis*.

But sectarian peace may not return so quickly to certain regions where the Shia–Sunni populations are in a state of equipoise and the Shia have the capacity to assert themselves. The Hazara community in Quetta in Balochistan is ghettoised to an extent that it will continue to attract Sunni violence, but sectarian trouble can be contained if the government is able to offer the Hazara Shias protection against the Taliban predominance in the city. The question of Parachinar in the Kurram Tribal Agency is, however, more complicated for two reasons: one, the historical nature of the friction between the tribes, and two the linkages the Turi Shia tribe of Parachinar have developed downwards into the settled areas of the North Western Frontier Province (NWFP), now Khyber Pakhtunkhwa. The neighbouring tribal agency of Orakzai and the cities of Bannu and Kohat in the NWFP have been 'Talibanised' by Sunni extremists, and the Shias living there are being forced to fight back. At the time of writing in 2007, Parachinar had seen 50 deaths in the sectarian battles between tribes still ongoing in the month of March.

Last but not least, the federally-administered Northern Areas of Pakistan may take time to control the sectarian violence that has gripped the region since 1988 when General Zia 'engineered a dramatic shift towards extremist Sunni political discourse, orthodoxy and a heightening of anti-Shia militancy' in the administrative centre of the Northern Areas, Gilgit.[26] The demographic balance in Gilgit is such that Shia and Sunni vote banks have polarised there like Iraq, but that is more owing to the government's refusal to allow the region to become devolved as a political entity. The army retains control of the administration of the Northern Areas because of the region's strategic location next to Kashmir. During the Kargil operation in 1999, which was carried out from base camps in the Northern Areas, ground was provided once again for the sectarian violence that followed into the new millennium. The militias Pakistan used at Kargil were all

Shia-killers.[27] The status of the region—a change which is bound to lead to the diffusion of sectarian tension—will be difficult to 'normalise' as long as the conflict with India over Kashmir is not resolved.

NOTES

1. *The Essential Rumi*, Translated from Persian by Coleman Barks with John Moyne, Penguin Books, 1995, p. 49. Jalaluddin Rumi (1207–1273) is a great Persian poet immortalised by Pakistan's national poet, Mohammad Iqbal, in his long poem, *Javid Namah*, as his guide through the various stages of Afterlife, on the model of Virgil in Dante's *Divine Comedy*.

2. The Census is a controversial institution although the state needs it for non-discriminatory purposes. The fundamental objection to the census is its policy of classification of citizens. In an ideal state, the census would simply be a head-count and not counting according to classifications. Modern states classify for purposes of affirmative action but such action can also attract discrimination against certain identities.

3. The demand for separate electorates by Jinnah was not on religious grounds as later claimed by the clergy in Pakistan. Jinnah simply wanted to 'negotiate' for more representation in the Muslim minority areas of India by giving away some seats in the Muslim majority areas.

4. CIA Fact Book. https://www.cia.gov/cia, 'Pakistani flag is green with a vertical white band (symbolising the role of religious minorities) on the hoist side; a large white crescent and star are centred on the green field; the crescent, star, and colour green are traditional symbols of Islam'. The flag was adopted on 14 August 1947. Prime Minister Liaquat Ali Khan, Jinnah's lieutenant and successor, echoed the liberal sentiments of Jinnah, the Quaid-e-Azam ('the great leader') when he explained to the Constituent Assembly at Karachi on 11 August what the Pakistani flag that he was about to unfurl stood for. He said: 'This flag is not the flag of any one particular party or community. This flag will stand for freedom, liberty and equality of all those who owe allegiance to the flag of Pakistan. As I visualize the state of Pakistan, there will be no special privileges, no special rights for any particular community or individual'.

5. *Tarjumanul Quran*, Journal of Jamaat-e-Islami, Pakistan, July 2000, The 'Stunt of Joint Electorates' Editorial: 'The identity of Pakistan was given a legal and practical shape first in the Objectives Resolution and then in the Constitutions of 1956 and 1973. It rests on three pillars, which are symbols of the nation's consensus: State's Islamic identity, its democratic order, and its federal system.... Those who are talking of joint electorate, pretending innocence and in the name of liberal democracy and equality, are, knowingly

or unknowingly, harming the foundations of Pakistan. They cannot be allowed to continue with this game'.

6. *The Friday Times*, 'Is the Two-Nation Theory still alive?', 1 September 2000: 'Pakistan's historian of the Pakistan Movement Prof. Shariful Mujahid stated that the Hindu members from East Pakistan chose to raise objections to the Objectives Resolutions only after consulting with the ulama in Lahore who resolutely opposed giving equal rights to the non-Muslims and the right to practise their religions 'freely'. He said this dichotomy between the thinking of the founding fathers and the ulama was highlighted by the fact that under General Zia, when the Objectives Resolution was made a substantive part of the Constitution, the word 'freely' was deleted without proper notification'.

7. The Shia clerical establishment compiled a volume proving that Muslims could not be declared non-Muslims and presented it to the members of the Senate and the National Assembly in 1993, *Firqa-Wariyat aur Uss Ka Sadd-e-Bab*.

8. Gregory H. Stanton, *The 8 Stages of Genocide*, University of Mary Washington, USA, http://www.umw.edu/cas/history/our_faculty/default.php. Stanton, President of Genocide Watch, enumerates eight stages out of which classification, organisation, polarization and denial presage the act of extermination. Under the organisation, he mentions the creation of militias as instruments of extermination since they assist in the creation of deniability.

9. David A. Hollinger, 'From Identity to Solidarity', in *Daedalus*, Fall 2006, p. 23: 'To share an identity with other people is to feel in solidarity with them; we owe them something special, and we believe we can count on them in ways that we cannot count on the rest of the population. To come to grips with one's true identity is to ground, on a pre-emptively primordial basis, vital connections to other people beyond the family'.

10. Ibn Khaldun, Abd al-Rahman (1332–1406) sees the historical process as one of constant cyclical change, due mainly to the interaction of two groups, nomads and townspeople. These form the two poles of his mental map; peasants are in between, supplying the towns with food and tax revenue and taking handicrafts in return. Nomads are rough, savage and uncultured, and their presence is always inimical to civilisation; however, they are hardy, frugal, uncorrupt in morals, freedom-loving and self-reliant, and so make excellent fighters. In addition, they have a strong sense of 'asabiya', which can be translated as 'group cohesion' or 'social solidarity'. This greatly enhances their military potential. Towns, by contrast, are the seats of the crafts, the sciences, the arts and culture. Yet luxury corrupts them, and as a result they become a liability to the state, like women and children who need to be protected. Solidarity is completely relaxed and the arts of defending oneself and of attacking the enemy are forgotten, so they are no match for conquering nomads. http://www.muslimphilosophy.com/ip/rep/H024.htm

11. Amartya Sen, *Identity and Violence: the Illusion of Destiny*, W.W. Norton, 2006, p. 17. Sen recommends plural identities for individuals under a state that does not 'classify' citizens. He thinks that imposition of a single identity is the state's pursuit of 'destiny' which is illusory and gives rise to violence: 'The descriptive weakness of choiceless singularity has the effect of momentously impoverishing the power and reach of our social and political reasoning. The illusion of destiny exacts a remarkably heavy price'.

12. *Tarjumanul Quran*, Journal of Jamaat-e-Islami, July 2000, Editorial: 'Besides other factors, which strengthened the secessionist tendencies in East Pakistan, one was the mode of election. The Government of Pakistan dismissed the proposal of separate electorates offered by the Christians of Pakistan and accepted the demand for joint electorates pressed by the Hindu community of East Pakistan. Consequently with the passing of time the group of Hindu voters in the representation of East Pakistan tightened and reinforced the secessionist movement. By abolishing the separate electorates it was indirectly accepted that Hindu and Muslim of East Pakistan were one nation'.

13. Khalid B. Sayeed, *Pakistan the Formative Phase 1857–1948*, Oxford University Press, 1968, p. 49. Jinnah denounced Gandhi's leadership of the Khilafat Movement, a movement based on religion which he thought would 'bring about conflict between Hindus and Muslims'. He resigned from the Congress on this point in 1920.

14. The discourse on this is differently interpreted by the secularists and the clergy. Jinnah constantly referred to Muslim identity on the basis of his knowledge of Islam as a lawyer. The clerics and rightwing politicians connect his speeches to what they think was his pledge to enforce the Sharia in Pakistan.

15. For instance, the 'excluded' Ahmedi community is punished under law if it calls its place of worship a mosque (*Masjid*) or publicly recites the '*kalima*' (declaration of Muslim faith). If an Ahmedi wants to acquire a Pakistani passport, he has to denounce his faith.

16. Akeel Bilgrami, 'Notes toward the Definition of Identity', in *Daedalus*, Journal of the American Academy of Arts and Sciences, Fall 2006, p. 5: 'Your subjective identity is what you conceive yourself to be, whereas your objective identity is how you might be viewed independently of how you see yourself'. Rejection of the old identity happens after 'discovery', a process that Amartya Sen denigrates the same way Aristotle denigrated it as a device of Tragedy.

17. Akbar S. Ahmed, *Islam under Siege: Living dangerously in Post-Honour World*; Polity Press, 2003, p. 113. The book denounces the clearly anti-Islamic writers in the West, giving rise to what has come to be known as Islamophobia, but more importantly it takes account of the extremist trend in Islam. He examines the central concept of Ibn Khaldun's study of society—the *asabiya*—and identifies in it the organising principle that allows people to survive collectively. It is the breakdown of *asabiya* that has scattered the identity of the Muslims. They no longer feel satisfied with the concepts

under *asabiya* that is no more. They feel dishonoured and denigrated by the world and desperately try to revive the sense of cohesion that has gone in such concepts as the *ummah*. Some among the Muslims become extreme in this search and wish the Muslim society to revert to old *asabiya* by force through such ideas as the *jahiliyya*. The violent principle of organisation Akbar calls hyper-*asabiya* and rejects it out of hand as being against the spirit of Islam. Post-modernity bothers the West—'a period of gentle apocalypse'— but it completely confuses the Muslims who had failed earlier to climb out of the colonial period into the twentieth century. Honour was the idea that they retained from their tribal past, and under globalisation—as the industrialised societies live completely without it—they seem determined to uphold it.

18. Ibid., Gregory H. Stanton, *The 8 Stages of Genocide*.

19. Amartya Sen, *Identity and Violence*, p. 37. Sen identifies discovery in 'installed locations' that deprive individuals of freedom of choice: 'The strongest reason for being skeptical of the discovery view is that we have different ways of identifying ourselves even in our given locations. The sense of belonging to a community, while strong enough in many cases, need not obliterate or overwhelm other associations and affiliations'.

20. Kwame Anthony Appiah, 'The Politics of Identity', *Daedalus*, Fall 2006, p. 20: 'If recognition entails taking notice of one's identity in social life, then the development of strong norms of identification can become not liberating but oppressive'.

21. In 1973, four Swedes held in a bank vault for six days during a robbery became attached to their captors, a phenomenon dubbed the Stockholm Syndrome. According to psychologists, the abused bond to their abusers as a means to endure violence.

22. Among the nearly one million Tutsis killed in a month by the Hutu militias there were all the moderate Hutus who would not support the massacres.

23. Ernest Gellner, *Post-modernism, Reason and Religion*, Routledge, 1992, p. 19: 'High Islam stresses the severely monotheistic and nomocratic nature of Islam; the most characteristic institution of Low Islam is the saint cult, where the saint is more often than not a living rather than a dead personage'.

24. See Khursheed Kamal Aziz, *Religion, Land and Politics in Pakistan: a Study of Piri-Muridi in Pakistan*, Vanguard Books, 1998. The author discusses in detail the dominance of the High Church madrassa in the cities and the Low Church shrine in the countryside in 1947.

25. The MQM is an ethnic party that wins federal, provincial and local government seats on a regular basis. Over the years the party has become acceptable to a majority of secular Pakistanis because the MQM is openly secular and violent and is thus willing to counter the violence of the religious parties and the seminaries in Sindh.

26. International Crisis Group, Report 131, *Discord in Pakistan's Northern Areas*, 2 April 2007, p. 16.

27. International Crisis Group, Report 131, *Discord in the Northern Areas*, April 2007, p. 172: 'The military's reliance on jihadis in its proxy war with India over Kashmir added a new dimension to sectarian conflict in the Northern Areas. In the 1990s, bastions of Sunni conservatism in the Northern Areas such as Chilas, Darel and Tangir became training grounds for the Kashmir jihad. Jihadi presence in the region increased markedly during the 1999 Kargil conflict, when the then-Army Chief Musharraf sent troops from the Northern Light Infantry and jihadi fighters across the Line of Control into Indian-administered Kashmir. Extremist outfits such as the Lashkar-e-Taiba, Jaish-e-Mohammed and Harkatul Mujahideen opened offices in the Northern Areas, which became hubs of jihadi training as well as anti-Shia activism. Despite the Musharraf government's ban on many of these groups, they still operate freely under changed names'.

1

The Shia in Pakistan

Two scissor blades make one cut.
And watch two men washing clothes.
One makes the dry clothes wet. The other makes
wet clothes dry. They seem to be thwarting each other
but their work is a perfect harmony.
Every holy person seems to have a different doctrine
and practice, but there's really one work.

— Rumi: *Two Friends*[1]

The two main warring sects in Islam are the majority Sunni and
the minority Shia. They originated in an early schism in Islam
about who should inherit the spiritual and temporal rulership of
the Muslims after the death of Prophet Muhammad (PBUH). The
Shia are as old in South Asia as Islam itself.[2] The Indian cultural
connection with Iran and its civilisation goes back to the Persian
Achaemenids (AD 550–330) who controlled some of the western
territory of what is today Pakistan and Afghanistan. Before Iran
became Shia in the seventeenth century, its Persian legacy was a
part of the culture of all Muslims in South Asia. The Sunni
prejudice against the Shia was tempered by culture and shared
mystical values that flourished in the Indian environment, but the
Sunni state remained sectarian till the establishment of the Mughal
dynasty (1526–1858). The Mughal state began a tradition of
sectarian tolerance that shaped Indian society down the centuries,
including reactions against their policy of tolerance.

The founder of the Mughal dynasty in India, Zahiruddin Babur
(reigned 1526–30) established the first friendly contacts with Iran.
The Safavid era, which made Shiism the religion of the state, was

to start 25 years later in Iran but the Sunni–Shia schism was already far advanced in Central Asia from where he hailed. Babur was beholden to the Shia king of Iran, Shah Ismail, for his survival in a battle against another warlord of Central Asia. As the Sunni founder of the Mughal Empire, he took the Persian crown as his head-dress and recited the *khutba* (authorised sermon) in his realm in the name of the Shah of Persia and inscribed the names of the twelve Shia imams on his coins. Babur counselled his son Humayun in his last will and testament: 'Overlook the difference between the Sunnis and Shias, otherwise the decrepitude of Islam would inevitably follow. Cleanse the table of your heart of religious bigotry and administer justice in accordance with the prescribed manner of each community'.[3]

Babur's son, Emperor Nasiruddin Humayun (1508–1556) was the first Indian ruler responsible for accepting a substantial influence of the Shia under the Safavids whose rise in Iran had coincided with his reign. He fled to Iran after being defeated by the Afghan invader Sher Shah Suri in 1531. There the Safavid King Shah Tahmasp pressured him into becoming Shia, which he did, and gave him 12,000 troops to reconquer India on the condition that Humayun give him the city of Kandahar located in today's Afghanistan. Humayun brought with him a lot of high Iranian culture. Mughal tolerance of the Shia became more pronounced under Emperor Jalaluddin Akbar (1542–1605) who encouraged pluralism and was especially attracted to innovative thought. His most learned minister, Abul Fazl (a very Shia name), belonged to a family spiritually linked to Mir Rafiuddin Safavi Shirazi, head of a Shia cult of Imam Mahdi. Another minister of his, Abdur Rahim Khan Khanan, was also considered a 'hidden' Shia because of his pluralist attitude. The anti-Shia trend in India came as a reaction to Akbar's policy of tolerance towards the Shia.

Akbar's son Nuruddin Salim Jehangir (1569–1627) married Nur Jahan, an Iranian lady who actually spread the Shia custom among the masses through her interest in art and social ritual. Her brother Asaf Khan was the power behind the throne, promoting the Shia penetration of the court. Jehangir, who represented Sunni coexistence with the Shia, faced Sunni reaction to Akbar's ignoring the boundaries dividing the two sects. He set aside the protest of Sheikh Ahmad Sirhindi (1564–1624) in the shape of a sectarian tract *Radd-e-Rawafiz* (Repudiation of the Rejectionists) and was able to put him in jail for his excessive millenarian claim of being a *qayyum* with a hint of equality with the Prophet.[4] (When Pakistan took Sheikh Ahmad into its nation-building pantheon, it ignored his sectarian and divine claims and focused instead on his protest against the pluralism of Akbar. He was useful as one who set up an early marker of Hindu-Muslim separateness, but he was to prove lethal when sectarianism invaded Pakistan in the 1980s.)

The Qutb Shahi Shia dynasty that ruled Hyderabad Deccan in what is today Andhra Pradesh in India began when Humayun was on the throne (reigned 1530–1556) and ended under Emperor Aurangzeb (1618–1707) when he crushed it in 1687. The Qutb Shahis were Turkmen Shia who produced a remarkable culture, mixing Telugu and Muslim traditions that gave rise to early Urdu literature. The dynasty ruled for over 150 years away from the centre of Mughal rule in Delhi. It was Aurangzeb who began Islamizing the Mughal state and soon turned against the 'heresy' of the Shia which his forebears had tolerated. He got several hundred Muslim clerics to compile Islamic Hanafi law in 33 volumes called *Fatawa-e-Alamgiri* which, among other judgements, also adjudged the Shia as heretics. Aurangzeb spent the last 27 years of his life fighting the Shia kingdom in the Deccan and died there during one of his campaigns. Annemarie Schimmel has made a very significant remark which should apply to the geopolitics of Pakistan today:

> The Shia kingdom of the South, which the Mughals had always regarded as a possible source of danger because of its friendly relations with Shia Iran, was thus eliminated [by Aurangzeb]; but now the Mughal Empire was left without the southern bulwark to protect it from the (Hindu warlords calling themselves) Marathas.[5]

When the anti-Shia *fatwas* were issued in Pakistan in 1986 they all referred to *Fatawa-e-Alamgiri* as their authority, while General Zia was busy in a countermove to neutralise the effect on Pakistan of Iran's Islamic Revolution! Schimmel also questioned the wisdom of a later invitation by another puritanical figure, Shah Waliullah (1703–1762), to the Afghan invader Ahmad Shah Abdali, as that facilitated the domination of India by the British colonial power. A votary of Pakistan's national poet Mohammad Iqbal, she marvelled at Iqbal's inclusion of Ahmad Shah Abdali in Paradise in his long poem on the pattern of Dante's *Divine Comedy*, *Javid Namah.*[6] What Iqbal definitely did not know were the letters written by Shah Waliullah to the courtiers of Ahmad Shah, asking him to kill the Hindus and the Shia in Delhi. As his son, Shah Abdul Aziz, recorded, Ahmad Shah did kill the Shias of Delhi together with the Marathas!

After the creation of Pakistan in 1947, the Sunni majority regarded the Shia minority with curiosity, but not with any rancour. There was intermarriage between the two communities and no one minded if the spouses continued to differ in their beliefs and rituals. Only in moments of curiosity did the Sunnis refer to the 'strange' practices of the Shia: their *kalima* (Muslim catechism) was different from the *kalima* of the Sunnis, their timings of *namaz* were different, they observed the month of fasting according to timings that differed from the Sunni timings, and they went to different mosques and followed different rituals of burial of the dead. This curiosity was not flecked with any suspicion or misgiving, yet anyone who pretended to have a deeper knowledge of religion tended to scandalise by pointing to the great Sunni–Shia quarrel of history and warning the 'less religious' about the danger of Shia heresy.

How much did the religious person know really? The Sunni clerics were supposed to know more than the common man, but repeatedly evidence comes to the fore that even the average cleric did not think it worth his while to inform himself about the facts of the Shia heresy. Nearly a century of the British Raj and its secular governance had put an end to the Sunni–Shia rioting that was normal before the arrival of the British in India. The sectarian hatred remained confined to the clergy. Because the population seemed insufficiently persuaded to focus on heresy under secular governance, the clerics of the two communities too avoided taking issue with one another. On the other hand, a century of secularism had persuaded both Sunnis and Shias away from any detailed knowledge of their sects. More than the Sunni, it was the Shia living among Sunni majorities who allowed himself to forget his own religion, particularly the tradition (hadith) part of it. Today, most Shias in South Asia will express ignorance about their funereal rites, which differ from those of the Sunnis: that there is a different method of bathing the corpse and there is the ritual of offering *talqin* (advice) before burial in a designated graveyard, etc.

There is evidence that in the days of the Prophet, *talqin* was practised among the Muslims. It is only after the 'conquest' of Hejaz (Makkah and Madinah) by the Wahhabi-Saudi warriors from Najd (Central Arabia desert) that it was given up among the Sunnis, although even today one can't claim *talqin* as a purely Shia ritual. Mai Yamani, daughter of the former oil minister of Saudi Arabia, Zaki Yamani, has this interesting observation to make:

> The considerable impact of Wahhabism on the conduct and site of Hijazi burial is clear enough, but despite the pressures for a particular brand of religious conformity the *awail* (families related to the tribe of the Prophet) continue to find some space for a certain measure of defiance. For example *talqin* (instruction of the dead) is still performed. Despite it being carried out in public and hence under possible surveillance, this custom is practised by most other Sunnis in Egypt, Malaysia, India and Pakistan. In Saudi Arabia, *talqin* is a controversial practice because the Wahhabis view it as unacceptable, excessive and unnecessary. Official Saudi doctrine holds that the Prophet never recommended nor practised the instruction of the dead. Members of the Committee for the Order of the Good and the Forbidding of the Evil will, therefore, reprimand any group practising it at the graveyard... *Talqin* is not taught in the country's school curriculum.[7]

Vali Nasr notes that 'many of Pakistan's leaders in the early years were Shias, including the country's founder and first governor general (Jinnah), three of its first prime ministers, and two of its military leaders (Yahya Khan and Iskander Mirza) and two later prime ministers, the Bhuttos'.[8] [He did not mention commander-in-chief Musa Khan who was a Hazara Shia and who by his will got himself buried in Mashhad, Iran, much before his community began to suffer extremist Sunni violence. Foreign Minister General (Retired) Yaqub Khan was Yakub Ali Khan from the Shia nawab family of Rampur but removed 'Ali' from his name after becoming foreign minister.] Nasr goes on to note that Bhutto's choice of colours for the flag of his party the PPP (black, red, green) were the colours of Shiism. After a born-again Deobandi General Ziaul Haq hanged a Shia Zulfikar Ali Bhutto in 1979, the parallel with the martyrdom of Husayn was not missed by some. A state-funded film on the theme, *The Blood of Hussain* by Jamil Dehlavi, actually deceived General Zia who could not grasp the strong symbolic presentation showing him as the usurper.

In a stunning irony, Pakistan's first president Iskander Mirza was not only a Shia but had descended from the family of Mir Jafar, the minister of Sirajuddaula, the ruler of Bengal. Mir Jafar is now a proverbial figure exemplifying disloyalty because he betrayed his ruler to the British. It is remarkable that while lionising Sirajuddaula, Pakistanis pay no regard to his Shia belief.[9] Iskander Mirza married twice and both times married Shia women, his second wife being from Iran.[10] His Shia ancestry was never called into question and no one ever thought it strange that he had descended from someone the Indian Muslims considered a traitor, Mir Jafar. (Attacks on him started only in the 1980s when anti-Shia trends became prominent in Pakistan under General Zia. For instance, he was condemned for designating the highest bravery award in Pakistan as the Nishan-e-Haider and not as the Nishan-e-Farooqi.)[11] On the other hand, clerical Shia prejudice was noted in Iran when some religious leaders condemned Pakistan's national poet, Allama Mohammad Iqbal for having written against the sixth Imam, Imam Jafar Sadiq, based on his line *Sadiq as Dakkan, Jafar az Bangal* in Persian for which the great Iranian intellectual Ali Shariati rebuked them.[12]

WAS JINNAH A SHIA OR A SUNNI?

After 1947, Pakistan adopted the position of denying that the population of the country was divided between Shias and Sunnis, among others. The census that followed took account of Muslims and non-Muslims but ignored the sects: it was also an indirect pledge of the state that it would not discriminate on the basis of sect. The founder of the state, Mohammed Ali Jinnah, although himself a Twelver Shia after conversion from the Ismaili sect, was wont to describe himself in public as neither a Shia nor a Sunni. His stock answer to a query about his sect was: was Muhammad the Prophet a Shia or a Sunni? Yet when he died in 1948, it was necessary for his sister Miss Fatima Jinnah to declare him a Shia in order to inherit his property as per Jinnah's will. (Sunni law partially rejects the will while Shia law does not.) She filed an affidavit, jointly signed with the Prime Minister of Pakistan, Liaquat Ali Khan, at the Sindh High Court, describing Jinnah as 'Shia Khoja Mohamedan' and praying that his will may be disposed of under Shia inheritance law. The court accepted the petition. But on 6 February 1968, after Miss Jinnah's demise the previous year, her sister Shirin Bai, moved an application at the High Court claiming Miss Jinnah's property under the Shia inheritance law on the ground that the deceased was a Shia.

Given the prestige of Miss Jinnah, she was allowed to dispose of all the property of her brother (as a Sunni she would have title to only one-half) and continued to do so till her death. After her death her sister Shirin Bai arrived in Karachi from Bombay, converted from Ismailism to Twelver Shiism, and laid claim to Jinnah's property. It is at this point that the rest of Jinnah's clan, still following the Ismaili faith, decided to challenge the authenticity of Jinnah's Shia faith. The High Court, which had earlier accepted Miss Jinnah's petition, now balked at the prospect of declaring the Father of the Nation a Shia. Needless to say, the case is still pending in Karachi. But Miss Jinnah's conduct showed that she was an observing Shia and took her brother's conversion to Twelver Shiism seriously. Why had Jinnah converted? It develops that he did it on his secular principle of freedom of religion. According to court's witness, Syed Sharifuddin Pirzada, Jinnah broke from the Ismaili faith in 1901 after his two sisters, Rehmat Bai and Maryam Bai, were married into Sunni Muslim families. It appears that this happened because the Ismaili community objected to these marriages. It also appears that the conversion to Isna-Ashari (Twelver) Shiism happened in Jinnah's immediate family, and not in the families of his two paternal uncles, Walji and Nathoo.

The court proceedings bear evidence of the last rites observed by Miss Jinnah immediately after her brother's death. Witness Syed Anisul Hasnain, a Shia scholar, deposed that he had arranged the *ghusl* (last bath) of Jinnah on the instructions of Miss Jinnah. He led his *namaz-e-janaza* (funeral prayer) in a room of the Governor-General's House at which such Shia luminaries as Yusuf Haroon, Hashim Raza and Aftab Hatim Alavi were present, while Liaquat Ali Khan, a Sunni, waited outside the room. After the Shia ritual, the body was handed over to the state, and Maulana Shabbir Ahmad Usmani, a breakaway *alim* of the Deobandi school of thought who supported Jinnah's Pakistan Movement but had recently apostatised the Shias, led his *janaza* (funeral) according to the Sunni ritual at the ground where a grand mausoleum was later constructed. Other witnesses confirmed that after the demise of Miss Fatima Jinnah, *alam* and *panja* (two Shia symbols) were discovered at Mohatta Palace, her residence.

Witnesses appearing at the Sindh High Court in 1968 to affirm Jinnah's sect were Mr I.H. Ispahani, a family friend of Jinnah and his honorary secretary in 1936, and Mr Matloobul Hassan Syed, the Quaid's private secretary from 1940 to 1944. Mr Ispahani revealed that Jinnah had himself told him in 1936 that he and his family had converted to Shiism after his return from England in 1894. He said that Jinnah had married Ruttie Bai, the daughter of a Parsi businessman according to the Shia ritual during which she was represented by a Shia scholar of Bombay, and Jinnah was represented by his Shia friend, Raja Sahib of Mahmudabad. (Raja Sahib was a close friend of Jinnah but differed completely from him in his belief. He was a devout follower of the Twelver Shia faith and ultimately chose to migrate from an independent India to Najaf in Iraq. His friendship with Jinnah has puzzled many. Apparently, the only bond they had was of the Shia faith.) He, however, conceded that Jinnah was opposed in the Bombay elections by a Shia Conference candidate. Ispahani was present when Miss Fatima Jinnah died in Karachi in 1967. He himself arranged the *ghusl* and *janaza* for her at Mohatta Palace according to the Shia ritual before handing over the body to the state. Her Sunni *namaz-e-janaza* was held later at the Polo Ground, after which she was buried next to her brother at a spot chosen by Ispahani inside the mausoleum. Ritualistic Shia *talqin* (last advice to the deceased) was done after her body was lowered into the grave. (Jinnah had arranged for *talqin* for Ruttie Bai too when she died in 1929).[13]

Fatima Jinnah's own funeral became something of a theatre of the absurd after her friends had given her a Shia funeral before the state could give her a Sunni one. Field Marshal Ayub Khan writes in his *Diaries*:

11 July 1967: Major General Rafi, my military secretary, returned from Karachi. He had gone there to represent me at Miss Jinnah's funeral. He said that sensible people were happy that the government had given her so much recognition, but generally the people behaved very badly. There was an initial *namaz-e-janaza* at her residence in Mohatta Palace in accordance, presumably, with Shia rites. Then there was to be *namaz-e-janaza* for the public in the Polo Ground. There an argument developed whether this should be led by a Shia or a Sunni. Eventually, Badayuni was put forward to lead the prayer. As soon as he uttered the first sentence the crowd broke in the rear. Thereupon he and the rest ran leaving the coffin high and dry. It was with some difficulty that the coffin was put on a vehicle and taken to the compound of the Quaid's *mazar*, where she was to be buried. There a large crowd had gathered and demanded to converge on the place of burial. This obviously could not be allowed for lack of space. Thereupon, the students and the *goonda* elements started pelting stones on the police. They had to resort to *lathi* charge and tear gas attack. The compound of the *mazar* was apparently littered with stones, Look at the bestiality and irresponsibility of the people. Even a place like this could not be free of vandalism.[14]

PAKISTANI NATIONALISM AND THE SHIA

Vali Nasr traces Pakistan's early indifference to sectarianism to the pan-Islamic nature of the Pakistan Movement, in the sense that it inspired Muslims of all sects, in contrast to Arab nationalism which remained Sunni in essence.[15] Yet the Pakistan Movement was not welcomed by the clerics who were politically mobilised at the time and decided to support the Congress rather than the Muslim League which they thought too secular. After 1947, however, the same clergy moved to Pakistan along with its sectarian baggage. The state thereafter began its journey from an unspoken semi-secular identity to the identity of a religious state. Much before the Islamization of General Zia in the 1980s, Pakistan felt the need to oppose an 'ideological' Pakistan to a 'secular' India. For purposes of legislation, it had to reintegrate the hardliner clerics of Deoband who had opposed the Pakistan Movement. The parts of India falling to Pakistan had responded to the Islamic appeal of the *pirs* (saints) and *mazars* (shrines) rather than the clerics and their madrassas (seminaries). To fulfil the need for Pakistan's Muslim nationalism it was considered proper to highlight the 'history' Muslims had in India.

Mohammad Qasim Zaman, on the other hand, thinks that Pakistan's trend towards sectarianism began quite early, from the early 1950s, with agitations against the Ahmedi community. According to his analysis, the apostatisation of the Ahmedis in 1974 put Pakistan on the slippery slope that reached its nadir in 1985 when Pakistan's first party devoted to the cause of declaring Shias as non-Muslims, the Sipah-e-Sahaba, was established.[16] Nasr and Zaman are both right in their views but there is evidence that it was the Pakistani state's need for nation-building under a new nationalism that actually began its anti-Shia orientation when the new textbooks were written for junior schools in the 1950s. Both Sunnis and Shias were required to read about a number of great religious personages of the past who were patently anti-Shia in their thinking. This emphasised a pre-British consciousness which had to be bowdlerised to suit the new nation-state. The bowdlerisation was simply a denial that the personages of Pakistan's pre-1947 and pre-British history were Sunni without an anti-Shia bias. The pro-Pakistan but anti-Shia Sunni clergy knew that the parts of Muslim history dug up for nation-building had an anti-Shia bias, but the politicians of the ruling Pakistan Muslim League were mostly unaware of the sectarian message buried in the new syllabi being taught to the children of the new state. The historian who helped create the new textbooks too would have known, but he helped by censoring the anti-Shia credentials of such textbook icons as the Mughal emperor Aurangzeb, the great Renewer of Faith, Sheikh Ahmad of Sirhind, and the great Joiner of the Community, Shah Waliullah, etc.

Pakistan ideology and Pakistani nationalism are expressed through its textbooks. One such textbook by M. Ikram Rabbani[17] pretends to prepare students for BA/BSc, Central Superior Services and Provincial Civil Services examinations. It has been the 'officially recommended reading' for passing examinations in Pakistan and has been criticised by local and foreign experts for expressing state biases against domestic communities and foreign states. In the context of sectarianism in Pakistan, the book follows the pattern traced by the state of Pakistan since 1947, that of asserting the Sunni view of history inducted into the Pakistan Movement, which in turn forms the single most effective component of Pakistani nationalism. It devotes seven pages to 'Imam Rabbani, Hazrat Mujaddid Alf-e-Sani Sheikh Ahmad of Sirhind' (AD 1564–1624) as the proponent of Pakistan's Two-Nation Concept:

Sheikh Ahmad was a staunch advocate of the separateness of the Muslims (from the Hindus) and desired to maintain the distinctive image of the Muslim Nationalism. He laid great emphasis on the separate identity of the Muslims and adopted a very stern attitude against the Hindus. Sheikh Ahmad firmly believed in the Two-Nation Theory. He was in favour of maintaining the differences between Hindus and Muslims. He wanted *jizya* (special tax on non-Muslim citizens) to be re-imposed on Hindus and demanded the destruction of Hindu temples.[18]

The book neglects to mention the anti-Shia orientation of the great Renewer of the Second Millennium as a pillar of Pakistan's ideology. It did not explain that Sheikh Ahmad was the author of the famous anti-Shia treatise titled *Radd-e-Rawafiz* (A Repudiation of the Rejectionists) which was to become central to the Shia–Sunni divide in Pakistan. The book does not mention that the Shia community had responded to the apostatising works of Sheikh Ahmad and had not accepted its rejection of the Shia as Muslims. It did not think fit to deal with the question of Sheikh Ahmad's designation of the Shia as non-Muslims while the Constitution of Pakistan did not do so. How could a Pakistani textbook ignore the Constitution while including seven pages of eulogy to an Islamic 'reformer' whose sectarian views were quite well known?

SECTARIAN AMBIVALENCE OF SHAH WALIULLAH

The textbook follows the recommendations of the National Curriculum prepared by the federal government of Pakistan, and the technique it follows in avoiding violation of the Constitution is simple: avoid mentioning the sectarian tracts if they are in existence and emphasise elements of sectarian harmony when sectarianism is vague or not blatantly expressed. This is the approach adopted by the textbook in respect of Shah Waliullah (AD 1703–1764), too, whose father, it says, was a compiler of the *Fatawa-e-Alamgiri* of Emperor Aurangzeb, a document that figures in the apostatising sectarian literature of the 1990s. In respect of Shah Waliullah, whom it treats in ten pages, it claims the status of a binder of the sects:

> He adopted a balanced approach and understanding towards religious matters. He thoroughly studied all schools of thought and expressed what was right and just in a mild and sophisticated way without hurting anyone. He removed misunderstanding, to a larger extent, between Shias and Sunnis, and in this way provided a spiritual basis for national solidarity and harmony.[19]

[The book replacing the above book in 2004, titled *Pakistan's Political, Economic and Diplomatic Dynamics*, edited by Javeed Ahmed Sheikh and published by Kitabistan Paper Products, Lahore, completely removes the focus of Pakistan Studies from the historical emphasis on Shah Waliullah and mentions him only in a list of saints that helped spread Islam in India.]

It is interesting that the *fatwas* published to apostatise the Shia in Pakistan steadily refer to Shah Waliullah as their authority. The clerical circles think of him as one of the foremost apostatisers of the Shia while non-clerical official scholars tend to protect him from this labelling. For instance, a work prepared by a government-funded institution has come to the conclusion that one well known anti-Shia tract was not written by Shah Waliullah. It describes Shah Waliullah as the biggest Muslim reformer of South Asia who was born in a period of Muslim decline. The book gives us the following truncated narrative:[20]

> The last great Mughal King Aurangzeb Alamgir was busy quelling the rebellion in the South while his sons Muazzam and Akbar secretly parleyed with his enemies. The Mughal empire was at an end, dying in an environment of chaos where Muslims and Hindus counted equally as enemies of the central government. The state of religion was abysmal. Muslim mullahs debated the status of Abdul Qadir Jilani and Sheikh Ahmad Sirhindi and fought for the supremacy of their conflicting schools of jurisprudence. Quran and hadith had been relegated to a secondary position by mullahs who wanted to show the supremacy of their *fiqh* (school of jurisprudence): some clearly stated that if any verse of the Quran or a hadith contradicted the ruling of their *faqih* (jurist) then it would have to be abolished. In 1731, Shah Waliullah travelled to Hejaz and met the Arab exponents of other jurisprudences and grasped the importance of bringing together versions of Islam greatly in need of a 'joiner' of the faith. It was in Madina that he became a formal pupil of the great teachers of the four schools of jurisprudence: Hanafi, Maliki, Shafei and Hanbali.

Shah Waliullah saw a dream in which he was appointed *Qayem al-Zaman* by the Holy Prophet to rescue the Islam of India from the power of Sikhs, Marathas and the Jats. Among the armies of the Marathas were also Muslim commanders with their myriad troops, which defined the chaos of post-Mughal times. Shah Sahib wrote a letter to the King of Afghanistan, Ahmad Shah Durrani Abdali, and asked him to break the power of the Marathas by invading India. The book also seeks to lay to rest another allegation that he wrote an anti-Shia book titled *Qurrat ul Ainain*. There is a letter in the book about the Shias that proves Shah's lack of sectarian prejudice. Therefore, *Qurrat ul Ainain* is not supposed to be authentic. Shah Waliullah himself has been inducted into the worldview of the extremist Deobandi warriors of our times, but, according to the book Shah himself was a 'binder' of the faith, not a 'divider' of it.

Why did Idara Saqafat Islamia, Lahore make an effort to deny that Shah Waliullah's book against the Shia was a forgery while most distinguished scholars in the past had accepted his *Qurrat ul Ainain* as an authentic tract?[21] One is forced to think that officially funded research scholars were given the task of disassociating Shah Waliullah from Pakistan's growing sectarianism. The followers of Shah Waliullah—the empowered Deobandi seminaries in Pakistan—were unaffected by this campaign. The *fatwas* of apostatisation of the Shia issued by a number of Sunni seminaries and individual Sunni muftis nonetheless refer to Shah Waliullah's own apostatisation of the Shia in his exegesis, *Musawwa*, of Imam Malik's work *Muatta*. Elsewhere, Shah Waliullah's view of the Shias as heretics has been clearly expressed:

> He was convinced in his *Tafhimaat* that the Shia did not believe in the finality of the Prophet, which is considered an act of apostasy by the Sunni clergy. The Prophet himself appeared in his dream to tell him that the Shia were wrong to oppose the caliphates of Abu Bakr and Umar. One reason, however, the Deobandi and Ahle Hadith scholars did not quote as much from him as his son Shah Abdul Aziz was that Waliullah did not believe that denying the Prophethood led to *takfir* (declaration as non-Muslim).[22]

This restraint on the part of Waliullah was, however, misleading because once anyone denies the Prophethood of Muhammad (PBUH) he is considered by the clergy to have forsworn his faith.

STATE INDOCTRINATION AND THE SHIA

The most confident verdict on Shah Waliullah comes in an article written by Bashir Ahmad Dar in 1965.[23] Dar quotes from his *Fuyuz al-Haramain* to tell us that Shah Waliullah had 47 spiritual experiences, mostly in the form of dreams, out of which the first eight were experienced at Makkah in the early months of 1731 while the rest were experienced at Madinah while pursuing his studies. *Fuyuz* was one of his first books to be written on his return to India and it explained his position vis-à-vis the religion of the Shia. In one of his dreams, claims Shah Waliullah, the Prophet appeared to him and told him to give up his view of Ali as being superior to Abu Bakr and Umar. Dar opines that Shah Waliullah came to an India burning with a Sunni–Shia controversy of great intensity and could not rise above it. He thinks that Shah Waliullah as a binder of the faith was limited only to the four schools of *fiqh* of the Sunni religion, but many writers keen to bind all *fiqhs*, including the Shia *fiqh*, as one nation in Pakistan, were persuaded to attribute to him the function of binding the Shia–Sunni divide. He traces the deliberate obfuscation of Shah Waliullah's sectarian role in the following footnote:

> It is often claimed that Shah Waliullah 'laid down lines of approach best calculated to remove the sectarian differences and to assist in the building of common, harmonious nationhood'. (Cf. S.M. Ikram, 'Shah Waliullah' in *A History of Freedom Movement* Vol. 1, p. 499).[24] This view seems to be based on a superficial acquaintance with the works of Waliullah. A thorough study of *Izat al-Khifa* and *Qurrat al-'Ainain* and the letters of Waliullah in *Kalimaat-e-Tayyabaat* will reveal that Waliullah called the Shias as *zindiq, nawabit* and *mubtadi*, i.e, heretics and innovators in religion, as did Sheikh Ahmad of Sirhind. Waliullah wrote his books about this controversy purely from the Sunni point of view, as was done before him by Ash'ari and Ibn Taymiyya. Nowhere do we find any attempt by him to bridge the gap between the Sunnis and the Shias, or between the Asharites and Mutazilites, as for instance, claimed by S.M. Ikram (*Rud-e-Kausar*, p. 516). These books of Waliullah intensified the Shia–Sunni controversy as a result of which his son Shah Abdul Aziz was forced to write another more

comprehensive anti-Shia book *Tuhfa Ithna Ashriyah* to defend his stand in these controversies which had assumed a more menacing form in his days. (See *Rud-e-Kausar* pp. 567–574.)

Shah Waliullah's effort to bind the four Sunni schools of jurisprudence may have actually hardened the Sunni way of thinking by linking it with the Hanbali trend that he encountered when he went on hajj in 1731. His stay in Makkah coincided with the period of education in Hejaz of Mohammad ibn Abdul Wahhab from Najdat al-'Uyaina who was the Hanbali founder of the puritanical form of Sunnism later known insultingly as Wahhabism. Shah Waliullah did not meet Wahhab, nor is he supposed to have been tutored by his teacher, but his stay in Hejaz did coincide with the rise of Hanbali thought in Arabia. Arabia was still under the control of the Ottomans and tolerated all the four schools of Muslims jurisprudence including the mystical tradition that was later to be rejected by most Arabs. According to one dream seen by Shah Waliullah in Hejaz, the Prophet asked him to treat all the four Sunni schools as equals. Another dream, however, had the Prophet telling him that the school most compatible with hadith was to be 'the most legitimate', which seems to suggest the superiority of Ahle Hadith over the other three.[25] This dream was to have a far-reaching effect in India. The Ahle Hadith were already given to a stringent form of fundamentalism; under Shah Waliullah's inspiration, the Deobandis, too, became hardliners. The sub-sect of the Hanafis, the Barelvis, however, remained less opposed to the Shias despite their acceptance of Shah Waliullah. They did not accept completely the joining of Indian Islam with the Hanbalite tradition. Today, Shah Waliullah is the founder saint of both the Ahle Hadith and the Deobandis. Both these schools look at the Barelvis with great suspicion and at times accuse them of being secretly in league with the Shias. More details about sectarian conflict between the Deobandis and the Ahle Hadith on the one hand and the Barelvis, on the other, will come in the later chapters.

Another apologist for Waliullah, M.D. Muztar is at great pains to differentiate between the thought of Shah Waliullah and

Wahhabism. He seems to think that Shah's lack of extremism and his acceptance of the four schools of Sunni *fiqh* set him apart from Wahhab, but he does recognise that Shah's admiration of Ibn Taymiyya brought him close to the Wahhabi creed. Shah Waliullah, during his stay in Hejaz, seems to have reached out to the new radical trend among the Arabs which later gave scope to the ideas of Wahhab. He translated a tract that must have appealed to the rising anti-Shia feeling in Arabia, which was exploited to the hilt when Wahhab came to share political power with the House of Saud. He translated into Arabic *Radd-e-Rawafiz* by Sheikh Ahmad and presented it to his teachers in Hejaz. Hatred of the Shia could yet bind the followers of Shah Waliullah to the Wahhabis as they arose in Arabia and made a strong appearance as Ahle Hadith at the Mughal court in the times that followed Shah Waliullah. Antipathy of Shah Waliullah towards the Shias was more veiled than that of his son Shah Abdul Aziz, but his letters to the courtiers of Ahmad Shah Abdali manifest his opposition to the presence of Shias in Delhi. Sayyid Athar Abbas Rizvi[26] tells us that because Shah Waliullah was upset over some of the Shia rituals in Delhi, he did ask the invading Afghans to oust the Shia community from the city and he reproduces his son Shah Abdul Aziz's remark: 'It so happened that my revered father said that next year, no *rafizis* (Shias) would be left in our town. This came to be true as the Durrani killed them'.

The textbooks in Pakistan began to blazon the names of a number of anti-Shia personages as markers of Pakistan's fledgling nationalism after 1947. This nationalism contained two strong negative and positive strains: the negative one being anti-Indianism, and the positive one, the Islamic identity. Unfortunately, it is in this positive strain that we find an unspoken negative evaluation of Shiism. However, it was not until 1986, when the first *fatwas* of *takfir* (apostatisation) were issued against the Shia, that the educated population of the country became aware of this tacit rejection of the Shia by Pakistani nationalism. The *fatwas* are on record since 1986 and continue to be circulated by certain organisations. It is not clear if they can be adjudged as illegal and 'terroristic' in nature under the Anti-Terrorism Act of 1997 or the 2001 Anti-Terrorism (Amendment) Ordinance meant to deter sectarianism.

ANTI-SHIA *FATWAS* AND ANTI-TERRORISM LAWS

After the Sunni–Shia conflict in Pakistan reached its first spike in the mid-1990s, the government passed an Anti-Terrorism Act of 1997, in which Section 8 related to 'Prohibition of acts intended to stir up sectarian hatred'. It has described the perpetrator of the terrorist 'act' as:

a) A person who uses insulting or abusive words or behaviour; or b) displays publishes or distributes any written material which is threatening abusive or insulting; or c) distributes or shows or displays a recording of visual images or sound recording of visual images or sounds which are abusive or insulting; or d) has in his possession written material or a recording or visual images or sounds which are threatening, abusive or insulting with a view to their being published by himself or another, shall be guilty of offence if (i) he intends to thereby stir up sectarian hatred or (ii) having regard to all circumstances sectarian hatred is likely to be stirred up thereby.

Two words—'threat' and 'insult'—are central to the framing of this apparently anti-sectarian law. Another law in the shape of an ordinance was promulgated in 2001, again with the intent of allowing the administration to move against violence against places of worship. The Anti-Terrorism (Amendment) Ordinance (2001) says:

An act of terrorism will have been committed if: (6/1-C) the use of threat is made for the purpose of advancing a religious, sectarian or ethnic cause; and (6/1-H) it involves firing on religious congregations, mosques, imam*bargahs* (Shia places of worship), churches, temples, etc.

Clearly, the intent here is to punish those who attack places of worship. Terrorist courts are summary courts where punishment is quickly dealt out and the amendment ordinance tends to increase the number of those who would be sent to the special courts and not tried at ordinary courts where delays and other means of obstruction can be employed to protect the perpetrators of attacks on places of worship. Once again the conditionality of 'threat' has been used for the coming into operation of the law. The question is: do *fatwas* fall in the category of written material that 'threatens' or 'insults'?

Sunni *fatwas* are in effect a Sunni objection to the 'insult' offered to the Sunni faith by Shia religious literature. They can be interpreted as threatening only indirectly since they place the Shia community outside the pale of Islam and thus 'threaten' their faith. Have the *fatwas* come before a court of law? What is the judicial mood in Pakistan about apostatisation or *takfir*? Unfortunately, the Constitution through its Second Amendment (declaring the Ahmedis non-Muslim) inclines in favour of apostatisation and exclusion and therefore does not directly discourage the concept of *takfir*. The truth is that the Constitution itself, through its definition of a true Muslim, commits *takfir* and exposes many potentially 'excludable' communities to the threat of apostatisation. The Shia were to be targeted by the *fatwas* later on the charge of not accepting completely the Prophethood of Muhammad (PBUH). The constitutional definition is given below.

Clause (3) The Constitution (Second Amendment) Act, 1974 was passed on 21 September 1974 and added to Article 260 of the Constitution that explains as to who is a non-Muslim. This Article pertains to definitions under the Constitution. The new clause stated that 'a person who does not believe in the absolute and unqualified finality of the Prophethood of Muhammad (PBUH) as the last of the Prophets or claims to be a Prophet, in any sense of the word or of any description whatsoever, after Muhammad (PBUH), or recognises such a claimant as a Prophet or a religious reformer, is not a Muslim for the purposes of the constitution or law.

Since this definition or explanation did not specifically refer to the Ahmedis, therefore, Article 106, which pertains to the formation of provincial assemblies and distribution of the seats within such assemblies, was also amended to make mention of Ahmedis amongst the non-Muslim faiths described in the Article for the purpose of reservation of special seats for them. They were referred to as 'persons of the Qadiani group or the Lahori Group (who call themselves 'Ahmedis').[27]

The *fatwas* against the Shia community rely on the phrase 'a person who does not believe in the absolute and unqualified finality of the Prophethood of Muhammad' to give their judgement against the Shia. As parallel but legally non-binding verdicts these *fatwas* contain the memory of early Islam when it was not judges with graduation from a law school but muftis who issued actionable decisions. Qasim Zaman is of the opinion that the tendency towards the apostatisation of the Shia grew after the passage of the Second Amendment against the Ahmedis in 1974.[28] Why is it that the 1986 *fatwas* were never brought before the court so that the issuing authority could either insist on their currency or plead that they were issued before the 1997 Act against sectarianism? The truth is that the first apostatiser of the Shia, Maulana Haq Nawaz Jhangvi, in his fiery sermons, used to challenge the courts to hear him out.[29] He was convinced, as he claimed, that no court of an Islamic state could ignore the opinion of the sacred personalities of the Islamic past and still maintain that Shia were Muslims. In 2003, when the Shia Hazaras were massacred in Quetta they made it public that the *fatwas* from the major Deobandi seminaries were in circulation in Quetta before the massacre, but no one took notice. In fact, the Hazaras later put them on their website straight from the 1986 collection of Manzur Numani, but again the government took no notice of them with a view to prosecuting the issuing seminaries under the 1997 and 2001 laws.

There could be a reason for not allowing a reference to the *fatwas* in the 1997 Act and the 2001 Ordinance. The *fatwas* are not directly 'threatening' or 'insulting' as defined in the laws; they are in fact a reaction to 'insult' found in the Shia tracts and practice.

Taking action under the new laws in 2001, the police swooped down on Shia bookshops and took away a lot of publications, included certain annotated editions of *Nahj al-Balagha*, the sermons of Ali, considered as acceptable Shia religious literature in the past. No such raids were carried out against Sunni books although some of them had been banned on other charges of heresy. For instance, Ghulam Ahmad Parwez's work on the unreliability of hadith was banned in the NWFP but no one minded his writings against the Shia, especially his book on Umar, the second caliph after the Prophet. His condemnation of the Shia could be taken only in the form of a protest against 'insult' offered by Shia tracts. In Pakistan, the institution of *fatwa* rests in the legal penumbra of the ideological state. Lawmaking so far has shied away from defining the legality of an opinion given by a certain religious authority. The Ordinance against sectarianism therefore, does not refer to the *fatwas* that have caused so much violence in Pakistan.

It seems that apostatisation as an illegal activity was officially taken note of in 1999 as a mode of an insulting exchange between the Sipah-e-Sahaba and Tehrik-e-Jafaria Pakistan (TJP) and a decision was made to punish the insulter of the Companions (Sahaba) and the apostatiser. The matter arose after Prime Minister Nawaz Sharif began taking firm action against the activists of the sectarian party. The then chief of the Sipah-e-Sahaba, Maulana Ziaul Qasimi, wrote, a friend of the Sharif family, Dr Israr Ahmad of Lahore, asking him to intercede with Nawaz Sharif to end the persecution of Sipah members. Dr Israr then addressed a letter to Nawaz Sharif's father, Mian Sharif, requesting him to arrange a meeting in which some decision regarding the sectarian conflict could be taken. Mian Sharif, harassed by the Sipah's terrorist activities against his sons, readily agreed and a meeting of three parties was decided: the leadership of the Sipah-e-Sahaba, the Tehrik-e-Jafaria, and the prime minister along with his brother Shehbaz Sharif and their father. The Shia side agreed that there should be life imprisonment for anyone insulting the Sahaba in return for strict punishment for anyone guilty of apostatisation (*takfir*). Qasimi proposed that anyone doing *takfir* be taken to court, and in case he fails to prove someone a non-Muslim, he should be punished under law. The meeting took place on 7 March 1999, but soon afterwards the Shia side expressed reservations about what it had agreed to: the adjudication of *takfir* in court of law. The negotiations could not proceed after that and the two sects fell back to what they were doing before. The TJP left the meeting saying, 'No assembly, court, or forum has the right to decide the faith of any Muslim'.[30] Upon reflection, the Shia side must have become aware that any court in Pakistan under Sharia would find it difficult not to accept the *takfir* of the Shia.

Pakistanis have been the victims of the 'nation-building' process undertaken by the state after independence was won in 1947. India and Pakistan have been 'built' up in conflict with each other. History has been selectively interpreted to fashion a citizen that is obedient to the state. Invariably the events emphasised in Pakistani 'nation-building' textbooks relate to a recall of Muslim history in India under the rubric of ideology in such way that it binds the population of Pakistan together while opposing it to the 'anti-Muslim' culture of India. In short, Islam is used to set Pakistan apart from India while binding its people together as one nation. In Pakistan, where ideology has made everything unsubtle, it is blatant and at times comic.[31] The ideological content in the Pakistani textbooks only indirectly attacked India, but its intensely Islamic content also targeted the Shia community at a subliminal level. The Islamic texts were, however, bowdlerised by secular historian-bureaucrats before being put in the textbooks. One can say that before the 1980s, Sunnis and Shias grew up as one Muslim community simply because they lacked knowledge of the origin of these texts. It is only after the clergy became aggressive in their sectarian views after the rise to power of the Islamizing military dictator in Pakistan, General Ziaul Haq, and the parallel rise of the theocratic state of Imam Khomeini in Iran, that the two communities began to acquire consciousness of their differences.

GENERAL ZIA'S HARDLINE ISLAMIZATION

Pakistan was Islamized gradually but when it reached a peak in this process in the 1980s, the country became vaguely aware of an extremism that the West called fundamentalism. When the international media began using the word there was an immediate reaction against it. The cleric and the intellectual both thought it an attack on Islam and began defending Islam instead of worrying about the growing extremism at home. Pakistan's fundamentalism was mobilised and made sectarian by the government of General Zia. It also became jihadi and terrorist with a lot of financial support from the United States and Saudi Arabia. The Americans were concerned only with winning the war in Afghanistan and defeating the Soviet Union, but the Saudis had ideological and sectarian aims. The United States ignored the Saudi policy thrust because of its own anti-Iran orientation after the 1979 Revolution and the hostage-taking at its embassy in Tehran by the Revolutionary Guard of Imam Khomeini.

To the extent that jihad in Pakistan responded to the financial stimulus of Saudi Arabia it became mercenary and cannot be discussed as a manifestation of Islam. It is quite certain that at the level of the jihadi leadership, the jihad was motivated by financial gains. Almost all the jihadi leaders came into possession of considerable wealth, which they shared with the state apparatus in Pakistan and—not in sufficient measure—with the young recruits who fought the war with deeply felt sectarian convictions. It is possible that among the majority of the rank and file of the jihadi youth there was belief in the spilling of blood in the name of Islam and belief in martyrdom. The same is true of sectarianism. The leader who plans the killings is working for money but the man who actually kills may be moved by religious passion. There is evidence that youth from the crime underworld also joined the jihad. One has to concede that in such cases the rank and file too were motivated by financial considerations. Jihad and the consequent 'weaponisation' of Islam have inflicted permanent damage on civil society and state institutions in Pakistan.

The Pakistan Movement was not clear about the kind of state it would culminate in. The clarity that we see today is a part of the nation-building process that began in 1949 with the adoption of the Objectives Resolution by the Constituent Assembly charged with the task of framing the country's first Constitution. Pakistan became an ideological state on the basis of the Muslim experience in India. Soon after 1947, the religious parties with strong grassroots presence in the cities began challenging the vague founding principles of the state. Scholars of great standing, like Maulana Abul Ala Maududi, relied on the early lineaments of the state in Islam in their rejectionist rhetoric. What helped in this was the inchoate theory of the state in Islamic history. After 1949, the process to transform Pakistan into a religious state *ipso facto* made the clergy the guardian of the new founding principle.

In 1958, the civilian politicians finally gave in and the army began to rule directly in Pakistan. The army, as an interest group, was brought down in 1971 by its compulsion to operate the state on the basis of conflict with India.[32] In the next phase, the growing power of the clergy, reacting to a decade of the Pakistan People's Party's (PPP) secularising policies, and the post-nationalisation industrial groups, sworn to revenge against the PPP's socialism, enabled the army to stage a comeback. The army under General Zia combined three interest groups: the army, the clergy and the industrial elite. The army broke from the past secular tradition of professionalism by adopting ideology as its strong plank. This gradually led to the Islamization of the army and the industrial elite. The democratic institutions opened up by General Zia, after amendments in the 1973 Constitution, allowed a fuller Islamization of the law, followed by Islamization of society.

The ideological state of Pakistan was one among many in the third world experiencing gradual loss of economic viability. The Pakistan army postponed an economic crisis by participating in the decade-long Afghan war in the 1980s, assisted financially by the United States and Saudi Arabia. The religious groups gained stature and power in this period. Islamization of law and society had already given them more power than any other interest group.

Islamization within the army had dimmed the dividing line between the clergy and the military officers increasingly drawn from the country's middle class. It was after the creation of local militias under religious leaders on the pattern of Afghanistan—for use in the low-intensity war in Kashmir after 1989—that the religious group became supreme in Pakistan, their supremacy based on the two principles embraced by the Pakistan army: Islamization and jihad, and in the latter case, the army's decision not to fight frontally but covertly through militias raised by the religious parties. The concept of jihad by non-state actors was allowed at the cost of internal sovereignty. Leaders of the jihadi militias as 'warrior priests' attained higher profiles than the elected leaders and even their military handlers. The idea of the state preached by the powerful religious leaders was utopian but it allowed them to constantly portray democracy as an alien system in which only the corrupt prospered. Democracy was acceptable to them only under Sharia but most clerics did not agree completely with the Sharia enforced by General Zia. Deprived of real power and uncertain of their tenure in government, the elected leaders took to embezzling state funds and taking graft far more single-mindedly than in the past. The enrichment of the religious leaders through even more dubious means, like non-disclosure of wealth and exemption from income tax, could not be challenged. The state began to be called a failing or failed state that could default on its debts.

PAKISTAN FROM LOW CHURCH TO HIGH CHURCH

Before 1947, East Pakistan was in the grip of linguistic nationalism centred in West Bengal. West Pakistan was Low Church in terms of religion as its incompletely settled land was still dominated by shrines[33]. Despite the world's biggest canal system established by the British to circumvent brackish underground water, which should have urbanised it and allowed the shrine (*mazar*) to be replaced by the seminary (madrassa), the region had not yet surrendered to the High Church seminary. The countryside dominated West Pakistan as opposed to Central India where the Pakistan Movement had taken birth in the Muslim-minority provinces. In the North West, Afghanistan was High Church, strongly aligned with the seminary whose graduates had trained at Deoband in India[34] and were traditionally aligned with the languishing Ahle Hadith (Wahhabi) movement which had retreated from Delhi after 1857 to Bhopal. The Pakistan Movement grew out of its leaders' rejection of the Khilafat Movement literally run by the Congress leadership. This led to the rejection of the Pakistan Movement by the strong city-based seminarian clergy. However, because of their rivalry with the more puritanical Deobandis and Ahle Hadith, the Barelvi clergy favoured the Pakistan Movement.

In West Pakistan, the cities had opened up to the seminaries but the countryside was predominantly shrine-oriented where mystical saints were celebrated as a part of the folk tradition.[35] Because Muslim-majority West Pakistan had not responded enthusiastically to the Pakistan Movement, Muslims and Hindus celebrated the same saints. The Deobandis opposed the mysticism of the shrine, the Barelvis accepted it. Ironically, a Low Church non-clerical Pakistan Movement was rejected by the High Church clergy of India but was accepted by the Low Church clergy, and was compelled later to govern the predominantly Low Church territory of Pakistan.

After 1949, the state started moving in the direction of Islamization as a nation-building tool. It began to realise quite early that Islamic law-making could not be achieved under Low Church conditions. The seminary had to be taken on board to give legitimacy to state institutions. A Council of Islamic Ideology (CII) was soon set up which was deliberately kept High Church, dominated by the Deobandi minority among the clergy. Mysticism could not be the foundation of the ideological state. Islamic scholars like Dr Fazlur Rehman were not tolerated for long in the Council; and the high water mark of the High Church dominance came when General Zia appointed Maulana Yusuf Banuri, the founder of the Banuri Mosque of Karachi, to the Council. The

NWFP was traditionally High Church because of its cultural proximity with Afghanistan. After 1947, the seminary there aligned itself with the pro-Congress National Awami Party (NAP). It should be interesting to investigate how the two parties, one secular-socialist and the other orthodox-puritanical, interacted in their pro-India orientations. Through the adoption of High Church the state managed to dilute the aggressive rejectionism of the seminary which had been opposed to the Pakistan Movement. When the war in Afghanistan began in 1979, the linkage of the mujahideen with the seminarian tradition increased the charisma of the seminary. The rise of the Taliban, and the induction of jihad by Pakistan into its Kashmir policy, drove the Barelvis out. No Barelvi could go to Afghanistan for training because he would be considered an infidel. Many boys from the Barelvi institutions had to change over to a Deobandi or Ahle Hadith seminary before going to Afghanistan. Funding of the High Church seminaries by Saudi Arabia and the Gulf States led to the decline of Barelvi power, and Barelvi mosques began to be forcibly taken over by the Deobandis with state help.

Shah Waliullah, the eighteenth century Muslim thinker discussed above, seems to have inspired both liberal and orthodox ways of thinking in South Asia. His most remarkable contribution was the linkage he formed between Deobandi Islam and the Hanbali Islam of Saudi Arabia during his sojourn in Hejaz. The rise of Saudi influence in Pakistan during the Afghan jihad against the Soviets cemented the old nexus further. The Saudi gift of seed money for General Zia's Zakat fund was conditional: a significant bequest had to be made to the Ahle Hadith seminary headquarters in Faisalabad—renamed to show gratitude to King Faisal of Saudi Arabia—the city where Al Qaeda's Abu Zubaydah was to be arrested in 2002. Army chief General Mirza Aslam Beg accelerated the spread of Deobandi seminaries in Bahawalpur and Rahimyar Khan so that their armed youth could be used as a 'second line of defence' against a possible Indian attack from Rajasthan.[36] The Arab sheikhs, who enjoyed extra-territorial rights, came to the area for hunting rare birds and began to fund the seminaries, thus allowing the rise of the Sipah-e-Sahaba under an intensely anti-Shia and anti-Iran leader, Maulana Haq Nawaz Jhangvi.[37] The Deobandi–Ahle Hadith tradition in India had always been coloured with strong sectarianism. Jihad in Pakistan brought to the fore the dominance of a Deobandi consensus together with a strong anti-Shia trend among the main jihadi groups.

Religious extremism gathered further momentum during the second jihad, which was the extension of the Afghan jihad against the Soviets, to Kashmir as a low-intensity conflict with India after 1989. The first jihad had empowered the Jamaat-e-Islami and its Pushtun leader, Qazi Hussain Ahmad. The sojourn of the Afghan jihadi leaders in Peshawar had begun a crucible process with the help of Saudi money. The High Church Afghans mixed with the local Deobandi consensus and tacitly agreed to oppose the Low Church trends in Pakistan. It was a 'hard' Islam Pakistanis knew nothing about. It came mixed with the even tougher tribal code called Pushtunwali that the 'settled' Pushtuns of Pakistan had gradually forgotten even in the tribal areas. The presence of the Arabs—especially the Egyptian runaways like al-Zawahiri—acted to further radicalise local Islam with *salafi* ideals overlaid with the Qutbite concept of the *jahiliyya* violence.[38]

The Deobandi seminaries became powerful on receiving *zakat* funds from the government of General Zia. After 1989, the empowerment of the Deobandis gained momentum as the jihad in Kashmir was restricted to the Deobandis and Ahle Hadith. The surrender of internal sovereignty to these militias happened first in the NWFP and the tribal areas; it later extended to a number of cities in Punjab, and in particular, Karachi, where the centre of the Deobandi consensus emerged at the Banuri Complex of seminaries. Increasingly, the youth joining the jihad were made conscious of the fact that somehow Pakistan had not enforced true Islam and that Pakistanis were living like infidels. More animus was shown towards the Shia community and to some extent the Ismailis.[39]

SHIA REACTION TO ISLAMIZATION

General Zia came to power in 1979 and immediately thought of promulgating new laws to enforce the Sharia in Pakistan. There were many reasons why he took the decision to Islamize Pakistan in a more strict fashion: first was his own personal bent of mind which inclined to strict Islam, the second was to meet the demand of those from among the right wing politicians and the clerical parties who had agitated against Prime Minister Zulfikar Ali Bhutto and brought him down with the help of the army; the third was the keenness with which Saudi Arabia, put under pressure by Imam Khomeini immediately on coming to power in Tehran in 1979, was pursuing the propagation of its own brand of Wahhabi Islam.

Saudi Arabia encouraged Pakistan to first proclaim the edict of *zakat*, the 2.5 per cent 'poor due' collected from all earning Muslims from their money and assets. King Faisal gave Zia the 'seed-money' to start the *zakat* system in Pakistan with the condition that a part of it go to the Wahhabi party, called Ahle Hadith in Pakistan. Having come under obligation to the Saudi king, Zia lost no time in signing the *zakat* and Ushr Ordinance (1980). He encouraged the clergy to open more seminaries to receive Rs 50,000 immediately from the *zakat* fund that he had started courtesy the Saudis. In a matter of months hundreds of new seminaries cropped up—some of them just signboards—on the Lahore-Islamabad highway, to net the funds being doled out. The distribution of *zakat* had been suitably reinterpreted as it did not allow payments to institutions. The Sunni madrassas increased from 401 in 1960, when Pakistan remained secular in governance, to 1745 in 1979, when ideology was emphasised and was finally enforced in the form of Sharia in two years of General Zia's government![40] And an Islamic University for Islamabad was decreed by the Saudi king to consolidate the growing involvement of Pakistan with hadith-based dogmatic Islam. This was the University where the intellectual founder of Al Qaeda, Abdullah Azzam, was to locate himself as a teacher.

The Shia in Pakistan did not accept the levy of *zakat*. General Zia and his fundamentalist advisers, particularly the Chairman of the Council for Islamic Ideology, Justice Tanzilur Rehman, knew that the Shia would not pay the poor-due tax to the state; instead their *zakat* was called *khums*—twice the amount the Sunnis paid—and it was traditionally paid to the Shia clergy, clearly a throwback to the history of Shias living as a suppressed majority or a minority in Sunni states. When the ordinance for the enforcement of *zakat* was promulgated, the Shia staged their biggest protest in the history of the country, coming to Islamabad in a large procession. They were led by Mufti Jafar Hussain (1916–1983), a graduate of Lucknow and Najaf who made his base in Sunni-dominated Gujranwala in Punjab and was proclaimed as the head of the Millat Jafariya of Pakistan. Known as a scholar before he decided to come out against General Zia, his exegesis of *Nahj al-Balagha* was popular in the community. In recognition of his learning he was appointed to the Council of Islamic Ideology repeatedly under Ayub and Bhutto and again under General Zia. Only under Zia did he resign his seat in the council in 1979 in protest against the inclusion of a majority of Deobandi and Ahle Hadith members who nursed a particular animus against his community. It is a tribute to his prestige among the Shia that after his protest General Zia had to announce an exemption for the community. *Zakat* has proved to be an unsuccessful religious tax in Pakistan, resulting in a lot of corruption. The exemption of the Shia community through the submission of an affidavit has permitted a lot of Sunnis to refuse to be a part of the corrupt law by declaring themselves Shia to their banks. The Supreme Court of Pakistan finally made the payment of *zakat* optional, thus negating the Sunni belief that it is compulsory under Islam.

General Zia's relations with Iran had worsened after the Revolution there in 1979. Imam Khomeini was not pleased by Zia's acceptance of the patronage of Saudi Arabia which exported its hard version of Islam. Zia had accepted a Saudi-funded Islamic University for Islamabad where Iran knew all the Salafi-Wahhabi teachers would gather from the Arab world. The jihad in

Afghanistan against the Soviet Union was not going well for Iran because the Saudi-backed Sunni warriors tended to ignore the Iran-backed Shia militias. Imam Khomeini periodically criticised Pakistan for doing the bidding of the Americans, while also implying subordination to Saudi Arabia.

Zia may have reacted by ignoring the anti-Shia stirrings among the Deobandi clergy in Pakistan. In the case of the Punjabi city of Jhang at least, there is evidence that the gathering sectarian storm was reported to him by the intelligence agencies, which he ignored.[41] The rise of Maulana Haq Nawaz Jhangvi in the stronghold of big Shia landlords in Punjab changed the sectarian scene in Pakistan. A full-fledged religious party called Anjuman Sipah-e-Sahaba of Pakistan (ASSP) came into being in 1985 under the leadership Jhangvi who was earlier the Punjab vice-president of the leading Deobandi party, Jamiat Ulema-e-Islam (JUI). In small towns, the old Shia–Sunni debate restarted with fury that had become dampened in the past. The tracts which carried this debate were scurrilous in the extreme and helped the clerics to whip up passions. The following year in 1986, General Zia allowed a 'purge' of the Turi Shias in the divided city of Parachinar (capital of Kurram Agency on the border with Afghanistan) at the hands of the Sunni Afghan mujahideen in conjunction with the local Sunni population.

Parachinar was the launching-pad of the mujahideen attacks into Afghanistan and the Turis were not cooperative. The Shia organisation Tehrik-e-Nifaz-e-Fiqh-e-Jafaria (TNFJ) had come into being under the leadership of a Turi Shia, Allama Ariful Hussaini in 1983. When the Parachinar massacre occurred, the party was led by him. Allama Hussaini was murdered in Peshawar in August 1988, for which the Turis held General Zia responsible. That was also the year of General Zia's death (within a fortnight of Hussaini's murder) in an air-crash in Bahawalpur, and for a time there was rumour of Shia involvement in his assassination although no solid evidence supporting this speculation was ever uncovered. The NWFP Governor General Fazle Haq, whom the Turis accused of complicity in the murder of Allama Hussaini, was ambushed and killed in 1991. (Mehram Ali, the Shia terrorist who blew up the Sipah leader Maulana Zia-ur-Rehman Farooqi at the Sessions Court in Lahore, was trained in Parachinar).

THE POLITICS OF *TAKFIR*

Mariam Abou Zahab tells us about the birth of the Sipah-e-Sahaba and how it turned Pakistani jihad into a sectarian crime and involved the state and its intelligence agencies in it.[42] The Jhang district (containing three cities, Jhang, Chiniot, Shorkot) in southern Punjab has a total population of 2.8 million out of which 25 per cent are Shia. (This is also the estimate about the total Shia population in Pakistan.) Half the population of Jhang are refugees from East Punjab who filled the vacuum created by the transfer of the non-Muslim majority of the district to India in 1947.

The Shia are divided among the refugees and the locals. So are the Barelvis, the locals among them integrated into Shia rituals and therefore are at peace with them. Most clerics in Jhang sought their careers in baiting the Ahmedi community of Rabwah which fell in Jhang district, but the Deobandis among them also began to take on the Low Church Barelvis and the Shia too, starting in 1950. The Shia power is represented by the strong Shah Jewna feudal landlords who are also divided into two hostile factions. Sunni feudals contesting assembly seats against the Shia feudals have played their role in strengthening the sectarian clerics. The refugee youth from the Arain peasant stock has arisen in the district as the most virulent sectarian and jihadi element over the years. The most remarkable figure to arise in this environment was Maulana Haq Nawaz Jhangvi (1952–1990) who founded the SSP in 1985, not a little assisted by the intelligence agencies spearheading General Zia's plan 'to teach the Shias of Jhang a lesson' for having opposed his *zakat* laws.

Iraq and Saudi Arabia funded SSP while the Shia were reactively funded by Iran. The politics of this funding culminated in 1989 when the Saudis ousted the Iranian jihadis from the Afghan interim government with the help of the ISI, of which more in later chapters. Jhangvi, a *khoja* graduate of a Deobandi seminary in the city, was vice-president of the JUI in Punjab till he became too big for the party. He acquired power by first attacking the Ahmedis, then the Barelvis. His hold on the administration (called *thanakutchehri*) increased over time till everyone with political ambition had to fund him. His denunciation of the Shia called for the apostatisation of the Shia on the order of the Ahmedis; it was followed by a similar denunciation of Imam Khomeini. According to Abou Zahab, funding for Jhangvi came from the marketplace, from businessmen and drug-dealers looking for protection. One major financier of SSP was Sheikh Yusuf, an MPA with contacts in the army who landed lucrative contracts for his construction company in the Lahore–Islamabad Motorway.

Another Sunni businessman, Sheikh Iqbal, fell foul of Jhangvi after he breached a pledge to foot the bill for weapons acquired by SSP elements. Jhangvi had put together a strong organisation of criminalised youth mostly from the *muhajir* (refugees from India) Arain community from East Punjab. He was eventually to die in the violence he had done much to instigate. According to Abou Zahab, he was killed in a local feud. Jhangvi was assassinated in 1990, followed by the murder of his successor Isarul Haq Qasimi in 1991 for which the SSP accused the civil servant son of Sheikh Iqbal, who was himself done to death by the SSP in 1995. Sheikh Yusuf, who funded the SSP, was known to have used its *goondas* (criminals) to hurt and kill his own business rivals, somewhat like the use made of the Sunni Tehreek in Karachi by a Memon businessman. In 1992, the new deputy chief of the SSP, Maulana Azam Tariq, tried to tame the *goondas* under Riaz Basra and his terrorists. Zahab tends to think that Azam Tariq had later nothing to do with Riaz Basra's Lashkar-e-Jhangvi. The truth is that Azam Tariq tried his best to prevent a Lashkar *goonda* from being hanged for an Iranian diplomat's murder. The Lashkar boss Riaz Basra, killed in a 'police encounter', was buried by him in a Sipah-e-Sahaba flag.

Jhang's main contribution was the SSP which served as the mother of all the Deobandi militias fighting the wars in Afghanistan and Kashmir. In Jhang, at least the rise of the SSP is located in a complex sociological matrix, but outside of Jhang, from Quetta to Kurram Agency and Kohat, to the Northern Areas, it is located firmly within the ideological paradigm of Pakistan and its logical progression towards a hardline Sunni state. When the SSP terrorist Haq Nawaz was to be hanged in 2001 for killing the Iranian diplomat in Lahore, the mainstream religious parties tried to save him. JUI, which had offered Lashkar-e-Jhangvi's main terrorist Riaz Basra a seat in the 1987 national elections joined the Jamaat-e-Islami and the SSP in trying to prevent his hanging. Maulana Azam Tariq tried to offer *diyat* (blood money) to Iran and the above-mentioned parties tried to persuade President Musharraf to exile Haq Nawaz as he had the former Prime Minister Nawaz Sharif instead of executing him. The clerical leaders were probably encouraged to make this proposal by Al Qaeda and some powerful personalities in the states of the Gulf.[43]

THE DEATH OF ZIAUL HAQ

General Ziaul Haq came to power in 1977 and was killed when his plane blew up in 1988 at the peak of the Shia killings in Pakistan. It was widely believed in Pakistan that his death was engineered by the Shia community in revenge. Zia began Islamizing the country under the tutelage of Saudi Arabia. By 1980, the first Islamic laws of the Sharia he enforced were backed by Saudi Arabia who sent special advisers at the time of framing them. In 1979, Iran went through its Islamic Revolution. Around the Gulf, the Arab states feared this development because most of them had Shia minorities they were not treating well. Saudi Arabia experienced the first uprising among the Shia of its oil-bearing Eastern Province in 1979, immediately after the Islamic Revolution. Every occasion of hajj began to be used by the Iranian pilgrims to stage protests. In 1981, Bahrain was nearly taken over by 72 Shia terrorists trained in Iran. In 1984, Iran sent its largest number of pilgrims, 154,000, to Makkah with a plan to stage a big protest, which led to rioting and Shia deaths. The same year Kuwait, where the Shia may number 25 to 35 per cent of the population, experienced terrorism which was traced to Iran.

In 1980, General Zia had to face Shia resistance to his enforcement of *zakat* on Pakistan's nearly 22 million Shia. In 1982, the Gulf States including Saudi Arabia set up the Gulf Cooperation Council (GCC) to face up to the threat of Iran. General Zia stayed away from providing it with military teeth, but he was clearly more under the influence of the Arabs than the Iranians by reason of a large expatriate Pakistani community working in the Gulf region and sending back nearly 70 per cent of the foreign exchange remittances coming in from all over the world. But in 1985, the anti-Shia organisation Sipah-e-Sahaba had already been formed. In 1986, an Indian Muslim scholar, funded by Saudi Arabia, asked the big seminaries in Pakistan to say whether the Shia were Muslims. Maulana Manzur Numani had earlier written a book against Iran and mentioned in it the 'near takeover' of Makkah by Iranian pilgrims in 1984. The seminaries in Pakistan sent to him *fatwas* saying that the Shia were not Muslims. The compilation of these apostatising *fatwas* later led to many Shia deaths in Pakistan.

Also in 1986, while the apostatising *fatwas* were being compiled, General Zia allowed the Sunni mujahideen fighting against the Soviet troops in Afghanistan to attack Parachinar, the capital city of the Shia-majority tribal area of Kurram near the Afghan border amid reports that the Shia were leaving for Iran 'by the truckload' for military training. Three years earlier, in 1983, the Shia of Pakistan had begun to be led by Allama Ariful Hussaini, who was a companion of Imam Khomeini during the latter's exile in Iraq.

Parachinar had no tradition of organised violence until Pakistan's interventionist policies in Afghanistan resulted in the influx of Afghan Islamist extremists and a flourishing trade in drugs and arms. Afghan fighters were brought into this area to attack Turi Shias because the

Zia government did not want any Shia pockets on the weapon supply route from Pakistan to Afghanistan. Since then, sectarian conflict has been endemic and bloody.[44]

The Kurram massacre of the Shias was still sending out waves of unrest in Pakistan when General Zia allegedly allowed another massacre of the Shia in Gilgit in the Northern Areas of Pakistan in April 1988. On August 5 of the same year, the Shia leader, Allama Ariful Hussaini, was murdered in Peshawar. Greatly offended, Iran sent a special high-level delegation to condole his death and take part in his funeral. Allama Hussaini's credentials were much strengthened as a scholar because of his association with Imam Khomeini during Khomeini's exile in Najaf in Iraq before the Saddam government ordered Hussaini out of Iraq.[45] Iran's special delegation was led by Ayatollah Jannati.[46] Then on 17 August 1988, General Zia was killed in an air crash in Bahawalpur in the south of Punjab while inspecting new American tanks that he wanted to buy, but his junior officers, including the local corps commanders, did not. The governor of the NWFP, whom the Shia community openly accused of being involved in the killing of their leader in Peshawar in 1988, was killed by unknown gunmen in 1991.

Zia's own aide de camp (ADC) Majid Raza Gillani was suspected of being involved in the killing of the Shia leader:

> The state appeal against the acquittal of those charged with the murder of Ariful Hussaini still continues to this day. The judge has delayed the appeal on 9 March 2005 on conflict of interest matters with one of the members of the judiciary. The accused are former government officials in the Zia regime, including ADC to the president Majid Raza Gillani, *whose apparent motive for such a crime would have been to counter Iranian influence in Pakistani domestic policy.*[47]

Azmat Abbas wrote,

> Shia outfit Pasban-e-Islam has been involved in several high profile murders, including the unsolved disappearance of Captain (Retired) Majid Raza Gillani who served as General Zia's ADC. In a verdict that was never accepted by many Shia organisations, Gillani was acquitted

in the 1988 murder trial of the Tehreek Jafariya leader Allama Ariful Hussaini. Gillani was shot, injured and abducted from outside his house shortly after his acquittal by a young man in a jeep and was never heard from again.[48]

Hassan Abbas connects him to the conspiracy of Zia's crash through the murder of Hussaini:

Intriguingly, Majid Raza Gillani who, according to an ISI insider, was a tool used in this sabotage, was in fact charged with the murder of Ariful Hussaini but was acquitted in 1993 by the district court in Peshawar. He also remained in ISI custody for some time after the August 17 crash but was later freed and thrown out of the Pakistan army.[49]

The Shia went in appeal later on, and in 2005, and quite in contradiction to the two versions above, Gillani was still under trial in Peshawar.

JUSTICE SHAFIUR REHMAN COMMISSION REPORT

Nobody can say for certain who killed General Zia. In 1992, Prime Minister Nawaz Sharif was forced by accusations of foul play from various quarters to set up a commission of inquiry into the Bahawalpur crash. (He was forced above all by a member of his cabinet, Zia's son Ijazul Haq, who constantly accused the army chief Aslam Beg, retired in 1991, of having killed his father.) The Commission was headed by the Supreme Court judge Justice Shafiur Rehman but it submitted a report of non-performance by clearly accusing the Pakistan army of obstructing its work. A summary of its report to the prime minister was published in an Urdu newspaper in Lahore and the report, too, may have been a public document but at the time of writing it has been sealed as secret and confidential by the Law Ministry.

The Shafiur Rehman Commission entertained three depositions made from the citizens: 1) the Ahmedis killed General Zia; 2) the Americans did it; 3) the Shias did it. No deposition said that the Pakistan army had done it. The conclusion, which accuses the army of putting hurdles in the way of the Commission's work, was reached by the Commission on its own. The theory that the Ahmedis did it, propounded in the deposition made by Manzur Elahi Malik, leader of Tehrik-e-Khatm-e-Nabuwwat, Kharian, was dismissed as absurd because it had named president Ghulam Ishaq Khan, General Aslam Beg, General Ahmad Kamal, General Durrani, Admiral Sirohi, and IG Punjab Nisar Cheema, as secret Ahmedis who killed Zia to avenge the anti-Ahmedi laws he had promulgated. The Commission ruled that killing Zia couldn't have rescinded the anti-Qadiani ordinance and therefore there was no logic in the theory.

The Commission also rejected the theory that the Shias did it. This theory was based on the 'fact' that Flight-Lieutenant Sajid, co-pilot in the ill-fated C-130, was a newly converted Shia, who had told his mother before his departure that he was going on 'a great mission', indicating the passion for *shahadat* (martyrdom) of the newly converted. Hassan Abbas has an inside track on what the ISI thought:

> At this stage, the planners of Zia's murder convinced Flight Lieutenant Sajid, a Shia who was co-pilot of the ill-fated C-130, that Zia was anti-Shia and had ordered the killing of Ariful Hussaini. So Sajid, according to the ISI report, was motivated to take revenge and crash Zia's plane.[50]

However, the Commission ruled out this version and any Iranian involvement, holding that the chemical which caused the crash couldn't have been taken into the plane by co-pilot Sajid without the help of Sunni officers.

The Commission examined the accusation that the Americans had killed General Zia and called up the records of the inquest held by the US Congress. It was revealed that ambassador Robert Oakley and General George B. Crist of CENTCOM had decided on their own not to involve the FBI in the investigation of the Bahawalpur crash in which the American ambassador Arnold L. Raphel and Brigadier General Herbert M. Wassom had been killed. They had instead got the Pentagon and the State Department to hold an inter-departmental inquiry. The Commission discovered that both Oakley and Crist had later apologised to Congress for having made this mistake. The Commission ruled that there was no evidence that the Americans were involved. In fact, it praised the US Congress for holding a proper inquiry, something that Pakistan had failed to do.

The Commission, however, called its work inconclusive because it was not allowed by the army to investigate the Bahawalpur crash fully. It was convinced that the air crash was an act of sabotage. It noted that the evidence was destroyed by the quick removal of debris and by an equally quick burial of the dead bodies without post mortem. The army refused to hand over the door with a hole in it, caused by the explosion in the cargo section, where a device was placed by loaders. (This door was noted in the photographs that were appended to an earlier air force inquiry.) The Commission complained bitterly about the fact that army loaders, who had placed some special cargo in the cockpit, were allowed to appear before it after great resistance, and that during their appearance in the court they were accompanied by army officers as 'minders' who obstructed testimony by their presence. The act of sabotage that killed 30 senior Pakistani army officers and two important Americans in 1988 will probably never be investigated properly.

Apart from the tense anti-Shia environment in Pakistan, the details of the crash still tended to point to a possible Shia conspiracy. Two pilots flying President Zia's C-130 plane were either reported to be Shia or their names recalled Shia identity. The pilot, Mashood Hassan, had a Shia-sounding name while his co-pilot Sajid was known to be a Shia. Epstein, who investigated the incident immediately after it had happened, dismisses the Shia conspiracy theory:

For its part, Pakistani military authorities attempted to foist an explanation that Shi'ite fanatics were responsible for the crash. The only basis for this theory was that the co-pilot of Pak One, Wing Commander (sic!) Sajid, happened to have been a Shi'ite (as are more than ten per cent of Pakistan's Moslems). The pilot of the back-up C-130, who also was a Shi'ite, was then arrested by the military and kept in custody for more than two months while military interrogators tried to make him confess that he had persuaded Sajid to crash Pak One in a suicide mission. Even under torture, he denied this charge and insisted that, as far as he knew, Sajid was a loyal pilot who would not commit suicide. Finally, the army abandoned this effort. The Air Force demonstrated that it would have been physically impossible for the co-pilot alone to have caused a C-130 to crash in the way it did. And if he had attempted to overpower the rest of the flight crew, the struggle certainly would have been heard over the radio. But why had the military attempted to cook up this Shi'ite red herring?[51]

There is a consensus among all those who have cared to look into the mystery of General Zia's death that it was no accident, that it was carried out by a group of people from within Pakistan, and that the Pakistan army consistently obstructed all efforts at finding out who had actually been a party to the conspiracy to kill Zia.[52] The 'Shia angle' was partially raised again in a long report that appeared in an Urdu weekly magazine *Takbeer* in 1992.[53] The 'suspected' army chief Aslam Beg had been replaced by General Asif Nawaz who was intensely disliked by the Islamist officers close to the ruling Prime Minister Nawaz Sharif. The contents of this unusual 32 page long report seem to have come from within the army when he was in office. The magazine published photos of the pages of an earlier air force inquiry into the crash and clearly tried to own a critical commentary on this report. Who from the army leaked this 'report on the report' to *Takbeer*? The army chief General Asif Nawaz was to die of natural causes—contested by his family—while in office in the middle of a dangerous row with the prime minister and his supporters among the serving and retired army officers.

The *Takbeer* report discusses the person of Flight Lieutenant Sajid in some detail. It contradicts Epstein's claim that he was security-cleared. Sajid and senior technician Abdul Aziz, both from Bahawalpur, were not security-cleared. It says that both left the

Bahawalpur airport for some time to meet their friends in the city. Sajid had also violated a rule. He had flown a plane to the dangerous mountainous region of Gilgit in the Northern Areas (a Shia majority region) a day earlier on 16 August and could not have flown again within 24 hours under the air force rules. Witnesses had told the investigative team that Sajid was tired when he reached Bahawalpur as a co-pilot of the president's plane. He was taken on board in a hurry and was not security-cleared. The magazine then discloses details that have not been noted so far: 'According to the ISI investigation, Sajid was first a follower of the Ahle Hadith school of Muslims and had converted to Shiism only three months earlier'.[54] It was Sajid's voice that one witness Wing Commander Munawwar Alam Siddiqi claimed to have heard over the radio while flying another plane in the vicinity. Sajid was calling out to Mashood, the senior pilot, before the plane went down.

What Sajid said to Mashood was precisely, 'What are you doing, Mr Mashood?' Startlingly, a report appearing in *Sunday Times* of 24 August 2008, reveals the following facts.

A postscript: Khan's activities give a new explanation for the crash of President Zia's C-130 plane in 1988, in which Arnold Raphel, the US ambassador, and General Herbert Wassom, head of the military mission, also died. Wing Commander Mash'hood Hassan, the plane's pilot, had also been flying Khan's centrifuge equipment to China. On one such trip he confided in a colleague of Khan's that he hated Zia, holding him responsible for the murder of a local religious leader: 'The day Zia flies with me, that will be his last flight.' The aircraft plummeted to the ground soon after taking off, killing all on board.[55]

This bit of information tagged to the main report tends to revive the controversy over the identity of the pilot Mashood Hassan who had a Shia-sounding name but has been somehow confirmed as not being Shia. It also links the crash to Dr A.Q. Khan through a friend who probably informed him that a pilot transporting his centrifuges hated General Zia enough to kill him through a suicide mission. At another place in this section, contacts between General Aslam

Beg and Dr A.Q. Khan are also discussed, but the latest information
given above tends to establish that Zia's death was linked both to
the sectarian war he had unleashed in the country—Mashood,
undoubtedly a Shia, was referring to a Shia spiritual leader, Ariful
Hussaini killed, according to the Shia, by Zia in Peshawar just a
week earlier—and the nuclear programme.

The *Takbeer* report disclosed that General Zia had stopped
travelling by air after the assassination of the Shia leader Ariful
Hussaini but was persuaded by senior officers twelve days after
Hussaini's death to fly to Bahawalpur despite the fact that he was
constantly hearing of conspiracies to kill him. While the drift of
the report was to focus on the senior officers, especially Corps
Commander Bahawalpur General Shafiq, on whose orders the
investigations were obstructed, it was hinted that the Shia officers
could have been made to participate on the basis of religion.
Although once military secretary to Zia, Shafiq was imprisoned in
the Major General Tajammul Case of a plot against Zia after a
conspirator's letter contained a reference to him. He was freed on
the request of General Musa, the Shia former commander-in-chief,
and was posted abroad. Later, Prime Minister Junejo was
instrumental in getting General Zia to promote him to lieutenant
general. Similarly, corps commander Multan, General Shamim
Alam Khan, could not have been greatly pleased with Zia as he too
was rescued from relegation by Junejo who pressured Zia to
promote him to the rank of lieutenant general after being told that
Zia was not promoting him despite his good record.[56]

An interesting testimony about General Shafiq's attitude comes
from the then corps commander Karachi, General Asif Nawaz
Janjua who was to succeed Aslam Beg as army chief in 1991.
General Asif Nawaz, upon hearing of the air-crash in Bahawalpur,
rang General Shafiq in Bahawalpur to ask what steps was the army
immediately taking and what orders had been issued in the wake
of General Zia's death. To his astonishment, General Shafiq replied
that Zia had met his end and there was no need to do anything
about it, clearly indicating Shafiq's intent to block all investigation
into the incident. The exact words he used were: 'He's gone; that's

it!' General Asif Nawaz, who was to succeed Aslam Beg as Pakistan's army chief, slammed the phone down in anger and said: 'He's not pushed! Something's not right!'[57]

ZIA AND SAUDI ARABIA; ASLAM BEG AND IRAN

The sectarian scene cannot be studied without the role played in it by Iran and the Arab states of the Gulf Cooperation Council (GCC) led by Saudi Arabia. The Iranian Revolution of 1979 took place when General Zia had just embarked on his campaign to Islamize Pakistan with the help of Saudi Arabia. His first Islamic Sharia laws were promulgated after being framed by an Arab scholar sent by King Faisal who had already given Zia 'seed-money' for his Zakat fund. Zia knew that he could not enforce the law of compulsory payment of *zakat* on the Shias, but he tried anyway in 1979, thus arousing the Shia to stage their first protest in 1980. The Quranic *hudood* laws based on a very strict literalist interpretation were actually first framed in Arabic by King Faisal's adviser (who also headed the World Muslim Council) and adopted in contravention of the recommendations by the constitutional advisory body, the Council of Islamic Ideology.[58] The full extent of Saudi 'help' is not known in this very delicate period for Zia who had referred in public to the 'empty coffers' left behind by the socialist government of Prime Minister Zulfikar Ali Bhutto—the popular Shia politician he hanged in 1979.

Saudi Arabia experienced its first Shia revolt in a long time in 1979 just after the Iranian revolution. Alarmed by Iran's revolutionary clout in the region, the Gulf states, in the tutelage of Saudi Arabia, set up the Gulf Cooperation Council (GCC). There was serious consideration given to the GCC having a military defensive aspect to it. Pakistan was the most natural ally from outside the region: it had a large expatriate population working in the GCC states and had a tradition of sending military advisers to them. Zia was close to the Arabs on many counts, having served as a military attaché in the region, but also had sense of a tradition of good Pakistan–Iran relations even though the pivotal role played by the Shah in them was at an end. While clearly an ally of Saudi Arabia, he was inclined to be neutral in the developing Iran–Arab confrontation. There were rumours in Pakistan in 1982 that the GCC states had threatened to expel all Pakistani workers if Pakistan refused to 'lend military teeth' to the GCC. There is very little on record because of the extreme caution exercised by the rulers of the UAE. Most books on the Gulf States discuss the GCC as a harmless organisation, but a clearer indication of what was at stake is indicated by Christopher M. Davidson. According to him, the plan for an anti-Iran axis existed up until 2001:

> Until September 11, 2001, many of the strongly anti-Iranian emirates had favoured a 'Sunni axis' comprising the UAE, Saudi Arabia, Pakistan, and the Afghan Taliban, in an effort to curb potential Shia expansion'. The author footnoted that his information had come from 'personal interviews, undisclosed locations, 2003.[59]

Zia had already had a bad meeting with Imam Khomeini. He had tried to play neutral in the Iran–Iraq war which had begun in 1980, but he could not please the Imam who had asked him to pardon Bhutto who was under the death sentence, only to be politely rebuffed by him. One meeting particularly went bad, as described by Vali Nasr, when Zia asked the Imam not to provoke the 'superpower' United States.[60] After that, quite illogically, he believed Khomeini when he accused the United States of backing a Saudi fanatic who tried to start a revolt in Makkah in 1979 after declaring himself Imam Mahdi. (The Mahdi was actually a Wahhabi named Qahtani put up by a rebel preacher Juhaima who harangued the hajj congregation about the arrival of the Muslim messiah which he significantly said was to come from the line of Ali.)[61] Zia repeated Khomeini's accusation on the television, which led to the destruction of the US embassy in Islamabad by mobs from a religious party included in his government. He later had to indemnify Washington for the destruction of its embassy. Discussing Zia's meetings with Imam Khomeini, Nasr says:

'Humiliated, Zia decided to take no chances by allowing Iranian influence in Pakistan and so had his Sunni fundamentalist allies reining in the Shias'.[62] Pakistani ex-ambassador to Saudi Arabia Shahid Amin records that Zia still played his cards carefully although his intimacy with the Arabs was a basic fact:

> During the Iran–Iraq war in 1980, Pakistan secretly tilted towards Iran while maintaining an overtly neutral attitude. Not surprisingly, Pakistan's help to Iran could not remain unknown for a long period of time. This brought complaints from the Gulf states with which Pakistan had always maintained very close relations and where hundreds of thousands of Pakistanis were gainfully employed.[63]

While the GCC was mulling the Iranian threat, Hojatul Islam Modaressi's terrorists struck again in 1983, this time in Kuwait, against the US embassy, through an explosive-laden truck driven by a Shia suicide bomber. The plot was uncovered through the impression taken from the thumb of the suicide-bomber which had remained intact. The trail led once again to Iran as the arrested men confessed. The following year, in 1984, Iran sent an unprecedented number of pilgrims to Saudi Arabia—over 15,000—with the intent of staging a demonstration in Makkah. Scuffles followed and the Saudi police ended up killing a number of pilgrims.[64]

Yet, while General Zia was clearly leaning in favour of the Arabs in the gathering Arab–Iran conflict, Pakistan was in the process of discussing a possible sale of nuclear technology to Iran!

Pakistan's nuclear acquisitions in the 1980s—thanks to the shadow of the superpowers' confrontation in Afghanistan under which it was proliferating—made Pakistan more challenging to India on Kashmir in the 1990s. Then, some of the North Korean syndrome got rubbed off on Pakistan. There were probably 60 to 70 nuclear bombs but no money to run the country's economy. The temptation to make money out of proliferation was great and was succumbed to. Dr A.Q. Khan, who ran the Kahuta Laboratory sat at the centre of a network of technology acquisition that stretched from North Korea to Germany, the US and Holland.

The Khan Network achieved a new level of illegal nuclear trade that challenged the non-proliferation regimes as never before. From the 1980s onwards, Dr Khan built centrifuges with imported parts, soon turning it into an import-export business covering Malaysia, Singapore, Turkey, South Africa, Switzerland, Dubai, and North Korea. Libya passed to him 450 tons of yellowcakes it obtained from Niger; in return Islamabad trained 18 Libyan scientists between 1973–1980. General Zia forced a cut-off in 1977, but Libya was able to revive its programme in 1995 through Dr Khan. In 1997, Dr Khan and his financier B.S.A. Tahir met the Libyans in Istanbul.

That was the year when Dr Khan sent Libya 20 complete centrifuges and material for 200 more. In 2000, Khan supplied two P-2 maraging steel centrifuges for testing. Libya ordered 10,000 P-2 machines from Dr Khan who made the delivery in December 2000. In 2003, Libya decided to abandon the project and come clean.[65] B.S.A. Tahir confessed to Malaysian authorities that Dr Khan supplied 1.87 tons of uranium hexafluoride to Libya in 2001. Dr Khan also supplied to Libya the complete nuclear component designs and instruction about how to build a nuclear bomb. The complete nuclear bomb would have resembled a Chinese nuclear bomb dating from the late 1960s. Since the last supply made was in 2002, the Libyan decision to come clean must have been sudden.

In February 2003, Iran told IAEA that it had been building two enrichment facilities at Natanz. In June 2003, Iran tested its first centrifuge, and in August 2003, began the test operation of the ten-machine cascade with UF6. In 2006, President Ahmadinejad announced Iran had enriched uranium. In 2007, he said Iran had 3,000 centrifuges enriching uranium and could graduate to the weapons level enrichment in a year. It is clear that without A.Q. Khan Iran could not have come to the threshold of nuclear power. Iran was the first country to receive centrifuges from Mr Khan. According to the IAEA, he made the sale to Iran of all the required elements in 1987 in Dubai.[66]

The one-page initial document of enrichment instructions by Dr Khan was shown by the Iranians to the IAEA. Iran contracted for 50,000 centrifuges from Khan for a price that ran into 'hundreds of millions of dollars' which included training of Iranian scientists in Pakistan in 1988. The Iranians complained about glitches in the P-1 centrifuges supplied earlier, but Khan developed P-2 centrifuges and supplied Iran with them to replace the earlier batch in 1993 and got paid $3 million for them. He also helped Iran with names of other suppliers that would sell to Iran. A Khan network scientist is quoted as saying,

> We confided in them [Iranians] about the items needed to construct a nuclear bomb, as well as the makes of equipment, the names of companies, the countries from which they could be procured. The Khan network's assistance enabled Tehran to contact suppliers in Europe, Russia, and Asia in order to acquire the nuclear technology and equipment.[67]

But let us take a look back into the past. Iran had asked Pakistan for 'nuclear assistance' in 1986, but General Zia gave strict orders to not give Iran anything substantial while himself signing an agreement with President Khamenei on peaceful nuclear cooperation. But Dr Khan got into the act through the chinks in the agreement which provided for training Iranian nuclear scientists in Pakistan at the Khan Research Laboratories (KRL). After Zia's death, army chief Aslam Beg (1988–1991) was in favour of giving Iran what Zia did not, and Dr Khan was most willing to oblige. Beg then threatened the Americans (Ambassador Oakley included) that he would transfer nuclear technology to Iran if America stopped the sale of weapons to Pakistan. Beg was aware of what Dr Khan was up to.

Benazir Bhutto, as prime minister, objected to sales to Iran but the army overruled her and the supplies continued. Islamabad had a troika system in which the executive authority of the prime minister was greatly diluted if not usurped. Dr Khan may have got the go-aheads but there was no systems impediment to his making money for himself too. His people—two are named, Sultan

Bashiruddin Mehmood and Chaudhry Abdul Majeed—also discussed all kinds of weapons of mass destruction with Osama bin Laden in Afghanistan.[68]

Gordon Corera says Pakistan's nuclear scientist and head of the Khan Research Laboratories (KRL), Dr A.Q. Khan was using Dubai, in the United Arab Emirates (UAE), as a base for meeting his suppliers. It is here in 1987 that he made a sale of crucial drawings and designs of a tested nuclear plant and received three million dollars in Swiss francs from the Iranian party.[69] Was this deal with Iran concluded with the consent of General Zia who was in the process of 'reining in the Shias' in Pakistan? After the massacre of the Shia in Parachinar he was to allow a *lashkar* (army) of Pushtun Deobandi fanatics to stage another massacre of the Shia in Gilgit, the Shia-majority capital of the Northern Areas, in April 1988. If he had given A.Q. Khan the go-ahead, did he realise that Saudi Arabia might get wind of it and retaliate against him? Zia was to die in an air-crash that year. Is it possible that the nuclear sale was made without his approval, that he came to know of it or was about to know it and might have acted against A.Q. Khan and his allies in the military establishment? And that he died because he had got close to the information in August 1988 about who had made the deal?

In a dossier released by the London-based International Institute for Strategic Studies (IISS) in 2007, a 'chronology of Dr A.Q. Khan's proliferation' indicates that he had visited Iran's reactor at Bushehr in 1986. It says that in 1987, the Iranian atomic energy commission 'concluded formal agreement on peaceful nuclear cooperation' with the Pakistan Atomic Energy Commission, something to which the Arabs would not have objected. But then Iran approached Dr A.Q. Khan's 'network' and 'Iran and the Khan network closed a $3 million deal for centrifuge technology'. The IISS dossier, distinguishing between 'Pakistan government' (meaning General Zia) and 'Khan network' (excluding General Zia), says:

At a meeting in Dubai, or perhaps later (Iran has not been forthcoming to the International Atomic Energy Agency or IAEA about the details) the network provided a 15-page document describing procedures for the re-conversion and casting of uranium metal into hemispheres, which IAEA Director General Mohamed ElBaradei later characterised as 'related to the fabrication of nuclear weapons' and a 'matter of concern'. Iran's claim that the Khan network provided the document on its own initiative is not consistent with what is known about the exchange of price lists.[70]

GENERAL BEG AND DR A.Q. KHAN

Is there enough circumstantial evidence to support the speculation that Zia died because of a secret pro-Iran nuclear policy followed from within the army which its supporters didn't want ended? Or that Zia first allowed and then decided to end the deal with Iran and was killed by those who didn't want the deal cancelled? Two streams of evidence seem to converge: that Zia's chief of staff or second-in-command, Lieutenant General Aslam Beg, was very keen about the nuclear programme and worked closely with A.Q. Khan; and that after the death of his boss was accused by Zia's son Ijazul Haq of engineering his death. After taking over as army chief, Aslam Beg began talking about 'selling' nuclear technology as a part of his 'strategy of defiance' of the United States. He knew that such nuclear cooperation with Iran was popular and that, within an increasingly anti-American army, Saudi Arabia and the Gulf Arabs were less popular as American clients in the region. The speed with which he declared the new nuclear policy leads one to speculate whether he simply wanted the 'obstacle' of General Zia to disappear from the scene. Zia was close to the Arabs, especially to Saudi Arabia, that had built a grand multi-million dollar mosque in Islamabad, the Faisal Mosque, where he was appropriately buried after his death.

Corera, too, wonders if the deal with Iran was 'official' or done without the knowledge of the 'government'—which was General Zia in 1987, Prime Minister Junejo being more or less a puppet by reason of the 8th Amendment in the Constitution passed by parliament which allowed Zia to dismiss him at his discretion. He records the official Iranian delegations—there was one led by president Ali Khamenei who was very keen to build the Iranian bomb—which must have clearly asked Zia for 'cooperation'. But the 'deal' in 1987 was concluded by a relative of A.Q. Khan in Dubai. This might point to Zia's reluctance to give the Iranians what they wanted in full public view, especially that of the Arabs, who had already reacted with alarm to the nuclear ambition of a friendly Shah in the 1970s. Corera makes the following interesting observation:

> But would Pakistan really want to see a neighbour with nuclear weapons? A few individuals might but not the whole government over an extended period. In essence, it appears that Khan could have received tacit approval and support from a small number of senior individuals but may have continued and deepened the relationship on his—or his network's—initiative.[71]

Then he provides a pen-sketch of General Aslam Beg:

> During the mid to late 1980s, when Pakistan and Iran were moving closer together and nuclear dealings began, General Mirza Aslam Beg was first vice chief from 1987 and then from 1988 to 1991, chief of the army staff.... As soon as he became vice chief he was 'made privy' to the nuclear programme for the first time. He supported a more overt nuclear policy and greater distancing from the United States and the West. According to his own writings, Beg thought in terms of 'democratising' the global nuclear non-proliferation order and moving to a multipolar world, which he believed would be safer than either a bipolar Cold War world or a unipolar world of American power.... Beg and A.Q. Khan were close friends and political allies and shared many of the same views.[72]

The IISS dossier on A.Q. Khan takes notice of the fact that he told his interrogators that he proliferated in favour of the Islamic world, but it rejects the claim because of his proliferation efforts in North Korea. What the dossier finds more convincing was the tendency to proliferate in favour of those states that defied the United States in particular and the West in general.[73] This brought his thinking close to the 'strategic defiance' doctrine of General Aslam Beg. In the case of both men, the general 'guiding principle' did not prevent them from personal enrichment. In the case of A.Q. Khan, two reprimands administered by General Zia to him for boasting about enrichment to the weapons' level in 1984 and 1987 may have strengthened his tendency to defiance based on resentment against Zia. Of this, more below.

In 2000, when General Pervez Musharraf ordered his National Accountability Bureau (NAB) to inquire into the affairs of Dr A.Q. Khan, NAB relied on an earlier investigation carried out under Prime Minister Nawaz Sharif by the ISI in 1998–1999 to confirm that Khan was 'buying too much material for Pakistan's own programme' and that 'he had given a house to General Beg and was paying off numerous Pakistani journalists and even funding a newspaper'.[74] The NAB report was kept without a number and the chief of the NAB left office concluding that Khan was too big a fish to tackle. General Musharraf later told *The New York Times* (17 April 2006) that once, when he asked for details of his forthcoming trip to the border city of Iran, Zahidan, Khan declined to tell him, claiming secrecy.

Musharraf is not as forthcoming about General Zia's death as he became about A.Q. Khan's connection with Iran. In his book he talks about the Bahawalpur crash but depicts it as a mystery, ending with a still more mysterious 'coda' to an event that should have caused him to look into what he clearly believes to be 'internal sabotage' meaning only the army as the perpetrator since 'internal' rules out 'external' parties:

The cause of accident still remains shrouded in mystery. The report did note that investigations found traces of potassium, chlorine, antimony, phosphorus and sodium at the crash site. Since these elements are not generally associated with the structure of an aircraft, the inquiry concluded that internal sabotage of the plane was the most likely cause of the accident. Mysteriously the case was not pursued further. The black box was recovered but gave no indication of a problem. It seems likely that the gases were used to disable the pilots.

But who unleashed them, we don't know. I have my suspicions, though.[75]

In 1987, someone in Islamabad sought to 'showcase' Pakistan's nuclear capability by arranging an interview between A.Q. Khan and Indian journalist Kuldip Nayyar with the help of Pakistani journalist Mushahid Hussain then employed with the Islamabad-based daily *The Muslim* and with known links to Iran.[76] Mushahid Hussain was an advocate of an 'overt' nuclear policy and was probably in contact with Vice Chief General Aslam Beg when he set up a meeting between Khan and Nayyar. Later, when Aslam Beg set up FRIENDS (Foundation for Research on Regional Defence and Security),[77] Mushahid Hussain joined it.

The IISS dossier points out that General Zia was not informed by A.Q. Khan about his 'great leak' to the journalist Nayyar. The general, upon reading what had happened, reprimanded Khan for the interview, proving once again that he was being kept 'out of the picture'. And this was not the first time General Zia had reprimanded him:

> The first time A.Q. Khan committed a problematic indiscretion was in April 1984 when a local newspaper quoted him boasting his achievement in enriching uranium to weapons' grade. This report caused considerable embarrassment for Zia.[78]

That the 1987 second 'disclosure' elicited a rebuke from General Zia who was chafing under the Pressler Amendment of 1985 in the aftermath of the first disclosure, leads one to assume that General Zia was kept 'out of the loop' on proliferation to Iran.

Following Zia's death, Aslam Beg became Pakistan's army chief and had his famous spat with the American ambassador in Islamabad, Robert Oakley, over his 'strategic defiance' thesis which he was free to parade after the US-imposed nuclear-related sanctions on Pakistan in 1990 had come into force. He also misinterpreted the 1991 American participation in the war against Saddam Hussein's Iraq after it occupied Kuwait. While Prime Minister Nawaz Sharif was visiting Saudi Arabia and ordering his troops to defend the sacred sites of Makkah and Madinah, Aslam Beg was making trips to Iran and predicting that the Americans would be defeated by Saddam Hussein after which Egypt and Saudi Arabia 'would be discredited' for being allies of the United States.[79]

Later, there were reports that Aslam Beg had gone to Tehran without informing Prime Minister Nawaz Sharif and had signed a secret agreement for 'military to military transfers' with Iran. Corera writes:

> Former Pakistani diplomats claim that Beg and the ISI chief General Asad Durrani approached President Ghulam Ishaq Khan with a proposal to sell nuclear technology in order to finance ISI operations that were ongoing in Afghanistan (but now without US financial support) and were just starting up in Kashmir. Sensing the potential political danger, the president, however, passed the issue on to prime minister Nawaz Sharif who declined the proposal.[80]

Journalist Zahid Hussain, in his book, also refers to Nawaz Sharif's Finance Minister, Ishaq Dar disclosing that 'Beg came back from Tehran with an offer of $5 billion in return for nuclear know-how, but Sharif rejected the offer'.[81]

Is it reasonable to assume that General Zia had not finally decided whether to give Iran the nuclear data it wanted while others around him were keen—anti-American feelings were building up in anticipation of the 1990 sanctions—to make a final break and join a regional phalanx of 'defiance' together with Iran? Was General Zia's death caused by this cleavage of opinion? Zia was actually fighting a sectarian war with Iran while secret contacts were being made by the nuclear scientists of Pakistan Atomic Energy Commission (PAEC) with their Iranian counterparts in Switzerland. Dr A.Q. Khan of KRL had also visited the Bushehr plant in Iran in 1987, but did Zia know that he had made a sale the same year at Dubai? Corera records that in 1989, the ISI chief General Hamid Gul had let President Ghulam Ishaq Khan know that 'there was evidence that A.Q. Khan was meeting with suspicious characters in Dubai'.[82] If the ISI got to know about the

Dubai contact in 1989, it is obvious that it could not have informed Zia about it in 1987. This strengthens the view that Zia was not informed about the deal with Iran. Was Zia thinking of 'cooperating' with the Iranians but was dissuaded from doing so for three possible reasons: his sectarian war against the Shia, his fear of Saudi and Arab wrath, and his fear of American sanctions which might include parallel retaliatory action by the Gulf States?

The Bahawalpur crash may have been engineered by collating a number of categories of elements willing to eliminate Pakistan's military ruler and yet a majority of the military personnel present on the occasion may not have known about the plot. Two facts about public opinion have stood the test of time: that Zia was killed by someone and that the army did not want his death properly investigated; and that his successor Aslam Beg had acted most strangely during the whole incident. Zia's son kept the pressure on Aslam Beg for some years till he got tired of it and became vague about who could have done the deed.

The *Takbeer* report of 1992, which reads like a 'leak' from the post-Aslam Beg military leadership, repeats some of the inconsistencies in Aslam Beg's statements that most Pakistanis have noted. When Zia asked Beg to return to Islamabad with him in his C-130, Beg said he had to go to Lahore on some other mission. This statement was given on 19 August 1988. But on 25 August he told some officers that he actually had to go to Multan and therefore had declined to go with Zia. But the log book of his plane mentioned no planned trips to either Multan or Lahore on the page-entry for 17 August. On 18 August 1988, in the presence of some American officials, Beg stated that Zia had been killed by the Russian KGB, Indian RAW and Afghan Khad working in tandem. After a few days, meeting the dead chief's family, he accused the Americans of having killed him!

The 'nuclear sale' story is the additional strand in the 'theory' of General Zia's death. The Shia 'strand' of it is present in this story through the newspaper *The Muslim* and its actively pro-Iran Shia chief editor and editor, and the Pakistani 'tilt' in favour of Iran by defying the pro-Arab trend set by General Zia. The 'theory' posits Aslam Beg as the central figure who is seen bringing together the various elements interested in killing General Zia. In the absence of any direct evidence or a confession, it remains a theory.

NOTES

1. *The Essential Rumi*, Translated by Coleman Barks with John Moyne, Penguin Books, 1995, p. 88.
2. The Sunni arrival in Sindh is dated from AD 711, while the Shia-Carmathian rule is witnessed by travellers in Sindh (Multan) in AD 985.
3. John F. Standish, *Persia and the Gulf: Retrospect and Prospect*, St. Martin's Press 1998, p. 39.
4. Saiyid Athar Abbas Rizvi, *Muslim Revivalist Movements in Northern India in the Sixteenth and Seventeenth Centuries*, Agra University, 1965, p. 207. Rizvi writes: 'He had written a repudiation of the Rawafiz (Shias). In the preface of the book he says that the Shias had written a treatise on the occasion of the siege of Mashhad to the ulema of Transoxiana in refutation of their letters which declared Shias as *kafirs* and exhorted the Sunnis to take forcible possession of the property and belongings of the Shias'.
5. Annemarie Schimmel, *Islam in the Indian Subcontinent*, Leiden, 1980, p. 104.
6. Ibid., p. 203. 'When one reads the terrible destruction that occurred during the mid-eighteenth century in northwest India, and for which Nadir Shah and Ahmad Shah Abdali are responsible, one wonders why Iqbal allotted these two rulers a special place in Paradise in his visionary poem *Javidname*'.
7. Mai Yamani, *Cradle of Islam: The Hijaz and the Quest for an Arabian Identity*, I.B. Tauris, 2004, p. 120.
8. Vali Nasr, *The Shia Revival*, Norton, 2006, p. 88.
9. Humayun Mirza, *From Plassey to Pakistan: Family History of Pakistan's First President Iskander Mirza*, University of America Press, 1999.
10. After his death in London, Iskander Mirza was buried in Tehran under orders from the Shah of Iran.
11. Mahmud Ahmad Abbasi, *Badshah Begum Awadh*, Maktaba Mahmud, (n.d.) p. 143.
12. Ali Rahnama, *An Islamic Utopian: A Political Biography of Ali Shariati*, by Ali Rahnama, I.B. Tauris, 1998, p. 212. Ali Shariati introduced Iqbal in Iran. The Iranian clergy objected to his Iqbal Lecture because they saw Allama as a Sunni philosopher. Some detractors even claimed that Allama Iqbal had insulted Imam Jafar Sadiq in one of his poems. It turned out that the said

poem was actually about two persons, Jafar and Sadaq of Bengal and Deccan, not the sixth Imam.

13. Liaquat H. Merchant, *Jinnah: A Judicial Verdict*, East-West Publishing Company, 1990. The book, source of the above narrative, contains the proceedings of the Sindh High Court on the question of Jinnah's faith. Well-known Karachi lawyer Mr Liaquat Merchant is the son of the daughter of Jinnah's sister Maryam Bai. Jinnah had four sisters (Rehmat Bai, Maryam Bai, Fatima Bai, Shirin Bai) and two brothers (Bundeh Ali, Ahmed Ali). Of the two brothers Bundeh Ali had died in childhood while Ahmed Ali had married a Swiss lady Emy and had lived in Bombay. They had a daughter Fatima who lived in Switzerland. The offspring of the granddaughter of Rehmat Bai, named Abbas Peerbhai, is in Karachi. Maryam Bai's two grand-daughters Zehra and Gulshan (his sisters) are also in Karachi. Mr Liaquat Merchant was born in Bombay and enrolled at the Bombay High Court in 1964 as a junior of his maternal uncle Akbar Peerbhai. Liaquat moved to Pakistan after Miss Fatima Jinnah asked him to do so in 1967. In Karachi he joined the office of the renowned lawyer Fakhruddin G. Ibrahim. Today he heads a number of organisations dedicated to the Quaid-i-Azam. In 1989, he set up the Jinnah Foundation Memorial Trust under which he set up a charity hospital and a school in Bath Island, and another charity hospital and school in Korangi Colony where 800 poor children were being educated. These schools and hospitals charge only nominal fees. In 1999, he also set up the Jinnah Society which has issued CDs and has a website majinnah. com.

14. Craig Baxter (ed.), *Diaries of Field Marshal Mohammad Ayub Khan 1966–1972*, Oxford University Press, 2007, p. 115.

15. Vali Nasr, *The Shia Revival: How Conflicts within Islam will shape the Future*, Norton, 2006, p. 88.

16. Mohammad Qasim Zaman, 'Sectarianism in Pakistan: The Radicalisation of Shi'i and Sunni Identities', *Modern Asian Studies* 32.3 (1998), pp. 689–716, Cambridge University Press, p. 691.

17. Ikram Rabbani, *A Comprehensive Book of Pakistan Studies,* The Caravan Book House, 1992.

18. Ibid., p. 37.

19. Ibid., p. 41.

20. *Nadir Maktubat Shah Waliullah* (Rare Letters of Shah Waliullah), researched and translated into Urdu by Maulana Nasim Ahmad Faridi, Idara Saqafat Islamia, Institute of Islamic Culture, 1994.

21. M. Mujeeb, *Indian Muslims*, George Allen & Unwin, 1967, p. 281.

22. A.D. Muztar in *Shah Waliullah: A Saint Scholar of India, Islamabad*, 1979, pp. 86–163 in *Shah Waliullah, His Religious and Political Thought*, edited by M. Ikram Chaghatai, Sang-e-Meel Publications, 2005, pp. 169–223.

23. Bashir Ahmad Dar, *Shah Waliullah and his Political Thought*, edited by M. Ikram Chaghatai, Sang-e-Meel Publications, 2005, pp. 19–50. Dar

originally wrote the article 'Waliullah His Life and Times' in *Iqbal Review*, October 1965, pp. 1–36.

24. Shaikh Mohammad Ikram (1908–1973) was an Indian Civil Service officer who cultivated a taste in history and arose to be Pakistan's leading historian after 1947. He was Visiting Professor in Indo-Iranian Languages and Culture at Columbia University in New York. On his retirement from government service, S.M. Ikram was appointed Director, Institute of Islamic Culture, Lahore. His work before 1947 reflects a historian's passion for facts, as shown by his trilogy *Aab-e-Kausar*, *Rud-e-Kausar*, and *Mauj-e-Kausar*, narrating the sectarian tendencies among the great Muslims of the past. In his other more political works like *Modern Muslim India and the Birth of Pakistan*, *Makers of Pakistan and Modern Muslim India*, *Muslim Civilization in India*, he doesn't emphasise the sectarian aspect simply because it did not appear important to him.

25. Ibid., p. 217.

26. Sayyid Athar Abbas Rizvi, *Shah Waliullah and his Times*, Ma'rifat Publishing House, 1980, p. 306.

27. Pildat: Pakistan Institute of Legislative Development and Transparency, Briefing Paper for Pakistani Parliamentarians, No 16, August 2004, p. 10.

28. Mohammad Qasim Zaman, *The Ulama in Contemporary Islam*, Princeton University Press, 2002, p. 113.

29. Jhangvi's taped sermons did the rounds in the mid-1900s in which he asked the courts to take cognisance of his *takfir* of the Shia. His tapes did insult the Shia but his reference to classical Islamic authorities—recognised as such by the courts—were all correct.

30. Zaigham Khan, 'Peace at Raiwind', *Herald*, May 1999, p. 48.

31. Krishna Kumar, *Prejudice and Pride: School histories of the freedom struggle in India and Pakistan*, Viking Press, 2001.

32. Hakeem Arshad Qureshi, *The 1971 Indo-Pak War: A Soldier's Narrative*, Oxford University Press, 2002, p. 247. Former Major General SSG (Commandos) points to the 'deliberate strategic conclusion that the defence of East Pakistan lay in West Pakistan'. The national defence doctrine was predicated on 'the defence of East Pakistan in West Pakistan' which was fortified on the calculus of Pakistan's challenge to India on the issue of Kashmir. East Pakistani military and civilian leaders were offended that the West Pakistan-based army had no real defence doctrine for East Pakistan.

33. *Daily Times*, Lahore (11 September 2003) quoted Ernest Gellner from his book *Post-modernism, Reason and Religion*: 'High Islam stresses the severely monotheistic and nomocratic nature of Islam, it is mindful of the prohibition of claims to mediation between God and man, and it is generally oriented towards puritanism and scripturalism. Low Islam, or Folk Islam, is different. If it knows literacy, it does so mainly in the use of writing for magical purposes, rather than as a tool of scholarship. It stresses magic more than learning, ecstasy more than rule-observance. Rustics, you might say,

encounter writing mainly in the form of amulets, manipulative magic and false land deeds. Far from avoiding mediation, this form of Islam is centred on it: its most characteristic institution is the saint cult, where the saint is more often than not a living rather than a dead personage (and where sanctity is transmitted from father to son).' Gellner was an outstanding theorist of modernity and a rare breed among late twentieth century scholars. He made major contributions in very diverse fields, notably philosophy and social anthropology. He is known for his path-breaking analyses of ethnicity and nationalism (*Thought and Change*, 1964; *Nations and Nationalism*, 1983), among other works.

34. Dr Rashid Ahmad Jullundheri, Journal *Al Ma'aref Quarterly*, (January–March 1998) Idara Saqafat Islamia. The issue contains a long survey of the Deoband seminary's birth and activities under the British Raj.

35. K.K. Aziz, *Religion, Land and Politics in Pakistan: A Study of Piri-Muridi*; Vanguard Books, 2002: Historian Khursheed Kamal Aziz has taken in hand an interesting but difficult theme from Pakistan's history: the relationship between ownership of land and the custodianship of grassroots spirituality as a power base for national politics. He was surprised to find that not much research work had been done on the subject. The most significant angle he provides to the understanding of the Barelvi dominance in Pakistan on the eve of 1947 is in his narrative of the participation of the Chishti order of sufi saints in the politics of a land that was dominated by Suhrawardi saints and Deobandi ulama. It was the Chishti success that brought in the Barelvi influence from Central India and converted what became known as Pakistan into a Low Church territory. This also makes known the Chishti support to the Pakistan Movement as opposed to the Deobandi ulama who opposed it.

36. This came up at a seminar in Islamabad. The information was given to the writer by a retired general of the Pakistan army.

37. There were secular beneficiaries too. A number of Sindhi families profited from the hospitality they offered to the Arabs who would spend an average of $1.5 million on each visit. The Mahr family of the chief minister of Sindh in 2003 is said to be one such beneficiary.

38. Khaled M. Abou El Fadl, *The Conference of the Books: The Search for Beauty in Islam*; University Press of America, 2003. The author traces intolerance to the anti-intellectual and anti-book nature of the *salafist* and Wahhabi Islam. He describes his argument with an Egyptian *salafist* priest who, when finding it difficult to answer some of the questions Khaled put to him, condemned him as a philosopher and a follower of traditions apart from the Quran and Sunnah. Khaled's main objection to the prevalent *salafist* trend is its total rejection of classical Islamic thinkers of the *fiqh*.

39. *Daily Khabrain*, 22 March 2003, published a brief biographical note on the late Allama Ehsan Elahi Zaheer of Jamiat Ahle Hadith who was killed by a bomb on 23 March 1987 in Lahore near Qila Lachchman Singh. Along with him four other Ahle Hadith scholars had also died. He had published a

number of virulently sectarian monographs in Arabic and was known to receive direct financial assistance from Saudi Arabia. Allama Zaheer was a great orator and an equally great author who was born in Sialkot in 1940 in the home of the Sethi branch of the Sheikh community. His father did not send him to school but had him taught the Quran and then sent him for more religious education to the Jamiya Islamiya in Gujranwala. In 1963, after qualifying, he was sent by the seminary to its headquarters in Madinah University from where he acquired the highest degree. Back home in 1967 he passed many exams: MA in English, MA in Political Science, MA in Persian, MA in Urdu and Law. He was made leader of prayers at the Wahhabi mosque in Chinianwali. As a speaker he was in the mould of Ataullah Shah Bukhari and took part in agitations against Bhutto. He wrote hard-hitting books on Shiism, Ismailism and other sects, in Arabic, and wrote equally hard-hitting books in Urdu. After he was killed by a bomb he was taken to a local hospital from where he was taken to Saudi Arabia on the orders of King Fahd of Saudi Arabia who sent his personal plane for him. He died in Madinah in 1987, and his funeral prayer was headed by the grand mufti of Saudi Arabia Sheikh Bin Baz, after which he was buried next to Imam Malik's grave.

40. Report of the National Committee for Deeni Madaris in Pakistan, Ministry of Religious Affairs, Government of Pakistan, 1979.

41. The writer as a Lahore-based journalist was interviewed by a committee headed by a police officer in 1984 about Jhangvi's activities. The committee was to report directly to General Zia. Later, the writer was told that the committee's findings were ignored.

42. Mariam Abou Zahab, *The Sunni–Shia Conflict in Jhang* in *Lived Islam in South Asia,* Social Science Press, 2004.

43. Suroosh Irfani, 'Pakistan's Sectarian Violence: Between the Arabist Shift and Indo-Persian Culture', in *Religious Radicalism and Security in South Asia*, Robert Wirsing and Mohan Malik (eds.), Asia-Pacific Center for Security Studies, 2004, pp. 147–169, 157. Irfani reports a similar effort from the religious parties not normally considered sympathetic to the sectarian killers.

44. International Crisis Group Asia Report No 95—18 April 2005. *The State of Sectarianism in Pakistan,* p. 4.

45. Mohammad Zaman, *Sectarianism in Pakistan: The Radicalisation of Shi'i and Sunni Identities*, in *Modern Asian Studies* 32.3 (1998), Cambridge University Press, p. 695. He makes reference to the fact that Hussaini had to quit Iraq after receiving orders of expulsion by the Saddam government, forcing him to return to Pakistan in 1978 after six years in the Najaf seminary. The writer of this book also learnt from Pakistan's scholar Qurayshpur on TV that Hussaini's death was commemorated in Iran with a postage stamp.

46. Mushahid Hussain, 'Among the Believers', *Herald*, September 1992, p. 39.

47. Saleem H. Ali, *Islamic Education: Conflict and Conformity in Pakistan's Madrassahs*, Oxford University Press, 2009.
48. *Herald*, November 2004, p. 38.
49. Hassan Abbas, *Pakistan's Drift into Extremism: Allah, the Army, and America's War on Terror*, ME Sharpe, 2005, p. 132.
50. Ibid., p. 126.
51. Edward Epstein, *Who killed Zia?*, Vanity Fair, September 1989.
52. Barbara Crossette, *Who Killed Zia?*, World Policy Journal, Fall 2005. Investigating US ambassador Dean's charge that the Israelis had got rid of Zia (and dismissing it), she writes: 'Given prolonged American involvement with Pakistan, isn't it time to look back with greater diligence and seriousness at this mystery? The longer the tragedy goes unexamined in any rigorous, if not conclusive, way, the more internally contradictory and bizarre this story becomes'.
53. *Takbeer*, 'Saaniha Bahawalpur main chand A'la Fauji Afsar Mulawwis hein', 20 August 1992. (Some high-ranking army officers are involved in the Bahawalpur tragedy).
54. Ibid., p. 21.
55. Simon Henderson, *Pakistan's Dr Nuke bids for the Presidency*, The Sunday Times, 24 August 2008.
56. Hassan Abbas, *Pakistan's Drift into Extremism: Allah, the Army, and America's War on Terrorism*, ME Sharpe, 2005, p. 121.
57. Interview (November 2006) with Shuja Nawaz, late General Asif Nawaz's brother, who was present when General Asif Nawaz rang Shafiq. Shuja Nawaz, after his career in the World Bank, lives in Washington DC. His book *Crossed Swords: Pakistan, its Army, and the Wars Within*, published in 2008, is on the Pakistan Army.
58. Syed Afzal Haider, *Islami Nazriati Konsal: Irtaqai Safar aur Karkardagi* (Council of Islamic Ideology: Evolution and Activity), Dost Publications, Islamabad, 2006. The book records that 'Dr Maroof Dualibi visited the offices of the Council' (p. 961). However, the Council's own report to the government in December 1981, observed that the Hudood laws were discussed by the Council and the Law Ministry 'under the guidance of Dr Maroof Dualibi who was specially detailed by the Government of Saudi Arabia for this purpose'. It seems as if Dr Dualibi sat in on discussions merely as a senior jurist and perhaps did not actually frame the laws. Just the opposite, in fact, happened. The CII report says that the recommendations on the Hudood laws made by it were set aside 'at the government level' before their promulgation as an Ordinance on 10 February 1979.
59. Christopher M. Davidson, *The United Arab Emirates: A Study in Survival*, Lynne Rienner Publishers, 2005, p. 206 and p. 244.
60. Vali Nasr, *The Shia Revival: How Conflicts within Islam will Shape the Future*, Norton, 2006, p. 162.

61. Dilip Hiro, *War without End: The Rise of Islamist Terrorism and Global Response*, Routledge, 2002, p. 139.
62. Vali Nasr, Ibid., p. 161.
63. Shahid M. Amin, *Pakistan's Foreign Policy: An Appraisal*, Oxford University Press, 2004, p. 141.
64. This was the 'Iranian takeover' as per the Shia prediction of Imam Mahdi's final takeover of Makkah mentioned in the prefatory article written by Manzur Numani to his collection of *fatwas* against the Shia. The *fatwas* were issued by Pakistan's major seminaries, many of them handsomely funded by Saudi Arabia, in 1986. But immediately after the Makkah agitation, it was the Sipah-e-Sahaba, the anti-Shia religious party, that made its sudden appearance in Pakistan in 1985.
65. Bhumitra Chakma, *Pakistan's Nuclear Weapons*, Routledge, 2009, p. 55.
66. Ibid., p. 111.
67. Ibid., p. 113.
68. Ibid., p. 125.
69. Gordon Corera, *Shopping for Bombs: Nuclear Proliferation, Global Security and the Rise and Fall of the A.Q. Khan Network*, Oxford University Press, 2006, p. 59–60.
70. International Institute of Strategic Studies, *Nuclear Black Markets: Pakistan, A.Q. Khan and the Rise of Proliferation Networks, A Net Assessment*, 2007, p. 69.
71. Ibid., p. 73.
72. Ibid., p. 74.
73. International Institute of Strategic Studies, Ibid., p. 85.
74. Gordon Corera, Ibid., p. 146.
75. Pervez Musharraf, *In the Line of Fire: A Memoir*, Free Press, 2006, p. 73.
76. The owner of *The Muslim*, Agha Murtaza Pooya, was a Shia and a votary of the Islamic Revolution with contacts in Tehran. The Editor of *The Muslim*, Mushahid Hussain was Pakistan's ranking journalist after his coverage of the 1983 military operation in Sindh. An admirer of Imam Khomeini, he was present in Makkah when the 1984 Shia pilgrims' protest there led to violence. He returned and wrote an eye-witness account of it for his paper.
77. Aslam Beg changed the 'defence' in FRIENDS to 'development'.
78. International Institute of Strategic Studies, Ibid., p. 94.
79. Gordon Corera, Ibid., p. 75.
80. Ibid., p. 76: Corera refers to Peter Lavoy and Feroz Hassan Khan, Rogue or Responsible Nuclear Power, Making Sense of Pakistan's Nuclear Practices, *Strategic Insights*, Vol. III, Issue 2, February 2004.
81. Zahid Hussain, *Frontline Pakistan: The Struggle with Militant Islam*, Columbia University Press, 2007, p. 166.
82. Gordon Corera, Ibid., p. 96.

2

The Sunni–Shia Schism

Knowledge that is acquired
is not like this. Those who have it worry if
audiences like it or not.
It's a bait for popularity.
Disputational knowing wants customers.
It has no soul.
Robust and energetic
before a responsive crowd, it slumps when no one is there.
The only customer is God.

— Rumi: *The Sheikh who played with Children*[1]

The Sunni–Shia split, often compared to the Protestant–Catholic
cleavage in Europe, happened immediately after the death of the
Holy Prophet Muhammad (PBUH) in AD 632 when the question of
succession of the head of the Islamic state had to be decided. A
faction led by the Prophet's cousin Ali ibn Abi Talib thought that
the Prophet had given enough indications that the mantle would
pass to him; others led by the companions of the Prophet, Abu
Bakr, the Prophet's close friend and father-in-law, and the strong
and influential companion, Umar Khattab, thought that succession
had to be decided through a vote in the council of elders. Once
the vote was cast in favour of Abu Bakr, Ali accepted the decision.
The best account of the origin of the schism and its later theological development is given by the great Iranian scholar, Hamid
Enayat.[2]

Abu Bakr was followed as the caliph of the Muslims by Umar,
Usman and finally Ali, and the four were called *rashidun*, or Rightly
Guided, by the Sunni Muslims down the centuries, implying that
their rule was exemplary for the purposes of settling questions of

Islamic jurisprudence. The followers of Ali however—called the Shia—did not agree that the three caliphs before Ali were exemplary, thus laying the foundations of a great schism in Islam.

The Shia object to Abu Bakr's convening of the council of Saqifah of the Ansar that awarded him the caliphate, fully supported by Umar, who proposed his name. After becoming caliph, Abu Bakr refused to accept the claim of Fatima, the Prophet's daughter and Ali's wife, to the property of Fadak, an oasis near Khaybar, owned by the Prophet when he was alive, relying on the Prophet's saying that no one will be his heir except the poor. The Shia object to Abu Bakr's offer of pardon to the general Khalid bin Walid after he had murdered a Muslim notable, just because Khalid's 'services were indispensable to the young Islamic state'.[3]

The Shia object to the caliphate of Umar most of all. They refer to the 'Thursday Calamity' incident on the day the Prophet died. He bade his companions to fetch him paper and inkpot to write his will so that they may not 'err after his death'—an indication that he was going to nominate Ali as his successor—but Umar stopped everyone from complying with the Prophet's demand by arguing that 'his illness had reached a critical stage, and he had become delirious'. Together with Abu Bakr, he refrained from executing a *munafiq* (hypocrite) whom the Prophet had found to be a renegade Muslim. They also objected to Umar making legal changes in the practice of Islam, like the prohibition of *mutah* (temporary marriage) which they thought was allowed by the Quran; and changing some rituals pertaining to hajj, and adding the phrase 'hasten to the best act' in the call to the prayer (*azaan*).

THE PERSIAN FACTOR

The Arab Sunnis have targeted Iran as the 'contaminating legacy' in the Shia tradition. Umar had defeated the Sassanian King Yezdigerd at Qadisiya in AD 637 and taken his daughters prisoners. According to legend, one daughter of Yezdigerd was given in marriage to Imam Husayn. The extreme views on this issue of Abdullah Muhammad al-Gharib, whose sectarian polemic most affected Al Qaeda through Abu Musab al-Zarqawi, have been noted by Nibras Kazimi:

> The esoteric *rafidha* (rejectionists) look upon Arab Muslims with malice and hate simply because they destroyed the glory of Persia and vanquished the rule of Cyrus. Al-Gharib asserts that the Persians turned to Shiism only because Imam Hussein married into royal Sassanian blood. The Persians also aided the Abbasids in dethroning the Umayyad dynasty, and then secretly sought to control them. Al-Gharib proceeds to describe the disruptive uprisings of the Qaramitah (Carmathians), the Buwayhids and the Fatimids, and how all these actions contributed to weakening Islam, adding 'they divided up the Islamic lands among them and spread unbelief wherever their feet trod'.[4]

A very popular book in Iran gives the following account of 'Iranian blood' in the Imams of Shiism:

Shia tradition has it that Sassanian-Iranian King Yezdigerd's two daughters were brought to Madinah after his defeat at the hands of an Arab army. Hazrat Ali, as guardian of prisoners, gave Shahar Bano's hand in marriage to Imam Husayn. She was to be the mother of Imam Zainul Abedin, the Fourth Imam. Her sister Kayhan Bano was given in marriage to the son of Hazrat Abu Bakr, Mohammad. She was to be the mother of Umme Farva who became the wife of Imam Baqar, the Fifth Imam. When Imam Jafar was born to Imam Baqar and Umme Farva 82 years after the *hijrat* (migration) of Prophet Muhammad (PBUH) (eighth century AD), he had blue eyes from his Iranian grandmother and great-grandmother.[5]

Here must also be stated that there has also been a deliberate Shia attempt to change the rituals of prayer in order to set Shiism apart from Sunniism. Liakat A. Takim notes:

> The addition of the phrase *I bear witness that Ali is the friend of God,* also called *wilaya,* was made by Shah Ismail (d.1425), the first Safavid ruler of Iran, who used the prevailing pro-Ali opinion to declare Twelver Shiism the official religion of the state.... He had the names

of the twelve Imams mentioned in the sermons in the mosques and issued a commandment stating that the first three caliphs were to be publicly cursed. Whoever refused to do so would be killed. He also issued a decree stating that the *wilaya* was to be mentioned in the *azaan*.[6]

The Shia objection to the third caliph Usman (Uthman) was of nepotism, especially in the case of the appointment of provincial governors, and his oppressive conduct towards the partisans of Ali, as in the case of Abdullah bin Masud, who was tortured, and Abu Zarr Ghaffari who was forced into exile at the governor of Damascus, Muawiyya's, insistence. They thought that Usman was not a worthy companion of the Prophet since he absented himself from the battles of Badr and Uhud, and from the fateful ceremony known as *bayat-ar rizwan* at which the Companions reaffirmed their allegiance to the Prophet. He is also criticised for abrogating the Quranic dispensation of allowing travellers to shorten their prayers. It is in the account of Abu Zarr (Dharr) Ghaffari that the objections become more detailed.

Shia Muslims believe that the Companion of the Prophet Abu Zarr was a strong supporter of Ali ibn Abi Talib in the political conflicts after Prophet Muhammad's (PBUH) death. However, his name is not mentioned as one of the prominent supporters of Ali by early historians. Abu Zarr is said to have served loyally in the Muslim armies and participated in the conquest of Jerusalem during the caliphate of Umar ibn Al-Khattab. According to the historian Wilferd Madelung, Abu Zarr fell into disfavour during the caliphate of Usman ibn Affan. Usman was appointing his relatives as governors and giving them money from the public treasury. Abu Zarr felt that this was a betrayal of the principles of Islam.

Abu Zarr had begun his agitation in Madinah after Usman had given 500,000 dirhams to Marwan bin al-Hakam, 300,000 to al-Harith bin al-Hakam, and 100,000 to the Madinan Zayd b. Thabit from the *khums* (poor due of the Shia) of the booty seized in Ifriqiya (Africa) in AD 647. He then quoted relevant Qur'anic passages threatening the hoarders of riches with hell-fire. Marwan

complained to Usman, who sent his servant Natil to warn Abu
Zarr, but to no avail. Usman displayed patience for some time
until, in the presence of the caliph, Abu Zarr launched an angry
verbal attack on Kaab al-Ahbar, who had backed Usman's free use
of public money. Usman now chided Abu Zarr and sent him to
Damascus.[7]

However, Abu Zarr was just as forthright in Damascus, where
he criticised the luxurious life and free spending of Muawiyya,
Usman's nephew and the governor of Syria. He was sent back to
Madinah, and finally, when he would not cease criticising misuse
of public treasury, he was exiled to al-Rabadha, in the desert near
Madinah, where he died. Madelung recounts that Ali felt that
Usman was wrong to punish Abu Zarr, who had been one of the
first converts and a favorite of Prophet Muhammad (PBUH). Ali
showed his sympathy by accompanying Abu Zarr to the edge of
town, thus sending him into his exile with good wishes and respect.
Usman had ordered that no one was to do this; Ali defied the caliph
to show kindness to Abu Zarr. Shia stories about Abu Zarr say that
he died of the lingering effects of beatings he had received at the
hands of Usman's soldiers, or, that he died of starvation in the
desert. There is a tradition that Prophet Muhammad (PBUH)
predicted this sad end, saying, *May Allah have mercy upon Abu Zarr!
Lonely will he live, lonely will he die and lonely will he be resurrected.*[8]
The Shia of Lebanon look at Abu Zarr as their progenitor, claiming
that he was exiled to Damscus by Caliph Usman, where the
governor, Muawiyya had disliked him equally and sent him into
further exile in Lebanon.

'Objections' to the three caliphs would have remained academic
and might not have led to schism had they not become scurrilous
in the extreme in the centuries that followed. The Shia
institutionalised these objections as a basis for abuse, which was
returned by the Sunnis with counter-accusations of offering insult
to the 'rightly guided' companions of the Prophet. The practice of
sabb (vilification) and *rafz* (repudiation of legitimacy) against the
first three caliphs became ritualised among the Shia clerics. With
the addition of Iranian nationalism to the schism, the situation

actually became worse. This happened with regard to Umar in whose caliphate the Arabs conquered Iran and destroyed its superior Sassanian-Zoroastrian culture, thus giving him a high place in Shia demonology. (Umar was killed by a Persian prisoner of war.)

Shia sources of criticism developed over time and by the tenth century AD Umar began to be attacked for having discriminated against the Iranian Muslims and for prohibiting marriages between Arabs and Iranians. The eighth imam Ali bin Musa al Raza was quoted as saying that Iranian Muslims had been accorded a higher social status after the death of Prophet Muhammad (PBUH). Seven hundred years later the great codifier of Safavid-Shia jurisprudence Mohammad Baqir Majlisi (d.1700) added that 'in the matter of faith, the Iranians are better than the Arabs'. He also quoted the sixth Imam Jafar Sadiq as saying: 'If the Quran had been revealed to the Iranians the Arabs would not have believed in it; so it was revealed to the Arabs and the Iranians came to believe in it'. Contrasts were made between the anti-Persian policies of Umar and Ali's equitable treatment of both Iranians and Arabs.[9] Umar was also the butt of jokes in burlesque *Umar kushaan* plays staged on 26 Zil-Hajj in Iran till the practice was stopped at the beginning of the twentieth century out of respect for the Ottoman Sunnis. Another object of hatred in Shia jurisprudence was Ayesha, the Prophet's wife and daughter of Abu Bakr, because of her known antipathy towards Ali, a fact that the Jordanian Shia-killer of Baghdad, Abu Musab al-Zarqawi, in 2006, mentioned on his website as a reason for his hatred.[10]

THE AUTHORITY OF IBN TAYMIYYA

From the Sunni side the quarrel was joined most effectively and taken to a higher intellectual level by Ibn Taymiyya (d. AD 1328). Reference to his work is found in the *fatwas* of *takfir* (apostatisation) issued against the Shia in Pakistan in 1986. His tracts were rejoinders to a famous Shia polemicist Allama Hasan bin Yusuf bin Mutahhar Hilli (d. AD 1325) but what is ignored by the Sunni

madrassa (seminary) of today in Pakistan is the fact that Ibn
Taymiyya's strongest apostatising criticism was against the extremist
(*ghulat*) Shia and the Ismailis, whom he dubbed heretics and
hypocrites, and not generally against the Twelver Shia whom he
considered only misguided.[11] However, among the Shia of Lebanon,
Ibn Taymiyya stands demonised as the jurist who ordered their
extermination. Nibras Kazimi gives the following note on him:

> Shaykh al-Islam Ibn Taymiyya (AD 1263–1328) was born in Harran
> (northern Syria) and died in Damascus. As part of his biographical
> lore, it has been recorded that he himself went on several Seljuk
> campaigns to quell Shi'i (specifically Nusayri and Druze) rebellions in
> Kisrawan, Wadi al-Taym and the Jurd Mountains of the Syrian
> coast.[12]

Taymiyya took issue with the idea of the imams as it was not clearly
expressed in the Quran; he equally rejected the idea of the Hidden
Imam and called the doctrine of the Shia Imamate impracticable.
About Ali his argument was that if Allah had designated Ali as the
successor to the Prophet, He must also have known that Ali would
be faced with disorder, and lack of knowledge was not expected of
Allah who was omniscient. He rejected the Shia idea of *ilm*
(knowledge) received by the Imams directly, first from the Prophet,
then from one another lineally. He thought that the Shia doctrine
of *taqiyya* (dissimulation) was a kind of mendacity which could not
be allowed. He preferred Sunni realism in accepting the incompetent
but powerful ruler to Shia idealism that confronted the powerful
and caused conflict. He denounced the Shia practice—which he
called mere superstition—of not naming the children after the first
three caliphs, and adulation of places expected to be the sites of the
reappearance of the Hidden Imam.

Early differences solidified further and moved the Muslim
community towards schism on the basis of the martyrdom of
Husayn, Ali's younger son, in AD 680, at the hands of an Umayyad
caliph, Yazid. In our times, sectarian passions are inflamed when
the Shia commemorate this martyrdom on the tenth of Muharram
(*ashura*) accordingly to the Islamic calendar. The tragic story of

Husayn is treated by moderate Sunnis as a symbolic challenge to the forces of injustice, but extremists on both sides of the divide challenge each other on details. Ali was challenged in his caliphate by the governor of Syria, Muawiyya, a Companion of the Prophet and son of Abu Sufian, the leader of the Arab opposition to the Prophet. Muawiyya's son Yazid was challenged by Husayn who did not formally accept his caliphate and was martyred by him. During the *ashura* the practice of condemning the killers of Husayn at times arouses opposition among the Sunnis who claim to venerate all Companions of the Prophet equally. A narrative of the Imams that followed Husayn is a tragic account of the unfolding of the schism in history, in which all the imams were murdered by Sunni rulers.

Sunni Arabs have inherited a more critical view of the Shia than the Sunni Muslims of South Asia. The reason for this is the cultural influence from Iran which came in through the Turkish and Mughal conquerors of India from Central Asia, which was for a long time an extension of Persian culture in Khurasan. For instance, the first Muslim king of India, Qutbuddin Aibak (reigned 1206–1210) began his career as a slave sold to the governor of Nishapur in Iran. Under him, Lahore became the 'Ghazni of India' (reference to a kind of cultural renaissance under Iranian influence) after the destruction of Ghazni in 1151. Scholars and poets from as far away as Kashghar, Bokhara, Samarkand, Iraq, and Herat, gathered in Lahore and made it the city of learning. The Mughals were greatly influenced by the Iranian civilisation and a special effort was made under Humayun—who found himself for a time in exile in Iran and was converted to Shiism by the Safavid king there—to actually inculcate Iranian culture in India. The advent of Islamic mystics to India also served to create a pro-Shia environment as sufism traces its inspiration to Ali. It was not until the enthronement of Aurangzeb Alamgir that the tide began to turn. Official Islam contained in the famous collection of *fatwas* of the Hanafi fiqh, *Fatawa-e-Alamgiri*, whose compilation was ordered by Aurangzeb, condemned the Shia as heretics, but at the grassroots level the cultural acceptance of the Shia remained intact. Aurangzeb's brother

Shah Shuja was a Shia and was killed by him in the fight for the Mughal throne. Another brother, Dara Shikoh, a mystic therefore inclined to Shiism, was also killed by him.[13]

Even the contact with Arabs during hajj did not change the Sunni tolerance of the Shia in India. Arabia was ruled by the Ottomans whose acceptance of mystical Islam and inclination to accept the Iranian culture made Hejaz a place of great Shia–Sunni interaction. It was the rolling back of the Ottoman empire and the rise of the House of Saud and the parallel authority of Wahhabism as a new Hanbali interpretation of Islam in the eighteenth century that changed the environment. The Arabs began reviving myths about the Shia provenance from ancient books and began using them as the verbal underpinning of the war with Iran. Under Saddam Hussein these myths were dug up in spite of the fact that the majority of Saddam Hussein's army was Shia and most of the casualties suffered by the Iraqi army in the war against Iran were Shia. Saddam's Baath Party made current the myth that the Shia had actually descended from a Jew named Abdallah bin Saba. Baghdad borrowed the theory from Saudi Arabia where it had been current for centuries.

The Baath Party found the work of the ninth century thinker and satirist al-Jahiz useful in its attempts to put Iraqi Shias on the defensive. Jahiz was a fervent defender of the Arabs and Arab cultural tradition against all latecomers to Islam, especially the Persians. One of his works that the Baath Party published with annotations was *al-Bukhala* (the misers) in which Jahiz used a wide variety of anecdotes to describe the character, lifestyle, and ethos of the 'misers' of Abbasid Baghdad.[14] Jahiz used the barb against the Persians whom he described as *shu'ubiyya* (splinter communities) who were different in culture from the Arabs. The epithet 'miserly' was meant to connect the Shia with the Jews. A reflection of this is found in the apostatising *fatwas* in Pakistan. In the case of Saddam Hussein, he applied the Abdallah bin Saba epithet only to those Iraqi Shias who did not participate in his war against Iran. The others were called the 'followers of Imam Ali'.

RISE OF ANTI-SHIA WAHHABISM

We have a vague understanding of Wahhabism as hardline Islam but know little about Mohammad ibn Abdul Wahhab (AD 1703–1792), who founded the creed, and how his legacy intertwined with the rise of the state of Saudi Arabia. Author David Cummins offers the background to what happened to Hejaz (Makkah and Madinah) under the Ottomans and how the transition from the Ottoman tributary Sharif of Makkah to the House of Saud was completed. The British successfully coaxed the Sharif to revolt against Turkish rule but could not remove the ambivalence of backing Ibn Saud as the rival claimant of the domain of the Sharif.

The story of the mission of Wahhab could not be complete without its merger with the fortunes of a Najdi conqueror, Abdul Aziz ibn Saud (1876–1953).[15] Raised in the austere Hanbali tradition, Wahhab travelled to Iraq and Syria to complete his learning, then evolved his own version of an uncompromising *tawhid* (unity) and condemned other schools of thought as admitting of *shirk* (dilution of unity through association of non-gods with God). The Hanbalites were more focused on preventing and punishing 'that which is forbidden' by religion. Imam Ibn Hanbal (d. AD 855) was for taking steps to stop and even chastise those found in violation of the divine edict. He was also in favour of taking action without reference to the government in power as he did not favour the ruler. Thus, it was a kind of vigilante action, but of a mild sort. The 'prohibited things' were usually singing, music and drinking called *munkiraat*. However, when we reach the times of the Hanbalite leader Barbahari (d. AD 941) the vigilante groups are 'plundering shops, raiding homes of citizens to search for liqueur, singing girls or musical instruments, challenging men and women seen walking together in public'. Vigilante action also prevented the normal burial of Imam Jafar Mohammad ibn Jarir al-Tabari (d. AD 923) because he was suspected of being Shia. The *nahi* (prohibition) also included action against the Shia community of Baghdad.[16]

People who hated Wahhab and his strict followers alleged that he had imbibed *khariji* rejectionism and had gone as far as the Iranian city of Qum to imbibe heretical views. Wahhab compiled the offences committed against *tawhid* (unity of God) from Hanbali sources in Basra but went so far ahead that the Hanbalis too took issue with him.

Wahhab rejected human intercession in worship as *shirk* and ordered the destruction of shrines, basing himself on hadith reports. He opposed Shiism as heresy and rejected Shia construction of mosques over graves. (Later, the sparing of the Mosque of the Prophet or Masjid-e-Nabwi was managed as a compromise between the Wahhabi ulama and politically more flexible Ibn Saud.) He also forbade worshipping at the graves of the Prophets and generally building an edifice on top of graves, basing himself all the while on hadith. While in Basra, Wahhab developed so extreme a puritan faith that he was expelled by the scholars there. In his book *Kitab al-Tawhid* he took his opposition to 'innovation' to such a level that his father, himself a Qazi in Najd, was put off. It was after his father's death that Wahhab really came into his own, much helped by his marriage into the family of a local ruler.

The period of 'commanding the right and forbidding the wrong' started in earnest first in the oases of Najd, culminating in the destruction of the structure built over the grave of Zayd ibn al Khattab, a brother of Caliph Umar, followed by the stoning to death of a woman guilty of fornication. Soon the local traditionalists took offence and persuaded the rulers to expel him. It was his shifting to the oasis of Al-Dirriya in 1744 that marked the most important event in his life. This city was ruled by Mohammad Al Saud. Wahhab told the ruler that the Muslims of Najd were living in the same state as when they were found by Prophet Muhammad (PBUH). Thus, was born the concept of the modern *jahiliyya*. Wahhab wanted his mission to cleanse the region with the support of Saud; the Saudi ruler wanted him to endorse his authority. The two joined in the most important secular-divine chemistry in modern Islam.

From 1744 to 1792 (when Wahhab died) the Saudis had conquered the whole of Central Arabia known as Najd. Wahhab also attacked the tradition of Islamic sufism, in particular, the teachings of Ibn Arabi (1165–1240), the only Muslim thinker followed by non-Muslim mystical cults in the West today. This suited the Saudis who wanted to oppose the mysticism-supporting Ottoman rule and conform to the more austere and literal Bedouin view of Islam. Among those who opposed him was his brother Sulayman who composed treatises of rejection against him, but now Wahhab had the power to punish. He punished those who read his brother's treatise. Sulayman himself was made to flee Najd and stay on the fringes till he too was brought in chains to Hejaz after the Saudi conquest of it and was allowed to die in confinement. Sulayman's critique was based on Hanbali sources and it condemned what today has become a burning issue: the dubbing of an entire community of a region as apostate-through-*jahiliyya* and then declaring it a 'land of war'.

The 'mission' went forward from there, justifying jihad-till-death against those People of the Book who did not accept their invitation to Islam. Outside Najd no one supported the 'mission'. Egypt was in Ottoman hands and Indian Islam followed the Ottoman-inspired Hanafi tradition of Central Asia. The mood was to reject Wahhabism and defend the Sharif who was applying the Hanafi law in a region dominated by Hanbali and Maliki schools. When the Sharif and his clerics compared Najd's rising Wahhabism to the Qarmatians, it appealed to everyone. (The Qarmatians had attacked the Kaaba and walked away with the Black Stone, calling it innovation.)[17] The Sauds took Makkah in 1803 and Madinah in 1805 and began tearing down the tombs. The Turkish ruler of Egypt, Mohammad Ali, marched into Hejaz and pushed the Sauds back into the desert of Najd in 1815.

What followed was the strengthening of the Ottomans in Hejaz and the exile of the Wahhabi preachers to Egypt where they deepened their knowledge in contact with Al-Azhar. The first Saudi emirate came to an end. A second one was besieged by infighting among the Sauds in 1834, and Mohammad Ali ruled Najd through a Saudi puppet till 1891. The third Saudi emirate was ushered in by Abdul Aziz ibn al Saud in 1902 after the conquest of Hejaz. Ibn Saud resorted to the authority of the scions of Wahhab and with it the challenge of the Najdi Islam, mainly based on Islamic xenophobia. Because of the Wahhabi influence among the nomadic tribes in Najd, a new community of the Ikhwan emerged that took Wahhabi Islam to another extreme. Ibn Saud became guardian of the Hajj and had to deal with all kinds of Muslim creeds while keeping at bay Wahhabism grown poisonously xenophobic with the Ikhwan brand of it.

The Ikhwan in Saudi Arabia were an offshoot of Wahhabism but they took the xenophobic aspects of it to such an extreme that Ibn Saud had to correct them through the authority of his Wahhabi ulama.[18] (They objected to Ibn Saud's British adviser St-John Philby roaming about and shaking hands with the Arab Muslims. Philby later embraced Islam and took many Arab wives, just to settle the score.) The Ikhwan reminded the Wahhabi establishment that Wahhab had ordained that no one leave Arabia as even the Muslim world outside was *jahiliyya* and therefore polluted. They rejected the technology of modern times as clashing with Islam and didn't want the Americans coming in to prospect for oil. Ibn Saud had problems with his Wahhabi ulama over loudspeakers, telephones and photographs, but could arm-twist them into agreeing to his policy of being moderate in order to satisfy Muslims from parts of the world for whom he was the Guardian of the Holy Places. The Ikhwan he had to quell with violence, especially as they were raiding into the adjoining territory of what is today Iraq then run by the British. And Ibn Saud was a British protégé! Ibn Saud proclaimed the Kingdom of Saudi Arabia in 1934.

Najd, however, remained hardline in contrast to Hejaz where foreign Muslims visited during Hajj. But news about this strange creed had reached countries like India, formerly under the Ottoman influence and not kindly disposed to the desert dogma also called *mutawwiyya*. The Wahhabi mission now included trying to disarm the Indian and African Muslims about Saudi Arabia's official religion. Books favourable to Wahhabism but published in Iraq and

India were imported, republished and distributed in large numbers. Because of this invasion of Wahhabi literature to South Asia, the Shia community in India became apprehensive although Ibn Saud was now careful with his Eastern Province Shias. Unfortunately, the Ikhwan raided the Shia province Al-Hasa, pushed the governor aside and banned all Shia rituals there and demanded their conversion on the pain of death as apostates. (Today the Shia community in Saudi Arabia is under pressure once again because of the hardening of the mind of the Muslim masses all over the world, and the rise of clerical Iran.)

WAHHABIS AS AHLE HADITH IN INDIA

One person who helped Ibn Saud and his ulama a great deal in improving the image of his Wahhabi kingdom in India was Nawab Siddiq Hasan Khan (d.1890) of Bhopal. He headed the Ahle Hadith school of thought, was a great scholar of the Arabic language, and reached back in his orientation to Shah Waliullah (AD 1703–1762) who had been to Arabia to bring back a new puritan trend with him. Waliullah's son, Shah Abdul Aziz (d.1824) then brought forward his legacy and finally Aziz's disciple Syed Ahmad Barelvi (1786–1831) took the dogma into practice through his jihad, although one can't be sure that he was influenced by the essential Wahhabism of Saudi Arabia. For instance, while he thought Sufism to be a kind of innovation he did not apostatise its votaries.

Siddiq Hasan Khan, whom Pakistani writer Shaharyar M. Khan[19] describes as a bit of an adventurer, succeeded in marrying a widowed Begum of Bhopal and was able to dominate her court. This opened the way for a steady trickle of extremist Wahhabi ulama to the scholarly haven of Bhopal, establishing a final and conclusive nexus between Saudi Wahhabism and India's Ahle Hadith. Saad Hammad, a Wahhabi scholar, was to stay in Bhopal for nine years and he was not the only Arab scholar influenced by Siddiq Hasan Khan. There was also the famous Kairuddin Alusi of

Baghdad whose hardline thoughts had greatly buttressed the Wahhabi tradition. He came across Siddiq Hasan Khan's work on Ibn Taymiyya in Egypt in 1878. What had been lost as a Wahhabi trace in India under the Mughals was now feeding back into Arabia with superior scholarship, spearheaded by Siddiq Hasan Khan.

Claudia Preckel gives the following assessment of Nawab Siddiq Hasan Khan:

> In the late nineteenth century, the Central Indian principality of Bhopal became the centre of a new Islamic movement, the so-called Ahle Hadith (people of the prophetic tradition). This movement drew on the ideas of the two famous Indian scholars Shah Waliullah (d.1763) and Syed Ahmad Barelvi (d.1831) as well as on the works of the Yemenite qazi Mohammad bin Ali al-Shaukani (d.1832). The Ahle Hadith aimed at religious reform (*islah*), criticising many religious practices as unlawful innovations (*bida*). As there are some similarities between the Ahle Hadith teachings and those of the Saudi Wahhabism, the question arises as to any connections between these two movements and if it is correct to label the Ahle Hadith as Indian Wahhabis.
>
> The principality of Bhopal was ruled by four strong Begums (female sultans) throughout the nineteenth century up to 1926, an unparalleled case in the history of India. The Begums built several mosques and religious schools and provided generous scholarships to religious teachers, architects and poets. The third Begum, Shah Jahan (reigned 1868–1901) married the Islamic scholar Siddiq Hasan Khan al-Qannauji who is considered to be one of the founding figures of the Ahle Hadith movement. He spread his views in more than 200 works in Arabic, Persian and Urdu. He also built a far-reaching network of representatives who had to sell his books throughout the Islamic world and to buy reformist writings which were sent to Bhopal and commented on. This challenges the common view that nineteenth-century India was only a 'periphery' which did not take an active part in the intellectual developments and trends of the 'centres' (Cairo, Makkah and Istanbul) of Islam.[20]

The second big support came from the reformist mufti of Egypt, Rashid Rida, in the 1920s. His *The Wahhabis and Hejaz* was written under the spur of Rida's hatred for Sharif Hussain and his Hashemite legacy in the Middle East. When in 1926, Ibn Saud held an international conference of Muslims on how to manage the Holy Places, Rida was his foremost supporter, while his *Al Manar* journal was being funded generously by Ibn Saud. The Muslim Brothers, who arose later in 1928 under Hassan Al Banna, took their inspiration from Abduh and Rida to become partly *Salafist*, but the founder Hassan al-Banna, together with Maulana Maududi of India, stayed away from the more extreme doctrines of apostatisation favoured by Wahhabism. It was Syed Qutb of the Muslim Brothers who took the legacy of Banna and Maududi to an extreme on the basis of Maududi's concept of *jahiliyya*. Maududi had taken it from Ibn Abdul Wahhab; Qutb simply took it back to Wahhab.

The common strand among the various trends expressed by Wahhab, Rida, Banna and Maududi was their antipathy towards Western domination and imperialism. There were clearly very deep cleavages in what they preached but they could come together on their shared hatred of the West. Today, the *wassatiyya* (moderate) scholars headed by the Qatar-based Egyptian thinker Qaradawi takes one back to the same single point of agreement over the nature of the West. Only, Maududi was able to give the idea of an Islamic state where an incremental process of rule by the exemplary pious (without violence) would bring about the ideal Islamic state. Syed Qutb read two books, the *Lectures* of Pakistan's philosopher-poet Allama Mohammad Iqbal, which he rejected out of hand 'as philosophy', and Maududi's book on the Islamic state which he welcomed, but added violence to both the concept of *jahiliyya* and to the achievement of the state. The violence arose among the Wahhabis of Arabia and the Muslim Brothers of a traditionally violent Egypt.

The last great representative of the puritan Wahhabi creed was Sheikh Bin Baz (1910–1999) who presided over Madinah University and spread the creed far and wide, but most of it in the carefully designated cities of Pakistan. He took issue in the 1990s with Syed Qutb for being critical of the Umayyad ruler Muawiyya (bribery and deception against Ali) as in his eyes Muawiyya's status as a companion of the Prophet absolved him of all criticism. (He called

Qutb's version of Islam's first civil war 'a repulsive slander'.) There was a strong anti-Shia side to Bin Baz's critique which Qutb could not have grasped had he been alive since there are no Shias in Egypt. He criticised Qutb again for refusing to accept the Wahhabi literalism of the God seated on His Throne or God's Hand, and making it symbolic. Because of Bin Baz's strong influence in Pakistan, many Pakistanis began naming their sons Muawiyya, a trend not seen before.

Bin Baz, the blind Saudi cleric, was unbending in his Wahhabi literalist belief about the solar system being earth-centric and the earth being flat and unmoving with mountains holding it down like nails. The Saudi king had to withdraw his book to avoid worldwide embarrassment. The hardness increased further after 1979 when Iran arose as a powerful revolutionary state and the Arab Shias began to assert themselves in the region. On the other hand, hatred of the West began to bother the Saudi masses as they saw their kings and the ulama lined up behind Western policies. The Shia arose during hajj and were put down; the Wahhabis arose under a pupil of Bin Baz and tried to take over the Kaaba in the name of Imam Mahdi. The Muslim Brothers from Egypt, whom the Saud had given shelter to when Nasser was hunting them, proved to be the new influence among those who questioned the kingdom.

Extremism was born all over the Islamic world challenging the impotence of the Saudi version of Islam which was once so masculine. Extremist scholars fled to the West to start challenging the Kingdom, not for the sake of democracy but for the re-establishment of the pure creed, not an elected parliament but a caliphate with a *shura* (council of the pious). People like Abdullah Azzam, Omar Bakri, Umar Abdur Rehman, Abu Hamza al-Masri, Aiman al-Zawahiri and Osama bin Laden were ready to take up arms against the West and were finding the House of Ibn Saud on the wrong side of the battle.

LEGACY OF WAHHABISM TODAY

In Pakistan, there was a *de facto* graduation of the state to hardline Islam with jihadis spearheading the movement. Columnist Irfan Siddiqi wrote in *Nawa-e-Waqt* (1 April 2005) an account of his visit to Madinah in Saudi Arabia. At Madinah he visited the famous Madinah Islamic University, set up 45 years ago with the advice of Maulana Abul Ala Maududi and Maulana Daud Ghaznavi of Pakistan. It was headed by its first vice chancellor, the great Sheikh Bin Baz. It welcomed 6,000 foreign students forming almost 80 per cent of the total student population. It gave generous scholarships plus an air ticket back home during vacations. Pakistani students came from Lahore, Faisalabad, Turbat, Mamo Kanjan, Karachi, Qasur, Gujranwala, Peshawar, Nowshehra, Haripur, Gilgit, and Mekran. Before 9/11, teachers of the university used to spread around the world picking up students but now that had ceased. Pakistan was no longer issuing no-objection certificates to its students for this university. There used to be 300 Pakistanis in the university, but now in 2005, the number has dropped to less than 200.

While accepting a dogmatic and strict variety of Islam from Saudi Arabia, the Muslims of South Asia applied their own regional filter and did not completely accept Wahhab's blanket condemnations of all the moderate thinkers of Islam. Islam faced the challenge of philosophy that came with Sufism early in its history, and its own Thomas Aquinas, Imam Ghazali, decided that philosophy was off-limits. But he adopted *ash'arism* (the anti-philosophy school that still used Greek tools of argumentation) and its logic which the Hanbalis rejected as *bida* (innovation), in the tradition of Taqi al-Din Ibn Taymiyya whose influence still marks the thinking of the Islamic world. He opposed *ash'arism,* and therefore Ghazali, and rebuked the Muslims who came to Makkah and Madinah and paid tribute to the saints they had set up there. He also vehemently opposed the cult of the grave as being *bida.* Wahhabism was not only against Ghazali but generally against the libertarian religion policy of the Ottoman Empire under which the Arabs lived.

The region of Saudi Arabia and its cities represented the periphery of the Ottoman Empire. It repeatedly gave rise to breakaway Islamic sectarian movements that defied the mainstream Sunni Islam of the Ottomans. Central Arabia gave rise to Hanbalism and later Wahhabism which recognised only early Islam. In Oman, the offshoot of the Kharijites, the Ibadi sect, took hold. The Carmatians were in Al-Hasa. The 'stepsons' of the Empire, so to speak, were putting the Ottomans on notice about their marginality. The Wahhabis thought of Prophet Muhammad (PBUH) as an ordinary man and banned praying to him instead of Allah and equally banned addressing the Prophet instead of Allah as heresy. But it is wrong to say that the Wahhabis recognised only the Quran and not the Sunnah. Wahhabism spread in Saudi Arabia and through the sacred places of Hejaz to the rest of the Islamic world, but the main element behind it was the rise to power of the clan of Al Saud who had adopted Wahhab as their spiritual leader against *bida*. When he died a prosperous man, Wahhab had 20 wives and 18 children; and his successor, son Ali, had 60 wives before he finally chose four. But among his descendants, none was like Mohammad ibn Abdul Wahhab, the great opponent of the heresy of *bida* in Islam.[21]

No one has explained the legacy of Wahhab in our times better than Khaled Abou El Fadl. His thesis relates to the current disorder in the world of Islam as moulded by the rich Saudi and Gulf Arabs who follow the Wahhabi–Hanbali creed and are scared of the new political developments in the region. Fadl, an Islamic jurist at the UCLA School of Law, challenges the extremists who arrogate to themselves the right to interpret Islam today and then feel they have the right to enforce their interpretation of it on Muslims. His views have been fully explained in his book.[22] The extremists are in a minority but moderates constitute the silent majority of Muslims in the world:

> But puritans have an impact on the religion that is wildly disproportionate to their numbers. Regardless of the present constitution of the Islamic world, the transformative moment of which I speak is embodied by the fact that there are two paradigmatically

opposed worldviews that are competing to define the truth of the Islamic faith.[23]

Mohammad bin Abdul Wahhab allowed self-proclaimed Muslims to be killed as heretics and hypocrites. The House of Saud provided him with the authority to carry out his purges among Muslims. He did not follow any school of Islamic jurisprudence, except that of Imam Hanbal partially and Ibn Taymiyya (d.1328) selectively, called himself 'non-imitative', and relied on a false tradition relating to the first Rightly-Guided Caliph Abu Bakr (d.634) to allow himself the killing of fellow Muslims for holding an incorrect faith.

Wahhab's yardstick of murder was easy. If a Muslim proclaims that the eating of bread and meat is disallowed in Islam (whereas it is allowed) then he renders himself an infidel and can be and should be put to death.[24] He found it equally easy to apostatise past jurists, as for instance in the case of Imam Fakharuddin al-Razi (d.1210).

All Shiites, without exception, and all jurists suspected of harbouring Shiite sympathies were also considered heretics. The significance of calling a Muslim a heretic was enormous: a heretic was to be treated as an apostate, and thus killing or executing him was considered lawful.[25]

Wahhab also included in heresy and *shirk* (association of others with Allah) any indulgence in rationalism and frivolity, such as music, non-religious poetry and art.

AN INDICTMENT OF SAUDI WAHHABISM

Khaled Abou El Fadl notes that Egypt's Omar Abdur Rehman and the Saudi Osama bin Laden both relied on the same texts as Wahhab in order to justify the killing of innocent people. The precedents that Wahhab defended were cited by them on websites set up by groups that butchered hostages in Iraq after 2003. The killing of the Shia in Iraq by terrorists led by Al Qaeda's Musab al-Zarqawi was clearly carried out in the same tradition, but since it appeared awkward at a time when the Shias were equally opposed to the American invasion of Iraq, Al Qaeda first denounced Zarqawi and then denied, after his death, that he was ever involved in sectarian violence, to claim him as a martyr.

Wahhab also carried out in his time an act that shocked the region: the stoning to death of a woman accused of adultery, although scholars researching Wahhab today may not agree that this extreme act of misogynism took place the way it is reported.[26] The jurists of the Muslim world were shocked by this act of cruelty because the punishment had not been carried out for a long time. Khaled Abou El Fadl points to the fact that today stoning to death is routine in Saudi Arabia but fails to mention that an equally hardline Islam in Iran has caused the stoning of many women; and that in Bangladesh village clerics have meted out the punishment to women after holding private courts in defiance of state authority. In Nigeria too, a number of northern provinces have tried to inflict *rijm* (stoning to death) on innocent women because of the growing Arab influence in the country. In Pakistan, despite clear opposition to *hudood* (Quranic) punishments, such as the cutting of hands, by the national poet-philosopher Allama Iqbal, and at least one dissenting judgment of the Federal Shariat Court, *rijm* remains on the statute books.

Wahhabism appropriated *Salafism*—a far more credible Islamic paradigm in Fadl's view—with the passage of time. Today Wahhabis in Pakistan tend to describe themselves as Ahle Hadith and Salafiyya, but *Salafism* as a creed was founded in the late nineteenth century by Muslim reformers such as Mohammad Abduh (d. AD 1905), Jamaluddin Afghani (d.1897), Mohammad Rashid Rida (d.1935), Mohammad al-Shawkani (d.1834) and Jalaluddin San'ani (d.1810). Some scholars take *Salafism* back to Ibn Taymiyya (d.1328) and his pupil Ibn al-Qayyim al-Jawziya (d.1350), the word *salaf* referring to the personalities living in the time of the Prophet Muhammad (PBUH) and his Rightly Guided Caliphs. In the early twentieth century, Wahhabis began to claim to be *Salafis* but it was not till 1970 that others began accepting them as such. By that time, however, *Salafism* itself had got lost in the extremism of the Wahhabis through Saudi patronage. The reformists mentioned above were far less intolerant of modern times and in fact sought to suit Islam to modernity by going back to the more 'reinterpretive' times of the early caliphs when the *fiqh* (jurisprudence) of *taqlid* (imitation) had not yet taken root. On the other hand, Wahhabism stood resolutely opposed to any change in the creed to suit modern times.

The theology of Puritanism of the Wahhabis and the latter-day *Salafis* was derived from the supremacist aspects of the writings of Abul Ala Maududi (d.1979) and Syed Qutb (d.1966) who expressed both *Salafi* and Wahhabi ideals.[27] Maududi exercised considerable influence over Arab scholars and the people at large in South Asia. Maududi followed Abdul Wahhab when he posited the concept of *jahiliyya* to which all Muslim societies had reverted because they were not living in an Islamic state guided by Sharia, but he stopped short of declaring all Muslims in these societies as apostates. Like Wahhab, he dreamed of a utopia based on the city state of Madinah but he advised waiting till the balance of power was in favour of the Muslims to actually start using force to achieve such a state.

Syed Qutb was not an extremist thinker till he was arrested and tortured under Nasser, after which he divided Muslim societies into the faithful and those living under *jahiliyya* and advised those living in *jahiliyya* to migrate (*hijra*) to lands where Islam was in force. Like Maududi and Wahhab, he thought that Islamic law was a clear and inflexible set of rules which could be easily taken out and applied once the Islamic state had been created. But Qutb joined Wahhab in believing that Muslims, after their *hijra* from the society of *jahiliyya*, would form a special community that would have to expand the creed by fighting against other Muslims to establish the true state under God's law. Khaled Abou El Fadl thinks Qutb was inspired by the German fascist Carl Schmidt when he thought on these lines.[28]

The upshot of this turn in religious thinking was that a kind of Salafi–Wahhabi assimilation took place in the 1970s represented by Egyptians Salih Saraya (executed 1975), Shukri Mustafa (d.1978) and Mohammad Abdus Salam Faraj (executed in 1982), who all formed their own organisations devoted to violent activity. It was Faraj's extreme position that not only did the rulers under *jahiliyya* have to be killed (which led to President Sadat's assassination) but also the Muslim common man in *jahiliyya* had to be eliminated. Was there no reaction from the genuine *Salafi* scholars on this development? In truth there was, from a prolific and influential Salafi jurist Mohammad al-Ghazali (d.1996) who launched a blistering attack on the Wahhabis, calling them Ahle Hadith (traditionally the followers of Imam Hanbal) because Wahhabi is not acceptable as a term to the Wahhabis: his main plaint was about literalism, anti-rationalism, and anti-interpretive approach of Wahhabism and their new Salafi allies.

The Saudi reaction to Ghazali was not kind. The Kingdom began a campaign of writings against him, reminding one of what it had done earlier to Salafist thinker Mohammad Amir al-Hussaini al-San'ani (d.1768) who had first praised Wahhab but later criticised him after learning about the atrocities committed by his followers. Even Rashid Rida, not willing to offend the Saudis, had praised Wahhab as a Salafi, but Rida's writings were still banned by the Kingdom. Even in Egypt, writings of such 'reactive' Salafis have become rare because of the rise of extremism among the Muslims. Khaled Abou el Fadl gives us the following formulation to explain the widespread extremism of the Muslims today:

> The bonding of the theologies of Wahhabism and Salafism produced a contemporary trend that is anchored in profound feelings of defeatism, alienation and frustration. The product of these two combined theologies is one of profound alienation, not only from the institutions of power of the modern world, but also from the Islamic heritage and tradition. Puritanism is not represented by formal institutions; it is a theological orientation, not a structured school of thought. Therefore one finds a broad range of ideological variations and tendencies within it. But the consistent characteristic of Puritanism is a supremacist ideology that compensates for feelings of defeatism, disempowerment, and alienation within a distinct sense of self-

righteous arrogance vis-à-vis the nondescript 'other'—whether that 'other' is the West, non-believers in general, so-called heretical Muslims, or even Muslim women.

In this sense, it is accurate to describe the puritanical orientation as supremacist, for it sees the world from the perspective of stations of merit and extreme polarisation. Instead of simple apologetics, the puritan orientation responds to feelings of powerlessness and defeat with uncompromising and arrogant displays of power, not only against non-Muslims, but even more so against fellow Muslims, and women in particular...Osama bin Laden, Aiman Al Zawahiri, the Taliban and other extremist Muslim groups belong to the puritan orientation. Wahhabism is strictly introverted; although focused on power, it primarily asserts power over other Muslims. Militant puritan groups, however, are both introverted and extroverted: they attempt to assert over and against both Muslims and non-Muslims. As populist movements they are a reaction to the disempowerment most Muslims have suffered in the modern age at the hands of harshly despotic governments and interventionist foreign powers. In many ways, these militant groups compensate for extreme feelings of disempowerment by extreme and vulgar claims to power. Fuelled by a supremacist and puritan creed, these groups' symbolic acts of power become uncompromisingly fanatic and violent.[29]

THE SECTARIAN *FATWAS* IN PAKISTAN

It is often said that the people of Pakistan are not sectarian. This is meant to point to the lack of a general anti-Shia animus at the popular level. Yet, Pakistan has seen a lot of sectarian violence in recent years. The truth of the above statement is substantiated by the pattern of killings: the Sunnis kill Shia at large, targeting congregations, and the Shias target-kill—with some exceptions— the self-proclaimed anti-Shia clerics. This pattern tells us that the Shias are aware that the Sunni majority does not hate them. It rather proves that Shia-baiting is a specialised function carried out in the tradition of certain schools of thought among the Sunni-Hanafi confession.

Is the state of Pakistan involved in this sectarian war? Brussels-based International Crisis Group in its Asia Report No. 95 titled *The State of Sectarianism in Pakistan* says:

> In 1988, the last year of Zia's rule, the longstanding sectarian peace in the Northern Areas was shattered by bloody anti-Shia riots. When Shias in Gilgit celebrated Eidul Fitr, Sunnis, still fasting because their scholars had not sighted the moon, attacked them. Since the initial clashes ended with a truce between local community leaders, Shias were caught unprepared when they were attacked by a Sunni *lashkar*.
>
> The *lashkar* consisted of thousands of people from Mansehra, Chilas, Kohistan and other areas in the NWFP. They had travelled a long distance to reach Gilgit, but the government did not stop them. No government force intervened even as killings and rapes were going on. Instead, the government put the blame on RAW (Research and Analysis Wing, India's intelligence agency), Iran and CIA. In the rampage that followed, more than 700 Shias were killed, scores of Shia villages were pillaged and burned, and even livestock was slaughtered.
>
> It was on Musharraf's watch as Army Chief that Pakistan's Kashmir jihad policy increased the ranks of Islamic extremists in the Northern Areas. In 1999 the Kargil conflict resulted in the influx of Sunni jihadi elements into the region. Extremist organisations like the SSP, Lashkar-e-Tayba, Jaish-e-Mohammad, Al-Ikhwan and Harkatul Mujahideen have since opened offices there. Places like Chilas and Gilgit have become the hub of Sunni jihadi training and anti-Shia activism. And every Sunni attack has resulted in a tit-for-tat Shia response.

The main reason for the 'hate specialisation' is the secret nature of the Shia faith (*taqiyya*) especially in some aspects of the historic quarrel with Sunni Islam. The clerics who target the Shias dig into early Islamic history to find evidence of 'insult' offered by the Shias to the Companions of the Prophet. The argument usually begins by the Sunni cleric positing that the Shias have a covert tradition of denouncing the fundamentals of Sunni Islam. The verdict of apostatisation is, therefore, purported to be 'reactive'. After that, the Shia tradition of offering *taveel* (secondary meaning) of the Quran is 'detected' and a *fatwa* of apostatisation is issued. Not all the Hanafi schools apostatise the Shias. The Barelvis are seen to offer a 'liminal' interface with them for which they are often denounced by the hard-line schools like the dominant Deobandi school. (Maulana Jhangvi, founder of Sipah-e-Sahaba, did that.)[30]

Islam has many sects. They are supposed to run into scores. Each region, however, chooses its own primordial hate-object which is then collectively apostatised. The Shias don't qualify as the 'death wish' object of hatred for Pakistan the same way as the Ahmedis. In Iran, it is not the Sunnis so much as the Bahais who arouse primordial hatred. In Pakistan, another sect with equally covert articles of faith—the Ismailis—don't arouse the same vehemence of feeling as the Ahmedis although hate material against them has recently come to light. The hatred of the Shia has focused on the clerics of Deoband and, after the Afghan war of the 1980s, on the Ahle Hadith. With the hardening of Islam in Pakistan the sectarian trend has grown. It could be predicted even in 1949 when the state of Pakistan embarked on the path of becoming an Islamic state and tacitly said goodbye to the *liminality* or cultural coalescence of the majority Barelvi school with the Shias.

ATTACKING THE SHIA TRADITIONISTS

Anti-Shia *fatwas* reveal the mainsprings of the sectarian dispute. The 'departure' or heresy of the Shias is seen in documents that don't have common currency in the country and only the orthodox practising Shias know about them. It is only after the polarisation caused by the Deoband-dominated Afghan jihad that some Shias have come to know about the early Shia writers like Kulayni and Majlisi[31] whose writings contain the kernel of the Shia–Sunni schism. Even the rise of Imam Khomeini in Iran did not bring about any considerable awareness among the Shias about the 'facts' of their case in the dispute, although an underground of denunciatory and abusive literature had always existed in some small cities away from the metropolises, usually a result of personal rivalries between local clerics on both sides of the sectarian divide. Marriages between Shia and Sunni spouses were quite common till the sectarian killings tended to increase the sect consciousness.[32] In some areas of the country cross-sect weddings have been disrupted by the local clerics under pain of violence.

The *fatwa* of apostatisation issued against the Shias by one the founders of Karachi's Darul Ulum at the Banuri Town mosque complex will make clear the basic features of the sectarian quarrel.[33] Mufti Wali Hasan Tonki issued the following judgement in 1986:

> The Shia believe that the Quran is created and not eternal and is lying safe with the Occult Imam; that the Quran has been changed as claimed in the works of Kulayni, Mullah Baqar Majlisi and Mohammad Taqi al-Nuri al-Tabarsi; that, like the Qadianis, the Shia accept Muhammad (PBUH) as the last Prophet only literally and not in the real sense and have set up a parallel system to his Prophethood in the concept of Imamate, equating one with the other; that the Shia reject the *ijma* (consensus) of the Muslim community on the caliphates of Abu Bakr and Umar; the Shia are therefore outside the pale of Islam.[34]

It is important to understand here the status of the Shia traditionists that the Pakistani ulama attacked in the above *fatwa*.

The author of *al-Kafi* was Abu Jafar Mohammad b. Ya'qub b. Ishaq al-Kulayni al-Razi. He died in AD 940. Very little is known of his life. He first worked as a religious scholar and *faqih* (student of *fiqh* or religious law) among the Imami-Shia scholars of al-Raiy in Iran. Then he moved to Baghdad and became head of the religious and legal scholars of the Imamis during the time when al-Muqtadir was Caliph. Al-Kulayni's life's work took place during the time of the *sufara'* of the Mahdi (the agents who acted on behalf of the Hidden Imam during the lesser occultation, *al ghaiba al-sughra*). Al-Kulayni is accredited with several works during this period. Among these are, as well as *al-Kafi*, a *Kitab al-rijal*, (a book in which men are assessed as authorities for traditions), *al-Radd 'ala 'l-Qaramata* (Refutation of the Carmatians, *Rasa' il al-a'immata,* Letters of the Imams and an anthology of poetry about the Imams. Only *al-Kafi* appears to have survived.[35]

Mohammad Baqir Majlisi, son of Mullah Mohammad Taqi, was born in AH 1037 and died circa 1700 and is buried in Atiq Mosque in Isfahan. He was a religious leader of the Muslims in Isfahan who controlled people's affairs through his wisdom and solved their problems. He was really interested in teaching and so many scholars took part in his classes. It is said that the number of scholars in Riyadh was estimated about one thousand. He travelled to Makkah and Iraq several times. His efforts to promulgate Islam were such that Shiism could be called Majlisi's religion, according to Shah Abdul Aziz's book *Tohfeh*. After Majlisi's book *Haqul Yaqin* was published, about 70,000 Sunnis of Syria converted to Shiism. He passed away when he was 73. Majlisi's works number more than 60. Some of his important works are: *Bahar Al-Anvar fi Akhbar Al-A'emah Al-Athar* (26 volumes), *Meshkatol Anvar, Eynol Hayat, Jala Al-Oyoun, Helyatal Motaqin and Hayat Al-Qollob*.[36]

There appear to be many Shia traditionists named Tabarsi but it is Nuri Al Tabarsi (d.1902) who comes under attack for claiming that the Quran was incomplete and would be revealed in its complete form by the occulted Imam Mahdi. But Tabarsi does not receive a consensual acceptance among the Shia because of his recent date. Yet, when the polemic is joined, there is a defence of Nuri Al Tabarsi which must be noted.

There are three individuals with the title of Tabarsi among the Shia. The one accused of writing a booklet on the incompleteness of Quran, is Husain Ibn Mohammad Taqi al-Nuri al-Tabarsi (c.1838–1902). Those who call the Shia *Kafir* due to this booklet, will be surprised to know that many of the Hadith reports that al-Nuri al-Tabarsi has quoted are, in fact, from the Sunni documents and were quoted from their most authentic books! Actually, his book has two parts. In one part he has gathered the Sunni reports and in the other part he provided the Shia reports in this regard. The Wahhabis, who have recently distributed copies of this book to attack the Shia, have intentionally omitted the part related to the Sunni reports! Nonetheless, the Shia scholars of his time disagreed with his conclusion regarding the alteration of Quran. This shows that the Shia scholars strongly believed that nothing is missing from Quran. We cannot call any person (Shia or Sunni) who claims Quran is incomplete, as *kafir*. This is simply because believing in the completeness of Quran is not an article of faith, nor do we have any tradition saying that anyone who claims Quran is incomplete, is a *kafir*. Also, the verse of Quran that states that Allah is the protector of the Reminder, can be interpreted differently. (Logically we cannot prove the lack of alteration in Quran by Quran!)[37]

The problem of the six accepted-as-true Sunni collections of hadith reports has cropped up in the past among the Sunnis too because of their objectionable content in the eyes of some scholars like Pakistan's Ghulam Ahmad Parwez (1903–1985) who rejected the Sunni hadith selectively because of reports found in it about the changing or withholding of certain sections of the Quran. There was intense reaction against him from Saudi Arabia and the Gulf. His works were banned in Kuwait and in the NWFP province in Pakistan. In Lahore, where his trust is located in Gulberg, there is always the threat of attack from radical militia-backed religious parties who don't agree with his Quran-centred and hadith-rejecting approach.[38] The irony of Parwez's work is that his writings reject the Shia faith while his critical examination of the Sunni hadith strengthens the Shia defence of the belief that the Quran had been tampered with. Parwez, of course, castigated the Sunni hadith for making this view current among the Muslims. His efforts were paralleled in Iran by Ali Shariati who objected to Shia hadith.

MANZUR NUMANI AND HIS ANTI-IRAN CAMPAIGN

A number of clerical leaders of Pakistan co-signed or confirmed the *fatwa* against the Shia in 1986. Among them were two well known names: Mohammad Yusuf Ludhianvi and Mufti Nizamuddin Shamzai. Both were to die in the sectarian upheaval that overtook Pakistan during the Afghan civil war of the 1990s and the jihadi reaction to the American invasion of Afghanistan in 2001. *Fatwas* of apostatisation are on record as having been issued from time to time from all the prominent madrassas of Pakistan. Darul Ulum

Haqqania Akora Khattak of Maulana Samiul Haq issued its own *fatwa* of apostatisation of the Shia in 1986 saying that eating food cooked by them, attending their funeral and burying them in Sunni graveyards stood banned. Another *fatwa* from Jamia Ashrafia Lahore, whose leader Maulana Mohammad Malik Kandhalwi known to be a relative of General Zia, declared the Shias *kafir* because 'they held that the Quran had been tampered with and gave Hazrat Ali a status equal to Prophet Muhammad (PBUH), claiming that angel Jibreel had made a mistake while taking *wahi* to the Prophet'.

The above *fatwas* were circulated in Quetta, Balochistan, in 2003 before the massacre of the Hazara Shias there on two occasions. Since no madrassa is required by the state to register all the *fatwas* it gives out to the people, the information given by the Hazara leaders on TV fell on deaf ears. However, a compilation of all the Shia-related Pakistani *fatwas* was made in Lucknow, India in 1987, thus offering research workers in Pakistan a glimpse into the activity of the madrassas which mostly disclaim that they are involved in anti-Shia crimes. Lack of knowledge of the Deobandi–Shia conflict of the past is yet another proof of the non-sectarian nature of the general public in Pakistan. It is not generally known that the founder of the state Quaid-i-Azam Mohammad Ali Jinnah was an Ismaili who chose to become Shia in the 1920s to help along his political career. (Shia faith was then more acceptable among Sunni Muslims than Ismailism.) It is also not known that Maulana Shabbir Ahmad Usmani who led the prayer of his public Sunni funeral (a secret Shia funeral having already taken place at night) had earlier signed a *fatwa* declaring all Shias as *kafirs*.[39]

The Sunni–Shia conflict as an Islamic schism died down in India under the British Raj simply because the British administrators dealt strictly and fairly with sectarian breaches of law. In Lucknow, for example, where the Shia community flourished, both the sects were forced to respect the municipal law under pressure from officers that had no religious affiliations. Had the local deputy commissioner not told a sectarian crowd that it could not take the law into their own hands, Lucknow's controversial poet, Yaas

Yagana Changezi, would have died as a lynched apostate. The same can be said about Ghalib in Delhi under the British Raj administration when he was accused of being a *rafizi* (converted Shia) by the Ahle Hadith who had dominance in the court of the Mughal King. Imam Khomeini's own family, fearing persecution in Iran, had migrated to India and lived in Lucknow for a time because they found the city safe.[40] Amir Taheri interestingly notes that Khomeini took the pen-name (*takhallus*) *Hindi* (Indian) in his poems and that his youngest brother Mohammad was named Syed Mohammad Hindi.[41]

Why were the series of *fatwas* apostatising the Shias issued in Pakistan in the year 1986? Why was there a simultaneity in the issuance of these *fatwas*? A book was put together in 1993 titled *Khomeini Aur Shia Kay Barah Main ulama Karaam Ka Mutafiqqa Faisla* (Consensual Verdict of the ulama on Khomeini and the Shia) in Pakistan by someone called Chishti Sabri and introduced by Khalilur Rehman Sajjad Nadvi. The text belonged to an Indian cleric Maulana Manzur Numani (d.1994) who claimed that 'it is a masterpiece of research'. Why should a collection of *fatwas* be described as a masterpiece of research? One comes to know that in fact, these *fatwas* were either never available freely in India and Pakistan or had become unavailable after their issuance simply because of the lack of habit of record-keeping in the country and the latter-day tendency of the madrassas to hide their sectarian past.

Maulana Manzur Numani was a graduate of Darul Ulum Deoband in India and had already written against Imam Khomeini in 1984, but in these writings he had not gone beyond accusing the Iranian Imam of heresy. But after that, he allegedly came across more solid evidence proving the Shias non-Muslim. He himself wonders that till the age of 80 he had not cared to look into the writings of the Sunni ulama down the centuries on the question of the real faith of the Shia. The 'masterpiece' he achieved came in the shape of a collection of *fatwas* printed serially in the Lucknow-based journal *Al Furqan* from December 1987 to July 1988. The *fatwas* were mostly issued in 1986 and their publication in

Al Furqan was undertaken the following year. What made him undertake his anti-Shia readings? He explains it himself. After the appearance of Imam Khomeini on the international scene in 1979, and after the 'anti-monarchical' inspiration of the Iranian Revolution radiated in the Arab world, many clerics in the United States began to worry about the future of their proselytising enterprise.

Numani says some ulama wrote to him from the US saying the American blacks were now being attracted to Shiism rather than Sunniism as in the past. Since proselytisation in the US was mostly leveraged with Arab/Saudi money, the fundamental Arab–Iranian religious contest too is visible in Numani's presentation of the case. He goes on to cite Imam Abu Hanifa's well-known edict that since the Shia were *ahle-e-qibla* (those who bowed to Kaaba) they should not be apostatised. He says Imam Abu Hanifa—the founder of the Hanafi school of jurisprudence—never meant it as a ban on apostatisation of the Shia who actually did not accept the Last Prophet sincerely. Quite the opposite of it, he points to the concept of the Hidden Imam in Shiism and says that the final aim of the Shias is to control the Kaaba and proclaim their ascendancy from there. He then refers to the 1987 clash between Saudi troops and the Shias doing hajj in Makkah and warns that a campaign to depose the Sunnis from the guardianship of the Kaaba could actually be taking shape.

There is an interesting precedent to Numani's book of *fatwas*. Numani had written an earlier book in 1984 titled *Iranian Revolution, Imam Khomeini and Shiism (Irani Inqilab, Imam Khomeini aur Shi'yyat)* with a preface written by a popular Indian religious leader Abul Hasan Ali Nadwi whom one least expected to endorse a sectarian tract. Vali Nasr met him in India in 1989 and this is what he writes:

> Nadwi or Ali Mian as he was popularly known was then one of the most senior religious leaders of India. He was a scholar and the rector of an important seminary in Lucknow as well as a trustee of Oxford University's Centre for Islamic Studies. He was also a leader of India's Muslim community, often interacting with politicians on behalf of

Indian Muslims and travelling across the Muslim world to represent them. Nadwi was an adviser to the Saudi Islamic World League. Although moderate in his views and a critic of fundamentalism, he nevertheless let himself be prevailed upon to lend his authority to Numani's attack—itself an ominous sign.

Numani saw Khomeini as the face of Shiism and pointed to Iranian excesses as proof that Shiism was beyond the Islamic pale. The book quickly made a stir. Numani and Nadwi were not marginal opportunists but senior Sunni ulama. Their commentary had the quality of a major *fatwa*. With Saudi financial support, the book was translated from Urdu into English, Arabic and Turkish for wide circulation across the Muslim world. A copy whether in English or Arabic was available to any interested person who requested one at the Saudi embassy in Washington, D.C. The book made Deobandis central to the ongoing sectarian confrontation in Pakistan.

When I visited Nadwi in 1989, I asked him about the book. I expected him to go into outspoken anti-Shia mode, but to my surprise he grew quiet. He preferred not to talk about the book. When I pressed him whether it was prudent to equate Shiism with Khomeini and to denounce the Shia faith so strongly, he demurred—it had all come down to the fact that Numani had been his friend, and that political circumstances had dictated the book's production. Moderate Sunnism was being pushed to adopt an unbending position toward Shiism. Nadwi had always been a pragmatic and temperate man. He had travelled to Iran during the Shah's days and until 1984 had not adopted an anti-Shia position. But, as he hinted, the Saudi–Iranian rivalry was imposing its own radicalising logic on sectarian relations.[42]

The lending of his name to Numani's book by Ali Mian is an extraordinary event. The profile of this great Indian Islamic scholar, provided by Yoginder Sikand, describes him as a very realistic man despite his correctly appreciated great scholarship. Sikand does not dwell on Ali Mian's anti-Shia leanings because there were apparently none, but he does list his deep contacts with the Arabs in general and the Saudis in particular. He received the King Faisal Award from Saudi Arabia in 1980 while serving as the rector of the Muslim seminary of Nadwatul Ulama, as member of the standing committee of the Darul Ulum Deoband, and participant in the working of many European institutions devoted to studying Islam.

He was member of the Standing Committee of Rabita al-Alam al-Islami (The World Muslim League), Makkah; member of the Consultative Committee of the Islamic university, Madinah. Sikand is of the view that his views were greatly moulded by his contacts with the Arabs.[43]

It is quite clear from the above that the 'inspiration' to write the books came from one source, Saudi Arabia, while a helping hand might have been provided by others. In 1984, Pakistan's General Zia had a bad meeting with Khomeini, after which in 1985 the anti-Shia organisation Sipah-e-Sahaba was allowed to be formed; in 1986 General Zia allowed the massacre of the Shia in Parachinar in Kurram Agency, and the same year the Deobandi *fatwas* were issued from the three top seminaries of Pakistan. In 1984, Numani in India got worried about Iran and wrote his book against Khomeini, which was picked up by the Saudis, translated and distributed all over the Muslim world. Then in 1987 Numani was prompted to put together all the *fatwas* against the Shia and write another book which has been noted above as the book published by a Pakistani in 1993.

Arab scholar Khaled Abou El Fadl explains the widespread puritanism among the Muslims of today as based on a textualism that leaves very little room for human agency in the interpretation of religion. He thinks that Saudi Arabia was able to guide the conservative Salafist trends among the Arabs towards a tough literalist faith after the collapse of Nasserism. Instead of putting the Quran and hadith at the top of all values in Islam, the puritans use them to empower themselves 'to project their socio-political frustrations and insecurities upon their text'. While the puritans seek to dominate and punish fellow Muslims, puritan militants like al-Zawahiri and Osama bin Laden, seek to punish the non-Muslims too. About Saudi patronage of this creed, he writes:

> Initially this process of dissemination (of Wahhabi ideology) consisted of lending financial support to fundamentalist organisations, but by the 1980s, this process became far more sophisticated. So, for instance, Saudi Arabia created a number of proxy organisations such as Rabita al-Alam al-Islami (Muslim World League, a sister organisation of

Mo'tamar al-Alam al-Islami or Muslim World Congress) that widely distributed Wahhabi literature in all of the major languages of the world, gave out grants and awards, and provided funding for a massive network of publishers, schools, mosques, organisations and individuals. The net effect of this campaign was that many Islamic movements across the Muslim world became advocates of Wahhabi theology.... In many parts of the Muslim world, the wrong type of speech or conduct (such as failing to veil or advocate the veil) meant the denial of Saudi largesse.[44]

Senior Pakistani journalist Mustafa Sadiq once wrote in Lahore's daily *Jang* (21 November 2003) that when he was saying his prayer in a mosque in Dipalpur, a small town in Punjab, he discovered pamphlets there penned by the great late Saudi scholar Sheikh Abdul Aziz Bin Baz. He was greatly impressed by the pamphlets and remembered that Bin Baz was rector of Madinah University and wielded a lot of authority with the Saudi royalty. The columnist went to Saudi Arabia in 1966 and interviewed Bin Baz, which he published on one full page of his paper *Wafaq*. Bin Baz could actually undo the punishments given out by the princes. He was so powerful he could open the door of the crown prince, the most powerful man in the kingdom, and enter at will. He wore his usual long robe but kept a big pocket in it. In the pocket was always a *mohur* (stamp). Whenever he wanted to give an order that the kingdom had to obey he took it out of his robe and affixed it on the paper carrying his instructions.

A PORTRAIT OF MAULANA MANZUR NUMANI

Qasim Zaman presents India's Maulana Manzur Numani (d.1996) as a populariser of Islam together with Yusuf Ludhianvi of Pakistan. Numani published his *Islam kiya hai* (What is Islam?) for the common Muslim reader and sold 70,000 copies of it in India and perhaps an equal number in Pakistan. By the late 1990s the book had been reprinted 38 times and many times more in other languages. Zaman categorises this kind of popular writing as a function of the ulama away from the usually specialised work not grasped by the masses. He refers to Mufti Yusuf Ludhianvi's similar contribution in a special column on Islam begun in daily *Jang* of Lahore in 1978.[45] The 'media mufti' was not popular among all the sects and was shot to death in 2000 in a market of Karachi. The Indian populariser Manzur Numani remained alive because he was in India and not in Pakistan where his book of *fatwas* would certainly have led to his death. It is quite possible that he was chosen to undertake the collation of anti-Shia *fatwas* because of his location outside Pakistan.

Zaman discusses Numani as a sectarian polemicist and mentions Saudi patronage in this regard:

> What has been labelled 'Saudi patronage' in this discussion comes not only from the state but also from Saudi-sponsored international associations like the afore-mentioned Rabita al-Alam al-Islami or from wealthy private individuals...Saudi patronage helped muster the support of many Sunni ulama against the Iranian revolution which the Saudis saw as a threat to the stability of their regime.[46]

He goes on to mention the efforts made by the Deobandi scholars to attract Saudi patronage in the form of money and training. He makes reference to a Deobandi seminary in Kohat in the NWFP which actually publicised the fact that it had 'formulated its goals in accordance with not only those of the other Deobandi madrassas of Pakistan and India but also with those of the Islamic University of Madinah and the Islamic Institute of Doha, Qatar'. The Jamia Farooqia of Karachi, which was to issue its most forceful *fatwa* of apostatisation of the Shia under Mufti Nizamuddin Shamzai (killed in 2004) was set up in 1967, but by 1991 it had 1,775 students. It was rated as the most successful seminary in terms of attracting aid from Saudi Arabia and other international sources. The curriculum of its language-learning department was a mix of styles found in South Asia and the Arab Middle East: 'Most of the students here are from the Fiji Islands, the Philippines, Indonesia, and Malaysia, and the institute itself is run by graduates of the Islamic University of Madina'.[47]

The Deobandis began their campaign for Arab funds after the rise of Imam Khomeini. A cable published by Iran from the documents (Vol. 2, p. 117) captured by Iranian youth after an assault on the US embassy in Tehran, records in 1979 a conversation between the chief of Pakistan's JUI, Maulana Mufti Mahmud and an officer of the American embassy in Islamabad. Mufti Mahmud asked, 'Why can the Arabs not spread their wealth among a broader cross-section of the rebels [in Afghanistan]?'[48] By 1986, only seven years later, the Deobandis were the largest recipients of Saudi funds.

Together with Hasan Ali Nadwi mentioned as Ali Mian by Vali Nasr, Numani began his career in the Tablighi Jamaat. While Numani was also a member of the advisory board of the Deoband madrassa, Nadwi was additionally a member of the Saudi-sponsored Rabita al-Alam al-Islami. Numani had engaged in polemics with the Barelvis early in his career and was sectarian-minded in his approach. His next step in the form of his *The Iranian Revolution, Imam Khomeini and Shiism* was a polemic against the Shia belief and quickly became a bestseller in the world, not a little assisted by Saudi funds and world-wide circulation in many languages. Then, in 1987, he put together the *fatwas* of *takfir* (apostatisation) that he had elicited from a large number of seminaries from India and Pakistan. First to be listed of course was the Jamia Banuri Town which was to be headed by the late Shamzai whose connection with Afghanistan's Mullah Umar was later to become well known. After 2001, his *fatwa* of *qital* (death) against the Americans became famous as he was known to be a moderate scholar.

Qasim is of the opinion that the mainstream Deobandi ulama engage in an academic polemic against the Shia but the killing is performed by the 'peripheral ulama and their operatives'. The leading ulama simply state that the Shia are 'infidels' because of their vilification of the great personages of Islam but do not directly prompt the Sunnis to kill the Shia.[49] This can be accepted as true but in the context of the Saudi–Iranian campaign of mutual contest, the issuance of *fatwas* in 1986 on the request of Numani has to be looked at differently. The truth of the matter is that the 'peripheral' ulama who carried out the killings were funded by the Saudis in equal measure with the senior ulama. It is quite possible that great scholars like Shamzai were persuaded to issue the *fatwas* without knowing that the prompting state had also organised the peripheral clerics to carry out the killings after the issuance of the *fatwas*. The creation of the apostatising Sipah-e-Sahaba in 1985, followed by the *fatwas* in 1986—which coincided with the massacre of the Shia in Parachinar—points to a programming that cannot be ignored. There is a crescendo pattern in this Saudi campaign involving the clergy and President Ziaul Haq of Pakistan who ordered another massacre of the Shia in Gilgit in 1988 and was to die on 17 August the same year after someone had killed the Shia leader Ariful Hussaini in Peshawar on 5 August.[50]

In his prefatorial remarks to his book of *fatwas*, Numani refers to all the great personalities that had gone into Pakistan's nation-building process. He refers to the first apostatiser of the Shia, Sheikh Ahmad of Sirhind and his famous tract *Radd-e-Rafawiz* (Repudiation of the Rejectionists) and points out that Sheikh Ahmad was writing to apostatise them when the Shia were influential in India. The queen of Emperor Jahangir, Nur Jahan, was a *ghali* (extremist) Shia and her father was prime minister while her brother was also highly placed in the Mughal court. He, however, remains selective in his account of Sheikh Ahmad and doesn't comment on Sheikh Ahmad's spiritual claims purported to elevate him to a status equal to that of the Prophet and higher than the Companions. He neglects to give the disapproving views of Sheikh Ahmad by the Sheikh's contemporaries like Abdul Haq Muhhadis and Manzur's own contemporary Abul Ala Maududi.[51] He then refers to Shah Waliullah, the patron saint of the Deobandi school, as another objector to Shia dominance in the aftermath of the long reign of anti-Shia emperor Aurangzeb when his weak successors were manipulated at will by powerful Shia persons in the court. Shah Waliullah wrote his voluminous work *Qurrat ul Ainain* against the Shia and in his letters clearly placed them outside the pale of Islam because of their doctrine of Imamat.

Numani proclaims that all Shia, whether clerical or not, have the doctrine of Imam Mahdi or the return of the Twelfth Imam inscribed on their hearts, and Imam Mahdi, after his arrival in Madinah, will exhume the corpses of Umar and Abu Bakr and punish them repeatedly with death each day for their transgressions of the past. After that Imam Mahdi will enforce *hadd* (Quranic punishment of death) on Ayesha too.[52] The invasion of Madinah by Imam Mahdi will be motivated by the aim of converting all the population to Shiism on the pain of death. Numani mentions this because he wishes to create a tradition of 'takeover' of the cities of Makkah and Madinah among the Shias to explain the trouble the Saudi government had with the Shia pilgrims from Iran in 1987.[53] He then quotes from Imam Khomeini's works that it was a religious obligation of the Shia to attempt the 'reconquest' of Makkah and Madinah whenever circumstances became favourable.

He quotes from the 350-page *Kashf al-Asrar* of Imam Khomeini that Abu Bakr, Umar, Usman and Abu Ubayda, etc, never became Muslims at heart but were *munafiq* (pretending to be believers) who had embraced Islam only to get close to the Prophet. These men went against the clear edicts of the Quran and ruled against the orders of the Quran. Had they found that they could not grab power without changing the Quran, they would have done so. They could have also manufactured new hadith reports to prove that the Prophet had actually ordained selection of caliph through council, not testament. In the end Numani quotes Khomeini as saying that Umar had insulted the Prophet at his death bed so grievously that the Prophet passed away nursing a wound in his heart. Numani invites all Sunni clerics to read Khomeini's book and let their Sunni followers know that all Shia were filled with the same poison against the Companions of the Prophet. He claims that Mullah Baqir Majlisi whom Imam Khomeini recommends to all the Shia, and whose works the Shia read with great relish at the popular level, had accused Ayesha of plotting with Hafza to poison the Prophet.[54]

Manzur Numani was responsible for spreading sectarianism in India too for which he used the famous Nadwatul ulama seminary. Yoginder Sikand, a noted Indian scholar of Islam, laments:

Even madrassas considered somehow more 'open' and 'modern' are not free from the virus of sectarianism. Consider the case of the Nadwatul Ulama in Lucknow, one of the largest and most influential madrassas in India. Established in the late nineteenth century, the Nadwa was intended as a bridge between the rigidly conservative Deoband madrassa and the thoroughly westernised Aligarh College. Its founders also envisaged it as broadly ecumenical, seeking to promote a sense of unity among the different Muslim sects. Among its early supporters and founder members were traditional Deobandi-type ulama, western educated Muslims, and even Shias and ulama of the Barelvi school. The Barelvi association with Nadwa proved short-lived, and the leading light of the Barelvis, Ahmad Raza Khan, went so far as to issue *fatwas* of *kufr* (infidelity) against the founders of the Nadwa. One of his main grouses against the Nadwa was that it had included the Shias, whom Khan considered to be heretics, in its programmes. The Nadwa did not go on to fulfil the hopes of its founders. Its early Shia supporters soon withdrew, and the Nadwa emerged as a centre for the promotion of Sunni orthodoxy, hardly different from Deoband. From the 1980s onwards, Nadwa began receiving generous Saudi patronage as part of the broader Saudi strategy of promoting conservative Sunni groups to counter anti-monarchical and anti-imperialist tendencies emerging out of Iran. One of the Nadwa's leading teachers, Manzur Numani, penned numerous diatribes against the Shias in the wake of the Iranian Revolution, branding them as infidels and insisting that Shiism had nothing to do with 'authentic' Islam whatsoever.[55]

LUCKNOW AND THE SECTARIAN MEMORY

As Indian scholars like Yoginder Sikand report a revival of the sectarian sentiment in Lucknow in the 2000s, sectarian publications in Pakistan seek to discredit the Shia faith by describing the eclectic culture of the Shia-dominated Lucknow as heresy. To understand why the anti-Shia *fatwas* were published by Manzur Numani from Lucknow, it is important to look at the city's sectarian past. Today the capital of India's largest state, Uttar Pradesh, Lucknow was once an annexed district of the Shia principality of Awadh. The state of Awadh itself was created in 1724 by an award from a declining Mughal king in Delhi. The man, Burhan al-Mulk, thus rewarded for military services to the king, was a scion of a family of Nishapur in Iran and was Shia by religion. A sectarian tract printed in Karachi describes the actions of the first ruler of Awadh as traitorous. Burhan al-Mulk, made ruler of Agra as well, was supposed to come to the help of the Mughal King when the Shia king of Iran, Nadir Shah, invaded Delhi and put it to the sword in 1739. The Awadh ruler advanced towards the army of Nadir Shah on his elephant but then allowed the animal to wander deep into the enemy lines till he was recognised by his Nishapuri friends in the Iranian army and accepted as an ally.[56]

The book describes the rise of the state of Awadh during the decline of the Mughal rule, which lasted for 140 years. The downturn of the Mughal rule is dated from the conquest of the Shia state of Deccan by the Mughal emperor, Aurangzeb, to give point to the fact that the Lucknow-centred Shia culture sprouted in the North after its first manifestation was destroyed in the South. Like the Qutb Shahi state in Deccan, the Shia state of Awadh was established in the midst of a majority Sunni population. The Author and translator Mahmud Ahmad Abbasi quotes from a literary figure of Lucknow, Abdul Halim Sharar, to describe the 'heresies' of the Shia rulers.[57] The book quotes Sharar on the Nawab of Awadh Naseeruddin Haider Shah (reigned 1827–1838):

Naseeruddin used to live among women and had become feminine himself, which affected Shiism in ways never heard of before. 'Wives of the twelve imams', selected out of the pretty girls of the realm, were made to re-enact pregnancies in anticipation of the birth of the occulted 12th Imam in rooms designated as special delivery rooms. The effeminate Nawab himself 'got pregnant' among these girls and pretended to experience the labour pains of the Mehdi, after which a mythical birth actually took place from his womb. After that, ceremonies of birth, cutting of hair and bath were also performed for the reborn Mehdi. The Nawab had no time for the affairs of the state as he was busy in carrying out these puerile rituals surrounded by women. Naseeruddin Shah had also started the 'innovation' of taking out the funeral processions of the imams who were actually 'buried' after a faked funeral prayer.[58]

Before Lucknow was made the capital of Awadh under Nawab Asaf al-Daula (reigned 1775–1797) Faizabad was the capital for nearly a half century. For the tract-writer in Karachi, however, it is important to note that Lucknow was never a Shia city and that till the end, when it became a Hindu-majority capital of India's UP province, it was firmly a Sunni city. It was Chief Minister Hasan Raza Khan under Nawab Asaf al-Daula who first sent money to Iraq for the building of the Hindiya Canal that transformed the desert cities of Najaf and Karbala into fertile land and made it possible for the Iranian scholars living in the shrines to convert Iraq's exclusively Sunni Arabs to Shiism. It was Hasan Raza Khan again who extended patronage to the Sunnis of Lucknow willing to become Shia. He is called '*ghali*' (extreme/abusive) Shia by the anti-Shia writers of later times. Sunni accounts give a lot of detail about how Shia mosques were built separately so that the Shia could manage to stop saying their prayers together with Sunnis. He also began to send Shia scholars to Najaf to absorb the true, as opposed the eclectic, Shiism of India, which is supposed to have led to the currency of the ritual of *tabarra* (abuse) of the Sunni caliphs and the modification of the call to prayers to include the name of Ali. This was followed by the first incidence of violent Shia–Sunni encounters in the city.

The spread of Shia faith in Lucknow was facilitated by the inclination of the Mughal court to favour Shiism, in some cases following the conversion of the Mughal king to Shiism. The reaction of the Sunni ulama to this development was understandably intense. Indeed, verdicts on the 'culture' of Lucknow were also intensely negative and were applied to the poetry produced in the city by the great Urdu poets, Mir Taqi Mir, Anis and Dabir. The poetry of Lucknow was considered lascivious and non-philosophical and totally given to hedonism.[59] The anti-Shia publications of the 1980s connected the 'literary decline' of Urdu to the 'effete' Shia rulers of Lucknow. The textbooks in Pakistan too looked down upon the highly cultured but militarily weak nawabs of Awadh as examples of Muslim decadence in India that the new state of Pakistan will shun.

A more reliable and scientific account of Shiism in Lucknow by David Pinault explains the character of the Shia faith in Lucknow as the religion of a minority community endeavouring to live in harmony with the dominant populations of Sunnis and Hindus. Official support to the Shia minority kept it from being discriminated against. Shia rituals were made compatible with Sunni and Hindu faith by toning down the *tabarra* tradition and by taking on board the *darshanic* tradition of the Hindu gods. Sunnis were thus enabled to grieve over the martyrdom of the family of the Prophet and the Hindus were enabled to see the rituals of martyrdom in the form of *darshan*, that is, treating the martyrs as deities in need of being looked after and decorated. The nawabs of Awadh therefore initiated a trans-communal sharing of religion under an *akhbari* Shia tradition in tune with local cultural accretions.[60]

Three factors changed the nature of Shia religion in Lucknow. First, was the arrival of *usuli* Shia ulama from Iran, including the forefathers of Imam Khomeini, who made it obligatory for the Shia society in Awadh to follow one supreme cleric (*marja taqlid*) and cleanse the Shia rituals of local Hindu accretions. The conversion to *usuli* Shiism forced the Shias to differentiate the Shia faith from the Sunni belief in 1803, thus removing the Sunnis from the rituals of Muharram. The second transformational event was the annexation of Awadh by the East India Company in 1856, removing the patronage of the rulers from the Shia minority population. The third event was the mutiny of 1857 that saw the Muslim community divided on sectarian lines. What followed was sporadic sectarian violence in Lucknow, reaching its high-water mark in 1977 when there were widespread riots, forcing the Shia community of India to firmly adopt the doctrine of *taqiyya* (dissimulation) and becoming a silent footnote to the religious politics of India.[61]

A PARTY DEVOTED TO APOSTATISATION

The three apostatising *fatwas* from Darul Ulum Banuri Town, Jamia Ashrafia and Darul Ulum Haqqania, Akora Khattak, were issued in 1986. Why were these issued the same year? If Manzur Numani had asked for them, who prompted him to make the request? Did someone or some agency ask them to issue simultaneous *fatwas* at the behest of the state? It is quite possible that in the mid-1980s, early contradictions between Iran and Pakistan were coming to the fore. (General Zia's intercessionary diplomacy in the Iran–Iraq war had failed because Imam Khomeini did not acknowledge his credentials as an impartial go-between. He was too aware of the billions of dollars Saudi Arabia and Kuwait had given to Saddam Hussein to take care of his Islamic Revolution. He also knew about the special relationship General Zia enjoyed with Saudi Arabia.) With this background the brazenly anti-Shia organisation, Sipah-e-Sahaba arose in the district of Jhang in Punjab in 1985. The *fatwas* followed soon after. In the years to follow, Pakistan was to cope with the post-Geneva Accord (and post-1989) situation in Afghanistan, facing an increasingly hostile Iran. Pakistan had already succumbed to the Saudi persuasion by ousting the Iran-based Shia jihadi outfits in the Afghan government-in-exile formed in Peshawar.[62] The ISI formed and executed Pakistan's jihad policy at this stage.

The foundation of the Sipah-e-Sahaba—the party that first demanded official apostatisation of the Shia in Pakistan—in 1985 is another factor that cannot be ignored. The founder became a rich man after coming into contact with the Arab princes in Rahimyar Khan where they have extra-territorial rights for hunting. The militia was set up in Jhang where a strong Shia presence was to be targeted. Aggressive sectarianism in Pakistan was born out of the decade of Islamic regimentation imposed on the country by General Zia and his decade of ideological control in the name of Islamization. International affairs, too, played a significant role in inclining the unwilling common man to the feeling of the sect. The rise of Iran as a theocracy exacerbated the sectarian scene in

Pakistan. In the initial stages, Imam Khomeini was looked at in Pakistan as an Islamic alternative and a messianic personality without any sectarian underpinnings. This helped move the formerly quietist Shia community to active approbation of the Islamic Revolution. Imam Khomeini himself reshaped the thrust of Iranian Islam to make it pan-Islamic rather than Shia. In the early phase, Iranian reforms abolished some of the extreme rituals of Shia Islam. To date, Shiism in some Sunni states remains wedded to more extreme ritual behaviour (for instance, violent self-flagellation) than in Iran.

The Iran–Iraq war, however, pitted Iran against the oil-rich but militarily weak Arab states in the region. Iran's aggressive conduct in the Gulf threatened these states. Iraq's Saddam Hussein exploited their military weakness and promised them security against Iran in return for liberal Saudi and Kuwait funding of the war against Iran. Pakistan tried to keep out of the Iran–Arab conflict—for instance, it refused to get involved in the plans to set up a Gulf Security Force—but was not able to sustain this posture for long. The biggest factor in this failure to keep neutral was the conflict in Afghanistan and its crucial financial hinge, Saudi and American funding of jihad.

A number of other factors combined to complete the sectarian developments in the region. The Shia clergy of Pakistan became aware of the charisma of Imam Khomeini and the purity of the new theocracy in Iran. In 1980, the Shia clergy had already refused to accept the new *zakat* laws promulgated by General Zia and was much strengthened in its resolve to defend its separate jurisprudence by the presence of a truly Shia-Islamic state in Iran. On the other hand, the mujahideen who fought the Afghan jihad against the Soviet Union had to be drawn from the Deobandi seminaries in Pakistan since Barelvi Islam was considered apostate in Afghanistan. In its very make-up, Deobandi Islam had a very strong anti-Shia background. Three other factors also weighed in.

The United States, that supplied the funding and the weapons to Pakistan for jihad in Afghanistan, had been greatly hurt by Imam Khomeini when he allowed over a year long but legally dubious siege of the American embassy in Tehran. Washington froze Iranian assets in the United States then crucially needed by the new Islamic regime; and the US Congress imposed sanctions on Iran. Washington also favoured a separation of the jihad on sectarian lines as that would keep Iran from exercising any influence on the war and the future political dispensation in Afghanistan. The parallel provider of funds, Saudi Arabia, actively sought the isolation of the Afghan Shia militias who relied on Iran for their strategy and survival. Funding was also provided directly to the Sunni militias in Pakistan through their seminaries.

With the funding came the Arab agenda. General Zia, and officers after him, favoured the 'downsizing' of the Shia factor because of the problems of the 'ideological disagreement' they faced with the Shia clergy.[63] The United States did not oppose the anti-Iranian trend and perhaps saw the increasingly anti-Shia pathology of the religious state in Pakistan as a positive factor in its regional strategy. Under the umbrella of the waiver of internal sovereignty by Islamabad in favour of the Deobandi warriors, the mujahideen were encouraged to adopt an aggressive sectarian posture. When the sectarian scene worsened in the mid-1980s as a result of these developments, the Shia found themselves defenceless. It is at this point that the Iranian funds—reactive and defensive in nature—began to come in. Leveraged with money, the sectarian war began in earnest in Pakistan, climaxing in the 1990s when the state in Pakistan had been leached of most of its internal sovereignty through covert wars in Afghanistan and Kashmir.

The third factor was the social impact of Pakistan's policy of sending workers to the Arab states. From Islamabad, there was no choosing where the country's surplus labour could be sent. They were absorbed by high-income low-population states across the Gulf and proved acceptable to the Arabs because of their apolitical identity in the intra-Arab ferment of ideas. Economists say large scale migration of Pakistani workers in the two decades of the 1970s and the 1980s dramatically altered the character of development in Pakistan and contributed to fundamental changes in the country's economy and society. In all, there are three million

Pakistanis working abroad sending home four billion dollars annually.[64] Out of them, two-thirds are employed in the Gulf region. While the people back home in general did not nurse any sectarian prejudice, their contact with a rising number of returnees from the Arab states tended to wean them from the more pluralist, low-church religion of the past:

> Attitude towards religion are also suggestive of some of the more complex conflicts engendered by the migration experience and contact with other Islamic societies, especially conservative societies such as Saudi Arabia which represented the heartland of Islam. Work in the Middle East allowed some migrants to complete what for many had been an impossible dream—undertaking the hajj and visiting the holy places in Makkah and Madina. There is evidence of substantial divergence in attitude on this point, suggesting that the greater choice brought about by the Middle East migration resulted in greater complexity and, on occasion, increased conflict at a local level. According to one village study, returnees disliked some of the more traditional aspects of rural Pakistani Islam, particularly special prayers on Thursday evenings and visits to the tombs of dead saints or *pirs*. Such migrants were referred to by villagers as Wahhabi because of their tendency to introduce and endorse new ideas stemming from Saudi Islam.[65]

NOTES

1. *The Essential Rumi*, Translated by Coleman Barks with John Moyne, Penguin Books, 1995, p. 46.
2. Hamid Enayat, *Modern Islamic Political Thought*, Islamic Book Trust, 2001. First published by Macmillan in 1982.
3. Ibid., p. 44.
4. Nibras Kazimi, 'Zarqawi's anti-Shia Legacy: Original or Borrowed?', in *Current Trends in Islamist Ideology*, Vol. 4, Hudson Institute, 2006, p. 56.
5. Kaukab Ali Mirza, *The Great* Imam*: Muslim Scientist and Philosopher Jaafar ibn Mohammad as-Sadiq*, Translated by Kaukab Ali Mirza, Iftikhar Book Depot Islampura, 1999.
6. Liakat A. Takim, 'From Bida to Sunna of Ali in the Shii Adhan', *Journal of American Oriental Society*, 120.2 (2002), p. 169.

7. Wilfred Madelung, *Succession to Mohammad*, Cambridge University Press, 1996, p. 84.
8. Wikipedia.org, see Ghaffari.
9. Hamid Enayat, *Modern Islamic Political Thought*, Islamic Book Trust, 2001, p. 46.
10. Martin Walker, 'The Revenge of the Shia', *The Wilson Quarterly*, Autumn 2006.
11. Hamid Enayat, *Modern Islamic Political Thought*, Islamic Book Trust, 2001, p. 48.
12. Nibras Kazimi, *Zarqawi's anti-Shia Legacy: Original or Borrowed? Current Trends in Islamist Ideology*, Hudson Institute 2006, footnotes no. 3.
13. Annemarie Schimmel, *Islam in the Indian Subcontinent*, Sang-e-Meel Publications, 2003, p. 102.
14. Yitzhak Nakash, *Reaching for Power: The Shia in the Modern World*, Princeton University Press, 2006, p. 91.
15. David Cummins, *The Wahhabi Mission and Saudi Arabia*, I.B. Tauris, 2006. The account that follows is gleaned from the book.
16. Michael Cook, *Commanding Right and Forbidding Wrong in Islamic Thought*, Cambridge University Press, 1990, p. 117.
17. The Black Stone of Kaaba or Makkah is called, in Arabic, *Al-hajar Al-aswad*. Muslims say that the stone was found by Abraham (Ibrahim) and his son Ishmael (Ismail) when they were searching for stones with which to build the Kaaba. They recognised its worth and made it one of the building's cornerstones. The official starting point of the walk around the Kaaba, that forms the core of the holy pilgrimage, is called the *hajj*. During the *Tawaf* (circumambulation) pilgrims kiss or touch the black stone as they circumambulate the Kaaba.
18. Not be confused with the Egyptian Ikhwan in the twentieth century.
19. See Shaharyar M. Khan, *The Begums of Bhopal: A Dynasty of Women Rulers*, I.B. Tauris, 2005.
20. Claudia Preckel, *Educational networks and scholarly culture in the Islamic principality of Bhopal: Mohammad Siddiq Hasan Khan (1832–1890) and the beginnings of the Ahle Hadith movement*, Roli Books, 2000. Claudia Preckel studied Arabic and Islamic studies and pedagogy at the University of Goettingen and Bochum. In 1997, she obtained her MA degree from Bochum University on the Begums of Bhopal. Parts of this work were translated into English and were published as *The Begums of Bhopal* by Roli Books in Delhi. (www.rolibooks.com)
21. See for summary Alexei Vassiliev, *The History of Saudi Arabia*, Saqi Books, 1997.
22. Khaled Abou El Fadl, *The Great Theft: Wrestling Islam from the Extremists*, Harper, 2005.
23. Ibid., p. 6.
24. Ibid., p. 48.

25. Ibid., p. 48.
26. Natana J. Delong-Bas, *Wahhabi Islam: From Revival and Reform to Global Jihad*, Oxford University Press, 2004, p. 221. The book argues that there is practically no violence in Wahhab's work *Kitab al-Tauhid* barring on the question of non-fulfilment of pledge. About the stoned women the book quotes at length from the biography of Wahhab to claim that the said woman fornicated again and again and came to him and declared that she committed adultery as a matter of habit and was not afraid of being stoned. Delong-Bas is of the view that Osama bin Laden has borrowed his creed of violence from Ibn Taymiyya and Syed Qutb and not Ibn Abdul Wahhab.
27. Khaled Abou El Fadl, Ibid., p. 80.
28. Ibid., p. 83.
29. Ibid., p. 101.
30. Mariam Zahab, 'The Sunni–Shia Conflict in Jhang' in *Lived Islam in South Asia*, Social Science Press, 2004. Founder of Sipah-e-Sahaba, Haq Nawaz Jhangvi (1952–1990), a *khoja* graduate of a Deobandi seminary in the city, was vice-president of the JUI in Punjab.
31. Colin Turner, *Islam without Allah? The Rise of Religious Externalism in Safavid Iran*; Curzon Press, 2000, p. 40. Mohammad Al Kulayni (d. AD 940) was the greatest compiler of Shia tradition, *Usul Arb'a*, his masterpiece being known as *Al-Kafi*; Mohammad Baqir Majlisi (d. AH 1110/AD 1679) arose as the most emphatic of the Shia traditionalists.
32. Leif Manger (ed.), *Muslim Diversity: Local Islam in Global Diversity*; Curzon Press, 1998. Tor H. Aase of the Department of Geography, University of Bergen, has taken a close look at what happened to society in the Northern Areas after migration and external confessional influences from Pakistan. The watershed event was the riots that broke out in Gilgit over the sighting of the moon and the observance of Ramadan fasting in 1988. Officially 300 people died but unofficially the count was 700. At least three Shia villages were wiped out in Gilgit as a result of the confrontation between the 'outside' parties, Sipah-e-Sahaba and Tehrik-e-Jafaria. The official blame was put on CIA, RAW, and MOSAD, while the people pointed to Hizb Allah and the Wahhabi movement. Sunni clerics routinely disrupted inter-sectarian marriages till the practice vanished.
33. Daily *Jang*, 14 June 2003, wrote that the founder of the Banuri Mosque complex was Maulana Yusuf Banuri (1908–1977) who was born in Basti Mahabatabad near Peshawar, son of Maulana Syed Mohammad Zakariya who was in turn the son of a khalifa of Mujaddid Alf-e-Sani. He was educated in Peshawar and Kabul before being sent to Deoband where he was the pupil of Shabbir Ahmad Usmani. He returned to join the seminary of Dabheel. In 1920 he passed the Maulvi Fazil exam from Punjab University. In 1928, he went to attend the Islamic conference in Cairo. He migrated to Pakistan in 1951 and started teaching at Tando Allahyar. He founded the Jamia Arabiya Islamiya in Karachi in 1953 while he led the attack against Pakistani Islamic

scholar Dr Fazlur Rehman. He was involved in the aggressive movement of Khatm-e-Nabuwwat from 1973 onwards and was made a member of the Council of Islamic Ideology (CII) by General Zia on coming to power. Today, Darul Ulum Banuri Town is situated in SITE, Karachi.

34. Mohammad Manzur Numani, *Khumaini aur Shia kay barah mein Ulama Karam ka Mutafiqqa Faisala* (Consensual Resolution of the Clerical Leaders about Khomeini and Shiism), Al-Furqan, 1988.

35. IKA Howard, *Great Shii Works: Al-Kafi of Al-Kulayni*, Al Serat Vol. 2, 1976. Published by the Mohammadi Trust of Great Britain and Northern Ireland. Reproduced with permission by the Ahlul Bayt Digital Islamic Library Project team.

36. Posted at http://www.irib.ir/Ouriran/mashahir/mazhabi/majlisi/html/en/page.htm, 12 October 2006.

37. Shia website: http://www.al-islam.org/encyclopedia/chapter8/5.html, accessed 13 October 2006.

38. Khaled Ahmed, 'The Genius of Ghulam Ahmad Parwez', *The Friday Times*, 11 December 1999.

39. Liaquat H. Merchant, *Jinnah: A Judicial Verdict*, East-West Publishing Company, 1990. The book is an account of a case in which the Sindh High Court sought to establish Jinnah's sectarian belief.

40. Baqer Moin, *Khomeini: Life of the Ayatollah*, I.B. Tauris, 1999. Ayatollah Ruhollah Khomeini (1902–1989) led the revolution against the Shah in Iran in 1979. The ancestors of Khomeini were Iranian settlers in the early eighteenth century in Kintur, a town of Oudh, not far from Lucknow in India.

41. Amir Taheri, *The spirit of Allah: Khomeini and the Islamic Revolution*, p. 315, (appendix) and Index.

42. Vali Raza Nasr, *The Shia Revival: How Conflicts within Islam will Shape the World*, W.W. Norton & Company, 2006, p. 165.

43. Ibrahim Abu Rabi (ed.), *The Blackwell Companion to Contemporary Islamic Thought*, Blackwell Publishing, 2006. Yoginder Sikand, *Sayyed Abul Hasan Ali Nadwi and Contemporary Islamic Thought in India*, p. 90.

44. Khaled Abou El Fadl in his book *The Great Theft: Wrestling Islam from the Extremists* Harper, 2005, p. 74.

45. *Jang* later gave Mufti Ludhianvi a weekly full-page in its sister English daily *The News*. This column was widely read by the more liberal section of the readers whom it shocked with its sectarian content. Mufti himself fell victim to sectarian violence in Karachi in 2000.

46. Mohammad Qasim Zaman, *The Ulama in Contemporary Islam: Custodians of Change*, Princeton University Press, 2002, p. 176.

47. Ibid., p. 175.

48. Mushahid Hussain, 'Among the Believers', *Herald*, September 1992, p. 36.

49. Mohammad Qasim Zaman, *The Ulama in Contemporary Islam: Custodians of Change*, Princeton University Press, 2002, p. 133.

50. Account of the Gilgit massacre is discussed in later chapters.

51. Annemarie Schimmel, *Islam in the Indian Subcontinent*, Sang-e-Meel Publications, 2003, p. 92: 'His dictum "Mohammad has become Ahmad" points to his own name, Ahmad. He also regarded himself as *qayyum* upon whom the world rests...towards the end of the seventeenth century Abdullah Khweshgi from Qasur accused the *mujaddid* of having arrogated Prophetic qualities, thus lately Maulana Maududi was very critical of Ahmad Sirhindi's claim to be the *mujaddid*'. And p. 91: 'Ahmad's fame rests on his 534 letters which were described by Jahangir as a "bunch of absurdities"...and had him imprisoned in the fort of Gwalior for a year'.

52. Manzur Numani, *Khomeini aur Shia kay barah main Ulama Karam ka Mutafiqqa Faisala* (Clerical consensual Verdict on Khomeini and the Shia), p. 31.

53. Dilip Hiro, *War without End: the Rise of Islamist Terrorism and Global Response*, Routledge, 2002, p.155. Iranian and non-Iranian pilgrims together took out a procession of nearly 100,000 which was stopped by the Saudi police amid violence that killed 402 people. After this, the Saudis brought the Iranian quota of pilgrims down to 45,000 from the traditional 150,000, which resulted in a boycott of the Hajj by Iran.

54. Manzur Numani, Ibid., p. 90.

55. Yoginder Sikand, Qalandar.com, 4 March 2004.

56. Mahmud Ahmad Abbasi, *Badshah Begum Awadh*, Maktaba Mahmud, p. 16. Typically undated, the book is a part of the anti-Shia campaign and revives an old publication written in criticism of the Shia culture as evolved in Awadh in general and Lucknow in particular. The central account concerns the lady rulers of Awadh and their religious practices, but it is the 166-page introduction to the old account that relates the heresy of Shiism to the situation in Pakistan after 1980.

57. Abdul Halim Sharar, Lucknow, *The Last Phase of an Oriental Culture*, Oxford University Press, 1994.

58. Mahmud Ahmad Abbasi, Ibid., p. 10.

59. Mahmud Ahmad Abbasi, Ibid., p. 126. The author questions the details deployed by Anis and Dabir in their poetic re-enactments of the Battle of Karbala and its *dramatis personae*.

60. David Pinault, *Horse of Karbala: Muslim Devotional Life in India*, Palgrave 2001, p. 17.

61. Ibid., p. 19.

62. Barnet Rubin, *The Search for Peace in Afghanistan: from Buffer State to Failed State*; Yale University Press, 1999, p. 105. Rubin says the Iranian *shura* (of mujahideen) was kept out because Saudi Arabia was against it. Saudi intelligence spent 25 million dollars per week during the discussions in Peshawar, and each delegate was paid 25,000 dollars to keep the Shias out.

The seven parties in Peshawar appointed all the 519 members of the assembly who were mostly Pushtun from eastern Afghanistan.

63. The Chairman of Council of Islamic Ideology Justice (Retd) Tanzilur Rehman was the spearhead of extremist anti-Shia thinking under General Zia, writing two books on the concept of apostatisation (*irtidad*) in which he included refusal to pay *zakat*.

64. *Dawn*, 24 July 2006, Sultan Ahmad, 'An outlook on home remittances': 'Having achieved a record rise in remittances of overseas Pakistanis to $4.6 billion in 2005, Pakistan now faces a prospect of falling inflows because of a big drop in the number of workers going abroad for employment.'

65. Jonathan S. Addleton, *Undermining the Centre: The Gulf Migration and Pakistan*, Oxford University Press, 1992, p. 158.

3

Soldiers of Sectarianism

> Someone puts a clump of burrs
> under a donkey's tail. The donkey doesn't know
> what's wrong. He just starts jumping and bucking around.
> An intelligent thorn-removing
> doctor must come and investigate.
>   – Rumi: *The King and the Handmaiden and the Doctor*[1]

Jihad and sectarianism intermingled in Pakistan. Because jihad in Afghanistan and Kashmir was controlled and conducted by the state of Pakistan, the involvement of the intelligence agencies in the sectarian strife could never be ruled out. There is evidence that when a jihadi outfit got into trouble as a result of its indulgence in sectarian or simple criminal violence, it was rescued by the intelligence personnel, usually drawn from the army. Because jihad was exclusively Deobandi and Ahle Hadith, both schools traditionally anti-Shia in their thinking, protection offered to them looked like state participation in sectarian mayhem. It is possible that at times personnel of the Inter-Services Intelligence (ISI) which ran the jihad, were themselves involved in the elimination of Shia 'obstacles' in the course of fighting. The jihadi outfits fighting against the Soviets and the Indians were well known and were the subject of much public admiration, but for the Shia community they were an affliction, especially as jihad was organised out of civil society and the jihadi outfits remained fully armed while located inside the cities.

On the *ashura* (10th day of the Shia month of mourning) of 2003 and 2004, the Shia Hazara community of Quetta in Balochistan was struck twice, killing 53 people. Pakistan blamed

India but the Shias were pointing clearly to the three well known sectarian militias and some quite respectable clerical leaders of Pakistan. When nothing was done and more Shias were killed at the Pakistan space agency SUPARCO in Karachi, someone hit back in a desperate gesture and shot dead a member of the National Assembly (MNA) Maulana Azam Tariq and leader of the anti-Shia religious party Sipah-e-Sahaba, in Islamabad. There have been many occasions in the past when the killings spiked because the state simply did not respond. The year 1986 was one such year the Shia of Kurram Agency were massacred. The Shia in Gilgit were gunned down in 1988, and Allama Ehsan Elahi Zaheer was killed in 1987 as a result of desperation because the state was either in collusion or simply unresponsive; and the Shia leader Ariful Hussaini was shot dead in Peshawar on 5 August 1988.

Pakistan was always mildly sectarian. It became more so after General Zia's Islamization and imposition of articles of Islam on which there is a Shia–Sunni difference of opinion. Jihad magnified the schism manifold, facilitated by money that came from Saudi Arabia and Iran. It should be noted that this money did not start the killings; it simply helped the two sides do the killings more efficiently. The state-backed jihadis became the foot soldiers of sectarianism. Some of them were exclusively anti-Shia and did jihad on the side, while others were devoted to jihad but did Shia killings on the side. Mariam Abou Zahab, Senior Fellow at the National Institute of Oriental Languages and Civilisation, Paris, has studied Shiism in Pakistan in general, and the phenomenon of the district of Jhang in Punjab and the rise of the Sipah-e-Sahaba Pakistan (SSP), in particular. She has visited Jhang regularly and lived among the family members of Maulana Azam Tariq to acquaint herself with it from the inside. She is considered an authority on the subject as far as Pakistan is concerned.

SIPAH-E-SAHABA: THE MOTHER OF ALL JIHADI MILITIAS

Mariam Abou Zahab tells the real story of Jhang which gave birth to the Sipah-e-Sahaba, turned Pakistani jihad into a sectarian crime and involved the state and its intelligence agencies in it[2]. The Jhang district (Jhang, Chiniot, Shorkot) in southern Punjab has a total population of 2.8 million out of which a quarter are Shia. Half the population of Jhang are refugees from East Punjab in India who filled the vacuum created by the transfer of the non-Muslim majority of the district to India in 1947.

The Shia are divided among the refugees and the locals. So are the Barelvis, the locals among them integrated into Shia rituals and therefore are at peace with them. Most clerics in Jhang sought their careers in baiting the Ahmedi community of a sub-district of Jhang, Rabwah, apostatised by the Constitution of Pakistan in 1974, but the Deobandis among them also began to take on the Low Church Barelvis and the Shia too. (Many scholars think that the idea of apostatising the Shia came after the apostatisation of the Ahmedis living in the same district.) The Shia power is represented by the strong Shah Jewna feudal landlords who are also divided into two hostile factions. Sunni feudals contesting assembly seats against the Shia feudals have played their role in strengthening the sectarian clerics. The refugee Arain (farmer) youth has arisen in the district as the most virulent sectarian and jihadi element over the years. In this environment of sectarian tension, Maulana Haq Nawaz Jhangvi (1952–1990) founded his Sipah-e-Sahaba Pakistan (SSP) in 1985, assisted to some extent by the intelligence agencies enforcing General Zia's plan 'to teach the Shias of Jhang a lesson' because they had defied his Islamization campaign.

Jhangvi was a JUI leader at the provincial level but his real power came from his ability to intimidate and use force through his seminarian youth. He was a firebrand orator and railed against the laxity of faith of the Sunni Barelvis and attacked the Shia for their heresy, targeting directly the Iranian spiritual leader, Imam Khomeini. As noted earlier, his power to intimidate attracted the market elements to him. He was able to obtain generous funding from the shopkeepers and take 'trouble-shooting fees' from businessmen involved in disputes. It was known for instance that he was financed by a businessman Sheikh Yusuf who had also got himself elected with Jhangvi's help to the Punjab assembly. Sheikh Yusuf was also linked to the army as a contractor whose construction company often favoured army officers. Jhangvi also punished businessmen who reneged on pledges of payment, as for instance, Sheikh Iqbal. Perhaps it was this aspect of his fund-raising that finally killed Jhangvi. Jhangvi was assassinated in 1990. Since he had abused the Iranian leader Imam Khomeini in his widely circulated audio cassettes, his party thought that Iran must be behind his killing. Then the man who replaced him Isarul Haq Qasimi, too, got killed in 1991, but this time the party blamed the civil servant son of Jhangvi's enemy, Sheikh Iqbal, and killed him in 1995. In 1992, Maulana Azam Tariq was recalled from Karachi and made chief of the SSP.

In the words of Zahab, Jhang succumbed to a very complex patchwork of conflict: 'Feudals versus the emergent middle class, Shias versus Sunnis, local Shias versus *muhajir* Shias, local Sunnis versus *muhajir* Sunnis, Shia local and *muhajir* Syeds versus lower class *muhajir* Sunnis, local Sunni Sheikh *baraderi* versus Arain Sunni *muhajir baraderi*, plus competition for dominance within the Sheikh *baraderi*. The local-*muhajir* conflict can also be analysed in terms of a conflict between two dominant castes, Sheikh versus Arain.[3] In Jhang, at least, the rise of the SSP is located in a complex sociological matrix, but outside of Jhang, from Quetta to Kurram Agency and Kohat, to the Northern Areas, it is located firmly within the ideological paradigm of Pakistan and its logical progression towards a hardline Sunni state.

THE RISE OF MAULANA AZAM TARIQ

Maulana Mohammad Azam Tariq, killed on 6 October 2003, along with four bodyguards in a drive-by shooting at a toll plaza near

Islamabad, was the son of Haji Fateh Mohammad. Born in March 1962 at Chichawatni in Punjab, Tariq obtained an MA in Arabic and also majored in Islamiat (Islamic Studies) from Jamia Islamia, a Karachi seminary. After completing his studies, he stayed on to teach at his alma mater. During that period he came under the influence of Maulana Haq Nawaz Jhangvi, the rabidly anti-Shia cleric from Jhang. In 1987, Tariq formally joined the Karachi wing of Jhangvi's Sipah-e-Sahaba (Warriors of the Prophet's Companions). He immediately shone with his organisational skills and was instrumental in streamlining the sectarian group's offices in Karachi. In the process, he caught Jhangvi's attention and the latter invited him to Jhang to run Jamia Mohammadiya, the SSP seminary set up earlier by Jhangvi.

Tariq's next move up the ladder was when he got elected as SSP's deputy patron-in-chief. He reached the top position in the group in 1997, getting elected as SSP president after Maulana Ziaur Rehman Farooqi was killed in a bomb explosion in Lahore. Tariq, who was with Farooqi at the time of the blast, survived after receiving severe injuries. At least 13 policemen and a press photographer were also killed in the carnage, one of the worst explosions in Lahore's history. Farooqi was the third SSP leader to die violently. Tariq was elected to parliament four times from the SSP stronghold in Jhang. He won the National Assembly constituency in 1990, 1993 and in October 2002. The 1990 election was a particularly big success when Tariq defeated the government-backed candidate Sheikh Yusuf by a big margin. In the 2002 election under Musharraf, he contested the election from jail. The government first let him contest the elections, then filed a petition in the Lahore High Court challenging the Pakistan Election Commission's decision to allow him to stand despite the cases against him.

Even before he became the SSP chief, Azam wielded considerable influence as an MNA. Seeking a greater political role for his party, he declared that law and order were a priority for the SSP. His party succeeded in getting two members inducted into the Punjab cabinet of Chief Minister Sardar Arif Nakai in 1995. However,

Tariq's accession to the party's top office came in the year the militant Lashkar-e-Jhangvi (LJ), an SSP splinter group, was at its most active in Pakistan. Although Tariq publicly dissociated himself from LJ, law enforcement agencies knew the SSP and the LJ were two faces of the same organisation. Indeed, close observers say creating LJ was a smart move since it allowed the SSP to put a political mask on its sectarian agenda. This fact was proved when Tariq campaigned to save the life of LJ activist Haq Nawaz, sentenced to the gallows for killing the Iranian consul general in Lahore.

The SSP was closely linked with Masood Azhar's jihadi outfit Jaish-e-Mohammed. Azhar, who was sprung from an Indian jail after the 2001 hijacking of an Indian airliner, was also a close associate of the founder Jhangvi. In fact, one of the reasons he broke away from Harkatul Mujahideen was because Harkat was trying to clean up its act and move away from the SSP–LJ sectarian terrorists. By creating Jaish, Azhar kept the links with his sectarian associates. In October 2000, Tariq unveiled his vision of an Islamic Pakistan at an international *Difa-e-Sahaba* (Defence of the Prophet's Companions) conference in Karachi.

He outlined his plan of converting Pakistan's 28 biggest cities into 'model Islamic cities' where television, cinemas and music would be banned. The SSP's vision was the same as the Taliban's. Tariq had close connections with the Taliban government in Afghanistan and was an important part of the Pak–Afghan Defence Council that opposed the American war in Afghanistan and the Pakistan government's decision to stop supporting the Taliban after 9/11. Such was his impact, despite being a Punjabi, that the rabidly anti-Shia Orakzai Pushtun tribes in the upper Miranzai Valley in Hangu and Tal had his and the SSP's name inscribed over hills around the town of Hangu. The area has seen much sectarian strife since the SSP made inroads there starting 1985.

Because of his close connections with Jaish, Tariq also supported the jihad in Kashmir, which was not possible without the tutelage of the ISI. Some observers say this allowed him to put a jihadi gloss over his sectarian activities. When Masood Azhar formed Jaish-e-

Mohammed to fight in Kashmir, Tariq pledged to send 500,000 jihadis to the disputed Valley to fight the Indian soldiers. Maulana Azam Tariq spent a total of 6 years in jail and had 65 cases registered against him. Out of these, 28 cases fell under the various provisions of the Terrorist Act. His lowest point came in August 2001 when General Pervez Musharraf banned seven terrorist organisations in Pakistan, including the SSP. He was sent to jail again and spent nearly a year, his longest spell behind bars. During this period, he made overtures to the military establishment and was allowed to contest the elections after he promised to support the government. He was released in November 2002 after being elected member of the National Assembly, after which he promptly decided to join the pro-Musharraf coalition. He was considered a natural ally of the six-party Muttahida Majlis-e-Amal (MMA), but said he would not support the MMA as long as Allama Sajid Naqvi, a Shia leader, and his party, were part of the alliance. In fact, his group supported the Pakistan Muslim League (Nawaz) candidate from Kohat, Javed Ibrahim Paracha, because Paracha's credentials as an anti-Shia leader were well-known and he was widely accused of fomenting sectarian trouble in the Upper Miranzai Valley as well as in the Orakzai Agency, which runs alongside and abuts the areas of Kohat, Hangu and Tal.

Amir Rana writes:

> Part of Tariq's agreement with the government was that SSP prisoners would be released. The MMA alleged that it was these released prisoners who were responsible for an attack on a Quetta mosque in July 2003 that killed 53 Hazara Shias. The MMA tried to come clean on the issue after the Hazara clerics accused the SSP, LJ and Jaish of perpetrating the violence, implying that the MMA knew of the SSP's sectarian designs. On 25 May 2003, Tariq announced the formation of a new party by the name of Millat Islamia Pakistan (MIP). He was on a countrywide tour to organise the party when he was gunned down. It was the fourth attempt on his life since the controversial sectarian cleric rose to prominence. He was first attacked in 1988 while he was associated with the group's Karachi chapter. This was followed by an attack on him with rocket launchers at Shahpur in 1993. The attack had left him badly injured. He was wounded again in the third

attack on 22 January 1997 in a bomb blast on the premises of the heavily guarded Lahore Sessions Courts. Tariq was one of the last major figures in the SSP to have been directly inspired by Haq Nawaz Jhangvi. The last surviving associate of Jhangvi in 2006 was Maulana Ali Sher Haideri.[4]

RIAZ BASRA AND LASHKAR-E-JHANGVI

The state of Pakistan treated Lashkar-e-Jhangvi as an organisation that could be conveniently blamed for all sectarian violence, thus implying that anti-Shia terrorism was not embraced by any other jihadi militia. There was much confusion every time the Shias were killed and the terrorists named in the press turned out to be members of other Deobandi organisations. There seemed to be an effort behind this focus on the Lashkar to somehow deflect attention from other religious organisations. Most jihad-watchers are, however, agreed that 'Lashkar' remains a blanket term for the sectarian aspects of all the Deobandi–Ahle Hadith formations. As the Sipah-e-Sahaba became more and more inclined to take part in formal politics, its need to separate the function of killing Shias in accordance with the apostatising mission of the founder of Sipah-e-Sahaba, Haq Nawaz Jhangvi, was recognised. As a result, several units with names like Jhangvi Tigers, al-Haq Tigers, al-Farooq, al-Badr and Allahu Akbar, were formed to spread terror in Karachi, Jhang, Chiniot, Samundari, and Faisalabad. All of them later became merged in Lashkar-e-Jhangvi in 1996 under the leadership of Riaz Basra, a central information secretary of the SSP.

Because of SSP's old contacts, the Arab hunters in South Punjab, the organisation was among the first to send recruits to Al Qaeda when it established its training camps in Afghanistan in the late 1990s. When LJ was formed it contained the best trained soldiers of the parent party. As time passed and LJ became a major player in the killing of Shias in Pakistan, there developed a division between Riaz Basra and the boys led by one Qari Abdul Hai who were associated with the training camps in Afghanistan. (Later on, the Basra group became active in Punjab while the Hai group was confined to violence in Karachi.) Hai was more in favour of carrying out missions for Al Qaeda against American and pro-American targets while Basra was determined to advance the cause of Jhangvi and kill Shias. For a time one saw a blending of the two positions in the killings that took place in Pakistan. Hundreds of innocent citizens died at the hands of Basra and his faction while Hai targeted Christians and Americans. LJ remained a Deobandi organisation and Basra was often seen attending the annual congregation of the Tablighi Jamaat in Lahore along with terrorists from other jihadi organisations but was never confronted by the police because of the large number of people present around him.

Lashkar-e-Jhangvi went on killing without much obstruction till General Musharraf was forced to heed the public protest against the organisation; he banned it in 2001. The following year Basra was killed by the police during an 'encounter' in Vihari, he had 300 cases of murder against him, including the Iranian diplomats, a commissioner of Jhang, and a number of prominent Shias from Punjab.[5] Also against his name was the massacre of 25 innocent Shias in Lahore's Mominpura. After 2001, LJ became a part of Brigade 313 to avenge America's invasion of Afghanistan, and was involved in a lot of Al Qaeda work, including the abduction and death of the American journalist Daniel Pearl in Karachi. LJ was close to Ramzi Yusuf, the man who used to carry out sectarian killings before he attacked the Trade Center in 1993, and to Khalid Sheikh Mohammad, his uncle, who planned the final assault on it in 2001. Mohammad was in charge of training Brigade 313 and LJ was a part of this Delta Force. Amir Mir writes that before his arrest, Khaled Sheikh Mohammad had assigned targets to his delta force, which included Musharraf himself and the corps commander in Karachi in 2004. LJ was involved in both attempts in tandem with agents directly commissioned by Al Qaeda.[6] At this point the intelligence agencies noted that Jordanian *Salafist* Abu Musab al-Zarqawi was seen in association with LJ, thus earmarking him as a sectarian killer before he went to Iraq and began his anti-Shia terror there.[7]

Riaz Basra was born in a village of Sargodha in Punjab in 1967. He was the youngest of four sons and two daughters. He was admitted to Government Primary School, Mauza Khurshid, but dropped out within a few months for lack of interest in studies. Later, for a few months, he received religious education from a local religious leader. When he was seven, his brother-in-law, Maulana Mohammad Feroze Madni, brought him to Lahore where he was admitted to Darul Ulum Islamia, Allama Iqbal Town. He studied here for two years before shifting to Jamia Usmania, Wahdat Road. It was at Jamia Usmania that he memorised the Quran and then started teaching it to children at home. According to police records, Basra joined the Sipah-e-Sahaba Pakistan in 1985. Initially, he was elected secretary of its Lahore district organisation. He was instrumental in raising funds for setting up the organisation's office on Lytton Road. In 1987, he became central information secretary of the SSP. In 1988, he contested a provincial assembly seat from Lahore.

He had started visiting Afghanistan, and according to police reports, received combat training at camps run by Harkatul Mujahideen (HUM), a militant group now banned in Pakistan. He also fought in Afghanistan against the Soviets and was wounded in the left leg. By 1990, he was involved in criminal and terrorist activities. The first group of people brought together by Basra for terrorist activities included Sheikh Haq Nawaz, hanged later for killing an Iranian diplomat in Lahore. Basra was first arrested on 5 June 1992, on charges of killing a Shia leader, Syed Sikandar Shah, and Sadeq Ganji, the Iranian consul in Lahore. On 30 April 1994, when he was brought to a special court set up on The Mall, Lahore for the hearing of the case, he escaped. On the assassination of Mr Ganji, and Basra's escape through the ISI, Hassan Abbas has to say this:

A former Pakistani intelligence operator reveals that Basra was operating in league with the ISI agents. According to his information, the other person on the motorcycle [as he shot Mr Ganji] was an ISI agent named Athar, a low-level officer from the Pakistan Air Force serving with the agency. However, it is not known if the act was approved by the ISI command or if some rogue element in the ISI had given the go-ahead on his own account, which was possible as some disgruntled elements in the ISI had started operating independently.[8]

Next, Basra founded Pakistan's most dreaded terrorist organisation, Lashkar-e-Jhangvi. The name hit the headlines on 7 March 1995, following the killing of Imamia Students Organisation leader, Dr Mohammad Ali Naqvi, and five others on Multan Road, Lahore. The reports of Basra's arrest had raised hopes of a trial that would not only boost the morale of the law enforcers but also expose those responsible for keeping alive the sectarian conflict. The government had tried to conceal the arrest but Basra's family was said to be aware of it. His mother, Jalal Bibi, was said to have identified a man in the custody of the law enforcing agencies as her son.

SECTARIAN VIOLENCE AND AL QAEDA

Osama bin Laden got offended with the government of Benazir Bhutto in 1989 because it was inclined to respond to the complaints of some Arab states that Arab terrorists doing jihad in Afghanistan were organising terrorism back home while based in Peshawar. Bhutto was reluctant to own the jihad legacy of General Zia and was still less inclined to kowtow to the aggressive power of the ISI in the country. Pakistani columnist and an interviewer of Osama bin Laden, Hamid Mir wrote in *Jang* (27 March 2006) that ex-ISI operative Khalid Khwaja had recently revealed that Osama bin Laden had paid Nawaz Sharif money to get rid of Bhutto's government in 1989, and that he himself had carried the money to Sharif. According to Hamid Mir, the truth was that Osama was not interested in bringing a no-confidence vote against Ms Bhutto, he was more interested in getting his Arab friends out of trouble in Peshawar. That year Hosni Mubarak, Qaddafi and King Hussein had asked Bhutto to get rid of the Arab terrorists in Peshawar. In the operation that was mounted, Abu Musab al-Zarqawi too had to spend six months in jail in Peshawar. After his release he was imprisoned in Jordan as well. Khalid Khwaja was then retired from the ISI but was personally serving Nawaz Sharif and flying Nawaz Sharif's plane between Rawalpindi and Lahore. He proposed that Osama pay money to end Bhutto's government so that his men would not be bothered anymore.

However, after getting cold feet, the plan was dropped because no head of state would be willing to protect Osama's men in Peshawar.

Jason Burke tends to confirm this and states that Sipah-e-Sahaba was one of the contacts the Arab terrorists exploited to put an end to Bhutto. Burke gives a large profile to Sipah-e-Sahaba in the terrorism that began in the training camps of Afghanistan. He claims that an attempt on Bhutto's life was unsuccessfully made by Ramzi Yusuf on the instigation of Sipah-e-Sahaba while the money came from his relative Khalid Sheikh Mohammad who was then living in Karachi disguised as a Saudi businessman. Ramzi got injured outside Bhutto's Karachi house when his bomb went off prematurely. Severely injured, he was visited in hospital by Sipah-e-Sahaba high officials. Bhutto, whose government was in coalition with Sipah-e-Sahaba in Punjab, accused Osama bin Laden.[9]

Osama bin Laden was inclined to remain above the sectarian conflict, although as a Sunni Arab and a follower of the school of Imam Hanbal and Ibn Taymiyya he was aware of the schism. But the jihadi outfits he supported were sectarian, including Lashkar-e-Jhangvi, which killed hundreds of Shias in Pakistan and took refuge in Osama's training camps in Afghanistan. Rohan Gunaratna takes account of the fact that Al Qaeda supported mostly the sectarian jihadi outfits and tolerated their Shia-killing activities.[10] Among his companions he had two mentors, intellectually-inclined Palestinian Abdullah Azzam, who wanted to target only the United States; and Egyptian Aiman al-Zawahiri who wanted to target 'friends of America' too; above all, Egypt. In the beginning, Al Qaeda was without a sectarian bias, but right from the start, there were Arabs in its fold who nursed antipathy for the Shia, like Kuwaiti-Pakistani Khalid Sheikh Mohammad and Ramzi Yusuf, and Jordanian Abu Musab al-Zarqawi. So great was the support of the two Kuwaiti-

Pakistanis—mainly because of the backing of funds from Kuwait's rich families scared by the Shia community which forms 35 per cent of Kuwait's population—that they could not be ignored. Far from dissociating itself from anti-Shiism, Al Qaeda called for a jihad for the release of Khalid Sheikh Mohammad and Ramzi Yusuf along with Egyptian cleric Umar Abdur Rehman from America's jail.

Ramzi Yusuf was associated with Pakistan's anti-Shia outfits in the 1990s whereas his association with Al Qaeda went back to the 1980s and certainly to the times when Al Qaeda was created in 1989. One of Pakistan's leading newspapers *The News* of 27 March 1995 published a long report on Ramzi and his Pakistani friends:

> Pakistani investigators have identified a 24-year-old religious fanatic, Abdul Shakoor, residing in Lyari in Karachi, as an important Pakistani associate of Ramzi Yousef. Abdul Shakoor had intimate contacts with Ramzi Ahmed Yousef and was responsible for the 20 June 1994 massive bomb explosion at the shrine of Imam Ali Reza in Mashhad in Iran.[11] The Iranian Government had earlier held the rebel Mujahideen Khalq group responsible for the explosion.

Independent reports suggested that during Moharrum in 1994, Ramzi travelled to Iran via Turbat in Balochistan. Abdul Muqeem, another long-time resident of Karachi and identified as a brother of Ramzi, had also spoken about Ramzi's involvement in the bomb blast at Mashhad. Ramzi is understood to have strong connections in the Pakistani and Iranian side of Balochistan. Abdul Shakoor shared with Ramzi, besides a Middle Eastern origin, some very strong anti-Shia feelings. Authorities said that Abdul Shakoor was also an active worker of the SSP, and during his interrogation, Shakoor provided interesting details showing that Ramzi also had some ties with that organisation. In 1994, Yousef's associates in Karachi were given the task of murdering Maulana Salim Qadiri, chief of the Sunni Tehreek, an organisation of moderate Sunnis from the Barelvi school of thought. Several important characters of the conspiracy were arrested in Karachi in 1995.

Pakistani investigators were sure of Yousef's ties with the Sipah-e-Sahaba. These ties flourished mostly in the military training camps inside Afghanistan designated for Arabs and Pakistanis. Orthodox Sunni religious schools in Pakistan served as feeders for these military training camps. Besides Shakoor, investigators believed that Abdul Wahhab, owner of Junaid Bakery in the Lyari area of Karachi, and the 'unit in-charge' of the Sipah-e-Sahaba in Chakiwara, a neighbourhood of Karachi, was another close associate of Yousef. Sources estimated that at least 2,000 persons, mostly Pakistanis and Arabs of different nationalities, were currently engaged in military training in the camps meant for jihad in Kashmir and elsewhere in the world. Another estimate had it that, since the expulsion of Soviet troops from Afghanistan, at least 10,000 Pakistanis belonging to the Islamic parties such as the Jamaat-e-Islami, Harkatul Ansar, Markaz Dawa-wal-Irshad, and Jamiat Ulema-e-Islam had acquired training in making bombs, hurling grenades, firing from light and heavy weapons and in laying mines.[12]

Abdul Shakoor, who himself was associated with a military training camp run by a Palestinian by the name of Abu Mahaz and a Pakistani named Commander Taslim near Kabul, stunned his interrogators by disclosing that his camp also provided training for hijacking. It was the first time that such a claim was made, but it was not confirmed independently. When Osama bin Laden returned to Afghanistan in 1996 from his exile in Sudan, he saw cadres of the sectarian jihadi outfits like the Sipah-e-Sahaba (SSP), Lashkar-e-Jhangvi (LJ), Harkatul Mujahideen (HUM) and Harkat-ul-Jihad al-Islami (HUJI) serving as soldiers of the Taliban. He must have known of an earlier association of his Al Qaeda cadres with some of these organisations controlled in varying degrees by the ISI. After the capture of Kabul by the Taliban in 1996, it was the elements of SSP/LJ who carried out the massacre of the Shias in the Hazara belt.

THE APOSTATISING SEMINARIES: BANURI TOWN MADRASSA

The Banuri Town seminary issued a *fatwa* of apostatisation against the Shia in 1986, which it accused them of declaring the Quran altered and claiming that the real Quran was in a cave near the Occulted Imam Mahdi, and claiming a status equal to that of the Prophet for the Shia imams, and separating themselves from the Sunni *kalima* and all other Sunni rituals like burial and fasting. It referred to *Fatawa-e-Alamgiri* of Emperor Aurangzeb and to the authority of Shah Abdul Aziz and declared the Shia non-Muslims. The *fatwa* is signed and endorsed by two leaders of the seminary, Yusuf Ludhianvi and Mufti Shamzai both of whom were later killed in the sectarian war. Shamzai issued another *fatwa* from Jamia Farooqia, Karachi in which he referred more specifically to Shia classical traditionists like Kulayni and Tabarsi and challenged their claim that Ali had a different Quran which would be manifested with Imam Mahdi. He pointed to the Shia insult to Abu Bakr and Ayesha as grounds for their apostatisation.[13]

The trend of apostatising was rife among the Deobandi seminaries, which were proliferating even after the ouster of the Deobandi Taliban from Afghanistan in 2001. According to Abdul Majeed Salik in *Jang* (6 January 2006), there were 11,221 religious seminaries (madrassas) in Pakistan in the year 2005. This number had grown from 6,761 in 2000. This meant that in the five years that also saw the terrorist attack of 9/11, the apostatising seminaries had almost doubled in Pakistan. There were 448 madrassas for women too. The largest number of madrassas, 8,191 belonged to Wafaq-ul-Madaris Arabiya, 1,952 to Tanzimul Madaris and 381 to Wafaq-ul-Madaris Shia. The majority seminaries are Deobandi. For instance, in Punjab 444,156 pupils are Deobandi as opposed to 199,733 Barelvi; 34,253 Ahle Hadith; and 7,333 Shia. The largest number of madrassas are in Bahawalpur, then in Lahore, Bahawalnagar, and Faisalabad.

The great seminary Darul Ulum at Banuri Town, Karachi is the largest and most influential centre of Deobandi Islam. It is said that

Allama Yusuf Banuri set up the Banuri madrassa (seminary) in
Karachi just after 1947, after coming down from the NWFP.
Another account says that the large Banuri Town complex of
seminaries was established by him much later. The headquarters of
what is certainly the largest Deobandi madrassa in the country is
in Banuri town spread over more than six acres. Jamia Banuria can
accommodate 2,000 pupils, while all its 12 branches in the city
accommodate 3,000 pupils.[14] The amount spent on its upkeep
comes to Rs 3.7 crore annually. The seminary has secular subjects
in addition to religious courses, but its graduates have figured
prominently in jihad. Its most well known pupil was Maulana
Masood Azhar who also taught here before becoming a jihadi hero
and leader of the banned Jaish-e-Mohammed.

Time magazine (7 September 2003) reported:

> Islam doesn't get more radical than the version taught at the Binori
> town mosque and seminary, which educates more than 9,000 students
> at branches across the city. There, in the feverish days after Sept. 11,
> sermons reviled President George W. Bush as a decadent Pharaoh and
> lauded Osama bin Laden as an Islamist hero. The school counted top
> Taliban commanders as alumni and served for years as a favourite
> rendezvous for al-Qaeda men passing through Pakistan en route to
> Afghanistan. In response to 9/11, the U.S. denounced these schools,
> or madrassahs, as terrorist-training academies and called for strict
> controls on their incendiary teachings. The U.S. hoped the newly
> cooperative regime of President Pervez Musharraf would rein them
> in.

Daily *Jang* (14 June 2003) wrote that the founder of the Banuri
Mosque complex was Maulana Yusuf Banuri (1908–1977) who was
born in Basti Mahabatabad near Peshawar. He was the son of
Maulana Syed Mohammad Zakariya who was in turn the son of a
khalifa (pupil) of Mujaddid Alf-e-Sani. He was educated in
Peshawar and Kabul before being sent to Deoband where he was
the pupil of the great scholar Maulana Shabbir Ahmad Usmani.
He returned to join the seminary of Dabheel, in Sindh. In 1920,
he passed the Maulvi Fazil exam from Punjab University. In 1928,
he went to attend the Islamic conference in Cairo. He migrated to

Pakistan in 1951 and started teaching at Tando Allahyar. He founded the Jamia Arabiya Islamiya in Karachi in 1953 while he led the attack against Pakistani Islamic scholar, Dr Fazlur Rehman. He was involved in the aggressive movement of Khatm-e-Nabuwwat from 1973 onwards and was made member of the Council of Islamic Ideology (CII) by General Zia on coming to power in 1977.

Maulana Mufti Rasheed Ahmad (1928–2002) was a companion of Maulana Yusuf Banuri and was a co-founder of the Banuri seminary. Rasheed became famous after his Al Rasheed Trust was banned for being linked to Al Qaeda. He became Sheikhul Hadith of the seminary and was greatly revered for his fidelity to the original Deoband seminary in India. He compiled 40,000 *fatwas* on different issues and authored 60 books. He set up the Al Rasheed Trust in 1996, the time of the arrival of Osama bin Laden back in Afghanistan. The Al Rasheed Trust had opened 40 branches in Pakistan in two years and collected charity second only to the Edhi Foundation. Mufti Rasheed began the journal *Zarb-e-Momin* which became the mouthpiece of the most radical jihadi outfits including Jaish-e-Mohammed. The Al Rasheed Trust spent its funds in Afghanistan, Chechnya, and Kosovo in the West; and Arakan in Burma in the East, helping struggling Muslims. The largest amount of money (Rs 20 million) was given to the Taliban government. The Trust was banned in 2001.

The most well known head of the Banuri complex was Mufti Nizamuddin Shamzai (1952–2004) who was counted as the most powerful man in Pakistan during the rule of Mullah Umar in Afghanistan. John K. Cooley writes that Osama bin Laden used Shamzai's Banuri Town seminary as his base in Karachi for some time.[15] Shamzai, together with Samiul Haq of Akora Khattak, was greatly revered by the Taliban leader, Mullah Mohammad Umar. Among his 2,000 *fatwas* the most well known was the one he gave against America in October 2001, declaring jihad after the Americans decided to attack Afghanistan. He had earlier in 1999 already deemed it within the rights of the Muslims to kill Americans on sight. (The *fatwa* was later modified in explanation.) He was the patron of the foremost Deobandi jihadi outfit Harkatul Mujahideen and was seen as an elder by the two leaders of Harkat: Fazlur Rehman Khalil and Masood Azhar. In 1999, after his release from an Indian jail, Masood Azhar quarrelled with Khalil and formed his own Jaish-e-Mohammed. Shamzai was clearly inclined to favour Masood Azhar and became a member of the Jaish *shura* (governing council). He was already a member of the *shura* of Jamiat Ulema-e-Islam (JUI) of Maulana Fazlur Rehman.

Daily *Insaf* (31 May 2004) wrote that Mufti Nizamuddin Shamzai, who was killed in front of the Banuri Town, Karachi seminary, was born in 1952 in Swat and taught hadith for 20 years at Saudi-funded Jamia Farooqia Karachi before joining the Banuri Town seminary in 1988. He had a PhD from Sindh University in addition to *fazil* of Dars-e-Nizamiyya from Jamia Farooqia. He was close to Osama bin Laden and was a close friend of Mullah Umar of Afghanistan. After 9/11, apart from his *fatwa* of death against the US, he took part physically in the jihad in Afghanistan and was banned from visiting the US and the UK after 9/11. Before that he had been visiting the two countries for *tabligh* (proselytising). He was a patron and founder of Jaish-e-Mohammed when it was formed and given its training camp in Balakot by the ISI. He issued a *fatwa* for support of the MMA. The Chief of Jaish, Maulana Masood Azhar, had gone straight to Karachi after his release from an Indian prison and held a press conference in Mufti Shamzai's apartment.

Shamzai was killed by a sectarian hit squad in 2004 at the height of attacks on Shias in 2003 and 2004, in which organisations linked to him through instruction and tutelage were involved. Columnist Khalid Masood Khan stated in *Khabrain* (3 June 2004) that four great scholars of the Banuri seminary in Karachi had been done to death: Dr Habibullah Mukhtar, Mufti Samiullah, Maulana Yusuf Ludhianvi and Mufti Shamzai. Mufti Shamzai was seen as a moderate scholar despite his pro-Taliban outlook. He had once helped the government open up the Karakoram Highway (KKH) blocked by protesting Sharia crowds belonging to his Deobandi persuasion. Because of lack of information from inside the state-directed jihad and the general silence over the *fatwa*-producing function of the seminaries, Shamzai continued to be regarded as a non-sectarian moderate among the Sunnis in Pakistan.

Karachi became the stronghold of Deobandi seminaries, all devoted to jihad and sectarianism. There are two reasons for this development. One early cause is the relocation of Deobandi scholars from northern India to Karachi as refugees after 1947. The second cause is the internal migration of the Pushtuns from the NWFP to Karachi in search of employment. Many Deobandi madrassas are, therefore, led by Pushtun clerics. Karachi has grown over time to be the locus of proliferation of extremist seminaries.[16] Countrywide the madrassa count is estimated to be 13,000 out of which nearly one thousand are in Karachi, but estimates given by politicians and scholars differ drastically. Ironically, while some Deobandi scholars deny a high count, some insist that they have 1,500 seminaries in Karachi.[17]

There is little doubt that most Deobandi madrassas were funded by Saudi Arabia because of the affiliation of Arab scholars with that school of thought. Most Pakistanis think that the Saudi and Gulf funding goes mostly to the Wahhabi or Ahle Hadith seminaries, but a few believe that the Deobandis are, in fact, more vigorously supported by the Arabs. In-house publications of these seminaries are most informative in this respect. A Wahhabi religious publication, monthly *Nida al-Jihad* writes about this in its March 1994 issue:

> As a result of the untiring and valuable efforts of Saudi scholars, almost every Arabic religious seminary has reformed its syllabus. Books about belief, philosophy and reason have been expunged from the syllabus. Now hadith has become an important subject at least in the Ahle Hadith seminaries. They should be thankful for Saudi scholars for bringing about this revolution in the old education system. Saudi scholars are running the affairs of Jamia Sattariya, Jamia Abi Bakr and Jamia Faruqia (Deobandi) Karachi. Saudi nationals are also looking after Jamia Salafiya, Faisalabad, and Wafaq al-Madaris al Salafiya Pakistan. Principal of Jamia Salafiya Islamabad is also Saudi while Jamia al-Ulum Asariya, Jhelum, Jamia Baltistan, and Darul Ulum

Ghavari, Jamia Ulum Zargari, Kohat, were also established by Saudis. The biggest seminary of Lahore, Jamia Rehmaniya was also funded and built by Saudis, half a dozen of whom are still teaching there.[18]

MAULANA MASOOD AZHAR, THE BRIDEGROOM OF JIHAD

The most famous alumnus of the Banuri seminary was Maulana Masood Azhar, leader of the banned Jaish-e-Mohammed. He is the son of Allah Baksh Shabbir, a teacher of the Quran, of Bahawalpur. His family was connected to the pre-1947 fundamentalist movement of the Ahrar. Azhar was born in 1968 and completed his religious training at the Banuri Mosque in Karachi and then taught there for two years till 1989. He was inspired to do jihad while at the Banuri Mosque. Masood's brother Ibrahim Masood went to Afghanistan at the age of 19. Later he took along his father too. A sister, Rabiya Bibi, worked for the Taliban government in Afghanistan. His elder brother is a computer salesman in Bahawalpur but made many trips to Afghanistan for jihad. Brother Ibrahim Azhar held the Bahawalpur office of the banned Harkatul Ansar and is said to have participated in the hijacking of the Indian airplane that sprung Masood Azhar from a jail in India in 1999.

Masood is the author of 29 jihadi tracts and was the organisational genius behind Harkatul Mujahideen, for which he toured abroad and collected funds. He was caught carrying fake dollars at Jeddah airport during one of these trips. He was instrumental in getting Harkatul Mujahideen (HUM) and Harkat-ul-Jihad al-Islami (HUJI) to merge for some time and was also the man behind creating a collective organisation named Harkatul Ansar. He was in Somalia in 1993 while Osama bin Laden was based in Sudan. Azhar was arrested in Anant Nag in Indian-administered Kashmir in 1994 while trying to coordinate the activities of Harkatul Ansar. He went to Saudi Arabia on a Pakistani passport, from where he went to Dhaka. When he flew to Delhi from Dhaka, he was carrying a Portuguese passport. Azhar is said to have met

Osama bin Laden in Madinah in 1994 when both were disguised. Masood's mission was to bring his jihadi organisation under the aegis of Al Qaeda. In 2000, after release from jail after his return from Afghanistan, he immediately announced the foundation of Jaish-e-Mohammed.

Masood Azhar was devoted to Maulana Haq Nawaz Jhangvi, the fanatically anti-Shia and anti-Iran founder of the Sipah-e-Sahaba, who was murdered in 1990, which in turn led to the murder of an Iranian diplomat in Lahore, thus starting the great sectarian war of the decade of the 1990s and attracting Arab funds to Deobandi warriors. Masood Azhar's Jaish first claimed the attack on the Indian parliament in 2001, then went back on it, but it remained the most aggressive fighting arm of jihad in Pakistan together with Lashkar-e-Taiba (LT). I: is said that his separation from HUM forced his co-leader Fazlur Rehman Khalil to move close to Osama bin Laden, but the truth is that Masood Azhar's trail in Somalia in 1993 links him with the adventure the Harkat recruits participated in from Sudan which resulted in 24 Pakistani troops (as part of a UN peace force) being killed in an ambush by Farah Eidid, the warlord Osama bin Laden was supporting. Later, in 1999, the kidnapper of Daniel Pearl in Karachi, Umar Sheikh, joined Masood Azhar and confirmed the strong bond between Al Qaeda and Jamia Banuria. Daniel Pearl's body was found in a property owned by Al Rasheed Trust in 2002.

The next renowned graduate of Banuri Mosque was Qari Saifullah Akhtar, born in 1958 in South Waziristan. The leader of Harkat-ul-Jihad al-Islami (HUJI), Qari Saifullah Akhtar first came to public view when he was caught in the 1995 unsuccessful army coup led by Major-General Zaheerul Islam Abbasi, but saved his skin by turning state witness. (Some say he was defiant but was still let off.) After that he surfaced in Kandahar, and from 1996, was an adviser to Mullah Umar in the Taliban government. His fighters were called 'Punjabi' Taliban and were offered employment, something that other outfits could not get out of Mullah Umar. The outfit had membership among the Taliban too. Three Taliban ministers and twenty-two judges belonged to Harkat. In difficult times, the Harkat fighters stood together with Mullah Umar. Approximately 300 of them were killed fighting the Northern Alliance, after which Mullah Umar was pleased to give Harkat the permission to build six more *maskars* (training camps) in Kandahar, Kabul and Khost, where the Taliban army and police also received military training. From its base in Afghanistan, HUJI launched its campaigns inside Uzbekistan, Tajikistan and Chechnya.

HUJI called itself 'the second line of defence of all Muslim states' and was active in Arakan in Burma, and Bangladesh, with well-organised seminaries in Karachi, Chechnya, Sinkiang, Uzbekistan and Tajikistan. Because of their common origin in the Banuri seminary, HUJI and HUM were merged in 1993 for better performance in Kashmir. The new outfit was called Harkatul Ansar, the first to be declared terrorist by the United States after one of its commanders, Sikandar, formed an ancillary organisation named Al Faran and kidnapped Western tourists from Kashmir in 1995. Qari Saifullah Akhtar fled from Kandahar after the fall of the Taliban and hid in South Waziristan for some time before reportedly being whisked away to some safe place in the Gulf by one of his Arab friends.

Umar Sheikh, the British national now under the death sentence for the murder of Daniel Pearl, had his beginning in England with the now-banned-in-Pakistan Hizb ut-Tahrir. He was caught in India trying to exchange British tourists that he had kidnapped in New Delhi for Harkatul Ansar terrorists held by India. He was released, together with Masood Azhar, in 1999 after the hijack of an Indian plane. After his release, Umar Sheikh tracked Daniel Pearl and kidnapped him in Karachi with the help of Jaish activists. Pearl was later kept by Khalid Sheikh Mohammad, the top Al Qaeda fund-raiser, who is said to have beheaded him. Umar Sheikh was also said to have been involved in Khalid Sheikh Mohammad's transfer of funds to the terrorists who flew two aircraft into the World Trade Center buildings in New York on 11 September.

AKORA KHATTAK: A MADRASSA
FOR THE TALIBAN

Darul Ulum Haqqania, Akora Khattak, near Peshawar, is one of
the Deobandi seminaries that issued 'simultaneous' *fatwas* of
apostatisation against the Shia in 1986. The brief *fatwa* refers to
the five-volume exegesis of the Quran *Al Safi* by the great Shia
scholar Mullah Mohsin al-Faydh al-Kashani and accuses the Shia
of allowing changes in the Quran. After making a broad reference
to 'other' heresies of the Shia, it says that to eat food cooked by the
Shia, to bury them in a Sunni graveyard, and to marry into the
Shia, was forbidden. The Shia are thus declared *murtad*
(apostates).

According to a 1978 editorial in *Al-Haq,* a publication of
madrassa Haqqania of Maulana Samiul Haq, the alma mater of
many of Afghanistan's Taliban leaders:

> We must also remember that Shias consider it their religious duty to
> harm and eliminate the *Ahle-Sunna*...the Shias have always conspired
> to convert Pakistan into a Shia state.... They have been conspiring with
> our foreign enemies and with the Jews. It was through such conspiracies
> that the Shias masterminded the separation of East Pakistan and thus
> satiated their thirst for the blood of the Sunnis.[19]

Darul Ulum Haqqania is one of the most well-known madrassas
with direct connections with the Taliban in Afghanistan. Mullah
Umar, the leader of the Taliban, was one of the graduates of this
seminary. The head of this impressive residential madrassa, Maulana
Samiul Haq, was elected to the Pakistani parliament of 2002 as a
senator from the clerical alliance the MMA. He presides over a
student body of 1,500 boarding students and 1,000 day students,
from 6-years-olds upwards. Each year over 18,000 applicants from
poor families compete for around 500 seats. Maulana Haq has had
a controversial past.[20] He was stopped by Belgian authorities at
Brussels airport on 22 April 2005. The Belgians had Maulana Samiul
Haq on a watch list and asked for protracted interrogation that he
refused. The Pakistani government promptly lodged a complaint

with the Belgian government in this regard and the public opinion in Pakistan too favoured this position.[21]

Samiul Haq was known for his personal closeness to Mullah Umar in Kandahar. How did the non-Taliban of Afghanistan look upon the Akora Khattak seminary? Here is an extract from an editorial of a Dari-Persian newspaper *Umaid* (15 January 2001):

> Last Wednesday, 10 January 2001, in Akora Khattak near Peshawar, they assembled. They who? They that have for the past eight years tyrannised and murdered tens of thousands of innocent Afghans, destroyed countless hundreds of Afghan villages, burned untold acres of Afghan farmlands and orchards, torched thousands upon thousands of ancient Afghan texts and artefacts, and basically ruined that which had survived the Soviet scourge. They congregated in a show of 'anger' and 'defiance' against the fresh United Nations sanctions against the Taliban militia. The list of attendees in Akora Khattak's Haqqania seminary included Pakistani terror masters Samiul Haq, Fazlur Rahman, Qazi Hussein Ahmad, Masood Azhar, Ejazul Haq, General (Retired) Hamid Gul and General (Retired) Aslam Beg.

GENERAL ZIA'S OWN: JAMIA ASHRAFIA

The Deobandi seminary of Jamia Ashrafia in India has always found more acceptance in Pakistan than the other Deobandi seminaries because its founder Maulana Ashraf Ali Thanwi (1863–1943) had supported the Pakistan Movement in India. So grateful was the Muslim League for getting this support that it encouraged Jamia Ashrafia to open its branches everywhere in Pakistan after 1947. When General Zia began his drive for Islamization he chose the Jamia for lavish handouts from the official Zakat fund. In some years it was the biggest recipient of state contribution to its treasury. The general had a special regard for the Jamia leader Abul Malik Kandhalvi who was also related to him. Zia's hardline Deobandi Islam was probably imbibed from his association with this madrassa.

Sheikhul Hadith at Jamia Ashrafia at Lahore, Maulana Abdul Malik Kandhalvi wrote in 1986:

The campaign of issuing *fatwas* of apostatisation against the Shia is very useful and necessary. The fact is that the way Iran has spread its faith in the past few years has no precedent in the past. It is a basic obligation on us to let the people know what is being done to their faith.

The observation was followed up by an official *fatwa* from Jamia Ashrafia which took issue with the famous Shia traditionists (Tabarsi, Kulayni, Nuri, etc) claiming that the Shia accepted the Sunni Quran only under the condition of *taqiyya* (dissimulation). The *fatwa*, endorsed by Kandhalvi, adjudged the Shia as *kafir* (non-believer).[22]

The most conspicuous of the seminaries in Lahore, Jamia Ashrafia, was founded only a month after the independence of Pakistan, on 14 September 1947, by Mufti Mohammad Hassan, a pupil of Maulana Ashraf Ali Thanwi. As the Jamia website proclaims:

> Due to great regards and esteem for his illustrious spiritual guide and in recognition of his services to prevail upon the ulama for united efforts for the creation of an independent land Pakistan for Muslims, Mufti Mohammad Hassan named this Institution at Lahore as Jamia Ashrafia.

Founded initially in an old quadrangular three-storied building in Nila Gumbad, Anarkali, at the centre of the thickly populated area of Lahore, the Jamia soon became recognised as the most authenticated pivotal seat of Islamic learning in Pakistan. Then Allah 'created means from the unknown' and a spacious area of 120 kanals ideally located piece of land between Canal Road and Ferozepur Road was purchased in 1955. In 1957, most of the staff and students had shifted to this new campus on Ferozepur Road, Lahore. Today, this main campus comprises a beautiful mosque, a huge administrative and teaching block, two spacious boarding houses—one for local and the other for foreign students—and a hospital with medical facilities for the staff and the students.

RAZA NAQVI AND SIPAH-E-MOHAMMAD

As the *Daily Times*, Lahore, reported on 25 June 2006, an Anti-Terrorism Court in Lahore sentenced two men to death for the murder of two associates of the chief of Sipah-e-Sahaba Pakistan (SSP), Maulana Azam Tariq. The court exonerated eleven others accused in the same case. The convicted men were Raza Naqvi and Shabbar Abbas. The two had killed Haji Imtiaz and Shahid, two SSP men close to Azam Tariq, in a failed bid to assassinate him in Sargodha in 1994. Azam Tariq was subsequently shot dead in October 2003 on the Lahore–Rawalpindi Motorway as he was entering Islamabad. Jihadi leader Qazi Ziaur Rehman was also killed in the attack.

The Pakistani press made no comment on the death sentence, nor was it made clear whether Raza Naqvi was in custody or had been given the sentence *in absentia*. He was no ordinary person. He was chief of the Shia sectarian organisation Sipah-e-Mohammad established to counter the sectarian terrorism of Sipah-e-Sahaba. Why did the press keep quiet? Firstly, because Pakistanis know very little about sectarian politics by reason of the general denial of sectarianism considered proper by them. Secondly, because the Sunni–Shia violence in Pakistan is carried out in the form of a vendetta by the clergy and their followers, away from the public eye. Thirdly, because talking about the schism might offend the grand jihadi alliance among Deobandi–Wahhabi militias with influence in the Urdu press. Fourthly, because either side of the schism can resort to violence against a newspaper thought to be reporting with prejudice. And lastly, because the English language press finds it difficult to grasp the sectarian debate while struggling with the English idiom.

Mujahid Hussain, *Daily Times*' reporter in Belgium, who had earlier reported on the Sipah-e-Mohammad beat in Lahore, wrote the following pen-picture of Raza Naqvi after the sentencing:

> Jarnail of Sipah Mohammad, Syed Raza Naqvi was unknown in Shia militant circle before 1990. In September 1990, he joined the Shia militant group Mukhtar Force while he served as a bodyguard of

Dr Mohammad Ali Naqvi of Lahore. Dr Naqvi masterminded the Mukhtar Force and later on founded Sipah Mohammad Pakistan (SMP). Raza Naqvi spent five years in the Iranian city of Qum as a student of Shia *fiqh* (jurisprudence) but soon abandoned his studies in favour of setting up a militant group of exiled Pakistani students under the name of Anjuman Fidayeen Ahle Bayt in Qum.

Naqvi appointed himself general with a uniform carrying five stars (panj tara) on its epaulettes. The five stars pointed to the Holy Quintet of the Prophet's family, as he explained in an interview in 1995 at the headquarters of Sipah-e-Mohammad at Thokar Niaz Beg in the suburbs of Lahore. (His stars coincided with the five stars on the flag of the opposed sectarian party Sipah-e-Sahaba, where four stars were the four Rightly Guided Caliphs and the fifth star represented three persons: Hasan, Husayn and Umayyad caliph Muawiyya whose son Yazid had killed the two grandchildren of the Prophet.) He was in this uniform when he was first arrested in 1996. (It should be noted that the Sipah-e-Sahaba chief Azam Tariq too had begun his anti-Shia sectarian career as a 'general'. An element of tit-for-tat is obvious in this, the Shia side being reactive to what the Sunni sectarians first do.)

According to the Shia sources in Pakistan, Naqvi developed a close relationship with Iran's Pasdaran Islam and got money and training in the Iranian military camps. When he returned to Pakistan in 1990, his first arrest in Jhang in April 1990 was in connection with charges of possession of illegal weapons. He spent five months in jail before being bailed out by Dr Mohammad Ali Naqvi. From 1990 to 1995, he was involved in several murders and bank robberies in Punjab, and the police set two million rupees reward money for his arrest. He was also involved in the murder of Sipah-e-Mohammad chief, Allama Murid Abbas Yazdani, in September 1996. After his arrest in December 1996, his militant group was almost finished and his close associates fled to Iran and some European countries.

Mazhar Zaidi in his article 'The Shias Strike Back' (*Newsline*, Feb. 1995) first took note of the rise of SMP after a shootout at Thokar Niaz Beg in July 1994, from the headquarters of the Shia force. That year SMP also staged its show of force at the historic Minar-e-Pakistan near the Badshahi Mosque in the heart of Lahore with Naqvi's guards firing in the air on his arrival at the venue, making the journalists flee in panic. As 'Aghaji' ascended the stage, he was already known as having been briefly jailed for robbery and attempting to kill the Sipah-e-Sahaba leader, Azam Tariq. Naqvi was full of resolve to counter and beat down the fanatic outfit of Azam Tariq. In 1995, he was already claiming to have killed two SSP clerics a day and a dozen SSP activists a week. The SSP alleged that governor Punjab, Chaudhry Altaf Hussain, was helping the SMP kill Sunnis.

At the height of his power, Naqvi got his followers to attack the newspaper *The Pakistan Observer* because it was not giving proper coverage to his party and because allegedly the owner of the newspaper had connections with the Arabs and with SSP. This could have been the first manifestation of the Arab–Iranian conflict in Pakistan, but caution was shown to play down the Arab–Iran factor when SMP's patron-in-chief Allama Murid Abbas Yazdani was sent to the office of the newspaper to apologise for the event. But Yazdani was arrested in Rawalpindi when he arrived in the city—in connection with an earlier event when the SMP had publicly announced that it would kill Azam Tariq if he addressed a meeting in Rawalpindi. The killing did not take place but the threat was culpable.

The Lahore police finally decided to take action against SMP. After nine hours of exchange of fire the police surrendered and its constables—whose weapons were confiscated by the SMP—were made to parade naked by Naqvi in a deliberate show of strength. SSP chief Azam Tariq accused the Tehrik-e-Jafaria Pakistan (TJP) of creating the SMP but evidence shows that the Shia rift was a long time coming. It began in 1988 when TJP's Sajid Naqvi abandoned the PPP, perhaps at the behest of Iran, and changed the name of Tehrik-e-Nifaz-e-Fiqh-e-Jafaria (TNFJ) to Tehrik-e-Jafaria Pakistan (TJP). In 2007, he was in the MMA, sitting together with the Deobandi–Ahle Hadith outfits with an anti-Shia orientation.

It appears that the SMP–TJP 'unannounced' break was genuine while the SSP–Lashkar-e-Jhangvi 'announced' break was not.

After the 1993 general election, the PPP had formed a coalition in Punjab which included Sipah-e-Sahaba Pakistan (SSP). The city of Lahore boasted torture cells guarded by the police where the SSP routinely tortured Shia activists. While Chief Minister Arif Nakai deferred to the wishes of the SSP minister in his cabinet and gave the SSP terrorists *carte blanche* to settle their scores with Raza Naqvi, the governor sought to balance the chief minister by leaning in favour of the SMP. Grasping this rift, the SSP staged a number of protests in front of the Governor's House, calling him a partisan of the Shia and an Ahmedi. (Ironically, it was not the governor but an earlier chief minister, Wattoo, whose father was an Ahmedi; and Wattoo had to 'clear his name' by not attending his father's funeral!)

In another account, Raza Naqvi was born in Abbaspur, a small town in district Khanewal, where he completed his schooling. He later got Shia degrees—Sultan-e-Fazil and Jaam-e-Mustafa—from two seminaries in Multan and Lahore. He was still at the age at which students normally complete their 12 classes when he was sent to Mashhad in Iran for three years for higher studies. He was sent into Afghanistan to fight together with the Hazaras after military training in Iran. He seems to have joined TNFJ after his return to Jhang in 1983. Naqvi set up his own madrassas in a village near Jhang in 1987 and was soon involved in violent crime (burning shops and assaulting Sunnis) in the district, as a result of which he had to spend three years in jail till he was set free by the Lahore High Court on the condition that he was not to set foot in Jhang again.

Naqvi finally moved to Thokar Niaz Beg as *khateeb* of the Shia mosque Ali Masjid and arose as the belligerent Shia leader in parallel to the more 'quietist' Sajid Naqvi (a graduate of the Najaf seminary in Iraq) of the mainstream TJP. He has been sentenced to death in an attempt made on the life of Azam Tariq in 1994, but his vendetta with the Sunni sectarian leader was also personal. According to one account, when the two rivals found themselves face to face in a district jail in Punjab, sparks immediately flew. After Azam Tariq slapped a Shia prisoner 'for being an infidel', Naqvi butted him hard on his face, making him lose two of his front teeth.

According to Mohammad Amir Rana,[23] SMP was created by Raza Naqvi, president of TJP Jhang, in 1993 because of the increasing quietism of Allama Sajid Mir, the TJP chief. He was joined by Dr Mohammad Ali Naqvi of Lahore who had already expressed his disenchantment with TJP by forming his Pasban-e-Islam. According to Rana, SMP claimed responsibility for the attempt on the life of Azam Tariq on the Sargodha–Khushab Road in 1994 for which finally the court sentenced Raza Naqvi to death in 2006. In its tit-for-tat vendetta with the SSP, the SMP was involved in 250 acts of terrorism between 1993 and 2001.

The decline of Raza Naqvi came after the break-up of Sipah-e-Mohammad in 1996 when the Punjab police decided to attack it in its stronghold in Thokar Niaz Beg. The attack was facilitated by an internal crack in the SMP which had led to the murder of Allama Murid Abbas Yazdani at the hands of SMP workers who confessed to the police that they had carried out the murder on the orders of Raza Naqvi. Naqvi had fallen out with Yazdani over the latter's participation in the Milli Yakjehti Council—a committee of reconciliation between the two sects—where allegedly Yazdani had agreed not to stigmatise the Truly Guided Caliphs. Also, the residents of Thokar Niaz Beg who had originally welcomed SMP as a defence against the tyranny of the SSP, were now reluctant to support it. When SMP was banned in 2001, it was hardly the aggressive outfit it was in the early 1900s.

THE ARMY OF THE 'SACRED ONES'

If you visit the Lake Road office of Hafiz Saeed in Lahore, the mosque inside the compound is named after Qadisiya, the place where in AD 636 the army of Caliph Umar destroyed the army of the Persians in a decisive battle. Why should Lashkar-e-Taiba adopt a name that clearly expresses a historic anti-Iranian sentiment? It also insults an Islamic Iran by giving it the pre-Islamic identity of a defeated nation. Iranian nationalist websites often proclaim:

> To all true Iranians: Feb 19 is the commemoration day of the start of the battle of Qadisiya. Qadisiya battle started on Monday February 19, 636 (AD) and lasted for four days, on the flat plains near the Euphrates River in modern Iraq between Kufa and Abu Sukheir. The Sassanian army under the command of General Rostam-e-Farokzad and the Arab army of caliph Omar under the command of Sa'd ibn Abi Waqqas clashed. Many Iranians fought bravely and died (more than 30,000 dead) in this battle trying to defend Iran from the nomadic Arabs attempting to convert Iranians to their Islamic religion. At the end of the battle Rostam was killed and the national flag (Darafsh-e-Kaviyani) was captured by the Arab nomads. This flag was taken to Caliph Omar who promptly removed all of the magnificent jewels set on it and then ordered it to be burned.
>
> After the battle the Arabs went to the capital Ctesiphone, the glorious capital of Sassanian empire and the largest city in the world at that time. The city was invaded, sacked, and functionally destroyed by the armies of Islam. The great Carpet of Baharastan, woven with threads of gold and silver in the great arched hall of the palace of Ctesiphone was cut up by the Arab nomads and distributed as war booty. (Note: this looting is still going on 1368 years later.) Gondi Shapour University and library were destroyed and its books were burned by the invaders. Most of Sassanian records and literary works were destroyed. This day February 19 should be commemorated by all Iranians nationally and internationally. This is our real national 'Ashura' not the one the mullahs force us to commemorate. Instead of going on a pilgrimage to Makkah and Karbala we should all go to Qadisiya to remind ourselves of the truth of what has happened to us over the past 1368 years.

Amir of the banned Lashkar-e-Taiba and the renamed Jamaat-ud-Dawa, Hafiz Mohammad Saeed, routinely issues criticism of the policies followed by the government under the tutelage of President Pervez Musharraf. After having abandoned the grand Muridke seminary which he ran under the Dawa-wal-Irshad cover organisation, he is now firmly established on Lake Road, near Chauburji,

Lahore, not lacking in financial and manpower muscle as always. Urdu newspapers print his almost daily diatribes against the misdirection of the country.

Hafiz Saeed is a Kashmiri *gujjar* whose family lived in Simla before partition. After 1947 he grew up in Sargodha where his family tilled the land they had got 'in claim' for the property they had left behind. Saeed's father, Maulana Kamaluddin, was a religious scholar, so was his uncle Maulana Hafiz Abdullah, who later helped in the organisation of Lashkar-e-Taiba. Abdullah's sons Abdur Rehman Makki and Abdul Mannan married the sisters of Hafiz Saeed. Makki later became number two in Lashkar-e-Taiba. Hafiz Saeed graduated from Sargodha Government College and later did his MA in Arabic and Islamiat from Punjab University. In the University Old Campus he was a *nazim* of the Islami Jamiat Talaba (IJT), the student wing of the Jamaat-e-Islami. Pakistan Muslim League (N) leader Javed Hashmi won the Punjab University Student Union elections under his *nizamat* (leadership) and rose on the Pakistani political scene.

After graduation in 1974, Hafiz Saeed was appointed lecturer at the University of Engineering and Technology (UET), Lahore, in the Islamiat Department. It is from here that he was sent for higher studies to Saudi Arabia. He graduated from King Saud University, Riyadh, and while in Saudi Arabia he was close to the famous Saudi scholar Sheikh Abdul Aziz Bin Baz who was the first to pronounce the *fatwa* of jihad in Afghanistan in 1979. After his sojourn in Saudi Arabia, he returned to Pakistan and was selected as a research scholar at the Council of Islamic Ideology, a selection made by a panel of High Court judges. While working at the Council, he retained his lien with the University of Engineering and Technology, Lahore.

According to the magazine *Nida-e-Millat* (22 March 2001) Hafiz Saeed took part in the election campaign of the Jamaat-e-Islami in 1970 but was put off by politics in general after losing. He turned against democracy and was traumatised by the fall of East Pakistan in 1971. It was after the *fatwa* of jihad in 1979 by Bin Baz that he turned to the war in Afghanistan and went to the training camp of

Abdur Rasul Sayyaf where he also met the teacher of Osama bin Laden and other Arab fighters, Dr Abdullah Azzam. He admitted that during his training he met Osama bin Laden a number of times. In 1986, the teachers of the Islamiat faculty of Lahore's Engineering University had founded Markaz Dawa-wal-Irshad, an Ahle Hadith organisation devoted to the Saudi brand of Islam and raising armies for the jihad in Afghanistan.

The most advanced seminary in Karachi, Jamia Abu Bakr al-Islamia in Gulshan-e-Iqbal Town, is also run by Jamaat-ud-Dawa under the leadership of Hafiz Saeed. Out of the 36 Ahle Hadith or Wahhabi seminaries in the city, the Jamia is the most sophisticated as it teaches the sciences and uses English as the medium of instruction. In the 1980s half of the enrolled pupils were foreigners, mainly from Indonesia, Malaysia and Thailand.

Jamia Abu Bakar gained international prominence in September 2003, when an Indonesian student, Gun Gun Rusman Gunawan, was arrested from its compound. His brother, Riduan Isamuddin, alias Hambali (a variation of Hanbal, Imam Hanbal being the greatest classical jurist of the Wahhabis), leads Indonesia's Jemaah Islamiyah, which was behind the Bali bombings of October 2002. The administrator of the madrassa, Abdullah Ghazi, denied that any student with that name or credentials was on its roll. Residents of the area, however, say that Gunawan was enrolled under the pseudonym of Abdul Hadi, and it is speculated that he was in Pakistan on a government-sponsored educational scholarship.[24]

Jamaat-ud-Dawa has 'maintained close links with other anti-Shia groups.[25]

THE LAHORE FUNERAL OF ABU MUSAB AL-ZARQAWI

Hafiz Saeed's sectarian connection became overt after he followed the Al Qaeda instructions with regard to Abu Musab al-Zarqawi in Iraq. At first Al Qaeda was put off by Zarqawi's campaign of killing Iraqi Shias, but after his death, Al Qaeda owned him and got its

Pakistani supporters and clients to declare that Zarqawi was not a sectarian man but was in Iraq only to kill the Americans. In fact, al-Zawahiri had written a letter to him, later shown on *Al Jazeera*, in which he had asked, 'Why were there attacks on ordinary Shias? Can the mujahideen kill all the Shias in Iraq? Has any Islamic state in history ever tried that?' Al-Zawahiri also didn't like Zarqawi's beheadings: 'We can kill the captives by bullet.'[26]

Reported in *Jang* (10 June 2006), Jamaat-ud-Dawa (old Lashkar-e-Taiba) carried out the *ghaebana namaz janaza* (funeral prayer in absentia) for Abu Musab al-Zarqawi in Lahore and condemned the Foreign Office for saying that the death of the Shia-killer in Iraq was an achievement in the war against terrorism. The congregation that blessed Zarqawi kept crying *zaar-o-qataar* (with great intensity) for the great *shaheed*. In the National Assembly, the MMA demanded *fateha* for Zarqawi but this was denied by the speaker. In *Nawa-e-Waqt*, the Jamaat-e-Islami leader Munawwar Hasan said that Pakistan was reluctant to call Zarqawi *shaheed* as that would offend Washington.

Columnist Hamid Mir wrote in *Jang* (12 June 2006) that Abu Musab al-Zarqawi listened to the lectures of Abdullah Azzam and Abdur Rab Rasul Sayyaf in 1988 in a mosque in Jordan and was convinced by Sayyaf to come and fight in the jihad against the Soviets. Azzam was a philosopher of jihad and had taught at the International Islamic University of Islamabad and then moved to Peshawar to set up what later developed into a fighting machine for Osama bin Laden. Zarqawi went to Peshawar in 1989 and was sent by Sayyaf through Miranshah to Khost where, together with Jalaluddin Haqqani, 'he drove the Russians out'. The Americans wanted the mujahideen to make peace and Islamabad was anxious to get rid of the Arabs in Peshawar. Zarqawi met al-Maqdisi in Peshawar and made him his spiritual father, but Maqdisi held an extreme position on the Arab–Israel accords of 1993. That year Zarqawi returned to Jordan and was arrested for opposing the accords and sentenced for life only to be let off in 1999 on the coronation of King Abdullah. He went to Peshawar and was imprisoned there too but influential friends got him out. Haqqani then sent him to Herat to train new warriors. From Herat he went to Kandahar in December 2001 where he was wounded by an American bomb. He then went to Tora Bora and joined Osama bin Laden, but his route out of Afghanistan was through Iran with Hekmatyar's help. He was not liked by Osama for his anti-Shia outlook but he soon gave it up and was thereafter owned by Osama.

It is clear that the Al Qaeda number two, al-Zawahiri, did not like to involve the organisation in sectarian mayhem. He shared his disinterest in killing the Shia with all Muslims unfamiliar with the schism because no Shia lived in their countries. Once a seat of the great Fatimids, Egypt is today without a Shia population and therefore doesn't share with the Arabs of the Gulf their fear of a Shia revival. But Al Qaeda in Iraq was manned mostly by Arab youths fired by the sectarian passions of the region and it became difficult for Al Qaeda to keep its sectarian side hidden after Zarqawi's death. In Pakistan, most Urdu columnists dutifully observed the martyrdom of Zarqawi saying he was no Shia-killer. The man was known to the reading public because of the publicity attracted by a case against two doctors in Karachi for having aided and abetted Al Qaeda by providing medical assistance to Zarqawi under the aegis of a terrorist organisation named Jandullah, which was controlled by Al Qaeda. Was Zarqawi innocent of sectarianism as proclaimed by the pro-Al Qaeda religious and jihadi organisations?

Pakistanis who stood in rows after Hafiz Saeed as he recited the funeral prayer for Zarqawi, were oblivious of the anti-Shia statement Zarqawi had posted on the internet before his death in June 2006:

> He declared that there would be no total victory over the Jews and Christians without a total annihilation of the Shia, whom he called the secret agents of the enemies of Islam. 'If you can't find any Christians or Jews to kill, vent your wrath against the next available Shia'. He claimed that his fellow-terrorists the Hezbollah in Lebanon, were only pretending to oppose Israel, while in reality their mission was to protect Israel's northern border. Zarqawi concluded with a formal

declaration of war on the Iraqi Shia leader Moqtada al Sadr'. (A large part of this bizarre and possibly unhinged outburst focused on slurs against the Prophet's wife Ayesha, on discussing Ayatollah Khomeini, and on assailing Shia).[27]

THE ANTI-SHIA JIHADI COMBINE

That the state was involved in Shia killings in Karachi was reported in the press in Pakistan. That there was a strong Deobandi–Sipah-e-Sahaba presence in Karachi with links to the Muttahida Qaumi Movement (MQM) Haqiqi, courtesy the intelligence agencies, was also noted. The most important person in this dominance of the seminary was Maulana Azam Tariq. Indeed, there were cities where his writ ran stronger than that of the state.

The press was careful in reporting the sectarian truth in Karachi but some signs of a desperate kind of journalistic courage came to light after the murder of the Shia doctors in the city. Amjad Bashir Siddiqi wrote in *The News* (5 August 2001):

> These sectarian organisations, with enormous money in their pockets, spend it without any limits to free terrorists or to bail them out, and more importantly, to penetrate into the administration. Recently, money was spent to free a terrorist from the custody of CIA (a Pakistani intelligence agency), who, three days later assassinated the chief of Sunni Tehreek, Saleem Qadiri. They also tried to wriggle free another activist of their party on death row and were ready to spend as much money as needed to ensure that Mansur, convicted for the killing of seven members of three families in PECHS back in 1993, got bail.

The article went on to describe how the Jaish-e-Mohammed leader Maulana Masood Azhar, whose entry was banned in Sindh because of the wave of sectarian terrorism, was stopped at Karachi airport and was asked to go back. Azhar phoned someone and the ban to allow him to enter Karachi was immediately lifted, after which he had a meeting with the home secretary, Sindh. Azhar also later went to Ghotki in violation of the ban and was ignored by the local administrative magistrate there. The officer was pulled up, but later still, when Azhar tried to enter Sukkur and was stopped by the district administration, the local bureaucracy was pulled up, this time for not giving him unhampered passage to anywhere in the city. The article adds:

> Another serious problem has been the criminalisation of the jihadi elements, some of whom have been involved in sectarian killings. Recently, commissioner Karachi Shafiqur Rehman Khwaja gave Rs 200,000 to the prime suspect of Saleem Qadiri's murder, Arshad Polka, as compensation money for being a victim of terrorism. Polka had died during the attack on the Sunni Tehreek leader.

Here was a blatant case of pro-sectarian bias: a dead man was disbursed state funds. The article goes on to link the state machinery with sectarian killers. Officers aligned to sectarian killers do two things: they get the criminals released in case they are caught after the act, and they see to it that the caught terrorists are not allowed to be linked to the jihadi militias.

Monthly *Newsline* (June 2001) actually wrote that the intelligence agencies were 'in' with the sectarian terrorists:

> The official quoted above has no hesitation in accusing the ISI of orchestrating such (Shia) murders through the militants of sectarian parties, adding that Sipah Sahaba terrorists are trained by the agency. The Sipah Sahaba killers are supported by the MQM Haqiqi Group. Sources reveal that Sipah Sahaba's Riaz Basra has been spotted in the company of a colonel who has also given him shelter in his house. Similarly, when three members of Lashkar Jhangvi (LJ) were picked up by the police, another colonel, who identified himself as their public relations officer, requested that they be released forthwith.

By 2002, Karachi had witnessed the death of 450 people in cases of sectarian violence since General Musharraf took over the government in October 1999. The killing became one-sided because the Sunni–Deobandi combine was simply too strong to be countered by the Shia organisations.

BARELVIS IN THE SECTARIAN CROSS-HAIRS

As described earlier, the sectarian Sunni clergy always regarded their fellow Sunnis of the Barelvi school of thought as renegades because of their sympathetic attitude towards the Shia. The Barelvi-baiting first began in Jhang but in 2006, it burst forth in Karachi in what is called the Nishtar Park massacre. Pakistan began its religious journey in 1947 as a Barelvi–Deobandi state (with 80 per cent Barelvi hinterland) under the Hanafi school of jurisprudence. The Barelvi school was dominant in Punjab while the Deobandi seminaries predominated in the NWFP and Balochistan among the Pushtun tribes. Because both were Hanafites, there was much common ground between them. However, the Barelvis inclined to popular Islam while the Deobandis inclined to puritanism on the basis of their superior ability to teach the Quran. Among the ulama, the Deobandis and the Barelvis at times refused to say their *namaz* together, but this divide was not apparent among the people. It was in 1996 that the rise of the Taliban brought to the fore a 'definition' of jihad as Deobandi. Afghanistan was always Deobandi-dominated, but the rise of Mullah Umar put the Deobandi stamp on it. Pakistan released 80,000 students of Deobandi seminaries in the NWFP and the tribal areas to assist the Taliban invasion of Kabul in 1996. The rise of the JUI as the champion of the war in Afghanistan started the process of Deobandi dominance in Pakistan.

The jihad in Kashmir, which began in 1988–89, was at first dominated by the non-Deobandi Jammu and Kashmir Liberation Front (JKLF) and the Jamaat-e-Islami, both able to gather militant support on either side of the Line of Control (LoC). However, as more and more mujahideen became available from the Afghan front, the Kashmir jihad began to show a variety of *mazhab* (schools of jurisprudence). Foreigners who came over from Afghanistan also introduced the Ahle Hadith or Wahhabi element into the war. The mujahideen began to demonstrate a new puritanism vis-à-vis the Muslim population in Indian-administered Kashmir. The rise of Harkatul Ansar (later Harkatul Mujahideen) as a fighting force inside Indian-administered Kashmir marked the rise of Deobandi *mazhab* in Pakistan as well. Inside Pakistani society, the Deobandi Sipah-e-Sahaba had already put forward its anti-Shia demands in 1985. Its power increased as its seminarians found their way into the Kashmir jihad through Harkatul Ansar mujahideen. By the year 2000, Afghanistan presented the scene of a Deobandi revolution become an Islamic emirate while Pakistan looked like embracing a purely Deobandi jihad.

The country reeled under its biggest-ever intra-Sunni sectarian blow as a grand Barelvi congregation celebrating the birthday of the Holy Prophet on *Eid Miladun Nabi* at Nishtar Park Karachi, was suicide-bombed on 11 April 2006. Out of the 1500 that had gathered, 57 died while over a hundred were injured. Witnesses differed over how it had happened. The official version was that the suicide-bomber was below the stage in the second row; Sunni Tehreek eyewitnesses said a man bounded like a monkey onto the stage and let off a home-made 5 kg device tied to his torso. Talking to Geo TV, Qazi Hussain Ahmad of the Jamaat-e-Islami referred to a Voice of America broadcast about an earlier incident at a Dawat-e-Islami mosque in Karachi and implied that the blast was plotted by the United States. He said it was tragic that the government too was aligned with the enemy. On the basis of his sources of information, he said it was no suicide-bombing; it was, in fact, a device fixed under the stage and ignited through remote control. He was proved wide off the mark soon enough.

Some explanation of Eid Milad (also called Mawlid) is in order. Eid Milad is the occasion of the birthday of the Prophet (PBUH). This yearly celebration is arranged by the Low Church Barelvi population of Pakistan. It is also embedded in the cult of the mystics who traditionally associate themselves directly with the Prophet (PBUH) rather than the orthodoxy in charge of the Quran and its interpretation. In all the old cities, the Milad celebrations are accompanied by people erecting small cardboard models of the mausoleum of the Prophet in front of their houses, and there is much expression of joy all around. The Deobandis and Ahle Hadith have always been opposed to the ritual of Milad and often label it *bida* (innovation). In Saudi Arabia it is actually banned. The attack on the gathering of the Barelvis in Karachi was an extreme interpretation of *bida* by sectarian terrorists. The intensity of the action could have come from the new Saudi and Arab domination of the madrassa in Pakistan. Mai Yamani speaks of the ban on Milad in Saudi Arabia:

> Two Hijazi traditions in particular are considered *bida* (dangerous innovation): the *mawlid* (the celebration of the Prophet's birthday) and the *hawl* (a memorial ceremony conducted on the anniversary of a family member's death that also involves chanting for the Prophet). Hijazis' frequent invocation of Mohammad for example during the *mawlid* is forbidden by thirteen *fatwas* (religious decrees) issued by Saudi religious authorities, who condemn as *bida* any elaborate use of the name and memory of the Prophet.[28]

Speaking to the same TV channel, Muttahida Qaumi Movement (MQM) chief Altaf Hussain, clearly said that the Karachi bombing on the occasion of Milad was a case of suicide-bombing by one 'particular' extremist organisation. He referred to the Hangu bombing on the day of *ashura* in 2006 (36 Shias killed) and clearly hinted at who the culprits were. (By the end of the year, the police were to declare that the Nishtar Park massacre was planned by Al Qaeda through its Deobandi henchmen from Waziristan.) Earlier, on April 7, Allama Hassan Turabi of Tehreek-e-Islami (Shia), after narrowly escaping a bombing in Karachi, had pointed to the acquittal of Deobandi Lashkar-e-Jhangvi–Sipah-e-Sahaba killers at the Sindh High Court a day earlier and complained that the same sectarian killers had done the deed. The suicide-bomber simply decapitated the militant Sunni Tehreek. Its current leader, Abbas Qadiri, deputy chief Akram Qadiri, and spokesman Iftikhar Bhatti were neatly eliminated. Along with them died others belonging to the moderate Jamat-e-Ahle Sunnat, like Haji Hanif Billo and Hafiz Mohammad Taqi. (Some Shia were in the *namaz*, which points to a Barelvi–Shia religious interface.) The Barelvi followers, much aggrieved by 'the government's neglect' in the past, then indulged in widespread vandalism, burning petrol pumps and cars and ambulances. The Edhi Foundation, with a hundred ambulances deployed, suffered the destruction of eight while the dead bodies were still inside. The vandalism ended after appeals from the MQM leaders.

While the MMA made a case for the MQM's involvement in the Nishtar Park massacre, President Musharraf called it a 'sectarian incident' although the Inspector General Police in Karachi was still 'defensive', employing the rhetoric of 'someone wants to divide the nation'. However, the evidence made public pointed to suicide-bombing, which, in turn, was taken to mean that a sectarian fanatic 'laid down his life for Islam'. Talking to Geo TV (17 April 2006) Mufti Muneeb-ur-Rehman—the Barelvi cleric who heads Pakistan's moon-sighting committee for Eid days and who was once roughed up by Deobandi ulama on the committee on difference of faith—stated that hundreds of mosques in the city were disputed between sects, and there had been violent confrontation over them in many cases. This was no Shia–Sunni conflict but a Sunni–Sunni one between Barelvis and Deobandis. According to the TV host, a hundred disputed mosques in Karachi had been locked up by the administration because opening them would immediately lead to violence. The *modus operandi* for 'repossessing' a mosque was never legal; the stronger party assaulted the mosques and took over.

Kamran Khan of GEO TV (12 April 2006) linked the Nishtar Park massacre to the Barelvi–Deobandi war in the Khyber Agency earlier in the month and noted that the Deobandi warlord in Bara, Mufti Munir Shakir was condemned in the 'wall-chalkings' that appeared in Karachi. (Statements against Mufti Shakir from the Barelvi ulama appeared in the press in Punjab too.) In fact, Sunni Tehreek was set up in 1990 against the growing Deobandi and Ahle Hadith dominance in Karachi, by Salim Qadiri, a member of Dawat-e-Islami (Green Turbans) who was himself shot down in 2001 at Chandni Chowk. The attackers were identified as members of the Sipah-e-Sahaba, from one of their men also killed on the spot. (The then Sindh government ended up paying compensation to his family as well!) Salim Qadiri left the party to Abbas Qadiri (now dead) under whom the organisation continued to flourish because of the ample funds it could access fròm the rich business community of Karachi looking for protection from the rival jihadi–sectarian organisations. There was also a strong MQM connection.

The jihad that began in 1980 empowered the Deobandis. The city of Karachi in particular experienced spasms of 'Talibanisation' when the madrassas decided to assert themselves. Because of the quietist nature of the Jamiat Ulema-e-Pakistan (JUP) leadership under Maulana Shah Ahmad Noorani, the Barelvis of Karachi remained peaceful even as their rivals became powerful owing to patronage offered by the state institutions handling jihad. The MQM was not able to exploit the Barelvi manpower of the JUP, but was moving in a direction that would bring the two entities together. (When Sunni Tehreek was set up in 1990, most of its militant manpower was drawn from the MQM while escaping the wrath of the army.)

In the 1980s, the decade was of Afghan jihad where General Zia had allowed, Jamaat-e-Islami to emerge as the most powerful organiser of militias. When the jihad evolved from Jamaat-e-Islami jihad to Deobandi jihad, the Barelvis of Karachi came under further pressure, this time because of the direct link of Afghanistan's Taliban leader Mullah Umar with the Deobandi headquarters at Banuri Town and with other Deobandi seminaries of the city. The state would have inducted the Barelvis into the Afghan jihad (as it did in some cases during the jihad in Kashmir) but it avoided getting into trouble with the Sipah-e-Sahaba-dominated militias operating in a predominantly Deobandi Afghanistan. The Barelvis were linked to the MQM because of their cadres but were not organised, mainly because of Maulana Shah Ahmad Noorani. Barelvi Ilyas Qadiri and his 'non-political' Dawat-e-Islami aggressively defended the community against Deobandi assertion mainly because of Dawat-e-Islami's wealth and internal discipline.

It was Salim Qadiri who, after breaking off from Dawat-e-Islami, put the claim of the Barelvi community on record and began challenging the state to pull back the Deobandi–Ahle Hadith dominance. In 1990 his Sunni Tehreek began its campaign to reclaim the mosques he alleged were originally Barelvi but were grabbed by the other hardline state-supported organisations emanating from Deobandi–Ahle Hadith madrassas. Salim was backed silently by the JUP—which gave him a ticket for elections to the Sindh Assembly in 1988 but he did not win—and other 'moderate' Barelvi organisations like Jamat-e-Ahle Sunnat. In the Memon community small businessmen, tired of the violence of the Deobandi hoodlums, began to fund Sunni Tehreek.

What followed was a kind of war with the Deobandis. Clashes followed in Karachi and Hyderabad and some cities in Punjab, in which mostly Sunni Tehreek activists were killed and wounded. Salim Qadiri boasted that his organisation had liberated 62 mosques in ten years from their wrongful occupiers. In 1992, he challenged the Karachi administration to help him take control of the Nur Mosque (which the rivals claimed had been built by Shabbir Ahmad Usmani, the great Deobandi leader, in 1948) and put his outfit in the limelight by getting dozens of its members arrested. When editor Syed Salahuddin of the weekly *Takbeer* was critical of the Sunni Tehreek, Salim's boys besieged his office. Later, the murder of Syed Salahuddin was blamed on the MQM. Three months later he tried to 'reoccupy' Ibrahim Raza Mosque in Burmi Colony, resulting in widespread riots, forcing the government to seal the mosque.

When things got too hot, Salim Qadiri was shot dead in Karachi in 2001 by a gang, which was clearly seen to be the Sipah-e-Sahaba because of the identity of one attacker who was killed in the crossfire. The state at this time was squarely behind the Sipah-e-Sahaba and its offshoots like the Jaish-e-Mohammed and Harkatul Mujahideen.

On 11 April 2006, in Karachi, the Sunni Tehreek workers were heard complaining that the state of Pakistan was still not willing to give the Barelvis the protection they deserved against hardline Deobandi outfits. After 1999, the Tehreek has seen a steady elimination of their leaders. Abbas Qadiri, chief of Sunni Tehreek, stated in the Barelvi weekly *Zarb-e-Islam* of 15 January 2002:

> The government is standing between us and the murderers. Our government is totally useless. It talks about putting an end to terrorists

and ends up patronising them. If the government had been strict with terrorists the federal interior minister General (Retired) Moinuddin Haider would not have had to shoulder the coffin of his brother today. I throw back the minister's words that he had no enemies.

Quoted in *Nawa-e-Waqt* (13 April 2006), a representative of Sunni Tehreek member Shahid Ghauri said in Karachi that the Nishtar Park massacre was committed to eliminate the leaders of the Sunni Tehreek. He said this act was connected with the killing of the founder of the Sunni Tehreek, Salim Qadiri, 'who was murdered by Sipah Sahaba in 2001'.

NOTES

1. *The Essential Rumi*, Translated by Coleman Barks with John Moyne, Penguin Books, 1995, p. 231, from the Mathnawi of Jalaluddin Rumi.
2. Mariam Abou Zahab, 'The Sunni–Shia Conflict in Jhang', in *Lived Islam in South Asia*, Social Science Press, 2004.
3. Ibid., p. 145.
4. Mohammad Amir Rana, *A to Z of Jihadi Organizations in Pakistan*, Mashal, 2004. The report was personally delivered.
5. Amir Mir, *The True Face of Jehadis: Inside Pakistan's Network of Terror*, Roli Books, 2006, p. 133.
6. Ibid., p. 135.
7. Ibid.
8. Hassan Abbas, *Pakistan's Drift into Extremism: Allah, the Army, and the War on Terror*, Pentagon Press, 2005, p. 207.
9. Jason Burke, *Al Qaeda: Casting a Shadow of Terror*, I.B. Tauris, 2003, p. 201.
10. Rohan Gunaratna, *Inside Al Qaeda: Global Network of Terror*, Berkley Books, 2003, p. 275.
11. B. Raman, *Massacres of Shias in Iraq and Pakistan: the Background*, South Asia Analysis Group, Paper 941 (2006), p. 3: 'On June 20, 1994 Ramzi Yousef and al-Zarqawi, at the instigation of the Iraqi intelligence, caused an explosion at Mashhad in the Iranian territory adjoining Pakistan which killed a large number of Shias. Zarqawi, along with the late Riaz Basra, the leader of the Lashkar-e-Jhangvi (LJ), the militant wing of the SSP, helped the Taliban in the capture of Kabul in September 1996'.
12. *The News*, 27 March 1995.

13. Mohammad Manzur Numani, *Khomeini aur Shia kay barah mein Ulama Karam ka Mutafiqqa Faisala* (Clerical Consensus on Khomeini and the Shia), *Al-Furqan*, 1991, p. 153 and p. 185.
14. International Crisis Group Report 130, 29 March 2007, *Pakistan: Karachi's Madrassas and Violent Extremism*: There are two seminaries named Banuri or Binori in Karachi. The important one is located in Banuri-Binori Town while Jamia Binoria is in the Industrial area called SITE.
15. John K. Cooley, *Unholy Wars: Afghanistan, America, and International Terrorism,* Pluto Press, 1999, p. 223.
16. *Daily Times*, Lahore, 4 July 2007: 'Karachi is a city of an estimated 0.3 million madrassa students at over 2,000 seminaries. The police cannot enter the premises of the madrassas. "The work of the police is to do duty outside the madrassa", said a Special Branch DIG. The madrassas of Karachi are divided into five broad categories: Deoband, Barelvi, Ahle Hadith, Jamaat-e-Islami and Shia. Many of them are members of the Ittehad Tanzeematul Madaris-e-Deeniya Pakistan and around 1,000 of them are Deobandi'.
17. International Crisis Group Report 130, *Karachi's Madrassas and Violent Extremism*, p. 5: The Ministry of Education's 2004 directory listed 979 Karachi madrassas; two years later the Sindh police claimed there were 970. Yet in 2004, the Deobandi Wafaq-ul-Madaris (madrassa federation) insisted it had some 1,500 of its own in the city. Thirty-nine non-Deobandi madrassa administrators claimed that Karachi had roughly 300 Barelvi madrassas, 36 Shia and 36 Ahle Hadith, bringing the total to around 1,800.
18. Mohammad Umar Rana and Mubasher Bukhari, *Arabs in Afghan Jihad*, Pak Institute for Peace Studies (PIPS), 2007, p. 55.
19. International Crisis Group Brussels, *The State of Sectarianism in Pakistan*, Asia Report No 95, 18 April 2005, p. 11.
20. Maulana Samiul Haq has always been an outspoken man, supporting the Taliban and Al Qaeda openly. The Taliban government had made him the clearing house for anyone seeking to meet Mullah Umar. All delegations going to Kandahar were vetted by him.
21. Saleem H. Ali, PhD: Conflict and Conformity in Pakistan's madrassahs, Oxford University Press, 2009.
22. Mohammad Manzur Numani, *Khomeini aur Shia kay barah mein Ulama Karam ka Mutafiqqa Faisala* (Clerical Consensus on Khomeini and the Shia), *Al-Furqan*, 1991, p. 192 and p. 194.
23. Mohammad Amir Rana, *A to Z of Jihadi Organisations in Pakistan,* Mashal, 2004, p. 415.
24. International Crisis Group Report 130, *Karachi's Madrassas and Violent Extremism*, p. 9.
25. Ibid., p. 9.
26. Martin Walker, 'The Revenge of the Shia', *Wilson Quarterly*, Autumn 2006, p. 18.

27. Ibid., Walker's astonishment arises from his unfamiliarity with the scurrilous sectarian discourse current these days in tit-for-tat publications in the Islamic world, especially where there is a sizeable Shia minority living among Sunnis.
28. Mai Yamani, *Cradle of Islam: The Hijaz and the Quest for an Arabian Identity*, I.B. Tauris, 2004, p. 22.

4

Narrative of a Fearful Asymmetry

Each of us touches one place
and understands the whole in that way.
The palm and the fingers feeling in the dark are
how the senses explore the reality of the elephant.
If each of us held a candle there,
and we went in together,
we could see it.

— Rumi: *Elephant in the Dark*[1]

There is no symmetry in the sectarian killings in Pakistan. The Shia are killed more often and in larger numbers. The Sunnis don't get killed in large numbers because the Shia terrorists select the extremists and then target-kill them. The thinking behind this pattern of killing is that the Shia are not many in Pakistan and can be 'finished off' if killed *en masse*. Therefore, the targeting of Shias is motivated by numbers to be killed; on the other hand, the Sunnis cannot be killed *en masse* because of their overwhelming numbers. Although the 'killers' are extremely limited in number and do not represent the social trend, the number of victims is quite high on the side of the Shia.

The Shia in Pakistan may be 15 to 20 per cent of the total population. Since no census figures are available, the percentage may be notional, comparable to a similar number of 15 per cent in Afghanistan and perhaps the same percentage in India. The Shia population in Pakistan is most often said to be 22 million, which makes it second only to Iran, the Shia majorities in Iraq and Lebanon being smaller than this. Also, the Shia community is spread all over Pakistan because of the absence of any obstruction to their upward economic movement. Successful Shias move to the big cities while the less developed populations tend to remain in their traditional habitat. There are certain regions and cities in Pakistan where the Shia population is either numerically significant or in a clear majority. In the tribal agency of Kurram they inhabit 80 per cent of the main city, Parachinar, although the figure is disputed by the Sunnis. In Gilgit in the Northern Areas, they constitute 60 per cent of the population. As for 'significant' presence, they are 10 per cent of the population in Quetta, Balochistan. There is a concentration of their more upward mobile members in Karachi where well-endowed traditional and new places of Shia worship called *Imambargahs* are numerically conspicuous.

Lahore has a large but uncounted presence of the Shia but here they are not targeted as often as in other cities because of the weak presence of the Deobandi–Ahle Hadith seminarian presence. The city has been dominated by the political and electoral presence of the Jamaat-e-Islami (JI) which remains non-sectarian as its founder Maulana Abul Ala Maududi refrained from engaging in the Sunni–Shia polemic. On the other hand, in Multan and other cities of South Punjab like Jhang, the dominance of the Deobandi seminary has resulted in sectarian conflict. Whenever Lahore has been made the scene of violence, non-involvement of the local population in the sectarian polemic has made it a special logistical effort for the 'outside' killers who have had to operate without local help. The British Raj ambiance of sectarian tolerance has continued in the city and its environs. In the 1960s and '70s, sectarian strife was almost unknown. A compilation of a 'calendar of death' made by the Shia starts with 1963 with an extraordinarily large casualty rate (118 killed) in a small city of Sindh but after that there is a gap of almost 20 years before the next incident is noted. As seen in the earlier chapters, sectarian violence assumed the proportions of war during the rule of General Ziaul Haq in the mid-1980s.

FIGHTING THE SAUDI–IRANIAN WAR IN PAKISTAN

There were many reasons for this, but one dominant reason was the regional politics of confronting the Soviet Union in Afghanistan. Even though the jihad was still non-Deobandi it tended to become divided between Pakistan and Iran. Saudi Arabia and its Arab allies—in the aftermath of Arab nationalism, which died with the Egyptian ruler Gamal Abdel Nasser in 1972—had aligned with Pakistan and the United States whereas Iran postured as a new power opposed to both the Soviet Union and the United States 'and its slaves'. It trained the Shia of Afghanistan in Iran for a separate jihad while Pakistan and its Arab allies put together a purely Sunni army of mujahideen. With the rise of Imam Khomeini and the Islamic Revolution in Iran, the Shia communities of some cities like Parachinar and Gilgit in Pakistan reacted with enthusiasm, and some Shias started going to Qum for training in religion and weapons. This aroused a reaction among the traditionally Shia-hating religious parties like the Jamiat Ulema-e-Islam (JUI), and sectarian disturbances began to take place in the mid-1980s. General Zia allowed the Deobandis some play 'to keep the Shias on the leash'. He also allowed the early raids on the Shia populations of Parachinar and Gilgit as a part of a policy of keeping the increasingly Iran-inspired communities under control. The Saudi influence on General Zia was clear enough. During the 1980s, the Pakistani–Saudi 'partnership' resulted in a proxy war with Iran and bore a bitter harvest in the 1990s. Vali Nasr writes:

> The Saudi and Iraqi involvement in effect transplanted the Iran–Iraq war into Pakistan as the SSP and its allies and the Shia counterpart TJP and its off-shoots began to do the bidding of their foreign patrons. The flow of funds from the Persian Gulf continued to radicalise the Sunni groups as they sought to outdo one another in their use of vitriol and violence in order to get a larger share of the funding, turning sectarian posturing into a form of rent-seeking. Since 1990 Sunni sectarian groups have assassinated Iranian diplomats and military personnel and torched cultural centres in Punjab. Attacks on Iranian

targets have been launched in retaliation for sectarian attacks on Sunni targets. By openly implicating Iran in attacks on Sunni targets and retaliating against its representatives and properties in Pakistan, Sunni sectarian groups have sought to complicate relations between Tehran and Islamabad and to portray Pakistani Shias as agents of a foreign power. When in September 1997, five Iranian military personnel were assassinated in Rawalpindi, the Iranian and Pakistani governments depicted the attack as a deliberate attempt to damage relations between the two countries. The killing of 22 Shias in Lahore in January 1998 escalated tensions between the two countries further as Iran openly warned Pakistan about the spread of Sunni militancy. The use of sectarianism to contend with the impact of the Iranian revolution thus produced a wider regional struggle for power that quickly went out of the control of the Pakistani state.[2]

It was the 'Deobandisation' of Afghan jihad which began the more intensified tit-for-tat war between the clergies of the two communities, most of it funded by Iran and the Arabs of the Gulf region. The rise of the Taliban, as facilitated by Islamabad, was accompanied by the rise of the Deobandi militias in 1994 under the tutelage of Pakistan's Inter-Services Intelligence (ISI). The 'calendar of death' shows a clear spike in sectarian violence in the mid-1900s, through the end of the decade into the new millennium. The Sunni sectarian killers trained with Al Qaeda and the Taliban and were protected by the Pakistan army as a strategic asset in Afghanistan. The civilian governments of the decade of the 1990s tried to halt the killings but failed because of their limited writ and the primacy of the war in Afghanistan. Karachi, strong with Deobandi seminarian presence after 1947, became a major scene of sectarian conflict. Incidents were repeated in the traditional strongholds like Parachinar, Gilgit, Jhang, Hangu-Kohat, and Quetta. One can see a clear pattern of external participation in this conflict. Only the Shia (Tewelvers) were targeted and not the Ismailis (Sixers) because of the lack of threat felt by the Arabs from the Ismaili community. Also, the Ismailis kept to their policy of quietism and were not inspired by the example of Iran into publicising their faith.

Aziz Siddiqi, writing in the *Herald* in January 1991, about the murder of Iranian consul Sadeq Ganji in Lahore, is clearly sensing the danger of a sectarian war. He is quite clear that the incident was the first of its kind and did not analyse too minutely the fact that Ganji's murder had followed the murder in Jhang of Maulana Haq Nawaz Jhangvi after an intensive anti-Shia campaign led by Jhangvi through taped addresses where he abused Imam Khomeini by name. Ganji had visited Jhang in February 1990 on hearing that Jhangvi was abusing the Imam—after making references to what he called Khomeini's heretical writings. Since Jhangvi was assassinated after Ganji's visit to Jhang in 1990, the Iranian consul was a marked man and was gunned down in Lahore the same year. Jhangvi was succeeded as the head of the Sipah-e-Sahaba by Isarul Haq Qasimi but he too was murdered in a by-election quarrel with local challengers. But his death was publicised by the Deobandis as a revenge of the Shia for Ganji's killing, and the clear hand of Iran in Pakistan's sectarian violence. The Shia organisation Tehrik-e-Nifaz-e-Fiqh-e-Jafaria (TNFJ) was named in the first information report filed at the police station. As a result of this death, the city of Jhang became divided, as the two communities began targeting each other's members straying into their sectors.

By the middle of 1992, Pakistan was seen by the monthly magazine, *Newsline* (May 1992) as a state in the stranglehold of an increasingly violent fundamentalist clergy. Another of General Zia's legacies, the Blasphemy Law was amended by the Muslim League (Nawaz) to make death the minimum punishment for insulting the Prophet of Islam and began to serve as a basis of targeting the Shia along with other minority communities, especially Christians. That year, Jhang returned a sectarian leader, belonging to the Sipah-e-Sahaba, to the Punjab Assembly while the Federal Shariat Court banned modern banking in Pakistan and put the government on notice for cleansing the financial system of usury. Another article in the *Herald* (September 1992) also took note of the rising power of the clergy but took consolation from the fact that the religious parties were still electorally weak. While the country succumbed to a wave of intolerance and religious militancy, Prime Minister

Nawaz Sharif had to say that 'he was not a fundamentalist'. A judge of the Supreme Court too said something to this effect. It was the beginning of a stiffening of religious identity in Pakistan. Later, even protestations of not being a fundamentalist became few and far between. By 1994, however, the country became aware of the presence of 'sectarian mafias' in Punjab without any accompanying analysis of why it was happening. When approached, the government still pointed to India as the mischief-maker, a clear reference to the pre-1947 non-support of the Muslim League by Deobandis, that is, India was acting through the Deobandis on the basis of the pre-partition Congress–Deobandi alliance.[3]

The rising graph of sectarian killings in 1992 prompted journalist Nasim Zehra to write in the *Herald* (August 1992) about the killing of 15 people during the *ashura* procession in Peshawar. A crowd of 5,000 Sunnis went on the rampage in the city, destroying public property and looting shops after accusing the Shias of desecrating a Sunni mosque and burning the Quran. The crowd belonged to a number of religious organisations (Jamiat Ulema-e-Islam, Jamiat Ahle Hadith, Sipah-e-Sahaba Pakistan) who were confronted by Shia snipers from the Imamia Students Organisation (ISO) representing the parent Shia organisation Tehrik-e-Nifaz-e-Fiqh-e-Jafaria (TNFJ). She noted that an earlier meeting in Multan had denounced the Shias and accused them of anti-Islamic practices, which was picked up and followed by the Peshawar clergy as many of them could be graduates of the Multan Deobandi seminary. She recounted three factors for the post-Zia spurt of sectarian violence: 1) Regional political change and rivalry between Iran and Saudi Arabia; 2) General Zia's encouragement to Sunni apostatisers to create their own violent outfits to seek revenge on the Shia community; and 3) the government's failure to punish the sectarian killers. Most deaths went unavenged and thus gave rise to more serial incidents of killing.

By 1995, the Pakistani press was writing about the rise of a Shia militant outfit Sipah-e-Mohammad Pakistan (SMP), appropriately named in opposition to the Sunni sectarian party Sipah-e-Sahaba Pakistan (SSP) and led by Shias trained in Iran. In Lahore, the SMP was more clearly organisationally divorced from the Shia mainstream political party TNFJ than was Lashkar-e-Jhangvi from SSP, because the Shia leader Sajid Naqvi refused to accept the new policy of confronting the Sunnis with arms.[4] One reason Naqvi was always lukewarm to the challenge of Sunni aggression was that he was a graduate of Najaf and not Qum, that is, not completely persuaded by the Iranian Revolution, although TNFJ was otherwise under the influence of Iran. Zahid Hussain noted that in the year 1995, up to the month of March, the country had seen 250 die in sectarian violence. He interviewed one Sunni killer in jail, Maulana Mohammad Ilyas, guilty of attacking Masjid Babul Islam in Karachi and killing nine people, and learned from him that he had been attracted to the anti-Shia sermons of Maulana Azam Tariq in a Karachi mosque and joined his organisation. He served Azam Tariq so well that he soon became secretary of the Sipah-e-Sahaba Karachi Division. He also killed 12 Shias in Masjid Hussaini on 10 March.[5] The same month *Herald* Karachi discussed why the Sunni terrorists were immune from police action. The officers interviewed by Aamer Ahmad Khan said that they could have brought down the SSP chief Azam Tariq as he fled an encounter with the police but were deterred by the thought that the public would turn against the police officers and the government would be forced to take action against them for murdering a religious leader. There is no doubt that, at a very tacit level, the killing of the Shia was beginning to be accepted by the people who were otherwise not sectarian.

THE SCORE CARD OF SECTARIAN DEATH

In 1997, Pakistan saw itself deeply involved in vicarious conflict against Iran in Afghanistan. Two Iranian diplomats had already been killed in Lahore and Multan, both belonging to the cultural centres of Iran dating back to the days of the Shah. Iranian consular officer Mohammad Ali Raheemi was killed in 1997 in Multan in retaliation for the death of SSP leader Ziaur Rehman Farooqi in the Lahore courts at the hands of a Turi killer Mehram Ali who had trained in Parachinar and could have also been trained in Iran. On 17 September 1997, five Iranian air force officials were ambushed and killed in Rawalpindi. The killers clearly had inside information about the movement of the Iranian officers and could have acted only after information about them was provided by someone from within the armed forces. As if in response, two respected teachers of Banuri Mosque in Karachi, Maulana Habibullah Mukhtar and Mufti Abdus Sami, were murdered in November 1997, which was followed by vandalism by thousands of Deobandi students of the seminary known to be influential in Kabul with Mullah Umar. Iran and Pakistan were in a way communicating with each other through sectarian violence. In an estimate published by *Newsline* in April 2001, the year 1997 was another peak year in terms of sectarian deaths. In all, 238 people were killed, and the next largest number in the past was shown to be in 1996 and 1994 with 73 killed. After 1997, another significant peak was reached in 1998 with 132 killed; and in 1990 with 102 killed. In August 2001, *Herald* published its list and found that a large number killed from 1999 to 2001 were in the Federally Administered Tribal Areas (FATA) with 61 killed, while Karachi followed with 54. Lahore was less than some smaller cities, with 14 dead.

The following year, in 1998, the killing fields of Hangu in Kohat district of the North Western Frontier Province (NWFP) saw 50 dead after the Sunnis tried to stop the Shia from celebrating the Iranian festival of Nauroz.[6] So far Nauroz was culturally associated with Iran under the Shah, and Afghanistan also celebrated it as a non-sectarian festival. (The Taliban changed the old Afghan 'Iranian' calendar and adopted the Islamic calendar in 1996) In Hangu, Nauroz had become associated with Iran as many young people from the area had started going to Iran for religious training. Led by Javed Ibrahim Paracha, the Kohat member of the National Assembly belonging to the Muslim League, the Sunnis attacked the Shia celebrants. Originally a member of the JUI and Sipah-e-Sahaba, Paracha easily moved into the Muslim League even though he was known as a sectarian fanatic to the party. Hangu was known for its sectarian ferocity which began after the entry into the area of the Punjab-based Sipah-e-Sahaba 'under Ziaul Haq's patronage in the early 1980s'.[7] Javed Ibrahim Paracha was to become the organiser of many sectarian clashes in Kohat and Hangu in the days to come before he became an advocate of Al Qaeda and welcomed its fleeing members into Kohat in 2003. In 2006, he was the leading lawyer in the NWFP defending Al Qaeda operatives caught and prosecuted by the government.[8] Zaffar Abbas, writing in *Herald* stated:

> After talks with the visiting Taliban, prime minister Nawaz Sharif led a delegation to Saudi Arabia to discuss the Afghan peace process, only to return after 23 March 1998 to read the following headlines in the press: '19 killed in Karachi', '13 more die in Hangu', One killed in Sindh Explosions' and 'PM dashed to Saudi Arabia.[9]

In 1999, Prime Minister Nawaz Sharif stopped holding 'open-court' complaint sessions at his house in Model Town, Lahore, after he was warned by his security staff that the sectarian outfit Lashkar-e-Jhangvi might be planning to kill him. The leader of the sectarian organisation Riaz Basra had actually visited one of the sessions addressed by the prime minister and had had himself photographed for proof. When the prime minister saw the photograph, he simply stopped holding the open court complaint sessions for the public.[10] The media covered sectarian deaths in the big cities but violence taking place in the small cities went unnoticed although the number of the dead was much higher and the incidents more frequent. For instance, in 1999, Muzaffargarh in South Punjab experienced violence, but thereafter there was a steady stream of deaths every year. The targeted people were always in large numbers, as in January when Muzaffargarh saw sixteen killed by a terrorist. Earlier, in 1994, ten Shias were murdered in a mosque while six more were killed sleeping by the roadside. One reason there was so much violence against the Shia here was that Abdul Hai, the second top man in Lashkar-e-Jhangvi, hailed from Muzaffargarh.[11]

The peak in 1997 can be understood in the light of the ongoing tug of war between the Taliban and the Northern Alliance forces in Afghanistan. The Taliban were supported by Pakistan and Al Qaeda while the Northern Alliance and its Shia component were supported by Iran, Uzbekistan and Russia. The Taliban had reached Mazar-e-Sharif and were in control of 90 per cent of the country but then suffered a set-back in the city, losing hundreds.[12] The revenge for this reversal was taken in Pakistan on the Shia population by the Deobandi militias fighting for or in sympathy with the Taliban. The anti-Shia terrorist alliance was led by Lashkar-e-Jhangvi whose killers routinely fled into Afghanistan after carnage and were given shelter and protection by the Taliban and Al Qaeda. In 1998, the Taliban finally conquered Mazar-e-Sharif and caught the Shia leader Ustad Abdul Ali Mazari after a slaughter of the Shia population there. Mazari was killed after he had surrendered himself to them. Among those killed in Mazar-e-Sharif were a number of Iranian diplomats, said to be secret agents like most other foreign diplomats, including those of Pakistan, serving in the consulates. Iran reacted furiously to the killings and brought its forces up to the Afghan border. For the first time a procession was brought out in Tehran against Pakistan which was held responsible. The hand of Al Qaeda was suspected by the Shia in Pakistan in the killings that followed in Pakistan. The Shia websites called all Deobandi killers Wahhabis, linking them with Saudi Arabia just as the Deobandis linked the Shia with Iran.

Mariam Abou Zahab states that the sectarian killers went to Afghanistan for training and sanctuary under the protection of Harkatul Ansar (HUA) led by Maulana Fazlur Rehman Khalil who was attached to Al Qaeda. She reveals that the man who killed Iranian consul Rahim in Multan, in March 1997, was made to escape from a Dera Ghazi Khan jail in December 1997 and was involved in the massacre of Shias at Mominpura in Lahore in January 1998 in which dozens died while saying their prayers. Khalil later changed his militia's name to Harkatul Mujahideen (HUM) and served the government of Pakistan closely through the ISI and is today living safely in Islamabad. His official line is that he does not indulge in the killing of the Shia, but he cooperates nonetheless with the Deobandi killers from SSP and its offshoots.[13]

Another sectarian peak took place in 2001 after the defeat of the Taliban and the fleeing of the Deobandi warriors to Pakistan along with their Wahhabi patrons. The areas most affected were in FATA and the NWFP where the two sects clearly saw their conflict as an Iran–Saudi war. The areas under fire were known to be inhabited by the Turis of Kurram Agency who were under Iranian influence. The first big killing, 22 dead, took place in Orakzai Agency in January 2001 when the Shias from around the area tried to visit a saint's tomb. (In the year 2006, the same shrine was again the scene of the killing of dozens of Shia.) This was followed in March 2001 by Hangu, a sub-district of Kohat in the NWFP, where twenty people were killed in a city-wide shootout. In May 2001, thirteen people were killed when the two sects exchanged rocket fire in Parachinar in the Kurram Agency, close to the Afghan border province of Paktia. In the NWFP and the tribal areas, the sectarian triangle of Parachinar–Orakzai–Kohat has yielded the largest number of dead in the sectarian strife. The Shia here are mostly Turis—many of them of historical Hazara origin—with Iranian contacts; the local Sunni tribes are aligned with the Taliban in Afghanistan and Deobandis in Pakistan.

A SPREE OF DOCTOR-KILLING

In 2001, Multan saw the killing of Pakistan's ex-foreign minister Siddiq Khan Kanju when he was campaigning for a candidate not favoured by the Sipah-e-Sahaba in the local bodies elections. July 2001 also saw the killing of the chief of Pakistan State Oil (PSO) Shaukat Raza Mirza in Karachi which shook the country. In 2002 a new category was added to men the Deobandis killed on priority: doctors. This started after a rumour spread across the country that Iran was funding Shia terrorists through Pakistan's Shia doctors. After that the most prominent doctors were earmarked for death.

Many of them had returned after making a lot of money in the United States and probably had nothing to do with Iran. Since most of them had set up their charitable and parallel lucrative practices in Karachi, the mega-city became the arena for the killing of these doctors. In all, around thirty doctors were killed, most of them in Karachi. The irony is that—without any apparent linkage to the killing of Shia doctors—Sunni doctors were mostly attracted to Al Qaeda and many of them were prosecuted for helping the terrorists sent out by Al Qaeda.

From the writings of India's Deobandi scholar Manzur Numani, one can easily deduce that the 'information' about the Shia doctors funnelling Iranian money to militant Shia organisations had come from Saudi Arabia. His anti-Iran and anti-Shia books from 1984 to 1987 sought to raise alarm about 'conversions' to the Iranian Revolution in the United States. Most of the Shia doctors killed had returned from the United States. Similarly most of the Sunni doctors prosecuted for connections with Al Qaeda and Arab warriors taking shelter in Pakistan were US returnees. A pattern emerges from the killing of the doctors in Karachi and Lahore.

Dr Ahmad Javed Khwaja, 63, was killed on 11 February 2006 by a bullet to the head as he was walking to his private clinic in Manawan, a border locality of Lahore. His death sparked angry protests by hundreds of his local admirers. They blocked the GT Road with burning tyres for three hours, chanting anti-American slogans. In their anger they even refused to release Dr Khwaja's body for an autopsy till they were persuaded to do so. Dr Khwaja had been arrested in 2002 for sheltering members of Al Qaeda in his village-clinic where he also tended to their wounds. When the FBI questioned him, he openly admitted that he was in sympathy with the cause of the Arab and Afghan warriors. He also told the Anti-Terrorism Court in Lahore that he was providing shelter to the Punjabi wife of an Arab member of Al Qaeda, Abu Yasir, after the invasion of Afghanistan in 2001. He was alleged to have visited Afghanistan three times after 9/11 and therefore had attracted a lot of suspicion as to his real intent. He was released in 2003 after the judge believed what he said and found no proof of his involvement in terrorism.

Dr Khwaja and his family were American citizens. He had graduated from King Edward Medical College in Lahore and then gone to the US to study and set up practice. His residence in the US from 1966 to 1982 got him his American citizenship while his two sons and two daughters were American citizens by birth. After obtaining his American citizenship he returned to Pakistan, took a piece of land in Manawan together with his brothers, and started living there. His brother's rubber factory provided the financial base while Dr Khwaja taught at different private medical colleges in Lahore. His hallmark was his free medical care to over a hundred patients daily without charge. He came from a deeply religious background. Another doctor who went and treated Osama bin Laden in Afghanistan was microbiologist Dr Amer Aziz whose family background was equally of great religious piety.

Dr Akmal Waheed and his younger brother Dr Arshad Waheed were convicted in 2005 by an anti-terrorism court in Karachi, and were sentenced to rigorous imprisonment totalling 18 years on charges of 'causing disappearance of evidence by harbouring and providing medical treatment to activists of banned Jandullah group'. The doctor brothers were prosecuted on charges of sheltering and training Al Qaeda–Jandullah activists, providing them funds and medical treatment, and sending them to training camps in South Waziristan. In 2004, it was the Jandullah activists who attacked and nearly killed the corps commander Karachi in what was clearly an Al Qaeda attack on the pattern of the ones earlier launched against President Pervez Musharraf himself. More ominously, there were reports in the press of the two doctors' contacts with Abu Musab al-Zarqawi who later went and killed Shias in Iraq on behalf of Al Qaeda. Dr Akmal Waheed and Dr Arshad Waheed had kept him in their house in Karachi and looked after him and then sent him to South Waziristan for onward journey to Afghanistan.[14]

No one found out who had killed Dr Javed Khwaja and the Lahore police announced, on the basis of sheer conjecture, that the

Indian intelligence agency RAW had killed him to take revenge for India's reversals in Afghanistan and Kashmir. The sectarian angle was completely ignored because no one, not even Dr Khwaja himself, could have realised that his support of the Arab (read Wahhabi) warriors could have offended the Shia militants waiting to avenge the killing of Shia doctors in Karachi. The peak of sectarian deaths in 2001 included a large number of doctors, most of them Shia. *Newsline* noted that out of the 83 people killed, over 50 were Shia, and out of the Shia, a dozen were doctors. After the killings, the trend of Shia doctors going back to the United States was also noted. At least 25 returned in 2001. One Sunni doctor killed in Karachi had actually renamed himself Amir Muawiyya, the historical Arab caliph who had fought against Caliph Ali and whose son had put Imam Husayn to death.[15]

Why were the Shia doctors targeted? And why were the Sunni doctors attracted to Al Qaeda? In the case of both categories, successful careers were made abroad and there was an apparent commitment to serve the country back home. Anyone attending a meeting of the association of doctors in Lahore would have been taken aback by their religiosity, as was the author himself in 2005.[16] An emphasis of religion in Muslim lives immediately highlights the sectarian cleavage and it should come as no surprise that the doctors too discovered it after embracing the new hardline creed radiating from Saudi Arabia and Iran. There could also be an element of professional rivalry. The Shias, however, did not target the Sunni doctors except when the 'Wahhabi' factor was proved beyond doubt, as in the case of Dr Ahmad Javed Khwaja of Lahore.

Does science, or more precisely, does technology nurture a sceptical and rational mind or does it strengthen an already faith-based worldview? Does rationality achieved through science always lead to enlightenment and its aspiration of global citizenship? Daryush Shayegan has discussed the problem with reference to technocrats serving in Revolutionary Iran and looks into their superficial grasp of culture and a consequent embrace of the more defined and water-tight categories of fundamentalist faith.[17]

Discussing the strict religiosity of nuclear scientists in Pakistan, Pakistani nuclear physicist Dr Pervez Hoodbhoy separates technology from the basic sciences. In his view the rational-enlightened worldview comes out of the learning and teaching of the basic sciences, while technology is simply a linear faith in the end-product, very similar to the 'certitude' of religion. He examines specific cases of Pakistani nuclear physicists' faith in jinns as producers of energy because the Quran states that the creatures are made of fire.[18]

STATE-SPONSORED JIHAD AND SECTARIANISM

The emergence of Jaish-e-Mohammed in 2000 added to the intensity of sectarian violence perpetrated by Lashkar-e-Jhangvi. Jaish was an important outfit fighting the Kashmir jihad while enjoying close contacts with Al Qaeda in Afghanistan. Because of the importance given to it by the Pakistan's intelligence agency, the ISI, and Al Qaeda, its status among the Deobandis had arisen. It was favoured by the country's most respected Deobandi seminary in Banuri Town, Karachi and owned as its own by the Sipah-e-Sahaba whose leader Azam Tariq had publicly declared himself to be the imitator (*muqallid*) of Jaish's leader Masood Azhar, the man for whom the 1999 hijacking of an Indian plane from Nepal was allegedly arranged by a combination of elements, named above, that valued him. Wrote Azmat Abbas: 'The SSP came to be the umbrella political group while Jaish-e-Mohammed and Lashkar-e-Jhangvi represented the organisation's jihadi and domestic militant wings respectively'.[19] Jaish was to cause a lot of embarrassment to its patron, the Pakistani establishment, when it attacked the Indian parliament and triggered a dangerous India–Pakistan military stand-off on the international boundary for nearly a year. A police officer in Karachi stated:

> We reported Jaish Mohammad's growing links with Sipah Sahaba and Lashkar Jhangvi leader Malik Ishaq [who had killed the Iranian diplomat Raheemi in Multan]. We requested that someone should talk

sense into him but we were told to mind our own business and not worry about Azhar.[20]

There can be little doubt that Jaish was 'protected' by the establishment in Islamabad. Also protected was Harkatul Mujahideen from whose larger cadre Jaish was created in 2000 to allow Masood Azhar to become a leader in his own right. Harkatul Mujahideen, led by Fazlur Rehman Khalil, had to be protected because of its role in the Kashmir jihad and his links to Al Qaeda and Osama bin Laden. The terrorist Ahmed Umar Sheikh, sentenced to death for the murder of Daniel Pearl, was known to be working in tandem with Jaish, but his links with Harkat were also known. Syed Shoaib Hasan wrote:

> Harkatul Mujahideen (HUM) is one of the largest militant organisations in Pakistan and its extensive network is based mostly in Karachi. While senior police officers are reluctant to concede such connections, several of the militants accused of spawning the current wave of terrorism in Karachi are known to have worked for Harkat at one time or another. Also amongst all the Pakistani militant outfits, HUM is reputed to be closest to Osama bin Laden. Ahmad Umar Saeed Sheikh, the principal accused in the Daniel Pearl Case, and Amjad Farooqi, currently the most wanted man in Pakistan, are said to have worked for HUM.[21]

In his memoir, Pakistan's ex-president General Pervez Musharraf named only Masood Azhar's Jaish-e-Mohammed while talking about attempts to kill him. His book abstains from mentioning HUM and Fazlur Rehman Khalil, probably fully aware of the protection provided to him by the ISI in Islamabad. The book gives a graphic account of how Amjad Farooqi was chased and finally killed in Sindh in 2005, but identifies him with Al Qaeda, and not with HUM. In fact, his book abstains from mentioning all the important jihadi outfits doing terrorism in Pakistan, including the Saudi-linked Lashkar-e-Taiba.[22]

The month of May in 2004 subjected Karachi to its worst sectarian trauma, beginning with the mass-killing of Shias and climaxing with the target killing of Karachi's top Deobandi leader,

Mufti Nizamuddin Shamzai. On 7 May 2004, a suicide bomber entered a prominent Shia mosque Imam Haideri in Karachi's famous Sindh Madrassa (where the founder of Pakistan, Jinnah, went to school) and blew himself up, killing 23 and injuring over a hundred. Riots broke out in the city in which an additional casualty is registered along with hundreds wounded. As usual, Karachi had to make the sacrifice of a lot of public property in the face of an extremely aroused Shia mob. There were other violent incidents in the city, like two bombs that went off in front of the American Consulate, and 17 killed in a by-election contested by the MQM and the clerical alliance, MMA, but the tit-for-tat came in the shape of the killing of Mufti Nizamuddin Shamzai on 29 May 2004. All hell broke loose in Karachi after that. Students of the dominant Deobandi seminaries came out and destroyed public property including the police station close to the Banuri seminary in Jamshed Town in front of which Shamzai was gunned down. It was clearly a sectarian murder, but Syed Shoaib Hasan writing a fortnight later actually wondered why such a non-sectarian (sic!) personality was killed:

> Mufti Shamzai was one of those highly complex characters that are typical of evolving societies. The West would perhaps brand him a terrorist; not only was he an extremely vocal opponent of the US-led war on terror, he had even given a *fatwa* of jihad against the Americans in 2001 when the latter was planning to attack the Taliban government in Afghanistan. He was held in high esteem by the now fugitive Taliban leader Mullah Umar and had led the delegation which the government of General Pervez Musharraf had sent to negotiate with the Taliban leaders in the run-up to the US attack on the Taliban. However, as a reputed Deobandi scholar, Mufti Shamzai had never been accused of instigating sectarian violence (sic!). To the contrary he was strong and vocal proponent of sectarian harmony. Besides, Mufti Shamzai had all but quit politics since helping Maulana Masood Azhar put together the now outlawed Jaish Mohammad.[23]

The writer was either writing defensively to protect himself against the wrath of the Deobandis in Karachi or was completely ignorant of what Mufti Shamzai had been doing since 1986 when he issued his own *fatwa* apostatising the Shia from Jamia Farooqia and endorsed the one issued by Darul Ulum Banuria.[24] In fact, Mufti Shamzai had also apostatised the Ismailis in a *fatwa* issued earlier from Jamia Farooqia.[25] This *fatwa* had followed on the heels of a *fatwa* issued by the Saudi grand mufti Sheikh Abdul Aziz Bin Baz. In the true Deobandi tradition, Mufti Shamzai was a sectarian cleric and was killed in the tit-for-tat situation created by the bombing of Haideri Mosque. Shamzai's death was avenged the following day, on 31 May 2004, when the city's well-known Shia mosque, Imambargah Ali Raza, was blown up by a suicide bomber, killing 26 Shias praying inside. The truth is that even General Musharraf was misled about Shamzai when he needed to send a delegation to the Taliban after 9/11. The ISI chief General Mehmoud who chose Shamzai as a member of the delegation was himself determined to actually ask Mullah Umar not to surrender to the Americans but fight a guerrilla war against them.[26] It is an intriguing fact that senior state officials continue to be ignorant about the causes of the sectarian conflict in Pakistan. It is quite possible that the briefing given to Musharraf did not explain the Mufti's penchant for violence and therefore his unsuitability as a peace negotiator.[27]

The Deobandi sectarians also developed a new outlook on religious parties not taking part in the sectarian war. They began targeting shrines where 'Low Church' Islam was mixing the two sects together. This tolerance of the Shia among the mystically-oriented Barelvis made the hardline Deobandis turn on them too. According to *Khabrain*, (26 February 2005) the police had arrested from the Rawalpindi–Islamabad area 35 terrorists, out of a total of 90, who had come from the Northern Areas to kill the ulama who would not take sides in the sectarian conflict of the country. These men had confessed to killing the *gaddi nashin* (custodian) of the Barri Imam (Shia) shrine near Islamabad. The name of the organisation to which the 90 belonged was being kept secret by the intelligence agencies for fear of arousing countrywide passions. The name could be guessed by the fact revealed by the agencies that the gang of 90 had come down to commit violence during the

Muharram *ashura*. The suicide attack on Barri Imam finally killed 20 Shias and Barelvis. Typically, the attack was blamed on the United States. Quoted in *Khabrain* (28 May 2005) MMA leader Samiul Haq of the Deobandi seminary of Akora Khattak stated that the act of terrorism at the Barri Imam shrine near Islamabad was carried out to stop the nationwide protest being staged against the desecration of the Quran at the American prison in Guantanamo Bay in Cuba. Talking to Iran radio, General (Retired) Hameed Gul, former chief of the Inter Services Intelligence (ISI), said that imperialist forces might have been involved in the Barri Imam incident. Gul said the US and Israel could not tolerate Muslim unity. He said the attackers were from abroad and that the secret agencies were brainwashing innocent people. He said the government was serving US interests by utilising all its resources in this regard.

Immediately after the Barri Imam incident in Islamabad, three terrorists attacked the Shia place of worship, Al-Jamia-tul-Arabia Ahsan-ul-Uloom, Gulshan-e-Iqbal, in Karachi, on 31 May 2005, but were foiled by the police in their project of mass killing. The assailants were spotted as suspects by the policeman on duty but they broke through, after which suicide bombing was resorted to. Because of the interruption to their plan, the blasts could not be properly targeted and only six people including one policeman and one citizen out of the 150 people worshipping inside the mosque lost their lives. Significantly, one terrorist was wounded and was apprehended. But the sectarian rage that followed later claimed the lives of seven people on the roads of the city. The death toll was finally 13. Rampaging youths burned 14 cars in the environs of Gulshan-e-Iqbal. Families were asked to get out so that their vehicles could be set on fire. Shopkeepers shut down their businesses because they knew that their shops would be burned down, but two gas stations were dangerously set alight and one KFC restaurant was burnt down with people trapped inside. As this was unfolding in the city, another terrorist attack took place in Landhi. Gunmen first abducted the Jamaat-e-Islami *naib amir* (Sunni) of the city, Aslam Mujahid, and then put bullets through his head and heart.[28]

THE PARACHINAR MASSACRES

Parachinar in the Kurram Agency plays a significant role in the chronology of sectarian violence in Pakistan. In this mountain valley, the Sunni–Shia conflict has played out like a vendetta dating back centuries. But Parachinar also establishes the rule of 'ghettoisation'—the concentration of the victim population at one centre for easy targeting—which can be applied to later such situations in Gilgit in the Northern Areas, Quetta in Balochistan, and to some extent to such cities of later Shia concentration as Kohat, Jhang, D.I. Khan, and Karachi.

Robert D. Kaplan, a rare visitor to the Kurram Agency, wrote in 2000:

> Parachinar, the largest town in the Kurram tribal agency, was a small market centre twelve years ago. Now it is a crowded city of 300,000, characterised by brutal concrete, electricity outages, water shortages, battles over property rights, and terrorism powered by guns that are filtering back into Pakistan from Afghanistan. When I asked the assistant political agent for Kurram, Massoud Urrahman, if military rule had made a difference, he replied dismissively, 'Whether the government in Islamabad is military or democratic doesn't matter. We have no civil law here—only Pashtoon tribal law'.
>
> The Pashtoon population of Kurram is split between Sunnis and Shias. In September of 1996, a gun battle among teenage members of the two rival Muslim sects escalated into a communal war in which more than 200 people were killed and women and children were kidnapped. A paramilitary official said that the atrocities were out of 'the Stone Age'; militants even executed out-of-towners who were staying at a local hotel. Now the situation in Parachinar is peaceful but extremely tense. Paramilitaries guard the streets around the Sunni and Shia mosques, which stand nearly side by side, their minarets scarred by bullet holes. Only a few weeks before my visit seventeen people had been killed in violence between Sunnis and Shias in another tribal region of the North-West Frontier Province.
>
> 'The Shias are eighty per cent of the Kurram agency', the Shia leader in Parachinar, Mohammed Anwar, told me. 'The problems have all been caused by Afghan refugees who support the Sunnis'. Yet the Sunni leader, Haji Asghar Din, claims that 75 per cent of the local population

is Sunni. He told me that Sunnis cannot buy land from Shias—'so how can we consider them our brothers?' The only certainty is that Parachinar, hemmed in by the Safed Koh Mountains on the Afghan border, has little more room to expand. A high birth rate and a flood of Afghan refugees have intensified the property conflicts. Population growth has also weakened the power of tribal elders and created extremist youth factions. The lack of water and electricity has increased anger. Meanwhile, the government schools are abysmal—often without teachers, books, and roofs. The poor, who form the overwhelming majority, cannot afford the private academies, so they send their children to Sunni and Shia madrassas, where students are well cared for and indoctrinated with sectarian beliefs.

Every person I interviewed was sullen and reticent. One day a crowd of men surrounded me and led me to the back of a pharmacy, where they took turns denouncing America and telling me that the Taliban were good because they had restored security to Afghanistan, ending mujahideen lawlessness. The 'external hand of India' was to blame for the local troubles between Sunnis and Shias here, I was told. Conspiracy theories, I have noticed, are inflamed by illiteracy: people who can't read rely on hearsay. In Pakistan, the adult literacy rate is below 33 per cent. In the tribal areas it is below that. As for the percentage of women in Parachinar who can read, I heard figures as low as 2 per cent; nobody really knows.[29]

The River Kurram rises in the Safed Koh (over 15,000 feet) and emerges in the broad valley of upper Kurram. Towards the southeast, the valley narrows to only four miles, till it opens on to Bannu and Kohat. From Tall, or Thal, as he calls it, Pennell observed in 1909 that the Turi tribe was originally from the left bank of the Indus at Kalabagh.[30] They had travelled to upper Kurram valley every summer to ply trade. Three hundred years ago the Turis fought their first battle with the Bangash (originally from Kohat) and came off victorious at a place in the upper Kurram called Burkha. After that they attacked and occupied the villages of Peiwar and Milana. Gradually, the Turis drove the Bangash down towards the south. As Pennell noted, upper Kurram was totally Turi, but down at Alizai their population was mixed with the Sunni Bangash, their Shia villages distinct from those of the Sunnis.

Under the British the war between the tribes ceased and the land was settled among them permanently. The original inhabitants of the valley were Arora Hindus and they were still around in 1890 in small numbers doing commerce.

Around the 1870s, the lower Kurram valley was inhabited by other Sunni tribes like the Mangals and Makbals. Above the valley, other tribes, all Sunni, clung to their mountainside villages. The Kurram valley was traditionally visited by nomadic tribes from all over the tribal land in Afghanistan. The Shia Hazaras visited Kurram valley and at times settled there, as under Amir Abdur Rehman, who hunted them out of their settlements in Central Afghanistan. As Pennell notes, Ghilzais from the area between Kabul and Jalalabad, and Khorotis (the tribe of Hekmatyar) also regularly visited the Kurram valley and at times settled there. He also notes that because the Turis and Hazaras were relentlessly persecuted by the Amir in Afghanistan and treated with hostility by the many Sunni tribes of the valley, the Shia tribes took easily to British control and were more ready to listen to 'the Christian message'.

As we can see, the Kurram valley vendetta between the Shia and Sunni inhabitants is quite old. Pakistan has inherited this situation. As the Afghan war loosened the control over the areas, and as Sunnis took part in the war as mujahideen and the Shias abstained, the administrative competence of the Pakistani officers in the Agency was eroded. The periodic battles that have taken place are also a Pakistani legacy, the lower Kurram valley being controlled completely by the anti-Shia organisation called Sipah-e-Sahaba (SSP). It is obvious that the SSP has taken advantage of the ancient tribal division on sectarian lines to spread their message. Azam Tariq, the Punjabi chief of the SSP, became a leader of these Pushtuns more than Jhang in Punjab from where he started, and the Kurram valley factor was clearly the cause of his strength vis-à-vis the Pakistan government. Under General Zia, the trend to attack the Shia began in Parachinar in 1986, when the mujahideen felt hampered by the Turis while marching into Afghanistan to fight the Soviet forces.

JAVED PARACHA AND
THE KILLING FIELDS OF KOHAT

The year 1986 is important in the history of Sunni–Shia conflict in Pakistan. An organisation advocating apostatisation of the Shia had been established with the tacit approval of the state in Punjab and was spreading its tentacles into the Kohat area from where a road connects with the Kurram Agency. General Zia allowed the mujahideen, then spearheaded by Hekmatyar's Hezb-e-Islami and local recruits backed by the Jamaat-e-Islami Pakistan, to 'remove the obstacle' in Parachinar. There was a sectarian stand-off for days while the Pakistani press was debarred from visiting the area. The Pakistan army had cordoned off the lower reaches of the area to prevent any eye-witness accounts. Hundreds of Turi Shias were put to death. One important factor was the leadership of the Pakistani Shias by a Turi named Allama Ariful Hussaini who was greatly revered in Iran because of his personal contact with Imam Khomeini. Because of him, the Turis were attracted to the training grounds of Iran where the Hazaras of Afghanistan were already training for jihad. The Sunni Pushtuns saw this development as a hostile act and feared a future clash with a much better prepared sectarian foe. Although Kaplan, above, refers to a 1996 clash, the sectarian violence in the Kurram Agency is a constant phenomenon, branching out into the lower districts of Orakzai Agency, Kohat and its sub-district, Hangu in the NWFP.

> Unlike Punjab and Sindh, where a majority follow Sufi Islam and its Barelvi component, in the Pushtun areas most Sunnis have gravitated towards a more puritanical version of Islam. Even before the current Deobandi ascendancy, the Afghan civil war and the resultant madrassa expansion had enhanced the JUI's political clout in Pushtun-majority areas. Since the province also has major areas of Shia concentration, such as Orakzai agency, Parachinar and Hangu in Kohat district, this rise of Deobandi extremism has heightened sectarian tensions and conflict, even in such Hindko(Punjabi)-speaking areas as Mansehra and Abbottabad.[31]

Kurram has been under pressure ever since the NATO invasion of Afghanistan in 2001. Fleeing Afghan Taliban have been coming into the agency and clashing with the Turi Shias who have always reported 'sympathetic attacks from Taliban every time they had trouble with the Sunnis'. After 2001, the incidents proliferated. Trouble trickled down to Hangu, a sub-district of Kohat, where there is a sizeable Shia Turi community settled alongside the local Sunni tribes. During the Afghan jihad of the 1980s and the Afghan civil war of the 1990s, Hangu experienced a stiffening of the Sunni attitude towards the Shia practices tolerated in the past. Understandably, the Sunni antipathy towards the Shia also translated as sympathy for the Taliban and Al Qaeda. When, after the Taliban defeat in 2001, some Al Qaeda elements decided to come down to the Hangu-Kohat area in search of protection, they were extended a warm welcome. However, when the Al Qaeda group arrived in Kohat it was greeted by a team of ISI officers who were probably there to arrest them. A misunderstanding led to an exchange of fire in which all the Al Qaeda members were killed. A host of the Al Qaeda 'guests', Paracha, and a long time self-confessed enemy of the Shia, described the scene as follows on a TV channel.

Geo TV (12 September 2003) host Hamid Mir investigated the well known mystery of the perfumed soil of Kohat after Al Qaeda mujahideen were gunned down there. The champion of the mujahideen cause was ex-MNA Javed Ibrahim Paracha who narrated the incident. After 9/11, Bulgarian and Chechen mujahideen fled from Afghanistan and came down to the tribal areas from where they came to Kohat, where already 27 Arab mujahideen were in jail. They were the offspring of the Sahaba (Companions of the Prophet) and were Ahle Bait (from the family of the Prophet). They were met by an ISI officer (*hassaas idaray ka afsar*) who assured them safe passage to Bannu, but when they approached the town they saw troops. Upon this, they shot the ISI officer. After that their Flying Coach vehicle was subjected to a barrage of bullets and all of them were killed. The last beautiful youth who died said that he was going to paradise. The entire surroundings smelled sweet with the perfume of the blood of the martyrs.

The people of Bannu were moved by the perfume of the blood and gathered around the dead bodies. They picked them up and took them to the CMH, planning to bury them in Bannu after medical care. But the administration took the dead bodies to Peshawar. A jirga was held in Bannu which decided to bury the mujahideen in Bannu. When the graves were dug the soil started smelling sweet. After which Javed Ibrahim Paracha went to Peshawar to demand the dead bodies. Paracha was arrested and taken to face the FBI where he said he did not know Osama but he thought him a soldier of God. He said he had named his own son Osama bin Laden. He then organised the construction of Shuhada-e-Islam Chowk (Martyrs of Islam Square) in Kohat. People had taken the perfumed soil soaked with the blood of the Al Qaeda soldiers and were keeping it in their homes. The Parachas of Kohat are known for their financial support to Al Qaeda. Javed Ibrahim Paracha fought the 2002 election for PML-N but was supported by the Sipah-e-Sahaba. He lost the election.

TROUBLE COMES TO ISLAMABAD

After the 7 July 2005 bombings in London (whose bombers were found to have Pakistani contacts), British Prime Minister Mr Tony Blair called on Pakistan to go after the seminaries involved in teaching and training terrorists. The police in Pakistan accordingly went after the extremists, after a pep-speech given to all heads of the department by the president (Pervez Musharraf) himself. In Islamabad, over 40 people were rounded up, including Mufti Ibrar, personal secretary to the leader of the opposition in the National Assembly, Maulana Fazlur Rehman. About eight seminaries were raided in the city, including Madrassa Jamia al-Hafsa commonly known as Lal Masjid (Red Mosque), which is said to be the most powerful stronghold of the Deobandis involved in a sectarian tit-for-tat with the Shia outfits, Jamia Farooqia, Madrassa Jamia al-Umar and a madrassa in Rana Market. No action had been taken earlier in the aftermath of the suicide bombing at Islamabad's Barri Imam shrine, which should have shaken Islamabad more than the bombings in London.

When the government had tried to smoke out the extremists of Lal Masjid and other seminaries in the neighbourhood, politicians like Imran Khan had intervened and prevented the operation. The Imam of Lal Masjid had escaped a number of sectarian attacks from the rival sectarian Shia party. However, neglect and political expediency led to a spike in the number of seminarians in the capital city. The police had to brave the onslaught of the seminarian boys and girls—estimated at 6,000 in the Lal Masjid complex alone, equivalent to numbers at a full-fledged university—who tried to prevent the operation. The head cleric of Lal Masjid was allowed to make good his escape, a feat he had accomplished in the past too.

In 2007, the government moved against the seminaries set up by the clerics of Lal Masjid, including the seminary Al-Hafsa meant for girls. Structures belonging to the seminaries were earmarked to be pulled as they were illegal constructions. Instead of going to court, the clerics decided to take action. The girls of Al-Hafsa were mobilised and they attacked and took over a neighbouring state-owned library. A stand-off followed during which the clerics threatened suicide-bombing. (After the threat, an Islamabad four-star hotel was actually suicide-bombed!) While President Musharraf seemed determined to follow the letter of the law on the illegal structures, the minister for religion in his Pakistan Muslim League cabinet, Ijazul Haq, kept promising the clerics a solution in their favour, with the result that the stand-off became prolonged and began to expose the government's lack of resolve to pursue the law against the clergy. The standoff against the Lal Masjid continued into May during which the clerics carried out vigilante action against certain households after accusing them of being brothels. In one house the women were dragged out bound in ropes amid shouts of 'Shia prostitutes'.[32]

Police raids also took place in Punjab, netting 30 'extremists' in Lahore alone where no hostile seminaries were ever mentioned before, but some of which were visited by foreign journalists and scholars like Harvard's Jessica Stern and labelled extremist. Raids were conducted in Khushab, Faisalabad, DG Khan, and Multan too, all known Deobandi and Ahle Hadith centres of power, linked to their Arab sponsors but also liberally supported by domestic 'philanthropists'. According to one source, donations from local philanthropists in the country amounted to about Rs 140 billion annually, of which some 90 billion was in cash and the rest in kind. Of this cash amount, some 80 per cent was received by religious organisations for running mosques, madrassas, orphanages and other such facilities. The 'extremists' arrested during this drive belonged to Lashkar-e-Jhangvi, Jaish-e-Mohammed, Harkatul Mujahideen and Hizb ut-Tahrir.[33]

GOVERNMENT ATTACKS LAL MASJID

Troops finally broke into the seminary of the Lal Masjid complex held by Maulana Abdur Rashid Ghazi and his foreign terrorists. The trigger was the kidnapping of some Chinese nationals from a massage parlour in Islamabad. The death toll among the seminarians was over 70, which immediately divided the nation, a majority siding with the rebel clerical leaders of the mosque, the brothers, Maulana Abdul Aziz and Maulana Abdul Rashid Ghazi.

Their father, the Lal Masjid founder, Maulana Abdullah, was killed in 1998 at the height of the sectarian war unleashed by Deobandi madrassas in 1986 after the issuance of apostatisation *fatwas*. Abdullah was a graduate of Jamia Banuria like Maulana Masood Azhar of Jaish-e-Mohammed whose trained terrorists are now found entrenched within Lal Masjid together with Maulana Abdur Rashid Ghazi. Ghazi echoed his father's sectarian worldview when he told a TV channel that the government might have brought out Shia warriors against his besieged acolytes.

The Aziz–Rashid duo began with a clear anti-Shia intent when they abducted a Shia lady in Islamabad after accusing her of running a brothel. Only the BBC website recorded the charge made by the lady that, while they were dragging her family out, the Lal Masjid vigilantes had referred to the Shia sect as a 'sect of prostitutes'. The duo had climbed to the top of the already dominant position of the Deobandi seminaries, counted at 88, in Islamabad by establishing contacts with the Taliban and Al Qaeda.

A Karachi journal summed up the incident thus:

The Lal Masjid movement was an extension of the growing religious extremism creeping into the cities from the Frontier region. Ostensibly, the clerics had developed a close nexus with Baitullah Mehsud, leader of the Taliban militants in Waziristan, and Maulvi Faqir Mohammed in Bajaur. They also had close links with Maulana Fazlullah, the firebrand leader of Tehreek-e-Nifaz-e-Sharit-e-Mohammadi (TNSM) in the Malakand region. TNSM, which was banned by President Musharraf in 2002, was founded by a pro-Taliban cleric, Sufi Mohammed, who is presently serving a prison term. The leadership of the movement has been assumed by his son-in-law Fazlullah, who rides a white horse.[34]

A PORTRAIT OF JAVED IBRAHIM PARACHA

William Dalrymple describes the Kohat champion of Sunni rights against the Shia in the following manner:

Javed Paracha is a huge, burly tribal leader with a granite outcrop of nose jutting out from a great fan of grey beard. In many ways he is the embodiment of everything that US policy makers most fear and dislike about this part of the Muslim world. For Paracha is a dedicated Islamist, as well as a wily lawyer who has successfully defended al-Qaeda suspects in the Peshawar High Court. In his fortress-like stronghouse in Kohat he sheltered wounded Taliban fighters—and their frost-bitten women and children—fleeing across the mountains from the American daisy-cutters at Tora Bora, and he was twice

imprisoned by General Musharraf in the notorious prison at Dera
Ismail Khan. There he was kept in solitary confinement while being
questioned—and he alleges tortured—by CIA interrogators.[35]

When the Lal Masjid crisis was at its peak in 2007, Paracha was
one of the 'mediators' brought in by the 'agencies' to break the
confrontation between the government and the avowedly anti-Shia
clerics of Lal Masjid, Maulana Aziz and Maulana Ghazi. The other
jihadi leader, with pro-Al Qaeda credentials, who was brought out
of his safe house in Islamabad, was the leader of Harkatul
Mujahideen, Fazlur Rehman Khalil. But Paracha was more
significant in that he was also a part of the anti-Shia agenda of the
Lal Masjid. Reports had linked him to some of the dubious
activities, like transfer of weapons, of the Lal Masjid. The
confessional 'opponent' of Lal Masjid in Islamabad was the shrine
of Barri Imam, a Shia estate with strong Barelvi attendance
characterised by mystical rituals of singing and dancing. Some
possibility of Paracha being linked to the Lal Masjid–Barri Imam
rivalry has been revealed by the British journalist, Jason Burke:

> Ershad [journalist friend in Islamabad] brought me up to date on what
> had been happening at the Bari Imam shrine. There was little good
> news. Drug traffickers had finally killed the cleric at the shrine a few
> weeks before, putting an end to his long campaign to end the sale of
> heroin in the local villages. Worse still, a suicide bomber in the middle
> of the shrine in the spring had killed dozens of worshippers. The
> bomber was linked to one of the groups that Javed Parachar was
> suspected of being involved with. I told Ershad about my interview
> [with Parachar] the day before. He shook his head and said
> nothing.[36]

Burke writes Paracha as Parachar, as a typically British speech quirk,
but he knew the man through earlier meetings and interviews. His
portrait of him tells us once again about Paracha's animus against
the Shia:

> One of my better contacts in the NWFP was Javed Ibrahim Parachar,
> a tribal chief who, like many such men, was both an elder and a

religious scholar. Both roles brought authority respect and, if managed correctly, wealth. Parachar, who had managed things correctly, lived in the town of Kohat.... As well as being chief and scholar Parachar was also a businessman, a farmer, a member of parliament, the vice-chancellor of an Islamic university and principal of a series of Islamic schools or medressas where several hundred young men, largely from poor families and attracted by free education, studied. When I first met him he had pointed to the bullet holes in his white Toyota pick-up truck and laughed heartily. 'They shot 170 bullets into this car', he said, chuckling, 'and six into me. But still they didn't kill me. God protects me because I do good for His people and I am a good Muslim'. The ambush, I knew, had followed a series of murderous attacks on local Shia Muslims which Parachar was reported to have instigated, funded and organised.[37]

Burke doesn't connect Paracha's strong sectarian bias to the suicide-bombing of Barri Imam because he was not told that Barri Imam was a Shia shrine. Most people who go to Barri Imam are Barelvi Sunnis and have forgotten the shrine's true identity. After the suicide bombing, its Shia custodian spoke up from his home in Multan, saying he was so disgusted at the incident that he was thinking of leaving Pakistan. What possibly had happened was a Lal Masjid action against its rival shrine, Barri Imam, with Paracha as the instrument of violence.

THE TRAGEDY OF THE NORTHERN AREAS

Originally a part of the disputed Jammu and Kashmir state, the Gilgit–Baltistan region was separated from Pakistan-administered Azad Kashmir and re-designated as the Northern Areas in 1949.[38] Because of the conflict with India, the region became strategically important. The Shia majority in the Northern Areas in no way disadvantaged Islamabad as it faced Ladakh on the Indian side. But the population began to pose a threat after 1980, after the Islamic Revolution in Iran and Imam Khomeini's difference of opinion with General Zia. Sectarian violence began here in 1988 as a result of Islamabad's Iran policy.[39]

The next bout of trouble took place in 1996 over the syllabus in the educational institutions, but from 2003, Gilgit and the region in its periphery have experienced violence of extreme intensity. The administration has played tough and imposed curfew and shut down the schools and colleges. Local journalists have been beaten up and threatened with death by three parties to the dispute: the two warring sects and the local civil–military administration. The fourth party, the Ismaili community, has kept out of the Shia–Sunni mayhem, but sporadic attacks on its welfare projects have taken place too, partly because of the religious alliance, the MMA's, campaign against the Aga Khan University in the plains.

According to K.M. Ahmad the most damning evidence against General Zia comes from the ex-commissioner of Gilgit:

In April 1988, armed rioters from outside entered the Gilgit environs. Eleven villages around town were torched, their wooden structures burnt to ashes and valuable goods looted. Around 40 persons were killed. Zia claimed that Junejo had failed to control the law and order situation, and removed him from office. This is a matter of record. What is not a matter of record is that this particular riot bore all the marks of a deliberately organised incident. It was not a local sectarian riot stirred up by Gilgit mullahs around the time of the holy month of Muharram. The civil administration did its best with the limited police force in Gilgit (which at least managed to save the town) and when it sought the help under aid to civil power provisions of the law (as the raiders started to move to the outlying villages), this help was denied on various pretexts. The same happened at Rawalpindi where the secretary to the prime minister could not persuade General Headquarters to direct the field commander in Gilgit to come to the rescue of the civil administration. It was clear to the Gilgit civil administration that the raiders, who were tribals and mujahideen *elements*, could not have reached this remote place from Peshawar without someone's blessing. The Frontier Constabulary, whose checkposts dot the Swat–Besham road and the Besham–Gilgit highway, did not act to intercept the raiders. The true significance of the Gilgit riot has never been highlighted by our media.[40]

Gilgit is the administrative centre of the Northern Areas which has five districts: Gilgit, Skardu, Diamer, Ghizer, and Ghanche. Three sects, Shia, Ismaili and Sunni are found in all the districts. F.M. Khan gives us a breakdown of the sects in the region: Today Gilgit is 60 per cent Shia, 40 per cent Sunni; Hunza is 100 per cent Ismaili; Nagar is 100 per cent Shia; Punial is 100 per cent Ismaili; Yasin is 100 per cent Ismaili; Ishkoman is 100 per cent Ismaili; Gupis is 100 per cent Ismaili; Chilas is 100 per cent Sunni; Darel/Tangir is 100 per cent Sunni; Astor is 90 per cent Sunni, 10 per cent Shia; Baltistan is 96 per cent Shia; 2 per cent Nurbakhti; 2 per cent Sunni.[41] No university in Pakistan has cared to send out its research workers to the Northern Areas to obtain a sociological profile of the area. Tor H. Aase of the Department of Geography, University of Bergen, writes that after the massacre of 1988, the pattern of relationships changed in the Northern Areas.[42]

In the past, intermarriage had taken place among the three communities, but in 1990 the sectarian poison had already been spread by the clergy. A Sunni boy from Chilas fell in love with a Gilgiti girl and marriage was arranged between them by their Yashkun families. The girl was in fact from Nagar and was Shia. When the marriage party went from Chilas to Nagar, the local Shia clergy declared the marriage *haram* (forbidden) and called people to arms. Even though the couple belonged to one Yashkun *qawm* they were forced to break off the match. No such *qawm* marriages are now permitted in the region by the *maulvis* (Sunni) and the mullahs (Shia) if they cross the sectarian boundaries.

Journalist Tanvir Qaiser Shahid in his comprehensive (unpublished because it is in Urdu)[43] report on sectarian violence in Gilgit says that on 8 January 2005, Shia leader Agha Ziauddin Rizvi was driving towards the city's central Shia mosque Jamia Imamia when three persons attacked his car, killing him and his guard. The killers were fired at by Rizvi's guards. One was killed on the spot and the other two were wounded. After the news reached the 60 per cent Shia majority of the city, mobs came out and began killing and burning. Dozens were put to death and much property was destroyed. Curfew was imposed on the city by the Frontier Corps with orders to shoot on sight. The following day the national press gave a small piece about the incident with no newspaper highlighting the importance of the Shia leader killed. This is, of course, quite normal in the national press. Most crucial details relating to sectarianism are either glossed over or are simply not available to a sector that is in the habit of denying sectarianism by ignoring it.

Agha Ziauddin Rizvi, 45, was the son of the most respected Shia scholar of the Northern Areas, Syed Fazl Shah. Rizvi went to Lahore's Shia premier institution Jamia Al-Muntazir after which he spent years at the famous seminary of Qum in Iran. He had led prayers at a London Shia mosque for two years before returning to Gilgit fifteen years ago. He became popular after he opposed the imposition of new textbooks on the Northern Areas by the federal government. The Shia community thought that the syllabus offended against their creed and preferred separate textbooks. In 1996, he was able to win 24 seats for Tehrik-e-Nifaz-e-Fiqh-e-Jafaria (TNFJ) in the Northern Areas Legislative Council (NALC), marking the highwater mark of his campaign. When in 2004, the Shia majority of the Northern Areas did not vote for his party, it demonstrated the community's distaste for sectarian politics, but the government in Islamabad was unable to make use of this trend by curbing the Sunni extremism of the area. In fact, it assumed that the Shia had given their tacit assent to a Sunni overhaul of the syllabus.

THE QUARREL OVER THE TEXTBOOKS

The failure of Pakistani journalism to report and discuss sectarianism has much to do with the tragedy of Gilgit. The 'politics' of sectarianism was moulded by the 'policy' of both communities to blame the violence on the United States. The blame Ayatollah Sistani of Iraq put on the Americans for the 2004 *ashura* massacre (a simultaneous bombing in Karachi was also blamed by the Shia and Sunni communities on the US) was echoed with great admiration by a number of columnists in the Urdu press. This pall of self-deception and sheer mendacity disabled the national press from examining in close detail the quarrel over the textbooks prescribed by the Musharraf government for the Northern Areas. The Education Minister, General (Retired) Javed Ashraf Qazi, was an outspoken secular person and was not expected to implement a hare-brained 'secularised' syllabus. The reports show that Rizvi was agitating against the exclusion of certain elements of the Shia syllabus while the Sunnis liked the exclusion:

> The ongoing sectarian tension started when the government introduced an Islamic Studies textbook, which showed the Sunni method of 'Namaz' as the correct way of offering prayers, as part of the curriculum. The book has been published by the Punjab Text Book Board. The majority Shia sect refused to accept it as a textbook. The government refused to accept the Shia demand and insisted on teaching the same Sunni textbook in the local schools. Consequently, the leading Shia *alim* (scholar) in the Northern Areas, Agha Ziauddin, called for a boycott of the textbook and the schools, resulting in the loss of one academic year in the Northern Areas. Eventually, the sectarian tensions resulted in an attack on Agha Ziauddin on 8 January 2005 and he succumbed to his injuries five days later. Agha Ziauddin's death led to more severe sectarian riots that claimed dozens of lives.[44]

The planning and writing of the textbooks for the Northern Areas became controversial as early as 2003. Shia leader Amin Shaheedi said:

> The controversial textbooks have been written by a panel of four authors, all of them Sunni and Deobandi by belief. So, you can imagine what kind of mindset they are likely to promote. The head of Curriculum Wing in Islamabad Dr Ms Haroona Jatoi admits the panel of writers didn't have any representation from the Shia community. She said she had asked them [Shia leaders] to provide her a list of their leaders that should be included in the committee of writers. She said the Wing had no objection to including them in the committee. Ms Jatoi agreed the textbooks should not carry pictures that can promote the rituals of only one sect. But many biased books were being taught in private schools and had been privately published.[45]

The press simply ignored the textbooks, perhaps refusing to read them as it had once refused to read Salman Rushdie's novel *Satanic Verses*. Islamabad, too, kept mum about its education policy in the Northern Areas, perhaps scared of drawing Sunni flak over an attempt at secularising the textbooks.[46]

The repercussions of the Gilgit killing of Allama Rizvi spread to the rest of the country. As if reacting to the indifference of the national press, Shia seminarians of Jamia Al-Muntazir attacked the press club of Lahore in January 2005, thrashed the journalists and burnt all the cars parked there. A few weeks later, as reported by *Khabrain* on 1 February 2005, popular religious leader Allama Ghazi Rashid of Islamabad narrowly escaped death when a car full of terrorists fired at him. He fired back as he was ready with his own weapons. He complained that his kalashnikov had been taken away by the police after this incident. A day earlier, a religious leader of the Sipah-e-Sahaba was killed in Karachi. According to the daily *Din*, the killers of Shia scholar Agha Ziauddin in Gilgit had computers and other electronic devices in their possession. The next day, on 2 February 2005, the daily *Khabrain* reported that the murder of Maulana Haroonul Qasimi in Karachi had been cracked by the police and some people were arrested. Maulana Qasimi was an important leader of Millet Islamiya (banned Sipah-e-Sahaba). The terrorists who murdered him also murdered four members of Tablighi Jamaat, which was not banned and is considered non-sectarian but not by the Shia. The paper did not mention the name of the banned outfit to which the murderers belonged. The banned Shia party (renamed Tehreek-e-Islami) was a part of the parliamentary alliance, the MMA.

Ex-inspector general of police, Northern Areas, Sakhiullah Tareen, was ambushed and killed on 23 March 2005 by unknown assailants on the Karakoram Highway. He had been removed from his job just a week earlier because of the rising controversy about him. The man was known to be imbued with extreme Sunni views and was inspired by the Taliban's sectarian politics from his days as a Pakistani diplomat in Afghanistan. Whether he was sectarian in outlook or not, the fact is that the

Shia community looked at him as a partisan 'of the other side' and claimed that during his tenure they had suffered the worst discrimination from the state authorities. His murder was certainly an act of revenge for the killing of Rizvi in Gilgit by Sunni fanatics. The Sunni sectarians struck back soon enough. On 1 April 2005, they killed the most revered teacher of Jamia Al-Muntazir in Lahore, Allama Najafi.

In May, the government seemed to have overcome the problems of public disorder and called the civil servants back to their offices in Gilgit. But then the textbooks once again became an object of conflict. As reported in the daily *Pakistan* on 12 May 2005, students in Gilgit came out on the streets to protest the teaching of a textbook they didn't like. The students belonged to the majority Shia community while the syllabus was seen to be imposed on them by the Sunni establishment. In the streets, the Sunni shopkeepers objected to their slogans, after which there was stone throwing. The police and the army came out and closed the markets down, and arrested 25 people.

In an interview conducted by Tanvir Qaiser Shahid, a friend of the assassinated Allama Rizvi, Ghulam Abbas Gilani in Gilgit, was of the view that the Shia leader had fallen foul of the government after he opposed the army's plan to build a military base in the Deosai plane. After his death, the government in Islamabad gave in to Shia pressure from all over Pakistan and revealed some details of the three men who had shot Allama Rizvi dead. It announced that it had arrested eight suspects. The Northern Areas administration kept a mysterious silence over this announcement. The question being asked in Gilgit was: who was the attacker who died during the ambush? And who was the bearded assailant who was injured during the ambush?

The local administration let it be known that it could not reveal the identity of the dead terrorist 'for security reasons'. The story in Gilgit was that one injured attacker who was arrested by the authorities had revealed that the dead terrorist was Mukhtar Ahmad, the son of a *pesh* imam (leader of prayers in a mosque) in Peshawar city, who had belonged to a banned religious jihadi organisation. On the day Allama Rizvi was murdered the authorities immediately cut off all telecommunication links of the Northern Areas with the rest of the country. The government also banned all air and road traffic into the region and stopped all journalists from reporting anything other than the official handouts. This kind of quarantine simply encouraged the terrorists to widen their activity. Instead of siding with the people the government seemed to join the extreme elements of the sectarian divide against the common man.

MUSHARRAF GOVERNMENT'S HANDLING OF GILGIT TROUBLE

Gilgit was transformed by the KKH joining Pakistan with China. Completed in 1986 at the height of the Afghan jihad and the rise of Imam Khomeini in Iran, it opened up Pakistan's Northern Areas to the rest of the country. In Gilgit property became valuable because of increased trade and tourism, but since the onset of sectarian trouble, no one has bought land there, and the prices of houses have fallen steeply. Lack of law and order has not only affected business it has also paralysed the administration. After the assassination of the ex-IGI, Sakhiullah Tareen, the chief secretary, the interior secretary and deputy commissioner of the Northern Areas did not attend office, and conducted their business from their homes. The district hospital of Gilgit was located in the Shia-majority area but its doctors were Sunni. Sunni doctors and Sunni forest officers were done to death in the wake of the killing of Allama Rizvi, and now no one was willing to work in their respective places of work. The shopping plazas and bazaars, where Gilgit's upscale market was located, were virtually closed down.

The Northern Areas Transport Organisation runs buses between the Northern Areas and the NWFP. Most of its 72 Shia drivers refused to get on the buses because they feared attacks on the way as the buses passed through Sunni-dominated areas like Kohistan and Diamer. One bus service was given personal guarantees by the chief minister of the NWFP, but when its buses passed through Diamer on 18 April 2005, they were fired upon. One bus got hit, 16 of its passengers received bullet wounds and the Shia driver was killed. The NWFP government declared the incident a robbery while it was clearly a case of sectarian violence. The KKH was also almost blocked at the time while illegal activity like the despatch of weapons from Peshawar went on unchecked. On 27 April, another spate of sectarian killing, claiming the lives of four Shias in Gilgit, forced the government to clamp down the law against public gathering known as Section 144 for another two months.

The Ismaili community has been retreating to high altitude localities and is the most scared local population. The warring sects can actually turn on them because the MMA, in which both the warring sects were represented, was engaged in a fierce propaganda campaign against the Aga Khan University Examination Board those days. Additionally, the Urdu press in Lahore was publishing articles about the possible creation of an Ismaili state in the Northern Areas outside Pakistan.[47] The army disrupted a meeting of the Aga Khan Rural Support Programme in Gilgit on 20 March 2005 on the excuse that the indoor meeting at the local council was violating Section 144. When the indoor nature of the meeting was pointed out by Nisar Abbas, correspondent for Jang and GEO TV, to a posse of army men who arrived at the meeting, one Major Rauf took the journalist outside and got his troops to give him a thrashing. The gathering was subjected to great violence by the army personnel. Those who received the beating included women and children, councillors from different parts of Gilgit, and a principal of a degree college.

Journalists in Gilgit went on strike and some of their protest was fleetingly covered by the private TV channels. The journalists complained that they were not allowed to report faithfully on what was really going on in the Northern Areas. They received death threats from the sectarian divide whose organisations wanted them to report only their handouts. The third offender against freedom of the press was the civil-military which didn't want them to report the sectarian war going on there. On 21 March 2005, a bomb exploded, in front of the house of Khursheed Ahmad, president of the Gilgit Press Club, to 'teach him a lesson'. Anyone who spoke on the phone with the BBC was punished by all the three parties ruling the region. On 21 March, the Union of Journalists of Gilgit–Baltistan and the Skardu Press Club held a meeting asking President Musharraf to apprehend and punish the army personnel who had subjected Nisar Abbas to such merciless beating.

One glaring example of Islamabad's lack of sensitivity came to the fore in 2005, the year when the new chief commissioner of Gilgit was appointed. After knowing full well that the Shias of Gilgit showed panic at the appointment of officers holding extreme Sunni views, the concerned ministry appointed a fundamentalist Sunni as chief commissioner. What it ignored was the message contained in the murder of a retired Sunni IG police earlier. Chief Commissioner Major (Retired) Nadeem Manzur, a strict practising Sunni officer in the Wahhabi tradition, a son-in-law of General (Retired) K.M. Arif, was posted to Gilgit. Major Manzur carried no blot but his almost fanatic observance of the Sunni faith should have alerted the ministry to his unsuitability. He proved ineffective and was quickly recalled. Why was he sent to Gilgit in the first place? Soon after his recall from Gilgit, Mr Manzur died of heart failure, which could be the result of living under tension there.[48] On the other hand, his appointment could have been motivated by anti-Shia sentiments at the higher levels of the Interior Ministry.

In 2005, the cities in the Northern Areas were tense; the villages too were bifurcated according to sect, and everybody was buying weapons. There were no longer any mixed localities. Populations were moving to create a region where sects live with a siege mentality. A Shia goatherd was killed at random in the Gilgit countryside, after which the two sides opened up with automatic weapons. When the smoke died down seven people had died and a large number had suffered bullet wounds. As weapons poured in across 120 inspection posts on the KKH, ex-army personnel in the two communities acted as 'testers' against fake sales. An influx of the population from the outlying areas into Gilgit followed. About

20,000 people of the Shia sect came into Gilgit to save their lives.

Tanvir Qaiser Shahid interviewed the Shia leader Allama Sajid Naqvi of Tehreek-e-Islami, the all-Pakistan Shia organisation now a part of the religious alliance, the MMA. He was clear why the Shia leader of the Northern Areas, Allama Ziauddin Rizvi, was killed. He discounted the report that Rizvi was agitating against the government for its establishment of a military base in the Deosai plain. He asserted that Allama Rizvi was also not greatly agitated against the Aga Khan Support Programme. The real cause of his death was his struggle in favour of a separate syllabus for the Shia students. Rizvi was for including in the textbooks content that would confirm the Shia creed. He also set aside the government suspicion that a foreign agency had killed Allama Rizvi to set alight the fire of sectarianism in Pakistan. Allama Sajid Naqvi accused the state agencies of facilitating the birth of sectarian terror. He referred to the 1988 massacre of the Shia community in the Northern Areas and a similar massacre of the Shia in the Kurram Agency in the tribal areas for which he held General Zia responsible. Naqvi accused Zia of being a Deobandi at heart. He pointed out that Zia was actually related to Abdul Malik Kandhalvi, the leader of one of the largest Deobandi seminaries in Pakistan, Jamia Ashrafia. For the government's part, it issued an advertisement on 17 April 2005 promising a reward of Rs 15 lakhs for anyone who would help in the capture of the killers of Agha Ziauddin Rizvi.

The International Crisis Group Report, *The State of Sectarianism in Pakistan*, says:

Like other sectarian minorities, those in the Northern Areas believe that political empowerment would enable them to contain Islamic extremism. Elections to even the largely ceremonial Northern Areas Legislative Council have exposed the limited support base of religious radicals. Says a lawyer in Gilgit, 'JUI could not win any of the 24 seats, not even in Sunni-dominated areas'. However, the way the 2002 elections were manipulated to counter the PPP bodes ill for sectarian peace as extremists continue to thrive in the political vacuum. Moreover, the Northern Areas remain in constitutional limbo, and the

centre resists even modest demands such as a reformed court system
and more powers for the elected council. Asadullah Khan, President of
the Northern Areas Bar Council, insists: 'Islamabad must devolve real
administrative and legislative powers to the elected Northern Areas
Legislative Council and settle the status of this region once and for all'.
With democratic governance, the moderate parties that enjoy
considerable popular support could easily check the growing power of
a clergy that has stakes in sectarian strife.[49]

The ICG view here links the resolution of the sectarian problem
with democratisation, which could have been relevant before the
state interfered in the Northern Areas against the Shia community.
However, after the creation of the sectarian conflict and the
segregation of the two communities into warring blocs, democratisation of the administration may initially intensify the problem.

THE ISMAILI FACTOR IN THE NORTHERN AREAS

A significant additional factor in the anti-Shia drive in the Northern
Areas was the anti-Ismaili campaign in the rest of Pakistan by the
religious parties, including such jihadi organisations as Lashkar-e-
Taiba, used by General Musharraf in his Kargil Operation. This
campaign had some ramifications that pointed to a split inside the
Pakistani establishment that was to bring Musharraf under pressure
and curtail his ability to control such jihadi militias as Lashkar-e-
Tayba that the state itself had midwifed into existence. The Ismailis
had been apostatised by Saudi Arabia's chief Mufti Bin Baz, which
was followed by a similar 'copycat' apostatisation by Mufti Shamzai
of Pakistan. Hence, there was a trend to look at the Ismailis and
the Aga Khan as apostate entities working against the Sunni
Muslims.

Saleem H. Ali, researching the madrassa phenomenon in
Pakistan, came upon this trend when he noted the religious
opposition to General Musharraf's decision to allow the Karachi-
based Aga Khan University to become the examination authority

in the country. He also noted the widespread suspicion in the national press about the coming into being of an Ismaili 'state' in Kashmir and the Northern Areas.

The Aga Khan Board controversy started when President Musharraf signed an executive order (the Presidential Ordinance of 8 November 2002) inducting the Aga Khan University Examination Board (AKUEB) into the national education system. The AKUEB was selected due to its excellent record in higher learning and would join the existing 24 examination boards nationwide. It was given the task of upgrading and modernising the declining standards of education and of holding examinations for private educational institutions.

The religious parties objected because the Aga Khan's followers are Ismailis who are not accepted as Muslims in the conservative circles. They added to the suspicion of examinership the involvement of the US funding. USAID, in funding some of the educational programmes of the Aga Khan Foundation, including a $4 million grant for the establishment of the examination board, raised the hackles of opponents of the Ismailis.

Sectarian politics was once again sparked by rhetoric from the leading madrassa Dawa-wal-Irshad in Muridke. In the internet edition of its weekly publication *Ghazwa* (4 Nov 2004), the madrassa warned against converting the Northern Areas into an Ismaili state. Hafiz Saeed wrote: 'Musharraf is working on making the Northern Areas an Ismaili state. He has been pressured by Christina Rocca (former US assistant secretary of state for South Asia) to hand over Kashmir to Prince Karim Aga Khan so that he could annex it with the Northern Areas and make it his fiefdom'.[50] What is worth noting is that the Lashkar chief has possibly been told by someone inside the establishment that Musharraf was promoting an American plan to cut the Northern Areas off from Pakistan and establish there an Ismaili state. What he was not told was that this state would have contained a Twelver Shia majority.

THE FATE OF THE QUETTA HAZARA

The Hazara Shia in Pakistan have been particularly targeted by the Sunni sectarian militias in the recent past. The Hazara are originally from Central Afghanistan, traditionally forming a marginalised and poor community in Kabul. Their persecution at the hands of the Sunni rulers of Afghanistan caused migration of the community into what is today Pakistan, mainly into Kurram Agency, and Quetta, the capital city of Balochistan. The Taliban rule in Afghanistan caused the biggest migration after 1996 and 1998. Most of the Hazaras came to Quetta and today number 200,000 in the city's 1.5 million population of Pushtun, Baloch, Uzbek, Tajik, and others. The intensity of the attacks on the Quetta Hazara increased after 2001 when the post-Taliban government in Kabul had a Hazara vice president. Like all communities under threat, the Hazara too have moved into one location in the city for the sake of security. Thus, apart from having the ethnic Hazara label they have the geographic label too. This constitutes two gradations (Hazara and Hazara Town inhabitants) from the original sectarian label which they share with the Shia community of Pakistan at large. It proves the theory that identity can manifest itself as religion, sect, ethnicity and border/geography. As proved in the case of Mumbai Muslims in India, concentration in one locality leads to 'ghettoisation' followed by targeting on the basis of geography.

According to a study by the Afghanistan Research and Evaluation Unit funded by the European Commission:

> The Hazara Shias are mostly concentrated in Hazara Town: Hazara Town is a lower-to-middle-income area on the outskirts of Quetta with a population of up to 70,000, of which an estimated one third are Hazara Afghans. The area was established in 1982 by Haji Ali Ahmed (an ethnic Hazara) who bought the land from a Kirani Baloch family and built housing there. Many ethnic Hazaras from Afghanistan who were living in different areas of Quetta moved to the settlement, attracted by cheaper land and the security of the scheme. Hazara Town is divided into nine blocks, and almost all the houses are made of concrete. Afghan residents are Persian-speaking Shias, originally from

various provinces in central Afghanistan—including Hazaras who migrated to Pakistan well before the war in Afghanistan as well as those who fled as refugees over the recent years of conflict. The community is a distinct minority in Quetta which is dominated ethnically by Pushtuns and is predominantly Sunni Muslim.

Most of Hazara Town's residents arrived as refugees in Quetta in 1996, when the Taliban regime in Afghanistan began to persecute Hazaras. They initially stayed in mosques in Quetta, then moved to homes with the help of local Hazaras who had arrived in Balochistan as early as the late nineteenth century. The refugees' local networks allowed them to bypass refugee camps altogether.... The ethnic Hazaras had close links with the old Hazara tribes with some political influence in the provincial government. Hazara refugees avoided the camps and settled in the city under the protection of their local Pakistani Hazara patrons.... They have, in contrast to other Afghan groups, actively invested in education. This has generally enabled them to participate more in the formal sector and, to some extent, in the public sector.... The importance of networks based on kinship, tribe and even religion cannot be over-emphasised. The Hazara ethnic group, for example, includes Shias, Sunnis and Ismailis, but only Shia Hazaras live in Hazara Town. In the mid 1980s there were religious tensions between Shia Hazaras and Sunni Pashtun groups in Quetta in which dozens were killed, and this tension and accompanying violence have persisted to some degree since then. The Hazara Shias have confined themselves to Hazara Town and Marriabad, an older settlement.[51]

The book, *War and Migration: Social Networks and Economic Strategies of the Hazaras of Afghanistan* by Alessandro Monsutti (Routledge 2005), encapsulated the Hazara past in Afghanistan as follows:

From 1878–1891: following the second Anglo-Afghan war, the first Hazaras came to Quetta to seek employment in British-run companies under the Raj. They are thought to have worked on the building of roads and the Bolan Pass railway as well as enlisting in the British army of India. At that time there could have been no more than a few hundred Hazaras in Balochistan. From 1891–1901: the subjugation of Hazarajat by Afghanistan's Amir Abdur Rahman, between 1891 and 1893, triggered a mass exodus of Hazaras to Turkestan, Khorasan and

Balochistan. From 1901 to 1933: the situation in Afghanistan returned to normal under Amir Habibullah (1901–1919), the son of Abdul Rahman. He offered amnesty to the Hazaras but this proved to be of little help in improving the lot of the Hazara community in Afghanistan. In 1904, the 106th Pioneers, a separate regiment for the Hazaras formed by the British, offered greater careers prospects, social recognition and economic success. From 1933–1971: the regiment of Hazara Pioneers was disbanded in 1933. Deprived of this social and professional outlet, Hazaras went to settle in Quetta between the 1930s and 1960s, although the process of migration never completely dried up. From 1971–1978: following the 1971 drought, Hazaras then settled in Quetta or went to Iran in search of work. Between 1973 and 1978, tensions over the Pushtunistan issue between the Daud government and Pakistan were an additional factor in the Hazara migration.[52]

Yet another wave of Hazara migration was experienced by Quetta in 1979 after the Soviet intervention in Afghanistan.

The Hazara of Quetta have attracted mischief from their Sunni neighbours on many counts. They are upwardly mobile in a conservative tribal society because of their focus on education and business. According to one Hazara professor of the University of Balochistan,

> The Hazara community is the most educated community in Balochistan. Some 50 per cent of position holders in the matriculation and FA/BA exams are from among us [Hazaras]. Hence the visible presence of Hazaras in the civil services, police, the IT market, small businesses and other professional sectors in Balochistan.

The Hazaras are clearly the most rapidly but silently emerging community in Balochistan. Hazaras have, by and large, come to be seen as an extremely hardworking people.[53]

The Hazaras chafe under the quota system that blocks them from more government jobs than they already have on merit. Their 'business' with Afghanistan (mostly cross-border smuggling) cannot flourish because of lack of cooperation from Sunni Pushtun intermediaries. As a consequence, they rely on cross-border 'business' with Iran where too the ethnic divide results in discrimination by the Iranians against the Mongoloid Hazaras, ignoring religious and linguistic commonalities. The Hazaras have infiltrated into Iran and even Europe in pursuit of their livelihood while ironically the local Pushtun impression is that the Hazaras are being preferred over them by the Quetta government. What must bother the government additionally is the Hazaras' ability to derive most of their income from smuggling with Iran. The Hazaras believe that sectarianism under General Zia has prevented them from integrating with the rest of the population of Balochistan.

In 2003, in one of the worst sectarian assaults in the history of Pakistan, some 58 people, most of them Hazara Shias, were killed while around 200 were injured when suicide bombers attacked Imambargah-e-Kalan in Quetta. Another 38 persons, mostly Hazara Shias, were killed in a sectarian assault on 2 March 2004 on the day of the *Ashura*. The incident left 200 people injured. Just before the 2003 attack, Quetta city was flooded with leaflets containing *fatwas* from the country's top-most ulama, declaring the Shia an apostate community. The 2003 massacre was preceded by widespread circulation of anti-Shia *fatwas* in Quetta, branding them *murtad* or apostate, a designation normally deserving death in the eyes of the pious Sunni Muslims.[54]

GEO TV (12 September 2003) had TV host Hamid Mir interviewing the imam of the Hazara Imambargah at Quetta where the Shia community had been blown up by suicide bombers. The imam said the attack was carried out by the Sipah-e-Sahaba, Jaish-e-Mohammed and Lashkar-e-Jhangvi, and this information had been given to the administration in Quetta. The leader of Pakistan's clerical alliance, the MMA, Qazi Hussain Ahmad was present at his side when he stated this. He added that Qazi Hussain Ahmad was a member of the MMA and should take measures to persuade others in the MMA to stop doing what was being done. Qazi Hussain Ahmad said instead that it was the responsibility of the government to end terrorism. The IG police Balochistan, Shoaib Sadal said that the mastermind of the Hazara killings in Quetta was related to Ramzi Yusuf who was now in prison in the United

States after being caught in Pakistan in 1995. He was a brother-in-law of Ramzi and thus the killings could be related to Al Qaeda.[55]

The 4 July killing was followed by the killing of six Shia employees of Pakistan's space research institution SUPARCO in an ambush in Karachi. On 6 October 2003, the killings were avenged with the murder of the Sipah-e-Sahaba leader Maulana Azam Tariq.

The year 2004 began ominously with a Shia procession on 10 Muharram being attacked by suicide bombers on 3 March. In all 47 people were killed and 160 injured. (Sectarian violence increased yielding more death and injury.) This was the first *Ashura* after the American invasion of Iraq and the attack was made to coincide with similar attacks in Baghdad and Karbala in Iraq. Gunmen had taken up positions on the balcony of a two-storey house on Quetta's congested Liaquat Road, while another group had mingled with the procession. A huge explosion sent a massive shudder through the mourners, followed by indiscriminate machine-gun and hand-grenade attacks on the procession. Two suicide-bombers detonated themselves in the middle of the procession. It was the third time in six months that the Shias of Quetta had been attacked. These massacres were avenged with the killing of the most revered Deobandi leader Mufti Shamzai of Jamia Banuria on 30 May 2004, which was followed by another massacre of the Shia in Ali Raza Mosque in Karachi on 31 May.

The *Ashura* killings in Quetta were made to coincide with the killing of Shias in Iraq. Grand Ayatollah Sistani of Najaf declared that the Iraqi killings were the work of the Americans and not of the Sunni Arabs.[56] This line was followed immediately by the Shia clerics of Pakistan who also blamed the Quetta killings on the Americans. The Pakistani Urdu press welcomed this development. Columnist Ataul Haq Qasimi wrote in *Jang* (5 March 2004) that he was greatly uplifted (*taza dam kar diya*) when he heard the Iraqi Shia saying that 200 of them killed in Iraq on *Ashura* was not the work of Muslims (read Sunnis) because no Muslim could do such a thing. The Shia in Iraq instead said that the evil deed was done by someone else (*kissi aur ka hath*). The columnist then said that the Shia of Pakistan should develop the same kind of thinking (*issi soch ki zarurat hai*) about the *Ashura* massacre of Quetta which killed nearly 50 Shias. Columnist Abdul Qadir Hassan wrote in *Jang* (5 March 2004) that the *Ashura* massacre in Quetta was just like the massacre in Baghdad and Karbala, and the Muslims were convinced that it was not done by the Muslims themselves. 'In present times, when America has unleashed its aggression on the Muslims no Muslim group can think of killing another Muslim'. In the case of the Quetta massacre another country (read India) could join America in committing this evil deed. 'Those who investigate the massacre should keep the idea of foreign hand (*beruni hath*) in their mind'. Columnist Irshad Haqqani wrote in *Jang* (5 March 2004) that a foreign office spokesman in Islamabad had stated that the *Ashura* massacre in Quetta had the hand in it of the Indian consulate in Afghanistan. In the Senate the opposition senators thought that it was a conspiracy hatched by a big foreign power.

Vali Raza Nasr presents another Sunni-Wahhabi angle on the *ashura* massacre:

On March 2, 2004, when a series of bombs in Baghdad and Karbala killed some 143 Shias who were commemorating *Ashoura*, a Kuwaiti Wahhabi cleric used his website to condemn this cherished Shia holy day as the 'biggest display of idolatry' and accused Shias of forming 'an axis of evil' linking Washington, Tel Aviv, and the Shia holy city of Najaf' to grab Persian Gulf oil and disenfranchise Sunnis. These sentiments were echoed by the Saudi Wahhabi cleric Nasir ul-Umar who accused Iraqi Shias of close ties to the United States and argued that both were enemies of Muslims everywhere. The language of Wahhabi ulama in Saudi Arabia echoed the anti-Shia vitriol, of the Taliban in Afghanistan and extremist Sunni forces in Pakistan.[57]

NOTES

1. *The Essential Rumi*, Translated by Coleman Barks with John Moyne, Penguin Books, 1995, p. 252.

2. Vali R. Nasr, *International Politics, Domestic Imperatives, and Identity Mobilisation: Sectarianism in Pakistan*, 1979–1998, Comparative Politics, Vol. 32, No 2, Jan 2000, p. 178.

3. Aamer Ahmad Khan, 'The Rise of Sectarian Mafias', *Herald*, June 1994.

4. *Herald*, February 1995, p. 54.

5. Zahid Hussain, *Newsline*, March 1995, p. 35.

6. The New Year holiday in Iran, Azerbaijan, Afghanistan, Pakistan, parts of India and among the Kurds, without regard to sect. It is also observed in many changed forms in parts of Russia, in such republics as Tatarstan. It falls on 21 March according to the Persian calendar. It is essentially a pre-Islamic Iranian festival and its spread denotes past Iranian supremacy in the region.

7. Rizwan Qureshi, 'The Road to Destruction', *Herald*, April 1998, p. 57.

8. William Dalrymple, 'Inside Madrassas', *The New York Review of Books*, 1 December 2005: 'Javed Paracha is a huge, burly tribal leader with a granite outcrop of nose jutting out from a great fan of grey beard. In many ways he is the embodiment of everything that US policy makers most fear and dislike about this part of the Muslim world. For, Paracha is a dedicated Islamist, as well as a wily lawyer who has successfully defended al-Qaeda suspects in the Peshawar High Court. In his fortress-like strong house in Kohat he sheltered wounded Taliban fighters—and their frost-bitten women and children—fleeing across the mountains from the American daisy-cutters at Tora Bora, and he was twice imprisoned by General Musharraf in the notorious prison at Dera Ismail Khan. There he was kept in solitary confinement while being questioned—and he alleges tortured—by CIA interrogators.'

9. *Herald*, April 1998.

10. *Herald*, January 1999, p. 101.

11. *Herald*, August 2001, p. 61.

12. The Taliban captured Mazar-e-Sharif in 1997 after a warlord from the enemy alliance made a deal with them. The Taliban later reneged on the pact and in turn were betrayed by the said warlord. Their assault on the culture of the liberal northern city provoked the population into confronting them.

13. Mariam Abou Zahab, 'The Regional Dimension of Sectarian Conflicts in Pakistan', Paper on the Internet.

14. *The Daily Times*, 13 February 2006.

15. *Newsline*, May 2002, p. 41.

16. Writer's comment: I was asked by the Lahore chapter of the doctors' association to address them on current national issues. I was prepared to discuss the problem of growing religious violence, but when I saw that most of the medical specialists in the high-income bracket were sporting flowing beards and already making speeches in favour of an Islamic revolution, I changed my mind and did not broach the subject of increased religiosity among the scientists in general and doctors in particular. The meeting was finally dominated by Dr Israr Ahmad, himself a medical doctor, and now

leading the *khilafat* revolutionary movement, and Dr Amer Aziz who had been to Afghanistan to treat Osama bin Laden.

17. Daryush Shayegan, *Cultural Schizophrenia: Islamic Societies Confronting the West*, Saqi Books, 1992, p. 32.

18. Pervez Hoodbhoy, *Islam and Science: Coexistence and Conflict*, Zed Books, 1991, p. 146.

19. *Herald*, February 2002, p. 35.

20. Ibid., p. 38.

21. *Herald*, July 2004, p. 33.

22. Pervez Musharraf, *In the Line of Fire: A Memoir*, Free Press, 2006, p. 261: Musharraf narrates the story of Amjad Farooqi together with Al Qaeda agent Abu Faraj al-Libbi but abstains from going into Farooqi's links with other jihadi outfits.

23. *Herald*, June 2004, p. 66.

24. Manzur Numani, *Khomeini aur Shia kai barah mein Ulama Karam ka Mutafiqqa Faisala* (Consensual Verdict of the Ulama on Khomeini and the Shia), 1987, p. 153 and p. 185.

25. Akbar Ali Ghulam Hussain, *Agha Khani Musalman kaisay*, (How can the followers of Aga Khan be Muslims?), Ismaili Namazi Committee, 1996, p. 140.

26. Kathy Gannon, *'I' is for Infidel: from Holy War to Holy Terror, 18 Years inside Afghanistan*, Public Affairs, 2005, p. 93: 'People present at the meeting and within the ISI revealed that General Ahmad had a message for Mullah Umar quite different from the one that Washington had pressed his government to convey. He took the slow-talking leader aside and urged him to resist the United States. He told Mullah Umar not to give up bin Laden. General Ahmad travelled several times to Kandahar, and on each visit he gave Mullah Umar information about the next likely move by the United States. By then General Ahmad knew there weren't going to be a lot of US soldiers on the ground. He warned Mullah Umar that the United States would be relying heavily on aerial bombardment and on the Northern Alliance.... Neither Osama bin Laden nor Pakistan's ISI chief explained to him the extent of the devastation that would be linked to his name and his movement'.

27. The writer lectured the Lahore Administrative Staff College on sectarianism with reference to Shamzai and asked the class of senior civil servants to especially investigate his Banuri seminary during their tour of Karachi. I was informed by them later that when they tried to confirm my facts with the Inspector General, Sindh, he lost his temper and praised Shamzai as a great non-sectarian scholar. The Mufti was to die a year later—a victim of sectarian violence.

28. *Daily Times* editorial, 1 June 2005.

29. Robert D. Kaplan, 'The Lawless Frontier', *The Atlantic*, September 2000.

30. T.L. Pennell, *The Wild Tribes of the Afghan Frontier*, 1909, ABI Publishing House, 1998 (reprint). Pennell was a British missionary-cum-doctor who

spread the Gospel and cared for health in what we call the tribal areas today. He found himself struggling to spread Christianity among these tough Muslims in the decade of 1890. He was accepted as a 'doctor padre' and was therefore able to pick up a lot of the Pushtun lore. He was in favour of the 'forward policy', requiring the Indian Government to spread its influence into the Pushtun–Afghan territory to control the foreign policy of the Afghan Amir while leaving him sovereign over internal policy. His hero was Sandeman who 'tamed' the tribes from Quetta to the Derajat. He favoured it because it gave him an opportunity to open hospices and spread the Gospel far into the North West. His ambition·was to reach Central Asia, which was not to be. Based in the Kurram valley, he concentrated on the Turi Shia tribe because they were receptive to his message. The account covers the last two decades of the nineteenth century.

31. International Crisis Group, *The State of Sectarianism in Pakistan*, Asia Report 95, 18 April 2005, p. 17.
32. BBC website, Urdu, 12 April 2007.
33. *Daily Times*, 21 July 2005.
34. Zahid Hussain, *Battle for the Soul of Pakistan*, Newsline, July 2007.
35. William Dalrymple, 'Inside the Madrasas', *The New York Review of Books*, Vol. 52, Number 19, 1 December 2005.
36. Jason Burke, *On the Road to Kandahar: Travels through Conflict in the Islamic World*, Thomas Dunne Books, 2006, p. 276.
37. Ibid., pp. 38–39.
38. Khaled Ahmed, 'How Azad is Azad Kashmir?' *The Friday Times*, 3 August 2001: 'In 1949, Pakistan decided to take over the administration of the Gilgit–Baltistan territory which is legally a part of Azad Kashmir. It concluded an agreement with the government in Muzaffarabad and simply delinked it from Azad Kashmir to call it the Northern Areas. Later on when it sorted out its frontier with China, some of this territory was ceded to China with the proviso that the settlement was subject to the final solution of the Kashmir dispute. Cases at the Azad Kashmir High Court challenged the authority of the federal government to take away the Northern Areas and wanted the territory returned to the administration of Muzaffarabad'.
39. Navnita Chadha Behera, *Demystifying Kashmir*, Brookings Institution Press, 2006, p. 197: '(Some scholars) believe (the policy) was initiated by General Ziaul Haq after the success of the Islamic Revolution in Iran in 1979, in order to counter the growing sectarian consciousness of the Shias and their demand for political and economic rights on par with the Sunnis'.
40. K.M. Ahmad, 'Recalling Ugly Use of Article 58(2)B', *Dawn*, 21 December 2002.
41. F.M. Khan, *The History of Gilgit, Baltistan and Chitral: A Short History of Two Millennia*, Ejaz Literary Agents, 2002.

42. Tor H. Aase, 'The Theological Construction of Conflict: Gilgit, Northern Pakistan', in *Muslim Diversity: Local Islam in Global Diversity*, Curzon Press, 1998, pp. 58–79.

43. Shahid is a Lahore journalist who has the reputation of being a maverick among Urdu journalists. He has a thorough grounding in international literature and reads English—unlike most of his colleagues. His investigative reports are often rejected in the daily *Pakistan*, Lahore because of their expected shocking effect. He permitted me to use his findings about Gilgit.

44. Pak Institute for Peace Studies (PIPS), Lahore, 2005.

45. Shianews.com: 5 July 2003.

46. A.H. Nayyar and Ahmed Salim, *The Subtle Subversion: A report on Curricula and Textbooks in Pakistan*, SDPI (Sustainable Policy Development Institute), 2003, updated 2006. 'One of the textbooks carries a sketch of a boy offering prayers in the Sunni way. The picture can mislead a Shia student about his/her religious rituals? Ali Ahmed Jan, a LEAD (Leadership for Environment and Development) Fellow, said. The textbooks hurt the religious sentiments of not only the Shias but also the Sunni-Barelvis. The Prophet is quoted as saying, 'God chastised the Jews because they began to worship their prophets' graves. Therefore, you should not worship my grave after my death'. This excerpt clearly provokes the Barelvis and the followers of saints like the Shia Barri Imam. Shia scholars also say the textbooks utterly ignore Hazrat Ali, the fourth caliph, whom the Shias revere. Moreover, while the books speak highly of the *sahaba* (Companions of the Prophet) they ignore important figures from Ahle-Bayt (family of the Prophet)'.

47. Akbar Ali Ghulam Hussain, *Aga Khani Musalman Kaisay Huay*, (How can the Ismailis be Muslims), Ismaili Namazi Mirror, 1996, p. 311 quotes weekly *Takbeer*, Karachi of February 1988 as saying that an Aga Khani state was in the offing after a meeting between the Aga Khan and General Zia. It said that an Ismaili army was being raised in Chitral with the help of Russia. The book quotes the daily *Inqilab*, Karachi which speaks of the creation of an Ismaili province in the North comprising Gilgit, Hunza, Chitral and adjacent areas. The author of the book, Akbar Ali Ghulam Hussain, was killed in a sectarian incident.

48. *Daily Times*, 'Failure to Tackle Gilgit Violence', Editorial, 7 December 2005,

49. International Crisis Group, 'The State of Sectarianism in Pakistan', Asia report 95, April 2005, p. 20.

50. Saleem H. Ali, *Islam and Education: Conflict and Conformity in Pakistan's, Madrassas*, Oxford University Press, 2009, p. 113.

51. AREU Case Study Series January 2006, *Afghans in Quetta: Settlements, Livelihoods, Support Networks, and Cross-Border Linkages*, Collective for Social Science Research, Funded by the European Commission and Stichting Vluchteling.

52. *The Friday Times*, September 1–7, 2006—Vol. XVIII, No. 28.

53. Inspector General Police Mr Shoaib Sadal, in a meeting in Lahore's National Institute of Public Administration (NIPA) in 2005, told the audience that the Hazara dominance of the Quetta economy had become a serious threat to peace because of the jealousy and hatred it aroused in the majority Sunni community.

54. The 'issuing authorities' of the *fatwas* were: Mufti Wali Hassan, Jamia-ul-Ulum Islamia, Karachi; Senator Maulana Samiul Haq, Head of Darul Ulum Haqqania, Akora Khattak, Peshawar; Maulana Abdul Haq, Member Pakistan National Assembly; Mohammad Malik Kandhalvi, Member Council for Islamic Ideology, Islamabad; Hafiz Hussain Ahmad, Member Balochistan Assembly, Government of Pakistan; Qazi Abdul Latif Kalachawi, Darul Ulum Deoband; Mohammad Ajmal Qadri, Imam Badshahi Mosque, Lahore; Mohammad Abdul Sattar Taunsavi, President Tanzeem Ahle Sunnat Pakistan; and Sheikh Abdullah Abdul Aziz, Grand Mufti of Saudi Arabia. These are the most well known *fatwas* from a much larger list on the Hazara website: shianews.com/hi/articles/politics/0000298.php—38k.

55. Dawood Bidani, a close relative of Khalid Sheikh Mohammad and Ramzi Yusuf, was the prime suspect in the 2003 attacks. Khalid, a close associate of Osama bin Laden, had reportedly spent a lot of time in Quetta before he was arrested from Rawalpindi in March 2003.

56. *Daily Times*, 4 March 2005, *Second Opinion*: 'Last year on the day of *Ashura* hundreds of Shias were killed in Iraq and Pakistan at the same time. It was decided by Ayatollah Sistani of Iraq that the killings were not done by the Sunnis but by the Americans and the Jews. This line was adopted by the ulama of Sunni and Shia communities in Pakistan too'.

57. Vali Nasr, *The Shia Revival: How Conflicts within Islam will Shape the Future*, Norton, 2006, p. 246.

5

Shias in the Middle East

This moment this love comes to rest in me,
many beings in one being.
In one wheat grain a thousand sheaf stacks.
Inside the needle's eye a turning night of stars.
                                    – Rumi: *Dance in your Blood*[1]

Because the recrudescence of the great Islamic schism took place after the Islamic Revolution in Iran and the Saudi–Sunni–Arab reaction to it, one can understand the sectarian violence in Pakistan—and to some extent in India—by surveying the schism among the states of the Middle East. The Shia diaspora is spread across a large part of the Middle East and is concentrated, barring Lebanon, in the states around the Gulf. The Arabs are generally known to represent Sunni Islam and often no importance is given to the Shia Arabs. Because of their marginal existence in the societies the Shia inhabit, the West has studied Islam more substantially as the unfolding of the Sunni religion. Iran has been looked at as a country of the Shia with a strong and impressive culture, but in this case too its pre-sixteenth century Sunni history has often been highlighted. The Shia Arabs who moved to Iran from the Middle East were ignored as heretics, but the truth is that their existence was coeval with the Sunnis, and as their residual pockets of location in many of the Arab states today suggest, they could have once been in the majority. The politics of oil has attracted the world's attention to the owners of the oil wells, to the Sunni Arab rulers in the Middle East, and to the Shah of Iran as a modern secular ruler before he was toppled in 1979. The security of the Middle East in general and the Gulf in particular has

engaged the West over the years only to realise that threats to Gulf
security had a very complex structure. Once again, the presence of
the Shia communities in the region was ignored simply because
they were marginalised and suppressed. This security map is
changing in 2006 and Western scholars are turning their attention
to the Shia faith and its followers as important inputs into the
security paradigm of the region.

Before we look at the 'Shia threat' within the states of the
Middle East, let us look at the complex pattern of threat perceptions
that the states of the Gulf possess, both within the region and
outside it:

> Leaders in the Gulf have no shortage of perceived adversaries. Saudi
> Arabia fears that Iran and Iraq harbour expansionist ambitions. Several
> GCC states may share these concerns and perceive Saudi Arabia's
> motives as hegemonic as well. Leaders in US-occupied Iraq continue
> to perceive the United States as the primary hegemonic threat in the
> region, working with its allies in Israel and the GCC to subjugate the
> regime in Baghdad and change the one in Tehran. The Saudis, Israelis
> and Americans used to advocate containing Iraqi and Iranian power in
> the 1990s. The Iranians called for the reduction of American influence
> in the area and advertised their sympathy for internal political change
> in the GCC states.[2]

Iraq invaded Iran in 1980 and then Kuwait in 1990, while
condemning the GCC states, basing its 'fear' on the loss of
territories through the drawing of frontiers its nationalism never
accepted.

PATTERN OF FEAR AND
LOATHING IN THE GULF

In respect of inter-state boundaries, the problem is much more
complex and gives rise to fears of irredentism as threat perception.
No treaty on the borders of the Arabian Peninsula has been ratified
except for a stretch of the frontier between Yemen and Aden. None,

the other states of the region, Kuwait, Saudi Arabia, Bahrain, Qatar, the UAE, Oman, and Yemen, could prove possession of their territories in a court of law without being challenged by their neighbours or by a third party. Even the Yemen-Aden boundary was challenged after the First World War when the Imam of the newly independent Yemen denounced it. The British had to send an army to Saudi Arabia to make it accept the boundary with Aden (South Yemen). Similar military forays into Oman, whose Imam was dethroned, and Abu Dhabi, had to be undertaken. A Saudi claim to the Gulf islands was resisted by the British who thought that they belonged to Bahrain and Kuwait. The borders between Saudi Arabia and North Yemen, and between South Yemen and Oman are disputed. Bits of land are still disputed among the seven members of the UAE. The states of the Arabian peninsula have territorial disputes with Iran, Iraq, Jordan, Israel, and Egypt. In 1961, the British prevented Iraq from occupying Kuwait.

One reason for this state of affairs is that the borders settled by the British were not recognised by the states. The other reason is the concept of territorial organisation prevailing among the tribes of the region from ancient times. The lines drawn in sand by the ruling British colonial power were not recognised by the states that emerged after the British went away. Thus, Iraq may not agree to respect its boundary with Kuwait. When the British were drawing these lines, there was no countervailing power to challenge the process, except for a weakened Ottoman empire and an equally enfeebled Persia. Thus, the *de facto* boundaries left behind by the British occasionally give rise to disputes and raids. The fact that international law is not equipped to handle boundary issues arising in a region where population mobility and tribal allegiance play a big role has complicated the issue.

Arabia was not endowed with riches of any sort before the mid-twentieth century, but its economy ran on the merit of its being a trade entrepôt. It controlled the trade routes that ran from its arid mass—through the Red Sea and the Gulf—to Egypt and the Mediterranean in the West and the Fertile Crescent in the north, and the Iranian plateau and the Indian Ocean in the east. The

Arabs also migrated to these lands of their trade. They were found in East Africa, on the Indian coast and the Far East. From Zanzibar the Arabs penetrated deep into the interior of Africa much before the Western travellers did, and to India and Southeast Asia and as far as Indo-China under the flag of Islam. The Arab trade with India was in the deficit but this was made up through export of manpower. The Muslim rulers of India established their factories on this route; for instance, Indian Muslim ruler Tipu Sultan's factories were functional in Yemen and Burma. But among the Arabs some regional tribes were more in control than the others and these were located at the strategic points of the trade route: Head of the Gulf, Strait of Hormuz, Bab al-Mandab, and the Oman coast.

When pearl became the big export commodity in the Gulf, tribes from the hinterland shifted to the coast. Kuwait, Bahrain, Qatar, and Abu Dhabi were the maritime bases developed by the Arabs of the interior. Inside the big desert, tribes benefiting from the income of the trade routes—protection and guidance—built medieval skyscrapers in Yemen, and impressive towns in Wadi Hadrmawt (from income from the Nizam of Hyderabad). On top of this came the Wahhabi movement that established the central state of Ibn Saud. The Ibadi Imams in Yemen and Oman disappeared towards the middle of the twentieth century, but the concept of the ancient frontier did not die away. In fact, it was revived by the Saudi state: mobility in space, with watering rights and tribal links which militated against the drawn boundary. After the oil company ARAMCO entered Saudi Arabia, its interest coincided with the Saudi instinct to expand into territories that the British-drawn boundaries had taken away. Saudi Arabia moved into the Buraimi oasis (disputed with Abu Dhabi) in 1952 and its case was presented by an American lawyer. Fouad Ajami describes the Pax Britannica, inherited by the Americans in the 1980s, thus:

British power had protected the smaller realms in the Gulf. Left to their own devices, the Wahhabi zealots of the second Wahhabi state (1824–1891) would have overrun Oman and Bahrain in the 1850s and 1860s. From the 1860s onwards, the small sheikhdom in Bahrain was sheltered by the British against the claims of the Persian state as well. Ibn Saud too had to be checked as he consolidated and expanded his realm. The temptation of the great desert warrior to claim the 'land of his ancestors'—in Qatar, Oman, and the states of the Trucial Coast—was discarded in favour of a live-and-let-live strategy with the British imperial power. Ibn Saud knew the balance of forces and the might available to the British. The zealots among his followers, the Ikhwan, (religious bands of warriors) who had served as his shock troops in the 1920s, wanted permanent warfare against the 'infidel' regimes in Iraq and Transjordan, and the conquest of Bahrain, Oman and Qatar. Of course it was the British who as late as 1961 defended the independence of Kuwait in the face of Iraqi claims.[3]

The British had inherited the region through conquest and by reason of devolution of empire from the Ottomans. By the time the British left the region in 1970, the boundaries were in place but disputed on the basis of complex claims put forward by the states. The boundaries had been created in light of the British imperial interests and had weak points in the legal context. As the status quo solidified and the region became transformed by the discovery of oil, the boundary disputes were swept under the carpet but did not die down.[4]

IRAN, THE ARABS, AND THE NATURE OF THE GULF

The Gulf itself became a sea of conflict between the Arabs on the one side and Iran on the other. The Gulf States were small and undefended while Iran had a population bigger than any Arab state, and an army to arouse fear in the neighbourhood. The Arabs feared Iran because of its Shia identity and thought Iranian irredentism against them might be based on the presence of disadvantaged Shia Arab communities living in their states. The Arab–Persian ancient rift was complicated by the Sunni–Shia split and was waiting to burst on the scene with the establishment of an Islamic state in Iran. Before 1979, when Iran flexed its muscles under the Shah it was an act of domination by a big power nextdoor, but when Iran began to export its revolution after 1979, it was the assertion of a Shia state challenging the Sunni Arabs for having suppressed their Shia minorities. Iran, in history, was never a naval power and therefore could not assert itself across the Gulf where European navies dominated. Even when Persia was an empire facing the Greeks, Themistocles, who defeated the Persian navy at Salamis in 480 BC, thought that the Persians under Xerxes were poor sailors.

The Gulf is 500 miles long and 180 miles wide at its widest point. The Strait of Hormuz, which forms the mouth of the Gulf to the Arabian Sea, is only 20 miles. Its coast on the Arab side has a shallow gradient because of the sand that keeps being swept into the Gulf by sand storms; on the Iranian side the Gulf is deep. This has made the Arabs good seamen and fishermen while the Iranians have remained non-sea-going. On the Iranian side, the Gulf is abutted by mountains, thus cutting off the Iranian hinterland and civilisation from water. There are only three historical outlets, Bushire, Kharg and Bandar Abbas. On the Arab side there are numerous outlets and civilisation is linked to the Gulf. Even in the Shatt-al-Arab estuary the Ottoman Empire was able to impose an unequal waters treaty on Iran, making the frontier run along the Iranian coast rather than in the middle of the waterway. The old Persian Gulf was not Persian at all. In fact, Iran was always dependent on other sea-going powers to give it control of it. On the Arab side, the tribes were arrayed against one another and therefore could neither control the Gulf nor oppose the Persian Empire unitedly. The trade through the Gulf had gone on from the days of the Silk Route which ran along the north of Iran. The Arabs took part in it but also lived off it through piracy. Only an outside power could impose peace on the waterway to make it fit for regular large scale trade. So in the sixteenth century the Portuguese got to the Gulf and established themselves near the Strait of Hormuz, picking up spices and silk for profitable trade in Europe. An envious England set up the East India Company in 1600 and made its way to the Gulf to compete with the Portuguese.

For the Portuguese it was easy to get Iran to sign contracts because the Iranians had no control over the Gulf; the Arabs were easy to control because they were fragmented and internecine. But the negative aspect of the Portuguese trade was that it was done in the name of the King, which usually resulted in maltreatment of the littoral states. The British advantage was that the East India Company plied trade as a private company and didn't bully the rulers in the region. Soon, the Arabs dumped the Portuguese and signed new treaties with the Company. The Iranians allowed it to locate trade offices in Bushehr, Kharg and Bandar Abbas in return for a fee. The Arabs learned to coexist with the Company 'residents' because of the latter's careful avoidance of local politics. Hormuz was captured from the Portuguese after a naval operation in 1622, and in 1654 the Company was able to snatch from them the crucial region of Muscat whose rulers had dominated the Gulf and East Africa from the Gulf of Oman. In 1739, Iran's Nadir Shah ransacked Delhi in India and carried off history's biggest loot back to Iran. With this money he was able to prepare for the rare battle in the Gulf from the Iranian side. With Indian money he built the Bushehr port, purchased ships from Surat (India) and Europe in 1741, and took Bahrain, and brought Muscat under his control. In 1747, Nadir Shah died, tilting Iran back into anarchy and losing his trophies in the Gulf. The Arabs turned into pirates, preying on the Gulf trade with their Qawasim headquarters in Ras-al-Khaima located on what was called then the Piracy Coast and is today known as the United Arab Emirates. The East India Company first arbitrated then got involved in local disputes on the pattern which had already become well known in India. Mahan's great military doctrine that naval power created world dominance on the basis of merchant marine received full application in General Keir's expedition in 1820 when agreements with the Arab sheikhs settled the piracy issue.[5] The Gulf Arabs were now controlled by the Company from Bombay. Iran became a 'partner' through a British charge d'affaires representing the Foreign Office in London.

Iran's weakness was always the Gulf because it had no navy to speak of. It relied on the British to defend itself against Ottoman pressures and incursions from the sea from Holland and France. It should be noted that Imam Khomeini was finally defeated in the Gulf through the American naval presence there in 1988—through an 'accidental' downing of an Iranian airliner by an American battleship. In 1837, Iran decided to take Herat while the Russians planned to ride into Afghanistan by aligning with the Shah. This raised hackles in London and Calcutta. In 1857, while mutiny was raging in India, Iran took Herat. It was time for the British to strike from the Gulf, Iran's weak point. Iran's defeat was facilitated also by the fact that Herat was a Sunni city and the Afghans simply would not accept Iranian rule there. This was ironic because a similar situation in Bahrain (where the majority population was Shia, as witnessed by Ibn Battuta in 1332) did not redound to Iran's advantage. London rejected Iran's claim on Bahrain on the argument that Iran had never held Bahrain for long and that the treaties of tribute signed by Iran with the various Arab rulers of Bahrain had been made under duress.

Today, the Gulf can function as a trade artery only if its freedom is guaranteed by an extra-regional naval power. The regional powers have deeply embedded rivalries that militate against freedom of passage in the Gulf. In 1971, the British rolled back their 'pax' from the Gulf and left it open. Iran's growing power caused the first disruption during the Iran–Iraq war when Iran bombed Kuwait and gave the Soviet Union its first opportunity to come in as a guarantor by flagging the Kuwaiti oil-carriers. The Americans effectively replaced the British in the Gulf through their own 'pax' and were able to 'save' Kuwait and Saudi Arabia when Iraq attacked the former in 1990. In the years following 1971, Britain, the USSR and the United States armed the states abutting the Gulf with weapons, sweeping up the petrodollars accumulated by these states after the oil crisis of 1973.[6]

IRAN'S RETREAT INTO RELIGIOUS IDENTITY

The Shah was toppled in Iran in 1979 and Imam Khomeini returned from his exile. Immediately, the 'revolution' he had started began to be exported across the Gulf. There were spontaneous riots in Saudi Arabia among the Shias living in the oil-rich province of Al-Hasa. In 1981, a conspiracy to overthrow the ruling Khalifa family in Bahrain was unearthed involving 72 men, all of them Shia from Bahrain and Iraq, but trained in Iran. In 1983, another terrorist attack in Kuwait revealed the involvement of the Kuwaiti Shia and the hand of Iran. In Lebanon, too, in 1983 a suicide-bombing against a US Marines barracks in Beirut revealed the hand of local Shia organisations acting on behalf of Iran. The Shia youth living in the Arab states had gone across the Gulf in dhows to take military training.

In 1979, Iran also challenged the United States by taking its embassy personnel hostage against all norms of international law, attracting an intense reaction from Washington. When Iraq attacked Iran in its own national interest in 1980, the Gulf States were relieved that Iran would now be engaged defensively elsewhere instead of following aggressive forward policies in the Gulf. The United States was relieved by the Iraqi invasion and assisted Saddam Hussein in what the Americans thought was the beginning of an effective containment policy against Iran. Under the Clinton administration, Iran was seen by Washington as a supporter of terrorism in the region, and in 1995, Congress set aside $20 million for covert activities inside Iran, clearly indicating its resolve for regime-change in Iran, in addition to sanctions already in place. The same year the US added military teeth to the doctrine of containment by stationing its fifth Fleet at Bahrain, the one state most at risk from Iran because of its majority Shia population.

Imam Khomeini's death in 1989 ended the era of challenge to the Gulf States. Under him, Iran pursued a forward revolutionary policy in its neighbourhood, especially states with Shia minorities under threat. The Gulf States, already persuaded that their security could not be assured by an outside power, had tried to create their Gulf Cooperation Council (GCC) in 1981 and were apprehensive about both Iran and Iraq as guarantors of their security. They had memories of pre-revolutionary Iran under the Shah which had acted as a guarantor with much encouragement from the US under

President Nixon. The 'policing' of the Gulf by Iran also provided Pakistan with 'strategic depth' against India.[7] Therefore, when the GCC tried to get Pakistan to act as its military protector, Pakistan balked. (Evidence emerged later that while Pakistan overtly remained neutral it has a secret understanding with the GCC in case of open war with Iran.)[8] It, too, had a memory about Iran as a security partner and wanted to act neutral. Both the Gulf States and Pakistan soon learned with a shock that Iran under Imam Khomeini was more interested in changing the status quo than protecting it. However, after the death of the Imam, Iran became more realistic and reached across the Gulf offering to create a security system from within the region to exclude guarantors from outside the region. The tenures of Presidents Rafsanjani and Khatami are often seen as a period of détente between Iran and the Arabs across the Gulf. Iran had the effect of uniting Arab entities historically suspicious of one another. The period of 'negotiation' with Iran demonstrated a unity of approach in the Gulf States caused by fear. Post-Khomeini Iran also shifted its focus from external perils to domestic problems. The period of détente did not last long. Ray Takeyh explains:

> Iran's new pragmatic rulers, led by Akbar Hashemi Rafsanjani, began discussing a regional security arrangement whereby the stability of the Gulf would be ensured by local regimes as opposed to external powers. After Saddam's eviction from Kuwait in 1991 and the deflation of his power the mullahs perceived a unique opportunity to establish their hegemony in the region. Instead of instigating Shiite uprisings and exhorting the masses to emulate Iran's revolutionary model, Tehran now called for greater economic and security cooperation. However, the success of this ambition was predicated on the withdrawal of American forces. This was to be hegemony on the cheap, with Iran's pre-eminence recognised, the US presence lessened, and a permanent wedge drawn between Iraq and the Arab Gulf States. The only problem with this proposal was that it remained fundamentally unacceptable to the sheikhdoms to whom Saddam's invasion of Kuwait had conveyed the danger of relying on imperious local regimes for their security.[9]

THE SAUDI SECTARIAN SCENE

Ayatollah Khomeini had advocated toppling the Al Saud kingdom but the Shia minority of Saudi Arabia's eastern province had more realistic demands: the right to observe Shia rituals, job opportunities, share in the oil revenues of the province, and social and religious infrastructure. In November 1979, the Shia, who make up 15 per cent of Saudi Arabia's 27 million population, defied the ban on the *Ashura* (ceremony of commemoration of the martyrdom of Imam Husayn) and came out in their thousands on to the streets of Safwa only to have 20 of their demonstrators killed by the Saudi National Guard. The Shias clashed with Saudi troops in the coming months, till the sheer intensity of government action made many of them go into exile. The battle gained in ferocity and the Shia continued to clash violently with Saudi authorities throughout the 1980s, which was also the setting of the sectarian battlefield lines in Pakistan. The occasion of Hajj became an annual event of Saudi–Iranian friction. In 1981, Iranian pilgrims, unusually large in number, began chanting Khomeini and Revolution slogans in Madinah. The police finally quelled the crowd but not without injury to 22 Iranians, which Radio Tehran reported with great fanfare as the defiance of the pilgrims; and there were processions in the streets of Tehran proclaiming the moral victory of Iran over Saudi Arabia. Imam Khomeini rang King Khaled to complain of the mistreatment of pilgrims, then got the Iranians in Tehran to demonstrate against the Saudi eight-point plan to settle the Palestinian–Israeli dispute. Saudi newspapers retaliated by calling the Iranian government 'irreligious'. The Saudi caution seemed to evaporate and Prince Naef said bluntly: 'The Iranians who said after the revolution that they did not want to be policemen of the Gulf have become the terrorists of the Gulf'.[10]

In 1980, Iraq's dictator Saddam Hussein began his war with Iran hugely subsidised in his effort by Saudi Arabia and other Gulf States scared of Iran's new assertion. The Gulf States created the Gulf Cooperation Council (GCC) to counter the Iranian threat, with Pakistan inducted secretly into it even as it pretended to be neutral. As Vali Nasr wrote:

> Saudi Arabia was wary of Iran's ideological and military threat and was leading a bitter campaign to contain Iran's revolutionary zeal and limit its power in the Persian Gulf region. Since then Saudi Arabia has sought to harden Sunni identity in countries around Iran, a policy that extends into Central Asia. Pakistan was important in the struggle for control of the Persian Gulf as well as in the erection of a Sunni wall around Iran. As Saudi Arabia and Iraq therefore developed a vested interest in preserving the Sunni character of Pakistan, the primary beneficiary was the Sipah Sahaba.[11]

Then, in 1988, as the Iran–Iraq war ended, General Zia of Pakistan was killed, followed by the death of Imam Khomeini in 1989. The Shia leaders in exile took a more nuanced position and demanded rights while seeking better relations with the Saudi regime. The regime began to respond, and in 1993, King Fahd sent out a directive to curb discriminatory practices and to remove the anti-Shia insulting references from the Kingdom's school textbooks. After that, Shia leaders met the king and agreed with him to let thousands of Shias return from exile in various neighbouring states, including Iran.

Thus came to an end the intensity of the 1980s sectarian war during which the Saudis had clamped down hard on their Shias. In 1990, when Saddam Hussein invaded Kuwait and brought his troops close to the Saudi border, the Shia of Kuwait formed most of the resistance to the Iraqi forces, which elicited appreciation and gratitude from the Kuwaiti Sunni population and from the Saudis.[12] But not all the Shias were in favour of accepting the leniency of Al Saud. Organisations such as the Saudi Hezbollah, with Iranian help and training in Lebanon, continued to inspire them with fear. Many Saudi Shia leaders exiled in Iran or in the neighbouring Arab Gulf States were reluctant to make peace because of disbelief in the possibility of a change in the Wahhabi creed. Thus, in 1991, Abdullah al-Jibrin, a member of the Higher Council of Ulama issued a *fatwa* designating the Shia apostates and condoning their killing. In 1996, the bombing of an American military housing compound in Shia-majority Khobar caused the Saudis to suspect—ultimately without proof—the Shia radicals under Iranian influence, although many Shia leaders were of the moderate variety and were more influenced by the Iraqi Grand Ayatollah Sistani rather than Khomeini. The Saudi clerics defied the efforts made by King Fahd to quieten the Shia with concessions and kept issuing *fatwa*s of apostatisation. They boycotted the 'national dialogue' organised by the government on the question of the rights of the Shias. In 2002, Saudi police assaulted the houses of Pakistani and Indian Shias observing the *Ashura* rituals within their houses and worsened the situation.[13] In 2003, Wahhabi clerics issued the typically confusing opinion in writing that Iraq's Shias were aligned with the invading United States. This accusation tended to associate the Saudi Shias, too, with the United States. However, in March 2005, the king finally moved to partially open the local government representation to the Shias of the Eastern Province. Needless to say the Shias won almost every seat in the province. There were also signs that the Shia of Saudi Arabia were moving away from a narrow definition imposed on them by Wahhabi reaction. Seeing that Al Saud are coming under pressure for their propagation of hardline Islam, they began to invite the king to see the Shia in the light of broader Saudi nationalism:

> Breaking from a narrowly sectarian agenda, some Shiite political activists called for broad institutional and political reform, the easing of restrictions on speech and a more participatory political system. Several signed the January 2003 petition, *A Vision for the Present and Future of the Nation*, that sparked broader discussion of reform. At the core of their approach is the conviction, expressed by Najib al-Khunayzi (a Shiite liberal activist who signed the petition, was arrested in March 2004 and has since been released), that change was inevitable but the country would be better served if managed by the al-Saud... King Abdullah, widely believed to have been at the forefront of efforts to engage Shiites and promote their integration, may now be in a position to effect greater change. Already, in 2003, while Crown Prince, he took an important step by creating a framework for Sunni and Shiite religious leaders to engage in direct dialogue, and there is

reason to believe he wishes to pursue this path. But even assuming this goal, he faces considerable obstacles.[14]

Like anywhere else, the Shia, as a minority community have tried to integrate in Saudi Arabia when Wahhabism appeared to weaken as a doctrinal hurdle. When Arabism seemed to assail Saudi Arabia despite the Al Saud rule, the Shias became attracted to the ideas made popular by Nasser in Egypt and the Baath in Iraq. (There was a Shia demonstration protesting Shia rights coinciding with Nasser's visit to Saudi Arabia in 1956). Even communism held its appeal provided it could integrate them with like-minded Saudi Sunnis. But in 1979, there was a revisiting of the Shia creed, inspired by Iran. In 1991, in the defeat of Iraq at the hands of the international coalition of forces led by the United States, the Shia of Saudi Arabia saw the coming era of civil rights and restoration of religious rituals. After the 1991 defeat of Saddam Hussein, the Saudi ulama, Safar al-Hawali, Dean of the Islamic College of Umm Al-Qura University in Makkah, and Nasir bin Sulayman al-Umar, Professor of Quranic Studies at Al-Imam Muhammad ibn Saud Islamic University in Riyadh, sent out a memorandum warning that 'a block of the Shia could emerge, one that would include Iran, Syria (under the Alawis) and Iraq, the Shia of Saudi Arabia as well as the other monarchies in the Persian Gulf'. The memorandum contained a comprehensive programme for the eradication of Shiism in the kingdom. Seeking to placate the frightened Wahhabi clergy, the government in 1992 'imprisoned and executed a number of Shias and razed four Shia mosques'.[15] Then in 2003, with the American invasion of Iraq and the promise of the restoration of the rights of the Iraqi Shias, the Shia of Saudi Arabia began to demand their rights as a minority. Parallel to these developments, the Wahhabi scholars of Saudi Arabia began to see America's moves in the Middle East as aimed at strengthening the Shia in the region.

After 2003, another phase in the life of the Shia in Saudi Arabia is at hand. Although muted, Saudi protest at the prospect of the United States' army leaving Iraq in a 'cut and run' fashion is intense. The Saudis are not only assailed by fear that Iran might become a hegemon in the region—which must still be tempered by the thought that America's fifth Fleet will remain in Bahrain as would American troops in some locations inside the Gulf—but by the rise of the Shia as a ruling majority in Iraq. Will an *Usuli* Iraq join up with an *Usuli* Iran to dominate the Sunni Arabs of the region? The Sunni fear of this eventuality drives the sectarian violence in Iraq, but there are subtle variations inside the Shia faith that point in other directions too.

The real issue, for the Saudis, must be the demonstration effect that the achievement of even moderate Shia majority rule in Iraq turns out to have on other Shia Arabs in the Gulf. This effect will be mitigated somewhat by the different traditions within Shiism that are represented in the various states. Without recounting the entire schism-ridden history of Shia Islam, it is a matter of practical political importance that the dominant form of Shiism in Iraq is that expounded by the *Usuli* school. This strain of thought, which also prevails in Iran, accords a prominent role to eminent, seminary-educated jurist-clerics known as *mujtahids;* each believer is obligated to select one of these scholars as a 'model of emulation' and to follow his guidance on questions of law, religious practice, and morality. By contrast, the *Akhbari* Shias of Bahrain and the Shaykhis of Saudi Arabia's Eastern Province do not have this same tradition of deference to clerical authority.[16] As a result, it may not necessarily be the case that Saudi, Bahraini and other Shias will automatically follow the political lead of the Iraqi Shia leadership.[17]

Saudi Arabia has countered the rise of the Shia in the Gulf region by leaning on Pakistan. The Pakistan government reacted both to the dismissive attitude of Tehran after 1979 and the more forthcoming and helpful stance of Saudi Arabia. The arrival of the Arabs in Afghanistan during the Afghan jihad and the subsequent civil war in Afghanistan initiated a bonding between Wahhabi warriors and the Deobandi hardline jihadi militias of Pakistan, and inclined the Pakistan government to support the Pushtun faction. Pakistan, Saudi Arabia and the Gulf States were the only states to recognise the Pushtun-Taliban government in Kabul in 1996. One

Pakistani opinion about the Pak–Arab relationship explains the anti-Shia trends in Pakistan in the 1980s onwards:

> Pakistan has received more Saudi financial aid—starting in the 1960s—than any other country outside the Arab world. In return, the Saudis have received military and diplomatic help from Pakistan. In the 1960s, Pakistani instructors went to Saudi Arabia to train Saudis on the use of newly acquired British aircraft. An agreement reached in the 1970s made it possible to send 15,000 Pakistani military personnel to the kingdom. The money paid for their services helped Pakistan in its defence preparations.

The dictum in Islamabad was:

> The Saudis will not let Pakistan sink. When Pakistan did not have money to create a *zakat* fund, the 'seed money' for it came from Riyadh. In the 1980s, when Pakistan's military balance with India went awry, Saudi Arabia paid (approximately $1 billion) for a batch of 40 F-16 fighter aircraft. In 1998, then Prime Minister, Nawaz Sharif, facing bankruptcy in the aftermath of the nuclear tests, received a Saudi offer for providing up to 50,000 barrels of oil a day to Pakistan for an indefinite period on 'deferred payment' terms. (The first Muslim leader to visit Pakistan's nuclear installations was Prince Sultan, then Saudi Arabia's defence minister.) Reports that Pakistan might be helping the Saudis to develop their own nuclear weapons capability have been around although Saudi Arabia is a signatory to the nuclear Non-Proliferation Treaty (NPT). So far there has been no proof of such collaboration, but Saudi Arabia might well be counting on Pakistan's nuclear capability to shore up the Gulf region's security in the face of an Iran that has become increasingly unpredictable under President Ahmadinejad.[18]

In December 2006, when the world thought the United States was about to pull its forces out of Iraq to put an end to its invasion of 2003, Saudi Arabia reacted aggressively to the possibility of Iraq becoming the first Arab Shia state and going under the influence of Iran. Stratfor offered the following analysis:

Saudi Arabia's top strategic adviser warned on 29 November 2006 that Riyadh will intervene in Iraq to prevent Iran from gaining a foothold there if the United States withdraws its forces. The only viable option for intervention the Saudis have is to back jihadist forces against the Shiite-dominated government in Baghdad. In the short term, this could benefit both the Saudis and Washington, as it could lessen Iranian influence in Iraq; however, in the long term, it will empower transnational Islamist militants who will threaten both Saudi and US interests.[19]

REVOLUTIONARY IRAN IN THE REGION

Today, Iran has a population of 68.6 million of which 89 per cent are Twelver Shia. One can say that Iran is what it is today because of the over two hundred years' rule of the Safavids (1501–1736). The Safavid shahs consolidated the Twelver Shia Islam and made it subordinate to Sharia. The Persian language began its transformation under them and completed its transition away from the *majhul* vowels while they were still in power, thus separating itself from the Persian of Central Asia and Afghanistan: the 'a' sound became 'o' and 'e' sound became 'ee'. But it is in the consolidation of the Sharia that the Safavids will be remembered. After them, their Turkmen successors never really arose to the same eminence. The founder of the Safavids, Sheikh Safi al-Din (1252–1334) was probably a Kurd who belonged to the Sufi tradition in Ardabil. Although he was a Sunni, he traced his lineage back to Ali through Imam Musa Kazim, the seventh Shia Imam. It was, therefore, not difficult for the first Safavid ruler Shah Ismail (reigned. 1499–1504) to declare himself Shia and resolve to revive the Shia religion of the masses suppressed for a long time by Turkic–Sunni rulers. Early Safavid success was owed to the Turkmen followers of Sheikh Safi who had introduced the concept of *ghuluww* (exaggeration) into his mystical tradition. Shah Ismail's grandfather Junaid (d.1460), who spent ten years in Anatolia among his Turkmen followers, was believed to be God; his son, Haider (d.1488), was believed to be the son of God. When Ismail

declared himself Shia it was the early *Imami* version flecked with
the *ghuluww* favoured by his Turkmen supporters who were mostly
of the Qizilbash tribe and its two branches, Qajar and Afshar.

Shah Ismail's *divan* gives proof of the fact that his *Imami* belief
was greatly influenced by the faith of his Qizilbash followers. In it
he claims to be a reincarnation of the major prophets of Islam and
the Iranian heroes of antiquity. He also claimed to be the
reincarnation of Ali and all the twelve Imams. Laying claim to the
condition of *hulul* (merger with God), which was later declared a
heresy, his poetry shows him seated on the throne of God. Included
in this system was also the concept of the *mahdi* whose coming
became a part of the system of holy prediction in later years. The
Arab *Imami*s never really accepted this Qizilbash version of Shah
Ismail's faith. The tradition of *ghuluww* tended to destabilise the
Safavid state because of its neglect of Islamic law. That is why under
Shah Tahmasp, who succeeded Shah Ismail, the inclination to
enforce the Sharia of uniform authorised practice had grown
strong. The Safavids also felt the need to dissociate themselves from
the Qizilbash tribes to validate their rule over all Persians. Tahmasp
defeated the Qizilbash in the civil war that raged between 1524
and 1536 and took the state towards a more purist version of
Imamism. The genealogy of the Safavids was linked to Imam Musa
Kazim and delinked from Abu Musa and Mohammad bin
Hanafiyya. Under Shah Abbas (1585–1628) the Safavid empire
extended from Baghdad in the west to Kandahar in Afghanistan in
the east. It was during the period of turning away from the Sufis
to the ulama of Sharia that some of the great mystics of Iran were
ignored by the Safavids. For instance, Mullah Sadra (d.1640) failed
to gain recognition from the Safavid king because of this trend. So
ingrained has been the tradition of Sharia in Iran after the Safavids
that Mullah Sadra could never attain the status he deserved even
though his mysticism was rooted in Sharia. Even in our times,
Imam Khomeini is said to have studied Mullah Sadra secretly so as
not to give offence to his fellow-seminarians.[20]

Today's Iran is stamped with the Islamic Revolution of Imam
Khomeini who overturned the identity given to the state by the

Shah as the US-supported 'policeman of the Gulf'. Ayatollah Ruhollah Khomeini (1902–1989) led the revolution against the Shah in Iran in 1979. The early eighteenth century saw the ancestors of Khomeini as Iranian settlers in Kintur, a town of Oudh not far from Lucknow in India. They were *seyyeds* (bloodline of Prophet Muhammad [PBUH]) descended from Imam Musa Kazim and were therefore called Musavi. Originally from Nishabur, they returned to Iran in 1850 when Khomeini's grandfather Ahmed moved from India. His father, Mustafa, was a prosperous man of Khomein in central Iran 200 miles north-west of Isfahan, the old Safavid capital. Ruhollah Khomeini was born in Khomein in 1902. His father was murdered by a notorious marauding group of the area under an unruly Qajar administration. Thus, young Ruhollah, bigger and more athletic than most contemporary kids, grew up an orphan in a respected Musavi *Seyyed* family. He became the pupil of the famous teacher Sheikh Abdolkarim Haeri at Arak, wearing the black turban to indicate his *seyyed* extraction as opposed to the white turban worn by the non-*seyyed* pupils. In 1922, he followed Haeri to Qum, the town that housed the shrine of Fatima, sister of the eighth Imam, Ali Raza. The last Qajar King, Ahmad Shah, came to Qum to celebrate Haeri's move to Qum. Khomeini abstained from *muta*, the temporary marriage practised by his fellow-pupils, and led a pure life.

The Pahlavi state that Khomeini was to transform into a theocracy was founded by Reza Khan who was inspired by Turkey's secular revolution. Reza Khan used his Cossack power to overthrow the Qajars and become the first Pahlavi king, promising to treat the clergy well. But when his sister was reprimanded by an ayatollah at the Qum shrine for not covering her face, he entered the shrine with his shoes on and beat the ayatollah with his whip. Khomeini kept aloof from the furore that arose after the event. He got his 'permission' as *mojtahed* (re-interpreter) in 1936 at the age of 32. At that time *mojtaheds* were respectfully called *hojatal Islam* (proof of Islam). The term *ayatollah* (sign of Allah) was not traditional but had gained currency after 1906 when it was given to those *mojtaheds* who signed the charter of Constitutional Revolution, subjecting the Qajar monarch to a parliament.

Khomeini's seclusion at Qum was owed to his study of mysticism, not in favour among the Iranian clergy. He was attracted to the teachings of Ibn Arabi through the Safavid scholar-mystic, Mullah Sadra. He gathered his followers gradually who were later to become his revolutionary lieutenants. The great leader at Qum then was Ayatollah Borujerdi, the greatest orthodox *marja-e-taqlid* (source of emulation) of the Iranian Shia population. On the other hand, Mehdi Bazargan and Taqi Shariati led a school of moderates who favoured reform in Shia teachings. Khomeini came out with his first statement of Sharia as governance in his treatise *Kashf al-Israr* (1947), intensely critical of the reformers.

Then in 1951, Mossadeq emerged as the most powerful exponent of Iranian nationalism, immediately embraced by the reforming clergy.[21] But Mossadeq's contacts with the clergy of Qum couldn't be strengthened because Mossadeq couldn't accept Sharia as a way of government. It was under Mohammad Reza, the son of Reza Khan, when Khomeini came out publicly against the government. The cause was the Shah's permission to non-Muslims and women to take part in local government elections. Bazargan sided with him despite his moderation. Khomeini went to jail, but after Qum saw popular rioting in his favour, the secret agency Savak sent him to exile in Turkey. (Savak first offered to send him to Pakistan, encoding Pakistan insultingly as 'Banana' in its internal cipher telegram, but Khomeini refused, instead choosing exile in Turkey). After a year in Turkey he was sent to Iraq, where he stayed for 14 years, falling foul of the Baathist rulers who wanted the Najaf clerics to oppose the Shah's claim on Shatt al-Arab. It was here that his pupil Ayatollah Mutahiri, who ran the popular Hosseiniyeh Ershad pulpit in Tehran, asked him to disapprove of modernist Ali Shariati, its most popular speaker. (Ali Shariati had rejected the Shia hadith which offended the Sunni world in modern times.) Khomeini carefully avoided condemning Ali Shariati, but he never accepted the revolutionary message of Ali Shariati, and after his death in London, refused to call him *shaheed*.[22] In 1978,

76-year old Khomeini left Iraq for Paris after making a futile attempt to enter Kuwait.

In Tehran, after the Shah was besieged by protests and gradually abandoned by his supporters, things turned in Khomeini's favour. After the Shah fled, Khomeini's religious stature made him the natural leader of all the forces of the left and right arrayed against the Shah. He returned to Iran in 1979 in triumph, set up an interim government under liberal-secular Mehdi Bazargan and then proceeded to shore up his power. The liberal constitution he had endorsed was changed by him and subordinated to the concept of his theory of *velayat-e faqih* which put his authority above all state institutions. Instead of general elections, he first had the election of the Council of Experts, waving aside all protest by his secular partners. Khomeini's leadership was based on the ancient orthodox beliefs of the Iranians. He began to purge the Bahais, killing Ali Abbas Hoveida, the Shah's longest-serving prime minister and a member of the Bahai community, after a dubious trial conducted by his infamous hanging judge, Ayatollah Khalkhali. He sent a 'correction' to President Khamenei who had told students at Tehran University in 1988 that the Iranian state would be run under the laws set by the *velayat* (guidance) of the Prophet Muhammad (PBUH). The correction implied an assumption by Khomeini of the status of Prophet and the Imams when it stated that 'the new Islamic state could subordinate all Islamic law or Sharia to new exigencies'. This was an oblique reference to his personal divinity in which most Iranians already believed. Khomeini's implied assumption of the status of Imam made him inflexible. He kept the American embassy under siege for over a year till the international view turned against him.

His refusal to put a stop to the war with Iraq when circumstances were favourable to Iran, isolated Iran and caused what Imam Khomeini took as Iran's defeat, comparing the ceasefire to a 'poisoned chalice'. Moderate Islamists were gradually isolated and made to flee. Foreign Minister Qotbzadeh was executed after being accused of planning an overthrow of the Imam in collusion with the Azeri Ayatollah Shariatmadari, whom he had already punished, causing unrest in Tabriz. President Banisadr fled Tehran on an air force plane. Parties such as Tudeh and Mujahideen-e-Khalq were greatly purged through summary trials. The parliament was placed under the complete control of religious leaders owing allegiance to him. His own appointed successor Ayatollah Montezari was punished for his moderate objections and his supporters put on trial. The Revolution began to behave like most revolutions in history. In 1989, after Khomeini died, the *vali* who could abrogate the Sharia was also no more. On President Rafsanjani's testimony, it was decided that Khomeini had nominated Ali Khamenei as his successor. He was duly appointed the Spiritual Leader and made ayatollah although he was not strictly qualified for it as he had not written his *towzih al-masael* thesis. Iranian Islam and its anciently held orthodox views of charisma and reality had responded to the evil of the secular-absolutist Shah in the person of Imam Khomeini.[23]

Khomeini was the first cleric in the region who had acquired a state in modern times. Political Islam envied him, as did Pakistan's Sunni chief of the Jamaat-e-Islami, Abul Ala Maududi when he said on the death of Khomeini in 1989 that 'he wished he had accomplished what Khomeini had, and that he would have liked to have been able to visit Iran to see the revolution for himself'.[24] One detail that he would not have missed is Imam Khomeini's new perception of the Sunni world around him and his very clear intent to threaten it on behalf of the Shia minorities living in it.

Agha Shahi, Pakistan's Shia foreign minister under General Zia, reported that Khomeini once sent a message to the Pakistani military ruler telling him that if he mistreated the Shia he [Khomeini] 'would do to him what he had done to the Shah'.[25] When, despite the warning, Zia imposed the *zakat* tax on the Shia on the advice of Saudi Arabia, the Shia came out to protest in Islamabad in their unprecedented thousands and Zia had to relent and exempt them from it. Khomeini went on to stir the pot in the region, provoking Shia minorities in Afghanistan, Pakistan, Saudi Arabia, Kuwait, Bahrain, Iraq, and Lebanon to assert themselves politically. He supported with money the new Shia religious organisations joined by the Shia after abandoning their Arab nationalism on the Left. The groups who benefited from Iranian funding were: Lebanon's Amal Movement of Musa al-Sadr, Iraq's Al Dawa, Afghanistan's Hizb-e-Wahdat, Pakistan's Tehrik-e-Jafaria, Bahrain's Al Wifaq, and Saudi Arabia's Saudi Hezbollah and Halqa Islahiya al-Islamiya. Shia activists from these parties were whisked into Iran and given military training.[26]

Iran's first big training camp for the domestic and regional Shia youth was set up soon after Khomeini's return, in the Manzarieh Park on the southern slopes of Mount Towchal, dominating the affluent north Tehran suburbs. The Shah had used it for scout jamborees. By 1981, when the first terrorist conspiracy was unearthed in Kuwait, Manzarieh was already established as an elite guerrilla and terrorist camp, producing 175 Afghan and Arab soldiers of the Revolution. Its first commander was of mixed Iraqi–Iranian descent, trained as a commander in Syria. The next camp commander was a graduate of the Palestinian guerrilla training camps of Lebanon who shared with Khomeini his hatred of the Palestinian leader Yasser Arafat. The clerical leader in charge of the training camp was Ayatollah Mahallati, who took particular care to train Iranian Revolutionary Guards (*baseej*) and send them to Lebanon and to the Shia-dominated Hazarajat of Central Afghanistan to fight the Soviets. Before 1985, at least 15 more training camps were opened in the vicinity of Tehran and Qum, in particular Eram Park outside Qum where South Asian Shia terrorists were trained. Two training camps, Gorgon Plain which was 400 miles east of Tehran, and Vakilabad, 600 miles east of Tehran were also in operation.[27]

Khomeini banked on the rallying of the Arab Shia to his revolutionary cause. He saw his aggressive irredentism in the region succeeding in the initial stages and was emboldened to move ahead with his inflexible approach to regional diplomacy. It was a part of his temperament not to give ground and retreat from extreme initiatives. He was determined to cause unrest in countries—from Pakistan to Egypt—seen by him as serving the interests of the United States. He named a street in Tehran after Khalid al-Islambuli, the man who had killed the Egyptian president, Anwar Sadat. Later on, when the Arabs decided to counter Iran, some mistakes were made on the basis of their understanding of Imam Khomeini. Nasr speaks of the early efforts of the Arabs to placate him:

> Khomeini's style and the challenge he posed unnerved the region. When a delegation of Muslim heads of state went to Tehran to mediate an end to the war with Iraq, Khomeini made them wait for two hours, sat on the floor and spoke untranslated Persian for ten minutes while his visitors stood, and then left.

The story came from Pakistan's Foreign Secretary Niaz A. Naik who had accompanied Pakistan's President General Zia to the meeting.[28] Yet, in 1982, when the Iranian army besieged Basra in Iraq expecting that the Shia inside the city and Shia troops would revolt against their own Iraqi army and join the Iranians, it did not happen, and the Iranian offensive finally collapsed in the face of the Shia who fought back as Iraqi patriots.

It was in Lebanon that Iran had the most success. Historically the Shias of Lebanon have had a special relationship with the Shias of Iran. When the Safavids decided to turn Iran into a Shia state in the sixteenth century, they imported the Shia ulama from south Lebanon. Ibn Taymiyya (1263–1328), the presiding saint of Al Qaeda, had asked the Mamluk Turk invaders of Iraq to attack the Shias living in the mountains of Kisrawan in today's Lebanon.[29] Considering that Iraq's Shia population is of even more recent origin than Iran, it is in Lebanon that the oldest Shias were located after the region encompassing Saudi Arabia and the Gulf States. When the Shia of Lebanon got left out of the confessional contract of Lebanon despite their superior numbers, it was an 'exported' Iranian cleric Musa al-Sadr who led them to form a movement in the 1960s. The Amal Movement became a militia and fought for the rights of the Shia in Lebanon, but Imam Khomeini did not much like the negative way in which Musa al-Sadr had reacted to his concept of *velayat-e faqih* and decided to create Hezbollah, closely connected to Iran, and in times to come, the more aggressive and dominant of the Shia organisations.

After Khomeini, Iran has been able to break out of its isolation, thanks mainly to the growing Sunni sense of outrage against the United States. After 9/11, US policy in the region has benefited Iran. Iran has also reached out to India, China and Russia to relieve the isolationism of Imam Khomeini who adopted it as a philosophy of redeeming the honour of Iran. Policies based on national honour and nationalism tend to be isolationist and Iran could have suffered because of its tendency to express pride and courage in international affairs, had it not been for the United States that adopted a similarly isolationist view of the world under the challenge of 9/11.[30] It was not so isolated when it invaded Afghanistan in 2001 to destroy the one Saudi-erected Sunni challenge that Iran was most afraid of, but it was more substantially isolated when it invaded Iraq in 2003 and promised the Shia of Iraq their democratic rights. In consequence, Iran is in a position to deploy its strategy of domination in the Middle East through the rights of the Shia populations in the region.

THE SHIA OF IRAQ

Iraq did not exist till it was created as the British mandate in 1921. Before that it was a province in Syria under the Ottoman Empire. Before that, it was simply a zone of contact between the Ottoman and Persian empires. Najaf and Karbala attracted the Shia of the region but the population of Iraq itself was not predominantly Shia. The tribes of Iraq converted to Shiism around the eighteenth through nineteenth century. When the Safavids ruled Iran in the sixteenth century they often claimed Najaf, Karbala and other cities since the Ottomans were neither reverential towards them nor exercised too much control over them. Najaf is where Caliph Ali is buried. But before he ruled from Kufa in Iraq, Umar had defeated the Persian King Yezdigerd in the battle of Qadisiya, taking prisoners and slaves and converts from Iran. When Ali ruled, his support came from this community of Persian origin. After Ali, the rule of the Umayyads from Syria was oppressive towards the

Iraqis. Surprisingly, Iraq could not win against Syria because of internal divisions—typical of any melting-pot type of cultural contact zone.

At Qadisiya, in AD 637, 4,000 Sassanian troops from Daylam in Northern Iran (called the Asawira) joined the 12,000-strong Arab army in Southern Iraq and decided to fight against their own King Yezdigerd, on the condition that they be allowed to settle where they wished. In Iraq, there were a number of Iranian Muslims who were to join the Muslim army under the name of Hamra, 'the red army'. When Hazrat Ali faced the forces of Muawiyya bin Abu Sufian at Siffin, his 70,000 Kufan soldiers included 8,000 *mawali* (non-Arab Muslim converts from slaves) and *abeed* (slaves). Sassanian soldiers swelled the Muslim armies in later years, coming and settling mostly in Basra from as far away as Sindh in today's Pakistan. They were better archers than the Arabs and became a useful part of the Islamic army. However, the civil war that followed the assassination of Ali in Kufa in AD 661, and the civil war that took place earlier between the Syrian forces of Muawiyya and the Iraqis of Basra and Kufa, saw these Sassanian elements as weakening the solidarity of the Iraqis already undermined by the revolt of the Khawarij, a sect that arose at Siffin opposing both Ali and Muawiyya. After the murder of Caliph Usman in AD 656, those who were angry at the incident arose in Basra as the supporters of Hazrat Aisha, the wife of the Prophet, under the leadership of Talha and Zubair. Caliph Ali's army was Kufan and was pitted against the Basrans who were routed and both Talha and Zubair were killed. But this proved yet again the split in Iraq, which made Syrian dominance of the country easy later on when Imam Husayn was besieged by the Syrians under Yazid.

The first Iraqi weakness appeared when the Kufans arose in revolt after the martyrdom of Imam Husayn at Karbala in AD 683, the orders of the Syrian-Umayyad Governor of Kufa Ubaidullah bin Ziyad. The revolt came after the death of Yazid and the flight of Ibn Ziyad back to Syria. The battle which occurred finally in North Syria was lost by the Iraqis once again because of lack of cohesion among its various communities. Many Iraqis did not join after first promising to, while the Syrian army was united and larger in number. The Basrans and Kufans had finally to submit although they were larger in population and lived in the richest province. The Umayyads ruled their most precious territory from Syria by disarming the Iraqis, who were once the most warlike and numerically strong force, and by sending particularly tyrannical governors to keep them tamed. One such was Hajjaj bin Yusuf al-Thaqafi who was cruel towards the dissidents and benefited from the lack of loyalty of the Iraqi *mawali*. He was particular in not sending Kufan and Basran troops for conquests abroad. His nephew Mohammad bin Qasim al-Thaqafi was sent for the conquest of Sindh with a Syrian army. Later, the demilitarisation and civilianisation of the Iraqi warriors actually delayed the overthrow of the Umayyads by the Abbasids. Under the Umayyads, the soldiers began to get paid salaries. The custom of getting Muslim convert armies from other lands was started by Ali, continued by the Umayyads, and finally adopted in real earnest by the Abbasids whose bloodline was partly from Khurasan.[31]

Today, Iraq has a population of 26.8 million of whom 65 per cent are Shia while the Sunnis are 35 per cent. Like all minorities, the Shia of Iraq keenly joined political movements that took the confessional focus away from public affairs. They embraced communism and pan-Arabism in order to become integrated into a Sunni-controlled state. The Baath party with its Arab nationalist doctrine took over in 1963 and was intellectually guided, making it possible for the Shia to participate in its politics. But by 1968 the Baath was taken over by tribal Iraqis with a strong anti-intellectual bent, which included an ancient distrust of the Shia and the communists. The Shia aroused suspicion because of their closeness to their religious leaders despite the fact that these leaders remained mostly quietist so as not to attract the cruelty of the Sunni tribes. But there were occasions when the Baath bore down on the more outspoken of the Shia spiritual hierarchy formed around the internationally revered cities of Najaf and Karbala. The poverty of the Shia prevented them from becoming completely integrated into the secular order. Saddam Hussein perpetuated himself through organisation and unbending cruelty towards his opponents or potential opponents.

Saddam banned public celebration of Shia festivals and killed the Shia leaders who showed signs of rebellion. His method of killing them was most gruesome and was meant to discourage any future disobedience. For instance, in 1980, he killed the Shia cleric Baqer al-Sadr by driving nails into his head after al-Sadr had watched his sister being raped. In 1999, Saddam went on the rampage. He killed Grand Ayatollah Mohammad Sadeq al-Sadr along with his two sons (one son was Muqtada al-Sadr's father); he also killed ten brothers of Abdul Aziz al-Hakim who fled to Iran and set up his militia as Supreme Council for the Islamic Revolution in Iraq (SCIRI) with Iran's help and in 2006 fielded the largest bloc of elected members of the Iraqi cabinet. Saddam fought his war with Iran from 1980 to 1989 with the help of the Arab states in the region and American support. Although prosperous, Iraq lost much of its economic strength because of the war, and Iran was finally defeated because of its self-imposed isolation. In 1990, Saddam invaded Kuwait and began a reverse process: the world got together, isolated him and attacked him. Saddam was defeated and ousted from Kuwait. This was also a window of opportunity for the Shia of Iraq. They arose in rebellion and could have won against the Saddam regime had America decided to take the invasion to its logical conclusion by removing Saddam from power. Nasr reports that Saudi Arabia prevented the Americans from removing Saddam so as not to strengthen Iran in the region. President George Bush senior and his administration understood what they were doing when they let Saddam turn around and punish the Shias for their act of rebellion, which they had earlier instigated.

The 'second coming' of Saddam was the cruellest moment for the Shias of Iraq. Saddam crushed the religious leadership and top Shia politicians who had to flee to Iran and become dependent on Tehran's largesse. This affected the legacy of Grand Ayatollah al-Khoei who had refused to accept the concept of *velayat-e faqih* of Ayatollah Khomeini and weakened the autonomous status of the

Iraqi Shia. Ajami notes that President Bush senior did not go for regime-change in Iraq in 1991 because that would have Lebanonised Iraq and tilted the sects into fighting and killing each other. Chairman of the Joint Chiefs of Staff Colin Powell and Secretary of State James Baker seemed quite sure about what they had done by not removing Saddam from power:

> The spectre of Lebanonisation of Iraq stayed America's hand. The Bush administration did not trust its knowledge of Iraq and its distant ways and sects. America was haunted by the memory of Lebanon—the sects warring on the deadly fault-lines—and was convinced that the Shia of Iraq were destined to fall under Iran's sway. The Shia were the majority of Iraq's population, the Shia faith having spread in the nineteenth century because the nomadic tribes of Iraq had taken to it when they settled near the shrine towns of Najaf and Karbala in search of water for their agricultural work. There had been no racial divide, no clear-cut distinctions between the Sunnis and Shias of Iraq. All this was unknown to those who had waged the war against Iraq. America had seen the terrible harvest of aggrieved Shiism in Tehran and Beirut. No one wanted a replay of the past. Hard as the Shia leaders of Iraq would insist that they had no 'sister republic' of the Iranian theocracy in mind, they could get no hearing for their case.[32]

As Ajami seemed to lay the foundation of a 'neo-con' interpretation of what happened in 1991, plans for invading Iraq in 2003 were afoot. This time the Shia got what they wanted; but the experience of 1991 had flecked their perception of the United States with scepticism. They gravitated to religious leadership because that is what they had during long years of marginalisation and persecution. Strangely, the clergy guided them realistically albeit there were extremists like Muqtada al-Sadr who began to clamour for an end to American occupation soon after it became apparent that the Americans had little grasp of what it meant to restore the civic amenities destroyed by the war and what the US troops would be up against when the insurgency started. The Shia clergy, while representing the Shia community, got divided into three factions. The first faction was of the quietist grand ayatollahs of Najaf— Mohammad Ishaq al-Fayyad, Bashir Hussain al-Najafi al-Pakistani,

Said al-Hakim—led by Ayatollah Sistani, that kept alive the legacy of Grand Ayatollah al-Khoei and spread it through their representatives in all parts of Iraq and among the moderate exiles abroad. Khoei's son, Majid al-Khoei, returned to Najaf from London in 2003 only to be murdered by the supporters of Muqtada al-Sadr.

Young Muqtada al-Sadr was the extremist who ruled the riff-raff of the Shia slum dwellers in Sadr City, Baghdad. Other slums in Kirkuk and Basra too had his supporters and although Muqtada had failed to pass the seminary, he knew how to control his following, relying mainly on the welfare network left behind by his great father. He was violent in his actions but was weak in religion and therefore sought advice from Ayatollah Kadhim al-Husseini al-Haeri at Qum, but he too distanced himself after seeing Muqtada's tendency towards violence. Strangely, Muqtada became more relevant to Iraq as time passed and violence became common. Insurrection played right into his hands and everyone from Ahmed Chalabi to Sistani wanted to either use him or to have him around in case the Sunnis increased their pressure. He mixed nationalism with Islam and threw his organised youths named, Mahdi Army into the fray in 2004, asking the Americans to quit while confronting the Sunnis and other objectors from among the Shia, from such cities where he had established his power as Baghdad, Basra, and Karbala. The last-named city provided big income to him from the fee collected from pilgrims.

The third clerical outfit is associated with Abdul Aziz al-Hakim and his Iran-backed SCIRI and militia Badr Brigade. He and his militia stood between the moderation of Sistani and the extremism of Muqtada. During the December 2005 elections, Muqtada joined the other two factions of the Shia clerics to sit atop the biggest bloc of members in the Iraqi government. He was readily accepted by the other two because he had fire power and could do violence in return for the Sunni violence steadily coming from the old elements of the Baath and Saddam's disbanded army.

THE GRAND AYATOLLAHS OF NAJAF

Grand Ayatollah Ali al-Hussaini Sistani (b.1930) emerged as the highest cleric of Iraq because he inherited the mantle of the late Grand Ayatollah al-Khoei at the world centre of Shiism at Najaf. He is Iranian-born and hails from Mashhad with no connections to Qum, but has a large following in Iran because of the influence of his moderate-quietist master, Al Khoei, also an Iranian.[33] Sistani's strength lay in his great learning in Shia theology and his ability to stay clear of Iranian politics, especially when taking sides had become important. He stayed clear of the quarrel which took place between the Lebanese Shia and Tehran—over Musa al-Sadr's militia, Amal—and also remained silent over the split that happened in Iran between Grand Ayatollah Montezari and Ayatollah Khomeini over the doctrine of *velayat-e faqih* and revolutionary violence. His status in the Shia world can be judged from his ranking among the *marja's* (persons worthy of following) in the world. Out of all the living ayatollahs, Sistani has the largest global following, the largest in being in Iraq, followed by Iran. In Karbala, the authority belongs to Mohammad Taqi Mudarassi; in Lebanon, to Mohammad Hussain Fadlallah; at Qum, to Mirza Javad Tabrizi, Taqi Behjat and Hussain Ali Montezari. The ideologically oriented Shia follow the Spiritual Guide, Ali Khamenei, in Tehran.[34] But in deference to the sheer power of Qum and the increasing insecurity at Najaf, Sistani 'chose Qum as the headquarters for his internet operations sistani. org'.[35] So close is the Lebanese Shia thinking to the moderates of the Sistani school that Hezbollah's spiritual guide, Grand Ayatollah Fadlallah, originally from Najaf, seriously thought of moving to Najaf but was thwarted by Iraq's insecurity.

In 2003, the Grand Ayatollah Bashir Hussain al-Najafi was targeted by Saddam's *fedayeen* terrorists, but the grenade thrown at him only seriously wounded him. In Pakistan, very few outside of the Shia clerical hierarchy know about the only grand ayatollah produced by Pakistan. There are five grand ayatollahs living today and four of them are in Najaf, Iraq, headed by Sistani. Out of these four, only one is Iraqi-born, the others being from Iran, Pakistan and Afghanistan. (Grand Ayatollah Fayyad or Fayyaz is most probably a Hazara.) Ayatollah al-Uzma Sheikh Bashir Hussain Najafi, as described on his personal website, was born in 1942 in Jullundhar, India, and moved with his family to Pakistan in 1947 and memorised the Quran while studying Islam in Lahore. He moved to Najaf for higher studies and in his 40 year career in Iraq has never visited Pakistan. He registered in the *hawza* (complex of seminaries) of Najaf headed by Ayatollah al-Uzma al-Seyyid Mohsin al-Hakim. He was counted among the bright students of Ayatollah al-Khoei and Ayatollah Seyyid Mohammad Al-Rohani. After three years, Najafi was already teaching other students and was accepted as the first teacher from South Asia. Under Ayatollah al-Uzma al-Khoei he started teaching the highest course of the seminary in 1974. Among his students were some Shia leaders who became famous in Pakistan: Syed Sajid Ali Naqvi, late Syed Ariful Hussain Al-Hussaini, late Syed Ijaz Kazmi and Maulana Syed Nabi Hassan, etc. Among other pupils he counts the family of the famous al-Hakim clerics of Iraq, and the family of the 'hanging judge' Ayatollah Khalkhali of Iran.

The Najaf school never accepted the doctrine of *velayat-e faqih* propounded by Imam Khomeini after coming to power. Under this doctrine, about which he began thinking in 1971 during the celebration of the pre-Islamic identity of Iran by the Shah, the Shia jurist had to rule the state instead of just issuing opinion. The doctrine posited that the leading cleric could have something of the divine spark that illuminated the Imams. This controversially meant that now the chief jurist could share in the *ismet* (infallibility) of the Prophet and the Imams.[36] During Imam Khomeini's stay in Najaf, where he went in 1965, Pakistan's Shia cleric from Parachinar, Ariful Hussaini, at that time a pupil of now-Grand Ayatollah Bashir Hussain, came under his influence and became his companion. It is through Ariful Hussaini that the Shia of the region of Kurram Agency, down to the settled district of Kohat in the NWFP, began going to Qum and manifesting signs of following the Khomeini doctrine.

It was said that after Grand Ayatollah Sistani, Bashir al-Najafi would take his place at the top of the Najaf hierarchy, but as far as the administration of the seminary complex of Najaf was concerned, he was the heir to the legacy of al-Khoei who personally gave him charge of it. The seminary was shut for six months after Khoei's death but was revived by Najafi with his personal resources. It was destroyed again by Saddam in 1991 but Najafi was able to rebuild dozens of seminaries and hostels and resume studies there. The average supply of electricity in 2006 was for about eight hours a day. He bought six large power generators to provide electricity to the seminaries and 2,500 houses in the neighbourhood. Some knowledgeable bloggers, one among whom is said to be a well-known British journalist writing under a pseudonym, believe that Najafi is more anti-American than Sistani. His website doesn't mention Sistani, which may be significant. If the 'Najaf four' are killed by terrorists, the leadership of Najaf will pass to the 'fifth' Grand Ayatollah Kadhim Haeri in exile in Qum in Iran, who has broken with the Najaf tradition of Khoei and subscribes to Khomeini's revolutionary creed.

It is not known whether the three 'foreigner' Grand Ayatollahs (Sistani, Najafi, Fayyad) have been naturalised as Iraqis or whether they are still aliens with passports and visas which have to be renewed. Some concern was raised about this when Sistani did not vote in the 2005 general election. One blogger reported that they had to get their visas renewed regularly through a local guarantor. He also reported that in the 1990s, it was Muqtada al-Sadr who became their guarantors and wrote the required letter of recommendation for them, and that, once, to assert his authority vis-à-vis the Najaf trio, he did not issue the letter and the government had to renew the visas without a guarantor. Another well-known blogger says, quoting Iraqi newspaper *Al Zaman*: 'The provincial council of Najaf, now dominated by the Supreme Council for Islamic Revolution in Iraq (SCIRI), requested that the first act of the Iraqi parliament once it is seated on March 16 be to grant Iraqi citizenship to Grand Ayatollah Ali Sistani. Sistani's family immigrated to Iraq from Iran and settled in Najaf about a century ago, the paper claims, but could never acquire citizenship. The vice-chairman of the Najaf body, Shaikh Khalid al-Numani, requested that the parliament also give citizenship to Bashir al-Najafi (a Pakistani) and Ishaq Fayyad (an Afghan)'.[37]

NAJAF AND THE SHIA OF AWADH

The India-born 'Pakistani' Grand Ayatollah of Najaf, Bashir Hussain, belongs to the tradition that links South Asia to the Shiism of Iraq. It is quite possible that his handling of the administration of the mausoleums and the seminary complex of the city of Najaf is an extension of the past that shows India deeply involved in the consolidation of the Shia faith in Iraq. The faith itself has a pattern of 'transference' which is quite interesting. The Safavid conversion of Iran to Shiism at the beginning of the seventeenth century was owed to the Shia jurists who were brought in from Lebanon, the surviving cradle of the faith. The conversion of Iraqi Arabs was owed, among other factors, to the 'bequests' that came from Awadh[38] (Oudh) in India, first rescuing a waterless and desiccated Najaf from death, through the construction of Hindiya Canal from the Euphrates, then through permanent stipends to the Shia jurists of the city.

Najaf is where the first Shia Imam Ali ibn Abi Talib lies buried. Karbala is where his son the third Imam Husayn fought his battle with the Umayyad caliph and achieved martyrdom. Both cities were visited by the Shia pilgrims of Iran and India. A large number of Iranians and Indians were buried in Najaf and other shrine cities. Iraq remained Arab and Sunni but there were interregnums when it was ruled by Shia rulers like the Buyids (945–1055) who defended the Shia Imams and looked after the shrines of Najaf, Karbala, Kufa, Hilla, Samarra, Kazimayn, etc. After Iraq fell to the Sunni Ottomans in 1533, these shrines were simply tolerated as places visited by the Shia of Iran and India. The conversion of the Sunni Arab tribes to the Shiism of Iraq is dated from the eighteenth century, but more significantly from the nineteenth century. The dominance of the faith grew through the twentieth century too and in 1932 the Shia were recorded by the census to be 56 per cent of the population of Iraq.[39]

Najaf and Karbala would have remained desert marketplaces visited by the nomadic Sunni Arab tribes during spring had it not been for the construction of the Husayniyah Canal by the Ottomans that revived Karbala. But it was the Hindiya Canal that was to uplift the two cities and bestow on them the greatness they acquired in later times, and also led to the settlement of the Arab desert tribes and to their conversion. In the late 1780s, the chief minister of Awadh in India, Hasan Raza Khan, made a contribution of Rs 500,000 towards the construction of the canal, completed in 1803, that brought water to Najaf. So big was the diversion of the water from the Euphrates that the river changed course. The canal became a virtual river and transformed the arid zone between the cities of Najaf and Karbala into fertile land that attracted the Sunni Arab tribes to settle there and take to farming.

The Shia kingdom of Awadh (1720–1856) gave more than a million rupees annually from its treasury for the upkeep of the Shia shrines in Iraq. The money went to the Iranian Shia jurists settled around these shrines. Yet the most significant contribution emanated from a loan the Awadhi king Ghaziuddin Hayder extended to the governor-general of the East India Company during the Company's war with Burma.[40] The loan was never repaid but the interest on it was paid regularly according to the will of the king; and the payments continued after the British annexed Awadh in 1856. According to the will, the interest had to be paid to the four wives of the king, but after their demise it was to go in part—and in some cases, full—to the Shia of Najaf and Karbala, through the Iranian jurists there, also targeting the 'pauper' Indian Shias—getting one-third of the bequest—who had made their homes in the two cities. The fund was called the Awadh Bequest— amounting to nearly 200,000 rupees when 10 rupees were equal to a British pound—and was handled by the British Indian consulate in Iraq, at times with an intent to extend the influence of the Raj in Iran.

Litvak reports an interesting change in the disposition of the Bequest in 1867 on the request of Nawab Iqbal al-Dawla, the grandson of Nawab Saadat Ali Khan of Awadh, who lived in Kazimayn.[41] He accused the Iranian jurists of not using the bequest honestly and pleaded for the 'pauper' Indian and Kashmiri population living in Najaf. He was able to change the distribution pattern of the bequest and henceforth administered the 'sub-bequest' whose beneficiaries also included the pauperised descendants of the Awadh rulers now living in Najaf. It was only after the initiation of this bequest that more Indian 'paupers' were attracted to the holy Shia cities like Karbala where there were no Indians to begin with.[42]

Many factors persuaded the Arabs to embrace Shiism in the nineteenth century. The one big factor was the Corpse Traffic (*naql al-janaez*) that accounted for nearly 20,000 bodies of Shias from Iran and India for the purpose of burial at the shrines. The practice was old and had stemmed from the hadith of the sixth Imam Jafar Sadiq that 'being next to Ali a day is more favourable than seven hundred years of worship'.[43] The coming of the corpses had its own economics that attracted a lot of commerce to the city of Najaf. The fertility of the land around Najaf and Karbala attracted the desert Arabs to agriculture, while the Ottoman bureaucracy encouraged them to own land so that tax could be collected from them. The well-endowed Iranian Shia jurists, threatened by repeated raids from the Wahhabis of Arabia against the Shrines of Najaf and Karbala, began to proselytise intensively among the Arab tribes till most of them converted.

ELECTIONS UNDER THE NEW CONSTITUTION 2006

Sistani convinced the Iraqi Shias into agreeing that Iraq should not become a theocracy like Iran. He joined the various Shia formations together and got them to vote as a united front in the January 2005 elections, which were meant to form a transitional parliament and a transitional government to oversee the framing of a constitution for Iraq. The polls anticipated a political system based on proportional representation similar to the Lebanese model and not the Iranian one. The Shia grouping won the largest number of seats in the constituent assembly but the Sunnis by and large boycotted the election. Then in January 2006, elections were held under the new constitution. A month after the Iraqis voted to elect their first permanent parliament since Saddam Hussein's capture nearly three years earlier, the country's independent electoral commission finally announced the results. As expected, the Shia-led United Iraqi Alliance (UIA), which dominated the previous year-long transitional government, easily won, taking 128 out of 275 seats, with 41 per cent of the votes cast, down only slightly from its near-majority in January 2005. A Kurdish alliance of two main parties took 53 seats and 22 per cent of the vote, also down a bit from the previous January's total. Finally, the two main Sunni-led coalitions took 55 seats and 19 per cent of the vote between them, a big gain on the 17 seats the country's former ruling minority won a year earlier, when most Sunni Arabs had abstained.[44]

The way the confessional communities reacted to the constitution indicates some trends of concern. The constitution is federal and promises enough devolution for the Shias and the Kurds to start aiming at carving out their separate states ultimately based on ethnic cleansing. The Kurds want to make an independent state out of the three northern provinces while the Shia want the nine southern provinces to belong to them. Both groupings have large oil resources on the sharing of which the constitution shows remarkable ambivalence. Both groupings are interpenetrated with other confessional and ethnic populations. The Iraq Study Group Report put it succinctly:

> The Iraqi Constitution, which created a largely autonomous Kurdistan region, allows other such regions to be established later, perhaps including a 'Shiastan' comprising nine southern provinces. This highly decentralised structure is favoured by the Kurds and many Shia (particularly supporters of Abdul Aziz al-Hakim), but it is anathema to Sunnis. First, Sunni Arabs are generally Iraqi nationalists, albeit

within the context of an Iraq they believe they should govern. Second, because Iraq's energy resources are in the Kurdish and Shia regions, there is no economically feasible 'Sunni region'. Particularly contentious is a provision in the constitution that shares revenues nationally from current oil reserves, while allowing revenues from reserves discovered in the future to go to the regions. The Sunnis did not actively participate in the constitution-drafting process, and acceded to entering the government only on the condition that the constitution be amended. In September, the parliament agreed to initiate a constitutional review commission slated to complete its work within one year; it delayed considering the question of forming a federalized region in southern Iraq for eighteen months...Iraq's leaders often claim that they do not want a division of the country, but we found that key Shia and Kurdish leaders have little commitment to national reconciliation. One prominent Shia leader told us pointedly that the current government has the support of 80 per cent of the population, notably excluding Sunni Arabs. Kurds have fought for independence for decades, and when our Study Group visited Iraq, the leader of the Kurdish region ordered the lowering of Iraqi flags and the raising of Kurdish flags. One senior American general commented that the Iraqis 'still do not know what kind of country they want to have'. Yet many of Iraq's most powerful and well-positioned leaders are not working toward a united Iraq.[45]

If the sectarian-ethnic fallout of the American withdrawal cannot be controlled and channelled, the Shia majority may become more assertive politically, overshadowing the apolitical and mostly 'foreign' priestly leadership of the grand ayatollahs. At the time of writing, the non-Iraqi 'trio' is already dependent on the politicised religious leaders like Aziz al-Hakim of SCIRI and Muqtada al-Sadr of the Mahdi Army. The field will thus be open to Iran to benefit from the decline of the anti-Khomeini 'foreign trio' and the rise of the militias more willing to engage Iran politically. Both would require financial and military support in the early phase, which will make them more dependent on Tehran. It is quite clear that neither Bashir al-Najafi nor Ishaq Fayyad is likely to succeed Sistani whose health has not been good since 2004. The 'fifth' Najafi grand ayatollah is located in Qum and might be chosen on a political basis. Kadhim Haeri has broken from the Khoei tradition of Najaf and embraced the Khomeinist interpretation of Shiism.

THE SHIA OF LEBANON

Lebanon has a population of 3.8 million of whom 95 per cent are Arabs, 59 per cent of whom are Muslim and 39 per cent Christian. From among the 17 sects of different religions who live there, four are prominent: Shia, Sunni, Maronite, and the Druze. Lebanon was once the mountainous part of the province of Damascus and was settled for the Shias in the mid-seventh century by a Companion of the Prophet, Abu Zarr (Dharr) Ghaffari whom Caliph Usman had exiled to Syria. The governor of Syria, Muawiyya, was displeased with his way of presenting the legitimacy of the caliphate and expelled him to Lebanon. Abu Zarr did not limit himself to the mountains but went to what is today south Lebanon and established the Shia community of Jabal Amil. The Shia of Lebanon call themselves the children of Abu Zarr.[46] Early Shia rulers in the region caused an expansion of the faith: Hamdanids in North Syria and Iraq from 906 to 1004, the Fatimids in Egypt between 969 and 1171, and the Buyids who ruled Iraq from 945 to 1055. In Lebanon, the Shia became concentrated in four areas: Jabal Amil in the south, Bekaa Valley and Baalbek in the northeast, Kisrawan in the northwest and the Maronite districts in the north.

Shia expansion in Lebanon stopped in the thirteenth century when the great Sunni jurist Ibn Taymiyya got the Mamluks to attack the Shia in the mountainous region of Kisrawan north of Beirut, in 1291. After three expeditions against them, the Shia went into concealment throughout the fourteenth century and began living as Sunnis with Shafi'i orientation. Later the Druze dominated the region and converted it into their stronghold. In the eighteenth century, the Jabal Amil community in the south also went into decline because an Ottoman governor marched on them and punished them. This period led to the formation of a defeated mentality among the Shia and a fondness for certain 'golden eras' of their faith before the attacks took place. At the turn of the nineteenth century the Shia were concentrated only in the Bekaa Valley and Jabal Amil, the first looking towards and economically dependent on Syria because of its proximity; the second, as part of Sidon province, looked towards Palestine and the Mediterranean coast. The south became more free in observing the *ashura* and other markers of Shiism but in the north the restraint and concealment endured longer. It is from Jabal Amil that Safavid Iran borrowed the Shia preachers to establish Shiism there in 1501. Migrating from these two points, the Shia were to form the largest community in Beirut in the twentieth century, as if preparing the city for the coming assertion of the Amal and Hezbollah militias.

After the First World War and the collapse of the Ottoman Empire, the territory of what is now Lebanon was given to France under the Mandate of the League of Nations. When the French arrived in Lebanon in 1918 they were greeted by the Christians who formed the largest community, about 30 per cent of the population, followed by Sunnis at 22 per cent and the Shia at 20 per cent. The Sunnis did not like the idea of separating Lebanon from Syria and boycotted the new colonial masters, the French, while the Shia did not mind being independent from Syria. In the period following the boycott, the Christians managed to occupy most of the important jobs in the administration, the Shia being less educated and skilled. The Sunni community identified itself with the Arab community of Syria while the Shia could not say that Arab nationalism could include them, as they lacked an Arab patron state. Thus, Lebanon became the fulcrum of three finely balanced communities between Arab nationalism and Lebanonism, that is, the Maronite view of Lebanon as an ancient Mediterranean-Phoenician entity with a modern Christian particularism. Its independence from Syria was made possible by the Shia community's support, from 1918 and 1936, which went with the Maronite Christians in order to safeguard their own socio-religious environment. They were rewarded with the constitutional recognition of a separate confessional entity in 1926. When the confessional compact about power-sharing finally came in 1943, it designated three leading separate communities as co-sharers of power, with the Maronites on top. As one community, the Muslims obviously outnumbered them but as two sects treated as separate religions they had to accept lesser rights.

There was a difference of status between the Shia of the Bekaa Valley and Jabal Amil, the latter being more backward, but supported economically by remittances from expatriate Shia in West Africa. In 1969, when the Jabal Amil notables set up the Higher Islamic Shia Council, they found no great religious teachers of any stature and decided to get the Iranian-born Musa al-Sadr to head the Council. In the 1930s the Sunnis decided to enter the national politics they had boycotted earlier. This immediately changed the confessional scene in the country. The Maronites found it easier to align themselves with the urbanised Sunnis because of their contacts with the larger Arab world outside than the rural Shia already marginalised in two locations. The Sunni–Maronite alliance produced what is called the National Pact:

> In 1943 it was agreed that the Maronites would keep the presidency of the republic, while the prime minister would become the preserve of the Sunnis. After 1947 the speakership of the parliament came to be reserved for the Shia. Other government and public positions were distributed proportionally among the various Lebanese communities. The representation of Christians and Muslims in parliament was fixed at a ratio of six to five. The architects of the National Pact left no record of the manner in which they negotiated their deal.[47]

The 'confessionalism' of Lebanon has been copied in Iraq in the 2005 Iraqi elections, but back in Iran the new Shia assertion shows dissatisfaction with this mode of representation. As Atash remarks:

> Whereas, in 1932, the Maronites constituted the largest sect in Lebanon, they later lost this position to the Shia who, by turn of the twenty-first century, constituted 40 per cent of the population. Demography had caught up with the Maronites and continues to work for the benefit of the Shia.[48]

The dominant Shia are led by Hezbollah which superseded Amal, the most effective Shia organisation in the 1980s. Amal was a secular organisation although created by Ayatollah Musa al-Sadr with contributions made by the Shia population without any help from Iran. There was rapid growth of qualified Shia clerics in Lebanon in this period and the population began to shift their loyalties from politicians to religious leaders. Mohammad Hussein Fadlallah, who had come to Beirut from Najaf in 1966, remained aloof from Musa al-Sadr and politicised the Shiism of Lebanon, thus opening the door for the entry into politics of Hezbollah. The new party was blessed by Imam Khomeini. It was assisted from the start by Iran through funding. Soon it fell foul of Amal and there was a contest for power between the two which was won by a more overtly religious Hezbollah led by an aggressive Hasan Nasrallah since 1992. A truce was mediated between the two Shia entities by Iran and Syria in 1990. That year the Arab League endorsed the paramountcy of Syria in Lebanon in the Taif Accord which was accepted by the Lebanese parliament along with the proviso that the Lebanese parliament would be proportionally divided between Muslims and Christians on the 50:50 formula instead of the old one of 6:5. The Sunni-dominated Arab League apparently ignored the growing 'cooperation' between Syria and Iran during the Lebanese civil war from 1975 to 1990. Iran's success in Lebanon was marked by the transformation of Hezbollah from an armed movement to an armed party. Its financial strength and its armoury, financed by Iran, gave it an edge against other Lebanese parties. In 1992, it won 8 of the 118 parliamentary seats and got together with other affiliates to enjoy the largest bloc in the house. In the 2005 election, following the withdrawal of Syrian troops from Lebanon, it increased its seats to 14, making it a formidable force in the country.

Iran has moved steadily in Lebanon in defence of the Shia and has retained Syria as its steadfast ally to keep its links with Lebanon secure. It was Iranian clerics and Revolutionary Guards commanders who organised Hezbollah in the 1980s with funds provided by

Tehran. It controlled its real fountainhead of power by supplying it with weapons.

THE ZAIDI SHIA OF YEMEN

The Zaidi Shia of Yemen are said to be 20 and 45 per cent of the Yemeni population which also contains 2.5 per cent Jafari and Ismaili Shias. One million are believed to be living in Saudi Arabia too. Yemen has a rather large population by regional standards: 21.5 million. Some accounts describe Yemen as a Sunni-majority country with a total population of 19 million. The Zaidis, who form a rather large minority, believe in the fifth Shia Imam, Zayd (Zaid) bin Ali, son of the fourth Imam Zayn al-Abedin. The Twelver Shia believe in Imam Baqir, a brother of Zayd, who the Zaidis think deserved to be the next Imam because he fought the Umayyad rulers, while Baqir did not. Iran under Imam Khomeini decided to recognise the three branches of Shiism considered breakaway heresies by the mainstream Shia in the past: Ismailis, Alawites and Zaidis. The first Zaidi state was established in northern Iran in AD 864; it lasted until the death of its leader at the hand of the Samanids in AD 928. Forty years later the state was revived in Gilan (north-western Iran) and survived under Hasanid leaders until 1126.

The Zaidi Imamate in the lineage of Imam Hasan, the second Imam, was established in Yemen in 893, which was abolished by the revolution of 1962. Yemen, thereafter, went through a hostile ideological bifurcation but reunited in 1988. The Zaidi rebellion began in 2004 in the northeastern province of Saada under the leadership of Hussein al-Houthi. The Yemeni government accuses the Iranian government of directing and financing the insurgency, and the fighting is going on at the time of writing. The United States supports the Yemeni government to ensure cooperation against Al Qaeda which had significant sleeper-cells in the country. Yemen is the ancestral home of Osama bin Laden and is particularly vulnerable to terrorist attacks. The bombing attacks that targeted

US- and Canadian-owned oil facilities in the eastern provinces of Marib and Hadramaut in 2006, the October 2000 bombing of the ship USS Cole in Aden, and the October 2002 bombing of the French super-tanker Limberg, have cost the Yemeni government millions of dollars as insurance premiums for ship owners have soared, causing many of them to refuse to dock at Yemen's ports.[49] Both sides, Sunni and Shia, are prone to Iranian and Al Qaeda slogans of anti-American and anti-Israeli provocation, leaving the Yemeni government in a typical Middle Eastern and Muslim situation: sectarianism that is internecine while agreeing on an anti-American direction.

KUWAIT, BAHRAIN, DUBAI, AND AZERBAIJAN

Kuwait has a population of 2.5 million out of which only 45 per cent are Kuwaiti Arabs. There are 35 per cent Arabs of other origins, 9 per cent South Asians and 4 per cent Iranians. It has the largest proportion of the Shia—35 per cent—in the Gulf Arab states after Bahrain, but presents a contrast to the oppressive manner in which Saudi Arabia and Bahrain have tackled their Shia populations. The Shia of Kuwait, mostly migrants from Saudi Arabia, Bahrain and Iran, are the most integrated population living among Sunni Arabs, and this is owed to the ruling Al-Sabah family. There is evidence that the increasingly conservative merchant class of the Sunni Kuwaitis did not always agree with Al-Sabah's policy, which they saw as using the Shia to water down the Sunni strength in the country. There is evidence too that funds were made available from Kuwait's private sector to terrorists willing to attack the Shia in Pakistan and Iran. But the Al-Sabah policy has succeeded so well that Kuwait's Shia policy might become a model to emulate in the days to come for the other Sunni states in the region.

Proof of the soundness of this policy came when Saddam Hussein invaded Kuwait in 1990 to see that the Shia were the backbone of the Kuwaiti resistance to the Iraqi occupation and refused to give up against impossible odds while the Al-Sabah family fled to Saudi Arabia. When the ruler Jabir Al-Sabah returned to Kuwait after the Gulf War, the Shia reaffirmed their allegiance to him, viewing him as a symbol of national unity. Apart from this display of Kuwaiti nationalism under invasion, there is the factor of the tolerant policy towards the Shia during the twentieth century, although there was occasional discrimination. The Shia community has played an important role in the economy; its members are effective in parliament and hold key police and army posts. One can say that the Shia of Kuwait feel proud of being Kuwaitis in contrast to the Shia of Saudi Arabia—where they demand civic rights in return for loyalty—and Bahrain. That this is due to the 'undemocratic' intervention of the ruling *emir* is quite evident from the occasional angry reaction from the Kuwaiti Sunni clergy and an increasingly conservative population. It is even more striking when one recalls that the *emir* was nearly killed in 1985 when a Shia suicide-bomber attacked his car.

Fouad Ajami's experience in Kuwait illustrates how the Kuwaitis still resent the official policy of tolerance. Ajami's 1985 visit to Kuwait as a Shia intellectual from southern Lebanon had aroused hostility among the local intellectuals who saw his Shia faith in a negative light. The occasion was a conference in which Ajami was to read a report approving the teaching of political science in English in Kuwait. One Kuwaiti writer named Baghdadi levelled severe criticism on the organisers for having invited a *shu'ubi*:

> With this label Baghdadi went to the heart of the matter. The Shu'ubiyya movement had been a political-literary revolt by non-Arab (mostly Persian) converts to Islam in the early centuries following the rise of Islam.... The issue was rendered more transparent by the last names of the protagonists: Baghdadi from the city of Baghdad; Ajami from the country of Ajam, Persia.[50]

In 1983, there was suicide bombing of the American embassy in Kuwait while other places like the country's big oil refinery were also targeted but not harmed. The terrorists caught in connection with these actions had turned out to be Shia. In 1981, out of the seventy-two Shia men arrested in Bahrain for trying to blow up important sites there were some Kuwaiti nationals too. Some Shia reaction was a response to the 'tightening' of the identity of the Sunni Arabs in Kuwait. Opposed to the *emir's* enlightenment, Kuwaiti parliament and Kuwaiti society in general favoured a hard Islamic identity. At the university, young men and women wanted to adopt traditional dresses including women appearing in *hijab*, while the state encouraged a modern dress form. It was the intensifying religious reaction of the Kuwaiti merchant class that produced the two half-Pakistanis with Kuwaiti blood, Khalid Sheikh Mohammad and Ramzi Yusuf, who first took on Iran and indulged in sectarian violence before joining Al Qaeda in Pakistan. Ramzi Yusuf, part of the 'wall' the Gulf conservatives were building around Iran, caused a bomb blast in the holy shrine of Mashhad, Iran, that killed 24 in 1994.[51] Later on, Khalid Sheikh Mohammad was able to collect a lot of funds from the rich Kuwaiti merchants for Al Qaeda and became the thinker behind the destruction of the Trade Center in New York and the attack on the Pentagon in Washington on 9 September 2001.

Bahrain has a population of 700,000 of which 80 per cent are Shia. They are *Akhbari* and therefore different from the *Usuli* population of neighbour Iran. The Shah of Iran claimed Bahrain but in a referendum in 1970 the population of Bahrain chose not to join Iran, perhaps because of their *Akhbari* origin in addition to abhorrence of the Shah's good relations with the Sunni Gulf states and the United States. The Shia of Bahrain have mostly migrated out of Al-Hasa and Qatif oases of the eastern province of Saudi Arabia under threat from the zealots of Wahhabism. The ruling Al-Khalifa clan have also come from central Saudi Arabia and conquered Bahrain in 1783 from their base in Qatar where they had moved from Arabia earlier. Bahrain was a possession of Safavid Iran from 1602 onwards and was ruled by the Arab clans living in Southern Iran. The Khalifas paid tribute to Iran in the beginning and did not deny Iran's ownership of Bahrain, but were invaded by their neighbours frequently. For instance, Oman attacked and occupied the islands in 1800, and after that Bahrain had to submit to the rising Al Saud. But Bahrain's security was finally provided by the British who concluded treaties with the Khalifa rulers in 1892, making Bahrain a protectorate that lasted till 1971.

Bahrain is troubled by the Shia demand for majority rights. The Shia have suffered as second class citizens under Sunni rulers who have actively encouraged Sunni immigration to water down the presence of the Shia, with the result that the Shia mostly inhabit villages while the Sunnis live in cities. According to Nakash, the Shia of Bahrain have nursed the myth of utopian prosperity in the distant past before they were suppressed and deprived by their Sunni rulers.[52] Their sufferings in Al-Hasa and Qatif have been enhanced in Bahrain because of the increasing Saudi influence on the Khalifa rulers. After Bahrain became independent in 1971 and the British left the region, King Faisal of Saudi Arabia reached an agreement with the Shah of Iran over the Saudi 'area of influence' over the Gulf States. In return, Faisal recognised Iran's role as a guardian of the Gulf waters. Eight years later, the revolution in Iran disturbed this arrangement and both Saudi Arabia and Bahrain became concerned over Iran's willingness to help the Shia populations in the Gulf States to agitate for their rights. During the Iraq–Iran war (1980–1988) Bahrain formally accepted Saudi Arabia as its guardian. In 1986, the King Fahd Causeway actually joined the two states territorially. In 1996, when the Bahraini oilfields dried up, Saudi Arabia began to finance its annual budgets till half of the revenue was provided by Saudi Arabia. After the British withdrawal Bahrain was approached by the United States for port facilities for the US Navy, which the Khalifa rulers accepted keenly given their difficult economic position. There are '21 US ships manned by 15,000 sailors and 12 more ships with equipment for ground troops in Bahrain, in addition to 10,000 American troops in other Gulf States'.[53] The base was used against Iran—and was directly responsible for the Iranian 'defeat' in 1988—and then against Iraq in 1991 when Iraq attacked Kuwait. After 9/11 Bahrain was declared a major non-NATO ally by Washington which signed a free trade agreement with it in 2004.

Bahrain's economic success in recent years has been at the cost of the Shia majority. The Shia began as divers in the pearl industry and as tillers of the soil in the villages, but as the Khalifa clan expanded, its members increasingly sought land in the Shia villages, further squeezing them. Bahrain also moved to develop its services sector in the economy after running out of oil. For this it had to import a large number of workers from India and other neighbouring countries. The ratio of foreigners to local population was 20 per cent in 1935 but reached 65 per cent in 2002 when the banking sector boomed. Skilled foreign workers have occupied jobs that would have gone to the local population, which now has an unemployment rate of 15 per cent generally, but 30 per cent for the Shia. In 1973, the rulers granted the state a constitution under which a parliament came into being with Shia presence in it, but the *emir* dissolved it in 1975 when the demands of the Shia for political rights became too loud for neighbouring Saudi Arabia to tolerate. Thus, hardly a decade after the Shia of Bahrain had rejected Iran in a referendum they welcomed the revolution of Imam Khomeini with great enthusiasm. In 1981, the first attempt by the 'Islamic Front' of Bahrain was foiled, and the men caught in this connection turned out to be a mix of Iraqi, Kuwaiti and Bahraini Shia youths trained in Iran. The 1980s were the darkest period of Shia struggle. This was also the period in which the local Shia clerics finally rejected the Iranian brand of Shiism and evolved their own style of struggle promoted by the top Bahraini cleric Abdul Amir al-Jamri who adopted the Gandhian mode of disobedience to get his demands accepted.

In 1994, Bahrain saw a one-year long agitation by the Shia for representation but they were forcefully crushed. In 1996, their leaders were accused of collaboration with Iran to topple the ruling family and replace it with a government dictated by Iran. A large number of Shias were arrested on the charge of having taken training from the Revolutionary Guards of Iran, a course of action which was tacitly approved by the United States. The Khalifa ruler Sheikh Isa also put off a general election alleging that it would produce a majority which would be pro-Iranian. Meanwhile, fresh Sunni immigrants from Saudi Arabia were being settled in the country. It is only after the death of Sheikh Isa and a cooling down of the Shia passions in 1999 that a reconciliation was finally effected, somewhat on the lines that took place in Saudi Arabia in 1993 under King Fahd. Sheikh Hamad removed some of the disabilities and improved the state's relations with its Shia majority, only to have everything reversed in 2001 after 9/11. The Sunnis have gone under the *Salafist* creed and the Shias have turned to Iran. Now a cartoon of Ayatollah Ali Khamenei published in Bahrain can attract a crowd of youth willing to offer themselves for martyrdom. In May 2004, when Muqtada al-Sadr's militia, the Mahdi Army, was fighting the American troops in Iraq, protesting crowds came out in Bahrain, demanding representation just like the majority Shia of Iraq. Nasr says:

> Bahrain's sectarian troubles will bear directly on the Shia–Sunni relations in the UAE, Kuwait and, most important, Saudi Arabia whose eastern province sits a stone's throw away from the causeway that links Bahrain to the Arabian mainland.[54]

Unlike Kuwait, the Bahraini Shia and the ruling Khalifa family have no history of accommodation and integration. The Shia community has always been poor and the Sunnis have acted as the privileged class. Historian Sugata Bose, in his book on the Indian Ocean, takes note of the traditional enmity between the poor Shia pearl divers of Kuwait and their rather callous Khalifa ruler. After an unsuccessful agitation to get their salaries raised, the Shia divers resorted to a strange show of contempt towards the *emir* and his family: 'While returning from Manama Shaikh Abdullah, brother of Sheikh Hamad, had encountered two boatloads of divers and ordered them to stop. Instead they 'jeered at him and lifting up their clothes shook their *membra virile* at him', which apparently was the highest insult and set Abdullah seething with rage'.[55]

In December 2004, King Abdullah of Jordan warned that a vast stretch of the Middle East from the Mediterranean in the west to the Caspian Sea in the east was coming under the sway of the Shia branch of Islam. He added that this Shia population would take its direction from Tehran. And President Hosni Mubarak of Egypt said that 'most of the Shia are loyal to Iran, not to the countries they are living in'. Martin Walker commented on the two statements by writing:

> If the first battlefield was Iraq, the next would be the oil-endowed regions of the Persian Gulf, southern Iraq and Azerbaijan where Shia happen to live. In this scenario the ayatollahs of Shiite Iran could then secure control of the Iraqi, Saudi, and Caspian oil and gas fields by placing them under their own nuclear arsenal, thus establishing the first Islamic state to achieve great-power status since the collapse of the Ottoman Empire in 1918.[56]

East of the Suez Canal, the Shia seem to dominate, but this has come to the notice of outside observers only now when Iran seems to rise as their champion. Yet out of 1.3 billion Muslims only 150 million are Shia. In Iran, Iraq and Azerbaijan they are the majority population although there may be subtle ethnic and confessional differences among them. One should keep in mind that out of Pakistan's 150 million people a fraction of 15 or 20 per cent makes a Shia population less than the Shia of Iran only. In India too they probably form the same proportion of the 150 million-strong Muslim minority. The total figure for the Shia could therefore be misleading because of the omission of India. Although historically a nursery of the Shia land-holding elite, Bangladesh has very few Shias in its population of 150 million.

Nasr notes that the states of the United Arab Emirates (UAE) have always had Shia minorities who learned to hide their identity more easily because they were involved in commerce and were not the working class as in Saudi Arabia and Bahrain:

> The main market in Doha, Qatar, is called the Irani Bazaar. The trading class in Dubai and Kuwait has always had a large Iranian component. I once shared a ride with a senior official of the UAE. As soon as we were alone in the car, he began speaking to me in fluent Persian. Noting my surprise, he discussed his belief that a healthy majority of the official citizens of Dubai, the UAE's expatriate-heavy economic boomtown, are of Iranian origin. Ethnic Iranians, he added, are disproportionately well represented in the UAE government and business ranks. Fear of Iran meant fear of the Shia, and this led the

Emirates to tie their fortunes to Arab identity in the hope of withstanding Iranian aggrandisement.[57]

The UAE has variously been claimed to have 6 and 16 per cent Shias out of a population of 2.45 million that is 70 per cent expatriate. In Qatar too, the sizeable Shia community has been assimilated over a long period of time for the same reasons. They Arabised themselves under the doctrine of quietism and have engaged in commerce and are accepted because of the free-market nature of the state despite the Wahhabi identity of the Qatar rulers. The UAE remains the most moderate society in the region because of its 'free market' orientation.[58]

Nasr's observation about the Shia presence in the UAE is substantiated by reports about the Iranian business interests in Dubai. The Iranian consulate in Dubai claims that at least 400,000 of the UAE's 4.1 million residents are Iranian and their numbers may have doubled since 2003. Located just 170 kilometres (105 miles) across the Strait of Hormuz, Dubai is frequently labelled a satellite state for Iranian capital. The Dubai Chamber of Commerce and Industry (DCCI) has 8,050 Iranian companies registered with it, ranging from banking to real estate and oil. Dubai's non-oil trade with Iran was worth eight billion dollars last year, a 30 per cent rise since 2004.

We estimate accumulated assets of Iranians in the UAE to be about 300 billion dollars, while trade between the UAE and Iran was about 11 billion dollars in 2006.[59]

Azerbaijan, a country no one discusses under the sectarian rubric, is exclusively Turkic Shia. It was also a member of the 'allies' that participated in the US invasion of Iraq in 2003. It is a former possession of Iran which used to produce the heir apparent to the Iranian throne traditionally inherited by Turk dynasties, the only Iranian one being the Pahlavi which produced just two kings before being overthrown by Imam Khomeini. The Turkic Qizilbash were the early Shias and Azerbaijan was the place of origin, but today the Azeri Shia of Azerbaijan are more sensitive to their ethnic identity than religion because of their life under Soviet rule for seventy years. After independence in August 1991, Azerbaijan thought of aligning itself with Turkey rather than with Iran. It had to seek cultural and linguistic commonalities in the West with Turkey because Iran had not allowed these cultural markers to its own Azeri minority. The assimilation of the Iranian Azeri in the Persian-speaking religious elite is complete with Azeri Supreme Spiritual Guide Khamenei sitting on top of the Shia hierarchy in Tehran. Ethnic Azeris constitute more than 90 per cent of Azerbaijan's 8.5 million population and enjoy a fully grown press in the Turkic Azeri language. This cultural wall has stood between the Shia of Azerbaijan and the Shia of Iran. It should be noted that a similar ethnic divide exists between Arab Shias and Iranian Shias, but the Arab Shia reach out to Iran because of their marginalised and oppressed status among the Sunni Arabs. It is possible that once the Arab Shia attain their rightful place in Iraqi society, they may become more sensitive to the ethnic-linguistic differences that separate them from the Iranian Shia. It is the independent status of the Azeri Shia that has stood in the way of a confessional merger with Iran. Azerbaijan will go on trying to balance its relations with the big regional power in the south by seeking cooperation with secular Turkey and through Turkey with NATO-West.

Azerbaijan began its career as an independent state in 1991 governed by the Azerbaijani Popular Front under the leadership of Abulfazl Elchibey who offended Iran with his extremely pro-Turkey Kemalist policies. He was succeeded by a more balanced Heidar Aliyev in 1993 who then improved the country's relations with Iran. There was no influential religious movement in Azerbaijan and the only Islamist trouble came from the 'imported' Wahhabi activists among the Sunni Lesgin minority. But as the government in Baku failed to achieve fulfilment of policies promised to the people, there was growing unrest among the Azeri Shia too. The seeds of an ultimate Shia religious upsurge are there in the movement headed by one Alikaram Aliyev in the village of Nardaran 20 miles from Baku, where the wife of the seventh Shia Imam Musa Kazim lies buried.[60] There was some protest in

Nardaran in 2002 which was put down. The following year there was a standoff between the government and the religious leader Ilqar Ibrahimoglu whose fiery sermons on Fridays in a Baku mosque persuaded the unemployed youth to call him the Azerbaijani Khomeini. While Baku fears little trouble from Iran it is taking measures to shield against the incursions of the Wahhabi warriors of Al Qaeda in the neighbouring Chechnya and Dagestan of the Russian Republic. Azerbaijan remains a transit corridor for the Sunni warriors making their way to the other states in the Caucasus.

NOTES

1. *The Essential Rumi*, Translated by Coleman Barks with John Moyne, Penguin Books, 1995, p. 278.
2. Gary G. Sick and Lawrence G. Potter, *The Persian Gulf and the Millennium: Essays in Politics, Economy, Security and Religion*, St Martin's Press, 1997, p. 37.
3. Fouad Ajami, *The Dream Palace of the Arabs: A Generation's Odyssey*, Vintage Books, 1998, p. 178.
4. John C. Wilkinson, *Arabia's Frontiers: The Story of Britain's Boundary-Drawing in the Desert*, I.B. Tauris, 1991.
5. Rear Admiral Mahan (1840–1914) was a United States Navy officer, geostrategist, and educator. His ideas on the importance of naval power influenced navies around the world and helped prompt naval build-ups before World War I. Several ships were named USS *Mahan*, including the lead vessel of a class of destroyers.
6. John F. Standish, *Persia and the Gulf: Retrospect and Prospect*, Curzon Press, 1998. Strategic description of the Gulf is from p. 76 in this excellent study. Chapter 4 (p. 117) describes Pax Britannica in the region. Reference to Nadir Shah is on p. 83.
7. Pakistan 'parked' its civilian aircraft in Iran during its wars with India. The feeling of lack of 'depth' vis-à-vis India intensified in the 1990s when Pakistan sought it in Afghanistan, this time to park its nuclear assets.
8. Christopher M. Davidson, *The United Arab Emirates: A Study in Survival*, Lynne Rienner Publishers, 2005, p. 206 and p. 244: 'Until September 11, 2001, many of the strongly anti-Iranian emirates had favoured a 'Sunni axis' comprising the UAE, Saudi Arabia, Pakistan, and the Afghan Taliban, in an effort to curb potential Shia expansion'. The author footnoted that his

information had come from 'personal interviews, undisclosed locations, 2003'.

9. Ray Takeyh, *Hidden Iran: Paradox and Power in the Islamic Republic*, Times Books, 2006, p. 66.

10. Robin Wright, *Sacred Rage: the Wrath of Militant Islam*, Simon & Shuster, 1985 and 2001, p. 160.

11. Vali R. Nasr, 'International Politics, Domestic Imperatives, and Identity Mobilisation: Sectarianism in Pakistan', 1979–1998, *Comparative Politics*, Vol. 32, No. 2, January 2000, p. 178.

12. Yitzhak Nakash, *Reaching for Power: the Shia in the Modern Arab World*, Princeton University Press, 2006, p. 101.

13. John R. Bradley, *Saudi Arabia Exposed: Inside a Kingdom in Crisis*, Palgrave Macmillan, 2005, p. 82.

14. International Crisis Group, 'The Shiite Question in Saudi Arabia', *Middle East Report* 45, 19 September 2005, p. 5 and p. 13

15. Yitzhak Nakash, *Reaching for Power: the Shia in the Modern Arab World*, Princeton University Press, 2006, p. 53.

16. *Usuli* are Twelver Shia Muslims who favour *fatwa*s over hadith when trying to determine what the Sunnah says about any specific topic. They form the overwhelming majority within the Twelver Shia denomination. *Akhbaris* are Twelver Shia Muslims who favour hadith over *fatwa*s when trying to determine what the Sunnah says about any specific topic. Unlike *Usulis*, the *Akhbari* Shia do not follow the *Marjas*, rather they follow the Imams. They are very few in number. Shaykhism is an Islamic religious movement founded by Shaykh Ahmad in the early nineteenth century Persian Empire. It began from a combination of Sufi and Shia doctrines of the 'end time' and the day of resurrection. Today the Shaykhi populations retain a minority following in Iran and Iraq. In the mid eighteenth century many Shaykhis converted to the Babi and Bahai religions, which consider Shaykh Ahmad to be a religious forerunner and predecessor of their own faith.

17. Joseph Mcmillan, 'Saudi Arabia and Iraq: Oil, Religion and an Enduring Rivalry', *United States Institute of Peace*, Special Report, January 2006, p. 9.

18. *Daily Times*, Editorial, 17 April 2006.

19. Strategic Forecasting Inc. 30 Dec 2006 <http://www.stratfor.com.

20. Charles Melville, (ed.), *Safavid Persia*, I.B. Tauris, 1996. The account is summarised from the book.

21. Dr Mohammed Mossadeq (1882–1967) was the democratically elected prime minister of Iran from 1951 to 1953. He was twice appointed to office by Mohammad Reza Pahlavi, the Shah of Iran, and approved by the vote of parliament. Mossadeq was a nationalist and passionately opposed foreign intervention in Iran. He was also the architect of the nationalisation of the Iranian oil industry which was dominated and exploited by the British through the Anglo–Iranian Oil Company (today known as British Petroleum [BP]). He was later removed from power by Mohammad Reza Pahlavi, in a

CIA-orchestrated coup, supported and funded by the British and the US governments.

22. Ali Rahnema, *An Islamic Utopian: A Political Biography of Ali Shariati*, I.B. Tauris, 1998. Shariati came from a family of great religious scholars who favoured reform of the Shia hadith, which set the Shia at odds with the Sunnis. Imam Khomeini represented the orthodox faith of the Shia even though he secretly enjoyed the writings of the mystics disallowed by orthodox Shiism.

23. Baqer Moin, *Khomeini: Life of the Ayatollah*, I.B. Tauris, 1999. The career of Imam Khomeini is summarised from the book.

24. Vali Nasr, *The Shia Revival: how Conflicts within Islam will Shape the Future*, W.W. Norton, 2006, p. 38.

25. Ibid., Vali Nasr, p. 138.

26. Ibid., Vali Nasr, p. 139.

27. John K. Cooley, *Unholy Wars: Afghanistan, America and International Terrorism*, Pluto Press, 1999, p. 101.

28. Vali Nasr, *The Shia Revival: how Conflicts within Islam will Shape the Future*, W.W. Norton, 2006, p. 141.

29. Yitzhak Nakash, *Reaching for Power: the Shia in the Modern Arab World*, Princeton University Press, 2006, p. 30.

30. Francis Fukuyama, *America at the Crossroads: Democracy, Power, and the Neoconservative Legacy*, Yale University Press, 2006, pp. 7–8: '...and there are [in the United States] what Walter Russell Mead labels "Jacksonian" American nationalists, who tend to take a narrow, security-related view of American national interests, distrust multilateralism, and in their more extreme manifestations tend towards nativism and isolationism. The Iraq war was promoted by an alliance of neoconservatives and Jacksonian nationalists, who for different reasons accepted the logic of regime change in Baghdad'.

31. Hugh Kennedy; *The Armies of the Caliphs: Military and Society in Early Islamic State*, Routledge, 2001.

32. Fouad Ajami, *The Dream Palace of the Arabs: A Generation's Odyssey*, Vintage Books, 1998, pp. 181–182.

33. Yitzhak Atash, *Reaching for Power*, Princeton 2006, p. 155. Says Sistani did not vote in the 2005 election probably because he was not registered as an Iraqi national.

34. Vali Nasr, *The Shia Revival*, W.W. Norton, 2006, p. 71.

35. Ibid., p. 218.

36. Daniel Brumberg, *Inventing Khomeini: the Struggle for Reform in Iran*, University of Chicago Press, 2001, p. 82.

37. http://www.juancole.com/>> Juan @ 3/15/2005 06:30 (Blogger Prof Juan Cole teaches at the University of Michigan and makes TV appearances in the US as an expert on Iraq.)

38. Awadh is a region in the centre of the modern Indian state of Uttar Pradesh, which was known as the United Provinces of Oudh and Agra before

independence. The traditional capital of Awadh has been Lucknow, still the capital of the modern State. The modern definition of Awadh geographically includes the districts of Ambedkar Nagar, Bahraich, Balrampur, Barabanki, Faizabad, Gonda, Hardoi, Lakhimpur Kheri, Lucknow, Allahabad, Kaushambi, Pratapgarh, Rai Bareilly, Shravasti, Sitapur, Sultanpur, and Unnao. The region is home to a distinct dialect, Awadhi. Literary Urdu has two competing accents, Dehlavi (represented by Ghalib) and Lakhnavi (represented by Mir).

39. Yitzhak Nakash, *The Shiis of Iraq*, Princeton Paperbacks, 1995, p. 13.
40. Meir Litvak, 'Money, Religion, and Politics: the Oudh Bequest in Najaf and Karbala 1850–1903'. *International Journal of Middle Eastern Studies*, 33, 2001, pp. 1–21. Litvak writes it was Nepal where the East India Company had planned its expedition.
41. The shrines of Musa al-Kazim and Mohammad al-Jawwad, the 7th and 9th Imams, are located in Kazimayn, now a Baghdad suburb.
42. Ibid., Meir Litvak, p. 6.
43. Ibid., Yitzhak Nakash, p. 186.
44. *The Economist*, 26 January 2006.
45. The Iraq Study Group Report: *The Way Forward—A New Approach*, Vintage Books, 2006, p. 18.
46. Jundub ibn Junadah ibn Sakan, better known as Abu Zarr, Abu Zarr al-Ghafari, or Abu Tharr al-Ghefari was an early convert to Islam. When he converted, the Prophet Muhammad (PBUH) gave him a new name, Abdullah. He belonged to the Banu Ghifari, the Ghifar tribe. No date of birth is known. He died in 652 CE, at al-Rabadha, in the desert near Madinah. Abu Zarr is remembered for his strict piety and also his opposition to the caliph Usman ibn Affan. For the Shia, Abu Zarr's fame is synonymous with his loyalty to Ali. He is considered one of the Four Companions, early Muslims whose loyalty to Ali never wavered. Shia believe that he added the phrase 'I witness that Ali is the appointed one by God' to the call to prayer (*adhan*), during Muhammad's (PBUH) lifetime and with his approval. Abu Zarr is said to have died as a result of his persecution, and thus is regarded as a martyr to the Shia cause. Because of his support for Ali, Shia accept hadith (oral traditions) traced to Abu Zarr. Lebanese Shia believe that Abu Zarr was the first to preach Shia Islam in Syria and Lebanon. There are two shrines dedicated to Abu Zarr in Lebanon: one in Sarafand near Sidon, and another in Meiss Al-Jabal in southern Lebanon.
47. Yitzhak Atash, *Reaching for Power*, Princeton, 2006, p. 108.
48. Ibid., p. 112.
49. Mohamed Al-Azaki, *Yemen on the Brink of Sectarian War*, Asia Times Online, 23 May 2007. Al-Azaki is an independent Yemeni journalist and researcher on Islamic militants at the Saba Centre for Political and Strategic Studies based in Sana'a.

50. Fouad Ajami, *The Dream Palace of the Arabs: A Generation's Odyssey*, Vintage Books, 1999, p. 157.

51. Vali Nasr, 'International Politics, Domestic Imperatives, and Identity Mobilisation: Sectarianism in Pakistan, 1979–1998', *Comparative Politics*, Vol. 32, January 2000, p. 178.

52. Yitzhak Nakash, *Reaching for Power*, Princeton 2006, p. 24. He connects the ancestral memory of the Bahraini Shia with the golden age of the Ismaili–Carmathian rule, which was witnessed by the great Ismaili traveler Nasir Khusrau when he visited Al-Hasa in 1051.

53. Fouad Ajami, *The Dream Palace of the Arabs*, Vintage Book, 1999, p. 191.

54. Vali Nasr, *The Shia Revival*, W.W. Norton 2006, p. 236.

55. Sugata Bose, *A Hundred Horizons: The Indian Ocean in the Age of Global Empire*, Harvard University Press, 2006, p. 91.

56. Martin Walker, 'The Revenge of the Shia', *The Wilson Quarterly*, Autumn 2006, p. 16.

57. Vali Nasr, *The Shia Revival*, Norton, p. 109.

58. Phebe Marr, *Iraq's New Political Map*, Special Report 179, United States Institute of Peace, January 2007. The Iraqi cabinet in 2007 had 13 'insiders' and 15 'outsiders' (exiles) and out of them the most moderate members came from the UAE: '(Five) have spent time working in Arab Gulf countries such as the United Arab Emirates (UAE), in a more open, commercial environment where different ideas may have had freer rein. (Abd Dhiyab al-Ajili, the minister of higher education and scientific research, is one such example).

59. John Irish, 'Dubai has become a Platform for Iranian Companies', Middle East Online, 21 March 2007.

60. Asbed Kotchikian, 'Secular Nationalism versus Political Islam in Azerbaijan', *Terrorism Monitor*, 10 February 2005, reproduced in *Unmasking Terror: A Global Review of Terrorist Activities*, Christopher Heffelfinger (ed.), The Jamestown Foundation, 2006, p. 386.

6

Transformation of Al Qaeda

Too often
we put the saddlebags on Jesus and let the donkey
run loose in the pasture.

— Rumi: *A wished-for Song*[1]

In 2006, Al Qaeda in Iraq was killing the Shia. This was a new phase in the growth of the organisation. It came into being vaguely as a promoter of jihad against the Soviet Union, then against the United States. Its intellectual origins were confused between a sense of the global and the regional. It set off on the global level but was soon diverted to focus on the region of Islam. Its internal debate pointed it to seeking revenge against Muslim states collaborating with the United States and Israel. Thus, a dynamic of change was built into its growth. It moved towards a consolidation of its identity along with the condition of change determined by the nature of the intellectual leadership offered by its charismatic leader Osama bin Laden. It is, therefore, wrong to be surprised that Al Qaeda is killing Muslims in Iraq.

The first deviation took place when Al Qaeda attempted to kill the Egyptian President Hosni Mubarak and bombed the Egyptian embassy in Islamabad in 1995. But this was Sunni-killing-Sunni and was justified by the *salafist-jahiliyya* trend of thinking rampant in the Islamist radicals of Egypt. Earlier, in the 1980s, Al Qaeda had allowed, or supported, its Pakistani ancillary jihadi militias to kill the Shia of Pakistan. These killings were underpinned by *fatwas* issued by Pakistan's Deobandi seminaries and the content of these *fatwas* relied heavily on the *salafist* objection to the Shia faith by Ibn Taymiyya. Al Qaeda supported the Taliban as they destroyed the Buddhas of Bamiyan and killed the Shia Hazaras of Central Afghanistan. But when Al Qaeda killed the Sunnis of Egypt it was not yet called sectarian. It is only in Iraq that it had to accept the intellectually demeaning (among Muslims) epithet of sectarian.

The first instinct behind what later became Al Qaeda was the concept of jihad, fighting in the way of Allah. It was of a piece with the age-old motivational force of Islam as a 'venture', as explained by Marshall G.S. Hodgson, that is, Islam as a venture of ultimate domination.[2] Even the moderate Muslim clerical leaders seek domination of Islam as a religious duty albeit with peaceful means, through 'invitation' (*dawa*). Sheikh Qaradawi, the Qatar-based middle-of-the-road (*wassatiyya*) interpreter of Islam said in Ohio in 1995: 'We will conquer Europe, we will conquer America, not through the sword but through *dawa*'.[3]

THE FOUNDING GENIUS OF ABDULLAH AZZAM

In Afghanistan the Arabs changed the often peaceful efforts at conversion (*dawa*) to war (jihad). The man who led the new movement was Abdullah Azzam (1941–1989), a Palestinian Arab who travelled to Damascus University in Syria for higher studies and joined the Muslim Brotherhood (Ikhwan) there. He then went to Al-Azhar University in Egypt and completed his PhD there in Islamic jurisprudence (*fiqh*) in 1973. He met the family of Syed Qutb, the Ikhwan leader who gave a new meaning to the concept of *jahiliyya* (Age of pre-Islamic Darkness) after reading it in the works of Pakistan's Maulana Maududi, and by bringing it closer to the way it was earlier understood by Mohammad ibn Abdul Wahhab of Saudi Arabia.[4] It is from Syed Qutb that Islamic radicals learned to apply it to the Muslims who actually professed to be Muslims but did not follow the true Sharia.

Abdullah Azzam thereafter taught at the University of Jordan in Amman but was dismissed from his job because of his involvement with the Brotherhood. After that he moved to Saudi Arabia and

joined the brother of Syed Qutb, Mohammad Qutb, on the faculty
of King Abdul Aziz University. It was here that Qutb and Azzam
met and influenced their pupil, Osama bin Laden. Azzam wrote
his tract *Defending the Land of the Muslims is Each Man's Most
Important Duty* and acknowledged the influence of Hanbali-
Wahhabi thinkers on his work, especially Sheikh Abdul Aziz Bin
Baz, the chief mufti of Saudi Arabia, who had declared jihad
obligatory on all Muslims—instead of the Islamic state—while
addressing the mosques of Jeddah and Riyadh. Azzam also quoted
Ibn Taymiyya:

> If the enemy enters a Muslim land, there is no doubt that it is
> obligatory for the closest and then the next closest to repel him,
> because the Muslims lands are like one land. It is obligatory to march
> to the territory even without permission of parents or creditors.[5]

It was under Azzam's inspiration and a direct reference to Ibn
Taymiyya that Osama bin Laden would challenge the stationing of
American troops in Saudi Arabia in 1991. But by planning to strike
at the enemy at his home base, he broke with Azzam, as will be
seen below.

The invasion of Afghanistan by the Soviet Union presented
Azzam with a situation where he was able to apply his theory of
jihad. After he left his position in Jeddah, the Muslim World
League (Rabita al-Alam al-Islami) appointed him to the International Islamic University in Islamabad, Pakistan, in 1984, where
he taught jurisprudence and his theory of jihad while handling the
affairs of the Muslim World League, already a major source of
funding of scholars engaged in anti-Iran and anti-Shia sectarian
writings. The World Muslim League office was later put in the
charge of the Jordanian, Mohammad Abdur Rehman Khalifa, who
ended up marrying one of Osama bin Laden's daughters. In time,
the League office in Peshawar became a great feeding mechanism
for what became Al Qaeda. Azzam also ran the Muslim Brotherhood
office in Peshawar. Another important person who joined him in
Peshawar in 1985 was Sheikh Omar Abdur Rehman, the blind
Egyptian cleric who would be involved in the first terrorist action

against the World Trade Center by half-Kuwaiti-half-Pakistani Ramzi Yusuf, whose trips to Islamabad also included staying in the hostels of the International Islamic University. Rehman was apprehended in the US and Ramzi Yusuf was handed over to the United States by Pakistan.

Azzam opened his Maktab Khadamat al-Mujahideen (Afghan Service Bureau Front or MAK) in Peshawar and was apparently working in tandem with the Pakistani authorities:

> Azzam worked closely with Pakistan's intelligence agency, the ISI, while Osama bin Laden served as his deputy. They were helped significantly by Saudi Arabia and its numerous private donors while Muslim Brotherhood remained an important background influence. The ISI was both the CIA's conduit for arms transfer and the principal trainer of the Afghan and foreign mujahideen. The CIA provided sophisticated weaponry including ground-to-air Stinger missiles and satellite imagery of Soviet troop deployments.[6]

Azzam has been called the founder of Hamas too, but when he was killed in 1989 he was more convinced of fighting the global jihad than the more restricted and less effective jihad in Palestine or in Egypt. His thinking went into the founding principles of Al Qaeda when it came into being soon after his death. Another person arrived from Egypt to become close to Osama and change the direction of the new-born organisation.

AIMAN AL-ZAWAHIRI TAKES OVER

Aiman al-Zawahiri came from a privileged family of doctors in Egypt aligned with an equally privileged family of scholars and lawyers on his mother's side, the Azzams. Himself a qualified physician, (he was to acquire a PhD in surgery [sic!] later from a Pakistani medical university while living in Peshawar)[7] he was inspired by the Quranic exegesis of Syed Qutb and was able to radicalise its message even further by applying violence to end the *jahiliyya* of Muslim societies not living under Sharia. Some think that al-Zawahiri was violent right from the start and that he became a hardliner after he moved to Afghanistan. The watershed event was the assassination of President Sadat in 1981 by al-Gama'a al-Islamiyya and an alliance of extremist outfits called Islamic Jihad. Hundreds of activists of both were imprisoned. Al-Zawahiri was tortured till he betrayed his closest recruit in the Egyptian army, Al Qamari, an act that would shape his later career through contrition. The trauma bestowed on him the unbending quality that he in turn inculcated into Al Qaeda.

Earlier, when Gama'a Islamiyya had chosen Sheikh Omar Abdul Rehman as its leader, al-Zawahiri had protested saying the Sharia did not allow a blind man to be the imam of an organisation. This was an early sign of toughness from an otherwise soft-spoken and self-effacing al-Zawahiri, an attribute that continued to arouse deep loyalty among the warriors who followed him. Al-Zawahiri left Egypt because it was too 'free' a society for his ideas to spread without being critiqued in its free press. He first went to Saudi Arabia and joined the Abdul Aziz University in Jeddah to be with two intellectual giants of jihad, Mohammad Qutb—the brother of Syed Qutb—and Abdullah Azzam, the inspiring Palestinian thinker profiled above. Al-Zawahiri had already visited Afghanistan after the war there in 1980 and had worked at Sayyida Zainab Hospital in Peshawar run by the Ikhwan. He was imprisoned for the assassination of Sadat in 1981 on his return, for three years; he came back to Afghanistan in 1986.

In Afghanistan (with a free run of Pakistan too) he had to marry his plan of terrorism against Egypt with Osama bin Laden's money and his wider confrontation. (Al-Zawahiri called America the 'far enemy'; but the 'near enemy', Egypt, had to be attacked first.) Abdullah Azzam, however, was in charge of operations in Peshawar. Al-Zawahiri possibly had Azzam and his two sons murdered in Peshawar in 1989 to get the full attention of Osama bin Laden and take over the burgeoning organisation. A Gama'a member was seen having an argument with al-Zawahiri on the streets of Peshawar in the course of which al-Zawahiri accused Azzam of being an 'agent' because he had good relations with Gama'a. He attended the funeral of the 'imam of the mujahideen' the next day!

Al-Zawahiri attacked not only Gama'a for going quiescent after the 1997 massacre at Luxor, he had earlier attacked the Ikhwan in his book *The Bitter Harvest* for giving up violence. He held to his view that Egypt had to be attacked because that was where the West had to be fought first. Located in Peshawar, he repeatedly tried to assassinate Egyptian ministers and civil servants suspected of persecuting the Islamists. His recruits narrowly missed two government figures in Cairo but killed one informer. He had accused the Egyptian Islamists of randomness but they too accused him of randomness when he tried to destroy the Egyptian embassy in Islamabad in 1995, succeeding only partially. Pursuing Osama bin Laden's agenda against the Americans after the setting up of Al Qaeda, he tried to blow up the US embassies in Nairobi and Dar-as-Salam in Africa in 1998, succeeding only partially. However, he was able to inflict more successful damage in Yemen and Al Khobar.

AL-ZAWAHIRI'S REDIRECTION OF ISLAMISM

Al-Zawahiri and bin Laden had to leave Afghanistan in 1994 for Sudan because of the infighting among the Afghan mujahideen during the presidency of Rabbani. They returned in 1996 after striking a deal with Mullah Umar after the latter's Taliban had established almost total control over Afghanistan. Pakistan was on the side of the Taliban and was weaned from it only after 9/11. It had also expressed its inability to the Clinton administration to make the Taliban expel Osama bin Laden. Al-Zawahiri accepted the tough Islam of the Taliban even though it would not sit well with the Islamists back in Egypt who were liberal with regard to women. The Taliban accepted a 'Wahhabised' radicalisation of their projection of ideological power because they got bin Laden's money in addition to the assistance they had from Islamabad. Pakistan was greatly influenced by this Taliban–Al Qaeda fundamentalism in its own ISI-driven internal transformation into an Islamized society.

Some Gama'a members of Egypt accuse Al Qaeda and especially al-Zawahiri of causing great harm to the Islamist cause. In violation of past practice, al-Zawahiri and Osama bin Laden would not own up to acts of terrorism till the 9/11 incident, when both came on TV to only hint at having done it. Al-Zawahiri was accused of having miscalculated the American response after 9/11. He thought it would be like the attacks that came in the wake of the African cases, that is, bombing of Afghanistan. But a full-fledged invasion of Afghanistan under a Security Council resolution under Chapter 7 of the UN Charter had damaged the Islamist cause beyond repair.

Kepel is of the opinion that al-Zawahiri began to monopolise Osama after the Arabs settled down in Peshawar with their wives and children and gradually managed to replace Azzam as Osama's spiritual mentor. He turned Osama off Azzam and his Ikhwan background by writing his anti-Brotherhood tract *Sixty Years of the Muslim Brothers' Bitter Harvest*.[8] He was not very effective when he recommended an anti-American course of action simply because the Arabs were being supplied weapons by the CIA, but later, as the Soviets prepared to leave, and the Americans looked like they were losing interest in Afghanistan, his argument tended to prevail. Kepel says that in this period there was a lot of violence among the Arabs, as a result of which Azzam was assassinated. Bergen adds that after Azzam was gone, the Arabs, inspired by Azzam, originally agreed to turn the jihad against the United States, as happened in the case of Mohammad Odeh, a Jordanian citizen of Palestinian descent studying in the Philippines in the late 1980s, and was inspired by a video message from Azzam. In 1998, he played a key role in the bombing of the American embassy in Kenya.[9] Bergen also mentions the changing orientation of Osama because of his closeness with the Afghan warlord Gulbuddin Hekmatyar who was host to the Egyptian Gama'a leader Omar Abdur Rehman in Peshawar in 1985. By 2004, around 25,000 Arabs had found their way to the training camps of jihad with Saudi airlines giving 75 per cent discount on air travel to and from Pakistan. Gunaratna is more precise:

The broad outlines of what would become Al Qaeda were formulated by Azzam in 1987 and 1988, its founding charter being completed by him in that period. He envisaged it as being an organisation that would channel the energies of the mujahideen into fighting on behalf of oppressed Muslims worldwide, an Islamic 'rapid reaction force' ready to spring to the defence of their fellow believers at short notice. Toward the end of the anti-Soviet Afghan campaign Osama's relationship with Azzam deteriorated, and in late 1988 and 1989, they disagreed over several issues. One of these concerned the Al Masada mujahideen training scamp on the Afghan-Pakistan border. In early 1989, Osama asked Azzam whether it could be turned over to Al Qaeda in order to become its principal base. Azzam refused, notwithstanding Osama's continued entreaties.[10]

AL-ZAWAHIRI'S 'NEAR ENEMY' AND THE DEATH OF AZZAM

The truth is that Osama was persuaded by Zawahiri's argument in favour of *al adou al qareeb* (enemy who is nearby) in opposition to Azzam's global vision of jihad which was described to Osama as *al adou al baeed* (enemy who is far away). This was in effect the beginning of the narrowing of the vision of Al Qaeda. Once this strategy was adopted the jihadists or mujahideen were permitted to vent their own local and regional angers, which finally came to focus on the Shia. The Arabs at first stayed aloof from the passions that swayed the Pakistani mujahideen whom Osama trained in his camps. The jihad that was fought against the Soviets was spearheaded by the ISI and Gulbuddin Hekmatyar, neither of whom was brought up on sectarian indoctrination. But starting 1985–86, the Saudis had begun their anti-Iran campaign among the seminaries in Pakistan, mainly among the Deobandi–Ahle Hadith ones. After that, starting with the Taliban and the return to Afghanistan of Al Qaeda from Sudan, the Arabs saw a changed battlefront. The Saudis had eliminated the Iran-based Shia mujahideen from the Afghan government in exile established in Peshawar in 1989, and the ISI was fighting its own war against

Iran. According to Barnett Rubin, in 1989, the Afghan mujahideen government-in-exile came into being in Peshawar after the Soviet retreat from Afghanistan. At the behest of Saudi Arabia, the exiled Shia mujahideen of Iran were not included in this government. The Saudis paid over 26 million dollars a week to the 519-member session of the mujahideen *shura* (council) as a bribe for it. Each member of the *shura* received $25,000 for the deal which was facilitated, according to Rubin, by the ISI chief General Hamid Gul.[11]

The Taliban were linked to the Pakistani mujahideen through their Deobandi faith mostly absorbed from the seminaries in the NWFP and the tribal areas of Pakistan. Fawaz A. Gerges, based on his extremely informative interviews among the jihadists, gives a more intimate account of how Azzam's vision was superseded within Al Qaeda:

> Azzam's followers accuse Zawahiri of precipitating the final divorce between bin Laden and Azzam—by spreading rumours that Azzam was an American spy. Osama Rushdi, a leader of the Egyptian Islamic Group who knew bin Laden, Azzam, and Zawahiri, blames Zawahiri for Azzam's murder. Abdullah Anas, Azzam's son-in-law and a senior jihadist who fought in Afghanistan along his side, recalled that Azzam had complained bitterly to him about the backbiting trouble-makers, Zawahiri in particular, who spoke against the *mujahideen*. In his memoirs Anas reported that Azzam would say, 'They have only one point, to create *fitna* (sedition) between me and these volunteers'.[12]

Azzam was a non-terrorist internationalist. His concept of jihad did not include the killing of innocent citizens as 'collateral damage'. With the removal of Azzam, Al Qaeda moved away from a defensive jihad against an invading Soviet Union and embraced terrorism as its methodology. Later, under the influence of Zarqawi, it would move from the empirical to the conceptual by condemning democracy to justify the killing of the Shia in Iraq 'because they had embraced democracy'. Gunaratna gives us yet another insight:

Though Azzam was the ideological father of Al Qaeda, bin Laden gradually assumed leadership of the group. Toward the end of the anti-Soviet Afghan campaign, however, bin Laden's relationship with Azzam deteriorated. The dispute over Azzam's support for Ahmad Shah Massoud, who later became the leader of the Northern Alliance, caused tension. Bin Laden preferred Gulbuddin Hekmatyar, former prime minister and leader of the Islamic Party (Hizb-i-Islami), who was both anti-communist and anti-western. Furthermore, together with the Egyptian members of Al Qaeda, bin Laden wished to support terrorist action against Egypt and other Muslim secular regimes. Having lived in Egypt, Azzam knew the price of such actions and opposed it vehemently. Azzam and bin Laden went their separate ways. Later, Azzam was assassinated by the Egyptian members of Al Qaeda in Peshawar, Pakistan. After the Afghan victory, bin Laden was lionised in the eyes of those who fought with him in the war as a brave warrior and selfless Muslim ruler.[13]

Through the slightly varying testimony of authors who watched Al Qaeda in that period one can draw the conclusion that Azzam was killed because of an internal organisational dispute, in which al-Zawahiri and Osama were able to join together to isolate him. There is also a general consensus that he was killed by members of Al Qaeda who accepted al-Zawahiri's leadership.

AL QAEDA ALLOWS
PAKISTANI SECTARIANISM

At the best of times, Pakistan's close relations with the Taliban did not result in the latter's acceptance of Pakistan's demand that sectarian killers belonging to Sipah-e-Sahaba, Lashkar-e-Jhangvi and Harkat-ul-Jihad al-Islami, who routinely escaped into Afghanistan after committing collective murders in Pakistan, be caught and surrendered to it. The Taliban themselves could not avoid a sectarian slant to their Sunni caliphate. They were not able to co-opt the Hazara Shia of Central Afghanistan in their drive to encircle and destroy the Tajik-Sunni warlord Ahmad Shah Massoud. In fact, the Taliban prejudice was quite deep-rooted and was responsible for the killing of many Hazaras who had fled into Pakistan. The siege of Bamiyan in 2001 killed thousands of Hazaras through starvation and sheer slaughter, in revenge for the 1998 massacre of the Taliban by the Hazaras when the Taliban army tried to conquer the northern city of Mazar-e-Sharif and ran up against an alliance of non-Pushtun forces. The massacres were carried out with the help of Al Qaeda and members of Sipah-e-Sahaba and Lashkar-e-Jhangvi, the sectarian Deobandi killers of Pakistan. This explains why the Taliban never responded to Islamabad's demand for the surrender of the Lashkar activists. That year the Taliban also destroyed the famous Bamiyan Buddhas after the Hazara pogroms had laid the region low. That Al Qaeda was involved in the massacre of the Shia was proved later when evidence came forth that it was Al Qaeda that had persuaded the Taliban to destroy the ancient statues situated in the territory of the Shia.

Mullah Umar didn't know Osama bin Laden before he arrived from Sudan in 1996 and was given into the safe hands of Maulvi Yunus Khalis in Jalalabad. Osama himself courted Umar with a wheedling letter which worked. They met finally after the Taliban had captured Kabul. Kathy Gannon narrates how the Taliban began by securing the Bamiyan Buddhas against vandalism by issuing edicts from Mullah Umar describing them as Afghanistan's cultural heritage in 1999.[14] In 2001, Osama bribed Umar's deputy prime minister and defence minister into convincing him to issue another edict for their destruction! The Taliban seemed to be religiously tentative. The hard Islam they adopted came from three sources: their Deobandi faith, the Pakistan army and its active arm the ISI, and the Wahhabi warriors of Osama bin Laden. And the most persuasive factor here was not religious conviction but money. After the Buddhas were destroyed, the Islamabad ministry for religious affairs issued a statement saying the destruction was according to Islamic principles. Pakistan was harder in faith than the Afghan medieval marauder Mehmud Ghaznavi who had spared the Bamiyan Buddhas but destroyed some of the most prominent temples of India in AD 1025.

In 2003, the Hazaras of Quetta became victims of terrorism amid reports that some important personalities connected with Osama bin Laden were living in Quetta, including the son of the blind Gama'a leader, Umar Abdur Rehman, now serving a life sentence in the United States for planning the attack on the World Trade Center in 1993. Osama Bin Laden was later to plan another unsuccessful terrorist-hijack plan to force America to free the blind Egyptian cleric. When the Al Qaeda 'number three' Ramzi bin al-Shibh was captured in Karachi in 2004, the planner of 9/11, Khalid Sheikh Mohammad was with him in the same safe house. He escaped to Quetta where he sought shelter in yet another safe house of the Jamaat-e-Islami.

After the defeat of the Taliban in 2001, many of its activists and the Al Qaeda Arabs fled to Pakistan. Karachi, which was to be transformed into the ground zero of Pakistan's sectarian massacres, became home to them. They were welcomed by the seminaries already funded by Saudi Arabia and by the religious parties that ignored or actively encouraged the anti-Shia campaigns of their youths. It was here that many terrorists from the Middle East and Southeast Asia were trained and then sent out on missions of sectarian violence. The tendency of not associating the Arabs and Al Qaeda with Shia-killing in Pakistan is quite pronounced and has accounted for the state's inability to effectively counter sectarianism. For instance, in President Pervez Musharraf's account of how he faced up to the attempts made on his life by the Deobandi militias and Al Qaeda, he completely ignores the sectarian activities of these entities. In chapter 24 of his book he gives a detailed account of Amjad Farooqi, the man who planned the attempts on his life in Rawalpindi in 2003, but does not refer to his links with Lashkar-e-Jhangvi while mentioning in passing that he had links with Jaish-e-Mohammed. In his three chapters devoted to terrorism, he simply ignored the thousands of Shia killed by the same people who had tried to kill him.[15]

A 'BLANKET' SECTARIAN OUTFIT

General Musharraf should have got his intelligence services to give him material for at least one chapter on the Shia killed by Al Qaeda and its Deobandi protégés on his watch. Amjad Farooqi, with a bounty of Rs 20 million on his head, was killed in 2004 in Sindh after a five-hour gun battle. He was wanted for two abortive attempts on the life of Pervez Musharraf in 2003, and the murder of the American journalist Daniel Pearl who was beheaded by Khalid Sheikh Mohammad. His strongest link with Al Qaeda was his involvement in the 1999 hijack of the Indian airliner IC-814 which sought to free a Harkatul Mujahideen leader, Masood Azhar, from an Indian jail. Although Pervez Musharraf clearly refers to Jaish as a terrorist organisation, it was not seen as such by Islamabad before it attempted to take his life at the behest of Al Qaeda. As noted elsewhere, the government of Pervez Musharraf handled him as its favourite after his release from the Indian jail and let him roam freely in the country despite his avowed terrorist and sectarian links. In fact, a lot of the sectarian slaughter that took place under Musharraf, would have been avoided had he moved to stop Masood Azhar.

Amjad Farooqi belonged to Harkat-ul-Jihad al-Islami, the largest jihadi organisation, with its headquarters in Kandahar and the largest participation in it of the Taliban fighters who later occupied important posts in the cabinet of Mullah Umar. One reason Musharraf did not discuss Farooqi in more detail could be that Farooqi's sectarian contacts went deep into the army too. A *Terrorist Monitor* report sketches the scene in Karachi in 2004:

> Karachi continues to be a safe haven for extremist religious groups like Lashkar Jhangvi and terrorist groups like Harkatul Mujahideen and Harkat Jihad Islami (HUJI). In fact HUJI runs 48 seminaries in Karachi. The biggest of these, Madrassa Khalid bin Walid, trains more than 500 students at any given point of time. It is the command headquarters of Karachi Muslims fighting the military regime in Burma. Their leader is Maulana Abdul Quddus, a Myanmarese Muslim who fled to India and made his way to Karachi where he received his

religious training before leaving for Afghanistan to join the jihad. A large number of his students fought the Northern Alliance during the Afghan wars of the 1990s. Some went to Kashmir with other HUJI members to fight Indian Security Forces but none returned to Myanmar or Bangladesh, choosing instead to make Karachi their home. Their collective objective is to turn Pakistan into another Taliban-style country.[16]

In 2006 a Bangladeshi, suicide bomber killed the top Shia leader of Pakistan, Allama Hassan Turabi, in Karachi after telling his parents through a video message that he was promised Heaven for doing the deed.

Because of the strong presence of the religious parties, their militias and the Al Qaeda Arabs, Karachi was chosen as the scene of regular Shia-killing. Akram Lahori, who took over Lashkar-e-Jhangvi after the death of Riaz Basra in a police encounter in 2002, was involved in the assassination of several prominent Shias including the brother of the federal interior minister, General (Retired) Moinuddin Haider. He also killed 24 Shias in Mominpura in Lahore and 11 at Imambargah Najaf in Rawalpindi, but his links with Al Qaeda came into the open through a man named Naeem Bukhari, whose involvement in the murder of Daniel Pearl was traced to the Yemeni elements of the organisation. Wilson John reports from the testimony of Fazal Karim, a Lashkar-e-Jhangvi activist picked up in Rahimyar Khan three months after the killing of Daniel Pearl: 'Al Qaeda had merged with various sectarian and criminal groups in Karachi to carry out terrorist attacks in Pakistan'.[17] There was a strong rumour in Pakistan that finally when Amjad Farooqi was killed in Sindh it was the intelligence agencies who refused to allow him to surrender as that would have revealed the hand of the state in his sectarian crimes on behalf of Al Qaeda.

In many accounts of the 1994 bomb attack at the mausoleum of Imam Raza in Mashhad, Iran, Al Qaeda's Ramzi Yusuf and Lashkar-e-Jhangvi are referred to as the perpetrators. In fact, it shows an early penchant within Al Qaeda towards sectarianism. Lashkar-e-Jhangvi is also mentioned separately from Sipah-e-Sahaba, its mother organisation and other Deobandi religious parties. Suroosh Irfani notes this blurring of the boundaries between the 'extremist' and the 'mainstream' in the Islamist spectrum:[18]

> If the JUI (Fazlur Rehman faction) allowed the SSP's leader Riaz Basra to contest the 1987 national election as its candidate both the JUI(F) and Jamaat Islami joined SSP in an effort to prevent the death sentence awarded to SSP's Haq Nawaz (for his role in the murder of the Iranian consul Sadeq Ganji) from being carried out. These Islamic parties reportedly went to the extent of demanding that if it was not possible for General Musharraf's government to pardon Haq Nawaz, he should be exiled like Nawaz Sharif to Saudi Arabia. Moreover, both the extremist outfits and the mainstream religio-political groups look up to bin Laden as a 'hero of Islam'. This is borne out by the reaction of the Mutahidda Majlis Amal (MMA) to the government ads carried in the national media in June 2002 portraying bin Laden and his Al Qaeda associates as religious terrorists.[18]

Just as there is evidence of mainstream religious parties' support to the sectarian killers, there is equally evidence of Al Qaeda supporting and patronising the sectarian outfits from its very inception, and much more openly after its return to Afghanistan in 1996 when it found the hardline Taliban ruling the country. Financial support from countries in the Gulf—where hatred of the Shia as a proxy of Revolutionary Iran was widespread—dented the early Al Qaeda resolve of staying away from internecine conflicts. Also, the induction of more and more Arab warriors from the Shia-hating regions into Al Qaeda gradually changed the character of the outfit. Finally, it was a consequence of the decision to move from Abdullah Azzam's 'distant enemy' thesis to al-Zawahiri's 'near enemy' thesis. Abou Zahab makes the following observation:

> The links between Pakistani Sunni extremists and Arab militants were forged in the training camps of Afghanistan during the Taliban rule; Pakistani militants belonging to Sunni extremist groups were involved in the massacre of Shias in Mazar-e-Sharif in 1997 and in Bamiyan in 1998. After the fall of the Taliban the local jihadis and sectarian groups which were already linked—many sectarian parties were part-time

jihadis and vice versa—became the voluntary foot soldiers of Al Qaeda networks in Pakistan and were instrumentalised for global interests. Some of them who seemed to work as freelancers and hired killers for foreign groups were used to launch attacks on Western targets.[19]

The effect of non-sectarian and less introverted Abdullah Azzam comes to the fore when one notes a lower sectarian profile of Deobandi–Ahle Hadith militias in Pakistan who came under his influence. When Harvard scholar Jessica Stern asked Fazlur Rehman Khalil of Harkatul Mujahideen (HUM) what book he revered most after the Holy Quran, he chose the writings of Sheikh Abdullah Azzam[20]. He then went on to praise the genius of Azzam as a thinker. Khalil's organisation has fractured under the pressure of a bifurcation it suffered in 1999 when its number two leader Maulana Masood Azhar broke off and set up his own Jaish-e-Mohammed with the help of his teacher Mufti Shamzai of Karachi's Banuri Mosque seminary. Harkat boys indulged in stray sectarian crimes only because Khalil's influence had declined and he was not always able to keep his militants under control.

Similarly, Hafiz Saeed of Ahle Hadith-Wahhabi Lashkar-e-Taiba has kept himself and his outfit away as much as possible from the Arab-driven sectarian wave in Pakistan. Saeed was a pupil of Azzam when he was in Saudi Arabia and was greatly inspired by him. His first great venture in Muridke, a city-like training camp behind walls just outside Lahore, was built with funds collected by Azzam. After Azzam's death he kept aloof from Shia-killing but could no longer avoid the influence of the Arabs and Al Qaeda because of his training camps in Kunar, the headquarters of all Arab warriors. His funds kept coming steadily from the Gulf States and the Pakistani expatriate community living in the UK and the US. In the end, on the occasion of Zarqawi's death in Iraq, he could no longer avoid owning up to his sectarian links when he held his *ghaibana* (*in absentia*) funeral in Lahore. When he moved to his new headquarters in Lahore on old Lake Road he named it Qadisiya, a symbolic anti-Iranian gesture.

ZARQAWI AND AL QAEDA'S POLICY ON SHIAS

Al Qaeda began killing the Shias of Iraq under the local leadership of Abu Musab al-Zarqawi who had fought as an Al Qaeda warrior from 1990 onwards. He died in Baghdad in June 2006 with $25 million on his head. The general impression in Pakistan is that Abu Musab al-Zarqawi was a soldier of Al Qaeda but was disliked by Osama bin Laden for his anti-Shia feelings. Zarqawi began his career as a jihadist in Afghanistan in the 1980s. In the 1990s, he established a training camp there to prepare guerrillas for rebellion in Jordan. He was jailed for seven years in Jordan on his return but returned to Afghanistan again. In Herat he trained jihadists and joined Osama bin Laden in Tora Bora in 2001. He got injured in Kandahar during the American invasion and was evacuated through Iran by Hekmatyar who had good contacts in Tehran. He moved to Iraq after that—well in time to see the Americans invade the country—and joined the Kurd-led jihadi militia Ansarul Islam there. Ansarul Islam was founded as a terrorist group by one Mullah Krekar who came to the Islamic University of Islamabad as a lecturer in the 1980s and later joined the jihad in Peshawar.

Zarqawi was born in 1966 in the town of Zarqa in Jordan as Ahmad Fadil Khalayleh and soon was seen as a bad student, given to using physical violence against other boys. (He later borrowed his name Musab from a Companion of the Prophet, Musab bin Umayr.) In 1987 he was arrested for inflicting a knife wound on a boy and was let off after his father paid a heavy fine. Two years later, at the age of 23, he went to Pakistan to join the jihad, only to find that the Soviet Union had already pulled out of Afghanistan. He began to frequent the inner circles of Al Qaeda which had just been founded by Osama bin Laden. He lived in Hayatabad, Peshawar, and met jihadi leaders like Abdullah Azzam, Hekmatyar and Burhanuddin Rabbani. He also met, for the first time, another personality who had arrived there from Jordan, Abu Mohammad al-Maqdisi. Maqdisi was to direct Zarqawi to a polemical opposition to democracy as a system destructive of Islam's cardinal principles.

He was sent to Khost where he simply arrived as a victor, the Soviets having already left, but he remained in Peshawar and Afghanistan till 1993, fighting against the pro-Communist factions under the Najibullah government.

Maqdisi was born in 1959 in Barqa in Nablus in the West Bank but was taken by his parents to Kuwait at the age of three. He was sent to Iraq to study Islam in the 1980s but his *salafi* faith and hostility to the Baath Party caused his arrest by the government. He was deported to Makkah, Saudi Arabia, where he soon impressed with his scholastic ability and was put in charge of the World Islamic League's missions to Afghanistan in 1984. In 1988, he joined the Society of the Revival of Islamic Heritage in Kuwait which is today banned in Europe and the US as a terrorist organisation. Maqdisi soon became the Arab world's leading thinker with a steady flow of tracts coming from his pen, mostly reacting to modernism as spearheaded by the West, in particular its liberal democracy which he thought as being against Islam. Eighteen of his articles were found in the personal effects of Mohammad Atta, the leader of the Hamburg Cell, who attacked the World Trade Center on 11 September 2001. Maqdisi remained in Peshawar for three years, hosted by the group Bafadat Mujahideen as a professor of religion. It is during this time that Zarqawi became a follower of Maqdisi. Brisard places Maqdisi in the ideological centre of Al Qaeda:

> According to the Jordanian police, in 1997 some of Maqdisi's terrorist activities were personally financed from Afghanistan by Osama bin Laden. The two men, said to be close, often met in Afghanistan at the time, especially in Pakistan, the rear base of the Arab forces. One of Osama's top associates in Afghanistan the Algerian mujahid Abdullah Anas, now in exile in London, recalls sharing a meal in Islamabad with Bin Laden, Abdullah Azzam and Maqdisi. In short, Maqdisi was at the heart of Al Qaeda.[21]

THE INFLUENCE OF MAQDISI

It is important to put Maqdisi in perspective as a terrorist ideologue to be able to understand the depth and significance of the split that took place later between him and Zarqawi. Through the 1990s, Maqdisi kept writing his tracts and forming new terrorist units as an instrumentalisation of his radical-Islamist views. His name cropped up in the confessions of the four citizens arrested in 1994 following the Al Khobar attack mounted in 1994 against the headquarters of the American soldiers stationed there, in which five Americans were killed, and for which the Saudis at first blamed Iran. The four men had been to Pakistan for the jihad and had met Maqdisi there and read his two books, *Clear Evidence of the Infidel Nature of the Saudi State* and *The Faith of Ibrahim*. Brisard refers to another terrorist, Azmiri, who was attracted to Maqdisi after reading his *Irrefutable Proof for Understanding Jihad*. Azmiri was involved in the so-called 1994 Bojinka plot to crash several airplanes simultaneously over the United States which became the forerunner of 9/11. Azmiri also took part in the aborted attempt to assassinate President Clinton in 1998.[22]

Maqdisi's second close friend in Pakistan links him to Khalid Sheikh Mohammad, the man who planned the 9/11 attack. Mohammad Shobana published an Islamist magazine *Al Bynyan Al Marsus* (The Impenetrable Edifice) which was supported by Khalid's brother, Abid Sheikh Mohammad. It was this magazine that first announced the foundational principles of Al Qaeda in 1989. And it was Shobana who recruited an almost illiterate Zarqawi into the magazine staff on Maqdisi's recommendation. Zarqawi's three sisters ended up marrying jihad veterans, including one given to a friend personally in accordance with the Arab practice of 'giving away' sisters and daughters as tokens of friendship. It was from his base in Al Bunyan that Zarqawi was to make his way to Sada camp of Abdur Rasul Sayyaf in Afghanistan and be in the company of Ramzi Yusuf and Khalid Sheikh Mohammad.

It is understandable therefore that when in 1992, he returned to Jordan from Afghanistan, Zarqawi went looking for Maqdisi. Maqdisi was ready to give him the next ideological injection. He had just published his new book *Democracy is a Religion*:

> According to this scathing diatribe against the West and its form of government, democracy is a social innovation condemned by the Quran, one that conveys heretical message. The citizens of democratic states are infidels soon to incur destruction. Democracy is a religion that is not the religion of Allah…. It is a religion of pagans…a religion that includes other gods in its belief…. In the democratic religion people are represented by their delegates to parliament…. They and their associates legislate in accordance with the religion of democracy and the laws of the constitution on which the government is based.[23]

Zarqawi set up a cell of Afghanistan veterans around Maqdisi in Jordan which was funded by Al Qaeda since it planned to attack important targets in Jordan, including blowing up the intelligence service headquarters, GID. In 1994, the leaders of the cell, including Zarqawi and Maqdisi, were arrested, the latter along with explosives in the false ceiling of his home. Both signed confessions that their planned terrorism was meant to target Israel and not Jordan. They were sentenced to prison for 15 years but were let out in 1999 when amnesty was offered to them on the death of King Hussein and the enthronement of King Abdullah. It was in part young King Abdullah's mending of fences with the Muslim Brotherhood whose leaders he then received in audience. (King Abdullah later regretted his decision to release Zarqawi.) Maqdisi was freed but kept under surveillance and was sent back to prison in 2002 where he was at the time of this writing.

In 1999, Zarqawi then made the big decision of his life: to leave Jordan and the teachings of Maqdisi behind forever. He left for Pakistan planning to stay on a six-month visa and landed in Hayatabad in Peshawar, the place connected to fond memories of the Afghan jihad. Once in Peshawar he was welcomed by the Pakistani Wafa Organisation, later banned by the UN, which provided Al Qaeda funds and false passports for the jihadists.

Finally, many of the important Al Qaeda terrorists including Khalfan Ghailani, the man who had planned the attack on US embassies in Kenya and Tanzania in 1998, were arrested from Hayatabad in 2004. Zarqawi's sister was already living in Peshawar married to a religious scholar. Zarqawi's mother came up to Peshawar to see her son settled there in 1999 and stayed there for a month. Soon his wife and children too joined him in Hayatabad. But he had only six months to get close to Osama bin Laden and launch himself at the head of a big operation.

In 1999, the international community became impatient with Pakistan and its intelligence agency, the ISI. From 1994 to 1999 almost 100,000 Pakistanis had been trained in the Afghan camps run by Al Qaeda, and the clerics of Pakistan, especially of the Deobandi variety, under the Jamiat Ulema-e-Islam (JUI), had begun to sense monetary and military advantage in aligning themselves with Osama bin Laden. Jordan too put pressure on Islamabad to arrest the planner of terrorism in Jordan, Khalil al-Deek, from his hideout in Hayatabad. When the ISI moved to arrest the Jordanian, Zarqawi too got arrested and was sent to jail. He was released after a week although he was listed as a terrorist in Jordan. With an exit permit in his hand, Zarqawi left for Karachi first, then decided to go to Kabul instead and be one of the trainers of terrorists in Al Qaeda camps. In Kabul he was given a house before being sent to Herat as a trainer. He called his family over from Hayatabad but not before he had married a young girl aged 13 in Kabul after falling in love with her. He was to marry yet another girl of 16 in Iraq.

ZARQAWI'S OPPORTUNITY IN HERAT

The break for Zarqawi and his band of Jordanians in Afghanistan came when Al Qaeda announced a big operation in the West and asked for recruits. It was Al Qaeda's famous recruiter Abu Zubayda, himself a Jordanian, who finally picked Zarqawi and his men for the important mission, lodging them in a house not far from Kabul in an area controlled by the Afghan warlord Hekmatyar.[24] By the end of 1999, Zarqawi had succeeded in becoming an important mid-level leader inside Al Qaeda. Al Qaeda papers found in Jalalabad after 2001 refer to him as a friend of Maqdisi, acknowledging the intellectual influence of Maqdisi on Al Qaeda. Later letters sent by Al Qaeda to Abu Qatada, the Al Qaeda leader in the United Kingdom (now in prison there), speak well of Zarqawi as a leader in charge of the camps in Herat.

Having sworn personal allegiance to Osama bin Laden, Zarqawi soon proved his efficiency in Herat where his camp, concealed inside a religious seminary, carried the signboard Al-Tawhid wal-Jihad which was to become the name of his outfit in Iraq later on. He sat on the Islam Qila crossroads giving access to Turkey through Iran, on the one hand, and to Chechnya through Turkmenistan, on the other. He was closely watched by the Iranians although there was agreement between Iran and Al Qaeda on the right of passage for mujahideen. Zarqawi knew that the Iranians were financing the Shia militias against the Taliban. Osama bin Laden was impressed with Zarqawi's efforts at training jihadists in explosives and chemicals (there was even a rumour that Al Qaeda's nuclear material was also stored in Herat) and therefore did not hesitate to give him $35,000 for his plan to carry out terrorist attacks in Israel in 2000. But Zarqawi's Jordanian bombers were arrested in Turkey after they had crossed through Iran.

Brisard explains that Zarqawi's maverick nature constantly induced him to rebel against his mentors while his brave leadership kept the Jordanian Al Qaeda in Herat intact as opposed to the Algerians in Jalalabad who had gone to pieces through factional infighting. After 1999, he had said goodbye to his first mentor Maqdisi; now in 2000 he wanted to break out of the ideological hold of Osama bin Laden and Aiman al-Zawahiri:

> In the past he had been careful to keep his distance from Maqdisi. Now he was trying to get free of the political line imposed by Osama himself, especially by Al Zawahiri. This wish for independence was reinforced by the geographical distance of the Herat camp and the recurrent criticism of Bin Laden on the part of many jihadists. The

Saudi had the reputation of constructing his own myth to the detriment of the common cause aimed at restoring the caliphate, and the two factions in Afghanistan, one of which was Zarqawi's, were said to be hostile to him. But in 2000 Bin Laden's financial and political support was still indispensable to Zarqawi, and he would have to be patient for another few months before breaking free. For it was only when he fled Afghanistan for Iran and then Syria that his expenses would be paid by his networks in Europe and the Middle East.[25]

ZARQAWI BREAKS FREE IN IRAQ

Zarqawi was in Iraq in 2001, two years before the Americans invaded in March 2003, after the US Secretary of State Colin Powell's public statement about him being Saddam's terrorist connection. Powell also named Zarqawi, wrongly, as a Palestinian terrorist. Zarqawi was, in fact, busy setting up an Arab militia in Kurdistan, already softened for the purpose by Saudi Arabia's generous funding there of a *salafist* movement. Soon, the predominance of the Arabs in Krekar's Ansarul Islam propelled an increasingly sidelined Krekar into making the decision to flee Iraq and seek asylum in Norway. The Islamic Movement of Kurdistan was based on the 500 Arab fighters brought in by Zarqawi. Soon, however, he ran into trouble with the Kurdish politician Jalal Talabani and had to fight his militia first. In 2003 the Arabs in Kurdistan faced an American offensive and had to run away to Iran and thence to the Sunni Triangle northwest of Baghdad back in Iraq.

While in the Anbar province in Iraq, Zarqawi and his Al-Tawhid wal-Jihad were to adopt a clear anti-Iran line, which simply goes to prove once again that he habitually 'transcended' the moral demands made on him by loyalty. There is proof that Iran rejected Jordan's request for his repatriation from an Iranian jail on the excuse that he was carrying a Syrian passport. (Iran repeatedly used the strategy of 'arresting' the Al Qaeda members it was facilitating.)

His Arab and Chechen trainees were allowed by Iran to routinely use its territory for transit. Iran's favours also included safe haven given to the son of Osama bin Laden, Saad, through the intercession of Hekmatyar. As he embarked on his war against the Americans from Anbar, he also reached a critical stage in his relations with his mentor and guide Abu Mohammad al-Maqdisi, then in a Jordanian jail. Maqdisi was of the opinion that Zarqawi should not wage jihad as a 'third party' when the main warring parties were both enemies of Islam. In his view Saddam Hussein and America were both enemies of Islam and Zarqawi should not help either one of them by intervening: 'Which Iraq are you talking about? The Baath Party of Saddam Hussein, the man who killed our clergy, who exterminated Muslims at Halabjah with his chemical gases? Where were you each time the United States supported Israel against our Muslim brothers in Palestine?'[26]

But this position changed soon. Al Qaeda announced its agreement with Zarqawi and ordered its warriors to wage jihad against the Americans in Iraq. Maqdisi seemed to recant his objection even as the Americans captured many of Zarqawi's warriors, including a Pakistani, Hasan Gul, from a number of places in Iraq in the autumn of 2003. Zarqawi finally struck back in April 2004, when he captured and beheaded the American hostage Nicholas Berg. In April he had already posted his lengthy justification for doing what he was about to do. He decided to kill Iraqi and Kurd 'collaborators' of America as a strategy of creating chaos in Iraq. By October he had killed Shias in Nasiriyah, Baghdad and Karbala, culminating in his murder of 50 Iraqi National Guards at a training camp in Kirkuk. (His most decisive act which unleashed the sectarian war in Iraq was the 2006 destruction of the tomb of Imam Askari in Samarra.)[27] He stole the salaries of the trainees in addition to getting private funding from Saudi Arabia and Jordan and remittances from the expatriate Muslim communities in Europe. In the beginning of 2004 he 'applied' to Al Qaeda for patronage clearly from a position of strength. It must be noted that he was already a member of Al Qaeda, having sworn loyalty on the hand of Osama bin Laden. What he now demanded was a change in the over-all strategy towards Iran and the Shia.

THE EXTREMISM OF NEW IDEOLOGUES

Al Qaeda viewed Iran as a kind of partner in its hatred of the Americans and their Saudi protégés. While it tolerated the Shia killing of its linked Pakistani jihadi organisations, it kept away from 'pronouncing' on the grand schism. It found Iranian cooperation useful when it was infiltrating into Iraq and the Caucasus. It was now swayed by Zarqawi because of his growing autonomous status and an increasing tendency among the Al Qaeda-backed Islamist jurists to persuade Muslims in the Middle East and Europe to approve Zarqawi's campaign on behalf of the Arab Sunnis of Iraq. The most persuasive cleric in this regard was the Qatar-based Egyptian jurist Sheikh Yussef al-Qaradawi, who had earlier approved of Al Qaeda's use of suicide-bombers. The Sheikh, characterised as moderate by author Raymond William Baker in his overly optimistic book, was put under a partial ban by the Qatar government after this opinion, to guard itself against the protest coming from the West. But the ban was soon ignored when Qaradawi gave a *fatwa* in September 2004 authorising abduction and killing of American civilians in order to 'force the American Army to withdraw'. Qaradawi was completely wrongly perceived by Baker as a representative of the *wassatiyya* school among the *salafists*. He called him the greatest living Muslim jurist of the twentieth century because his one daughter was a PhD scholar and working in the United States and his other daughters were studying for their doctorates.[28] After Qaradawi, another 'jurist' representing Al Qaeda in the United Kingdom, Abu Qatada—now in a London prison—too approved of Zarqawi's decision to spread chaos in Iraq by attacking 'America together with its collaborators'. Another statement by Zarqawi in October 2004 seems to confirm that Al Qaeda had finally yielded and approved of his strategy.

Maqdisi was in jail in Jordan when Zarqawi obtained the acceptance of Al Qaeda and renamed his organisation as Al Qaeda of Mesopotamia. He was greatly upset over the new strategy of using suicide bombers to kill people other than the Americans. He wrote two tracts as his reaction, *Al Zarqawi Advice and Support* and *An Appraisal of the Fruits of Jihad* (July 2004) criticising Zarqawi's action in Iraq. Seeing the rift, the Jordanian authorities released him in December 2004 in the hope of causing a rift in the movement. Maqdisi sent a taped message to Al Jazeera saying,

> My project is not to blow up a bar, my project is not to blow up a cinema, my project is not to kill an officer who has tortured me.... My project is to bring back to the Islamic Nation its glories and to establish the Islamic state that provides refuge to every Muslim, and this is a grand and large project that does not come by small vengeful acts. It requires the education of a Muslim generation, it requires long-term planning, it requires the participation of all the learned men and sons of this Islamic Nation, and since I do not have the resources for this project then I will not implicate my brothers...in a small material act that is wished for by the enemies of our nation to throw our youths behind prison bars....[29]

Maqdisi warned against indiscriminate suicide-bombing and against killing the Shia. Zarqawi, now a leader many people saw well set to supersede Osama bin Laden himself, thought it was time to respond to his old mentor at the same level of polemics. He shot back a tract titled *The Grandchildren of Ibn Alqema*[30] *have Returned* in which he railed against the Shia and called them reprobates and held that even if the Shia were not infidels they could be killed if they came in the way of his war against the Americans. Maqdisi stated in response on Al Jazeera that on the question of the Shias he agreed with Ibn Taymiyya in not declaring Shia laypeople as unbelievers, and that 'as [Ibn Taymiyya] says in his *fatwa* under the section of fighting the rebels that one should not equate [the Shia] with the Jews and the Christians as to how they are to be fought'. Maqdisi warned that taking the campaign against the Shia even further would lead to *fitna*, or upheaval, among the Muslims and would deflect energy and attention from fighting the enemy. He said expansion of the field of killing Shias and sanctioning the spilling of their blood was due to a *fatwa* that emerged during the Iraq–Iran War from the Sunni clerics as they defended Saddam Hussein in order to justify his war against Iran. There was no justification, according to Maqdisi, in targeting the mosques and holy places of the Shia, since 'the laypeople of the Shia are like the laypeople of the Sunna, I don't say 100 per cent, but some of these laypeople only know how to pray and fast and do not know the details of [the Shia] sect'.[31]

Zarqawi was cut to the quick and hit back with a vengeance. His repartee was carried by all the jihadi websites. Nibras Kazimi noted:

> Although maintaining a respectful tone towards his former tutor, he comes back to say that Maqdisi is essentially a relic of the past, and that Zarqawi is now 'a soldier of Osama bin Laden'. He hints that Maqdisi is being used as a tool by the enemies of Islam who are 'waging the largest crusader campaign of our times'. Feigning hurt and bewilderment, Zarqawi says that it is now clear to him after viewing the interview, and from the earlier letters, that the matter is beyond being a lapse of judgement on the part of his former 'friend'. Zarqawi goes on to say that Maqdisi was but one of several early influences on his thinking. He said that he never sought to emulate a teacher and if that had been his goal, he would have found someone more learned than Maqdisi.[32]

The Jordanian authorities, who had thought the rift would weaken Al Qaeda, now saw Zarqawi emerging as the leader of jihad, reinvigorating Al Qaeda with a new agenda. They quickly put Maqdisi back in jail.

ZARQAWI APOSTATISES THE SHIA AND IRAN

Two months before his death on 7 June 2006, Zarqawi recorded a four-hour interview that brought out in full his sectarian worldview.[33] One can say that the contents of this article by him mark a crossroads in the evolution of Al Qaeda. Zarqawi consciously ignored the earlier hesitations on the part of Al-Zawahiri and

Osama bin Laden to own his anti-Shia slant on the war against America in Iraq. His 'separation' from the worldview of Al Qaeda began to take place in 2004 at the end of which he needed to ask for a re-induction into Al Qaeda on the basis of his view of the war in Iraq, which Osama bin Laden accepted. By the beginning of 2006, he was ready to launch a different kind of war in which the number one enemy was not America but the Shias of Iraq and the Shia state of Iran. It is clearly with the intent of taking the leadership role that he recorded his thoughts on the Shia creed two months before his death. If there was any hope that his death would bring Al Qaeda back on its old tracks, it was soon betrayed. His successor at the head of Al-Tawhid wal-Jihad and Al Qaeda of Mesopotamia, Abu Hamza al-Muhajir (or al-Masri) immediately posted his own anti-Shia diatribe to ensure continuity to the ideology of the deceased leader.

In an excellent timely article posted on the Hudson Institute, Washington D.C. website, Nibras Kazimi quotes Zarqawi on his new strategy for Iraq and the Sunni Arab world:

The Muslims will have no victory or superiority over the aggressive infidels such as the Jews and the Christians until there is a total annihilation of those under them such as the apostate agents headed by the *rafidha* (rejecters or the Shia)...Jerusalem was only retrieved at the hands of Salahuddin, even though Noureddin Mahmoud [Zenki] was harsher on the Crusaders than Salahuddin. It was Allah's will that victory and the liberation of Jerusalem would come at Salahuddin's hand only after he fought the 'Ubeidi *rafidha* [the Fatimids of Egypt] for several years, and totally annihilated their state and overthrew it, and from then he could focus on the Crusaders, and victory was awarded to him and he retrieved Jerusalem, which had remained captive for years under their grip because of the treachery of the *rawafidh*. This is a very important lesson that history gives us that should not be overlooked at all: we will not have victory over the original infidels [*alkuffar alasliyeen*] until we fight the apostate infidels [*alkuffar almurtaddeen*] simultaneously along with the original infidels. The Islamic conquests that occurred during the reign of the *rashideen* [the Four Righteous Caliphs] only occurred after the Arabian Peninsula was cleansed of apostates. And that is why the most hated figure among the *rafidha* is Salahuddin, and they would tolerate death rather than tolerate him.[34]

There is no doubt that Zarqawi relied on the anti-Shia literature produced in the Sunni Arab world to flesh out his approach to jihad. Just as Abdullah Azzam and Aiman al-Zawahiri were inspired by the writings of Syed Qutb, he too was provoked by the new anger permeating the Sunni polemicists after 1979. There is a touch of al-Zawahiri in Zarqawi in so far as the former broke from Azzam's view of the global rival in the West and sought his targets nearer home, against the 'collaborators of the United States'. Zarqawi's variation on the theme was that he sought the 'collaborators' rather ham-handedly among the Shia. Intellectually more gifted, Azzam was murdered; and an equally bright Maqdisi was made to languish in jail. Al Qaeda's ideological journey was finally to be contingent rather than in accordance with a well-thought out and evolved strategy. Osama bin Laden improvised in order to overcome his intellectual deficiencies. One can say that, faced with practicalities, Osama bin Laden steadily allowed the non-intellectual to triumph over the intellectual in his organisation. This downward trend was encapsulated in a letter that Zarqawi wrote to Osama and al-Zawahiri in February 2004:

> The *rafidha* (Shias) have declared a secret war against the people of Islam and they constitute the near and dangerous enemy to the Sunnis even though the Americans are also a major foe, but the danger of the *rafidha* is greater and their damage more lethal to the *umma* than the Americans.[35]

As if in answer, Iran's first vice president Parviz Davoudi said, 'When a religion is to be abused to such an extent, the so-called group, Al Qaeda, would also come forward and abuse Islam to take up terrorist actions'.[36]

At first, Osama bin Laden was reluctant to accept the merger of Al-Tawhid wal-Jihad with Al Qaeda. He did not like that in addition to targeting the Americans in Iraq, Zarqawi was killing the Shias and the Kurds. Gerges opines:

In contrast, bin Laden was not in favour of civil strife between Shiites and Sunnis, lest it distract from the confrontation against the Americans. As a militant Salafi, bin Laden undoubtedly harbours anti-Shiite prejudices, but he views Iraq as a pivotal front in his global jihad and has called on Muslim Iraqis and non-Iraqis of all ethnic and linguistic backgrounds to cooperate in opposing the pro-American order being installed in Baghdad. He has shown similar indifference to ethnic, sectarian, and ideological distinctions in issuing condemnations of Iraqis, including Sunni Arabs, who collaborate with the coalition forces.[37]

However, in December 2004, bin Laden released a videotaped statement which accepted Zarqawi's argument, saying anyone joining or collaborating with the Baghdad government set up after the 2003 invasion was fair game for Al Qaeda killers.

ENTER AL-GHARIB THE ULTRA-SECTARIAN

The author Zarqawi appears to have followed most closely in his apostatisation of the Shia is Abdullah Muhammad al-Gharib, an Egyptian scholar, whose ideas had been expressed in his book *Then Came the Turn of the Majus*.[38] But soon the name al-Gharib was challenged because no one with this name was writing anti-Shia tracts in Egypt, and the real author, a Syrian named Sheikh Mohammad Suroor Zein al-Abedin, was instead revealed as the real author. He had moved to Saudi Arabia to teach jurisprudence there, after which he had transferred to Kuwait, and then finally settled in the United Kingdom in 1984. He may have taken a pseudonym for many reasons, one of which could be his failure to agree with the content he might have been writing for Saudi Arabia for money; or he may have felt ashamed, like most Muslim scholars, of writing on the subject of the grand Islamic schism. His first move to Saudi Arabia and the second move to Kuwait clearly indicate that he feared being punished by the Syrian government for writing against Iran. In Kuwait, where the Shia form 35 per cent of the population and find themselves in a position of some influence, he must have felt insecure, which might have caused him to decide finally to go to the United Kingdom, considered the safest place in the West for Sunni extremist elements. The UK later earned the reputation of being a 'Londonistan' for Al Qaeda.

As discussed in Chapter 2, the trend towards writing anti-Shia tracts began soon after Imam Khomeini's Islamic Revolution in 1979 and Iran's efforts in the early 1980s to 'export' the Revolution—through acts of terrorism—to the Sunni Arab states in the Middle East with oppressed Shia minorities. In India, an anti-Khomeini tract was first published in 1984 by Maulana Manzur Numani with funding received from the Saudi-backed World Muslim League. Al-Gharib is supposed to have written his book 'in the late 1980s', following Manzur Numani's, which was translated in many languages and distributed across the world by Saudi embassies. After that, in 1986 the major Deobandi seminaries in Pakistan (most of them funded generously by Saudi Arabia) issued *fatwas* of apostatisation against the Shia, which were then compiled in a separate volume by Numani again and became the basis of Shia-killing in Pakistan in the years to follow.

Zarqawi's 'scholarship' on the issue of Shia apostatisation relied on other Arab authors too, mostly of recent date, with most of them writing under assumed names. One such is Mamdouh al-Harbi, whose work is available only as audio files on the Internet. Harbi attacks the Saudi Shia community's petition sent to Crown Prince Abdullah in 2003, for the restoration of the Shia to normal citizenship in return for their loyalty to the House of Saud. Harbi reacted by pointing to 'the danger posed by Saudi Arabia's Shia who are "actively breeding" through community-funded mass nuptials, and who seek to control strategic businesses such as bakeries and fish markets', and that 'the Saudi Shia are similar to the Shia all over the world with regard to their heretical doctrine, paganism and grave-worship'. He accuses the Shia of plotting 'to use financial bribes to sway the rulers as well as making gifts of Persian female agents fluent in Arabic and with force of character and intelligence, in addition to being beautiful'.[39] He uses such sources as *The Protocols of the Elders of Qom* behind 'a fifty year plan being employed by the Shia to turn Sunnis to Shiism and to take over the Persian Gulf as well as Pakistan, Turkey, Iraq and Afghanistan'. Although the level of scholarship, in the tracts Zarqawi relied on, is abysmal, they do refer to much better regarded authorities of antiquity, such as Ibn Kathir whose book, *The Beginning and the End* (*Al-bidaya wel nihaya*), describes the Shia as betrayers of Islam. Ibn Kathir (1301–1373) was born in Syria's Horan plain and allegedly studied under Ibn Taymiyya and wrote multi-volume tracts on Islamic history containing virulent attacks against Shiism.

Ibn Kathir is referred to by Imad Ali Abdul Sami Hussein, who also claimed that the Shia Fatimid Caliphs were not descended from the family of the Prophet but from a Jewish blacksmith! Another writer, Abdul Muhsin al-Rafi, goes so far as to say that the Shia of Saudi Arabia were:

> demanding their rights in order to spearhead the execution of the aforementioned plan in dismembering Saudi Arabia and bringing the Shia to power, and giving the Crusaders control of the Holy Sites as they did in Iraq, thus fulfilling the dream of the Jews. And Iran's foreign policy encompassed a Rafidhi-Russian Alliance and another Rafidhi-Hindu Alliance, directed against the Muslims of the Caucasus and Central Asia along with the Muslims of the Indian Sub-continent.[40]

AL QAEDA DESCENDS INTO SCHISM

In 2007, the decline of Al Qaeda into a schismatic organisation is owed to a number of factors. First, it remained a predominantly Arab enterprise where authority was bestowed on Arabs or half-Arabs, in the latter case based on their linguistic ability. Second, it linked up in Pakistan with jihadist militias whose hinterland seminaries were already funded by Saudi Arabia to confront the sectarian challenge of Iran. Third, Al Qaeda tolerated the sectarian violence perpetrated by its jihadist protégés in a policy of *laissez faire* which nevertheless gave protection to them when confronted with state action from Pakistan. Fourth, because Al Qaeda relied on the approbation of the religious leaders in the Islamic world, it could not oppose their schismatic leanings, since Islamic sectarianism can be avoided only through non-religious nationalism. Fifth, because of the non-intellectual nature of Al Qaeda owing to the non-cerebral charisma of Osama bin Laden who allowed ideological transition from Abdullah Azzam to al-Zawahiri and al-Maqdisi and other Hanbalite thinkers without analysis. Sixth, ingress into Al Qaeda of Arab fighters who were hostile to Iran and indoctrinated by Saudi-funded Arab literature reacting to the aggressive policy of 'export' of the Iranian Revolution since 1980. Seventh, the American invasion of Iraq and the division of Iraqi society into three sectarian and ethnic domains and the compulsion of Al Qaeda to enter Iraq and confront America there.

The first consequence of this transformation manifested itself in Pakistan where Al Qaeda completely divested itself of its earlier hesitancy to link itself with Shia-killing. Three incidents of terrorism in Karachi in 2006—the blast at the US Consulate, the Nishtar Park massacre and the murder of Allama Hassan Turabi—were all carried out by the sectarian militia, Lashkar-e-Jhangvi, and were planned in South Waziristan under the tutelage of Al Qaeda. The new combination was Lashkar-e-Jhangvi, the Waziristan city of Wana and Al Qaeda. Lashkar-e-Jhangvi was the blanket term used by the state for all manner of jihad in which all the Deobandi–Ahle Hadith militants made common cause. All the three incidents were staged through the device of suicide-bombings and were traced to Wana in Waziristan by the Pakistani investigating agencies. The bombing jacket of the boy who killed Allama Turabi was made in Darra Adam Khel at the behest of Al Qaeda, the new activity now spearheaded by Abdullah Mehsud who was released by the Americans from Guantanamo Bay in 2003.

In 2006, too, Al Qaeda clearly chose Lashkar-e-Jhangvi as its instrument, marking its own transformation. A fresh targeting of the Shia community was launched in the cities where they are found in large numbers: Lahore, Rawalpindi, Gujranwala, Multan, Khanewal, Layya, Bhakkar, Jhang, Sargodha, Rahimyar Khan,

Karachi, Dera Ismail Khan, Bannu, Kohat, Parachinar, Hangu, Hyderabad, Nawabshah, Mirpur Khas, and Quetta. During the *Ashura* of 2007, some of these cities were actually attacked, killing and injuring state functionaries who had been forewarned. A kind of sectarian war of great intensity seemed to have taken hold of cities like Gilgit, Parachinar and Bannu, marking the 'sectarianisation' of Al Qaeda.

Will the 'sectarianisation' of Al Qaeda lessen its capacity to strike at the United States and its 'allies' in Europe? The diversion of its intensity to Iran will certainly affect its original jihad but the propulsion for this diversion will come from the Muslims who accept the politics of Al Qaeda.[41] The 'diversion' will be accomplished through a paradoxical 'explanation' of the Shia movement as a collaborator of the United States, as propounded by Zarqawi. On the other hand, the targeted Shia community will continue to think of their Sunni enemies also as collaborators of the United States. This is a typical sectarian formulation and was first noted in Pakistan in 2004 and welcomed by most columnists there as an 'America-did-it' explanation of the internecine sectarian violence in the country.

Ahmad Rashid wrote in the *Sunday Telegraph* that, in 2007, Al Qaeda will 'continue to develop its original aims of trying to defeat the West, carry out regime change in the Muslim world and increase its armies of supporters worldwide, to hasten the advent of its dream of a worldwide caliphate—Muslim state—ruled by Al Qaeda'. Instead, 2007 saw an unprecedented attack inside Iranian territory from Pakistan. In the Iranian border town of Zahidan an organisation named Jandullah, known to be linked with Al Qaeda, bombed the town on February 17, which killed thirteen people, including nine Iranian Revolutionary Guard officials. The attack was followed by another incident in which four people were killed, and two kidnapped from along the Pak–Iran border. Iran protested officially to Pakistan, but predictably, the Iranians, while executing one suspect, got the crowd to chant 'Death to America', implying that Al Qaeda was now a partner of the United States.[42]

The trend of popular support for Al Qaeda among the expatriate Muslim communities in Europe will increase, but most of it will be directed at Iraq, and after the withdrawal of the United States from Iraq, it will be directed against Iran and the Shia community. It is however possible now to argue that those who go to Iraq will target both the American troops and the Shia. An analysis of Muslim opinion in Europe reveals a very high proportion of it related to Iraq and a weakening trend in concern over Afghanistan. As far as Afghanistan is concerned the European Muslim community was able to produce only Sunni objectors while the Shia stayed away. No Shia jihadist was found entering Pakistan from the Arab world or from Europe to fight the Americans in Afghanistan. This trend goes back to the period of the Afghan war against the Soviet Union when Shia and Sunni jihadi militias fought separately from separate bases. The Sunni warriors were based in Peshawar in Pakistan while the Shia alliance was based inside Iran. Al Qaeda easily presided over these Sunni warriors. The Arabs among them were generally non-sectarian although those belonging to the Hanbali-Wahhabi background were open to anti-Shia thinking. On the other hand, all the militias from Pakistan after 1996 were Deobandi-Wahhabi with a highly evolved anti-Shia position inculcated since the early 1980s by Saudi Arabia.

In Europe, Muslim reaction against the American occupation of Iraq is very intense. This is a Sunni phenomenon which has been influenced by Abu Musab al-Zarqawi to a large extent. Before he died in 2006, his ability to attract funds from Europe for his Shia-killing enterprise became also the measure of how much Al Qaeda's purely anti-American stance had become watered down. In the event, sheer numbers—that Al Qaeda killed more Shias than it killed Americans in Iraq—tell the story. 'Londonistan' was a Sunni phenomenon and continues to be so. Before Iraq forced the sectarian obligation on the Muslims in Europe they did not consciously relate it to jihad. But they certainly felt the anti-Shia thrust of the radical Islam in the United Kingdom and in some parts of Europe. On a Pakistani TV programme, meant to bring the two sects together on the day of *Ashura* (10 Muharram), most

London-based Pakistanis rang up to criticise the Shia while there was no Shia positive response in favour of the effort being made by the channel. UK-based Pakistani youths interviewed on BBC invariably expressed their anger at the American occupation of Iraq. There is hardly any doubt that the European anger was related to Iraq at the outset and did not contain any anti-Shia element in it. But after Al Qaeda's change of policy under Zarqawi, the attitude must change, and it will be made easier because of the Wahhabi-Deobandi orientation of the community.

'CREATION OF CHAOS' AND AMERICAN WITHDRAWAL

Another awkward confluence was in the offing as the Americans prepared a change of policy in 2007. An American withdrawal from the scene would change the way Al Qaeda, under Zarqawi, had been projecting the conflict. Out of the 'two adversaries' only one will be left; yet, as seen above, his position was that it was the Shia and Iran that were more dangerous as foes than the Americans. After the Americans are gone, the majority population of Iraq would face the brunt of Al Qaeda's revenge, and most of the recruits it will deploy would be Sunni Arabs. From Europe too the supply of suicide-bombers would come from Muslims of Arab extraction although mixed with a rare Pakistani whose passion has become redirected by Al Qaeda towards sectarianism.

Because of the presence of the United States in Iraq, at least three entities (Sunnis, the Shia under Muqtada al-Sadr and Abdul Aziz al-Hakim, and Iran) were compelled to postpone strategy and think only of creating chaos, simply because the Americans were under an obligation to create order. Order meant the perpetuation of American control of Iraq and of the region. Chaos meant its opposite, but it also meant inability of the other parties to control Iraq. America was thus faced by three 'spoilers' threatening discomfiture through internecine violence. The killing of one American a day had to be matched with 100 Iraqis a day to secure this chaos. Iran and Al Qaeda, presumably the final protagonists of the war after the United States has left, are both 'spoilers' and have no considered plan for creating order in Iraq. Most Muslims, including the Muslims of the United States, presume that once the American troops are withdrawn, peace and order will somehow prevail in Iraq. In the words of a CAIR (Council on American–Islamic Relations) representative in Washington D.C., if the Americans left Iraq, the Muslims would be forced to come to a peaceful consensus.[43] When Iran was asked if it could cooperate with the United States to create peace in Iraq, the answer was 'first the Americans should leave'.

Iran's policy of supporting all the contenders for power except the Sunnis—who will not accept any overtures from Tehran—is 'chaotic' in the extreme. It supports all the warlords that field their militias in Iraq and are busy collecting their 'revenues' from the various city governments and oil while being a part of the government. Its support hardly inclines the warlords to mutual adjustment as a preparation for a post-American situation in the country. Iran also supports the ayatollahs of Najaf but hardly does anything to protect their authority from being undermined by the radical Shia militias. Najaf clerics are aware of the fact that Iran disagrees with their version of non-revolutionary and quietist Shiism which rejects the central concept of *velayat-e faqih* of Iranian Shiism under Imam Khomeini. Iran and Syria have kept their links with the Kurds in the north as a part of their old policy of supporting anyone in Iraq persecuted by Saddam Hussein. (Iraqi Kurd president, Jalal Talabani, held a Syrian passport till 2006.) The Kurds will make the third side of the warlike triangle reflected in the devolved 2005 Constitution of Iraq. After the American troops leave, Turkey is bound to follow an intrusive policy towards Kurdistan, thus presenting Iran with a tough policy choice if it wants to go on supporting the Kurdish cause.

Did the United States know that the execution of Saddam Hussein in December 2006 would become a world-wide sectarian event, meaning that its moral and legal status would not be accepted unanimously by the Muslims of the world? It was assumed in the West that since Saddam had been an 'equal opportunity' killer of all the sects and ethnicities, there would be a general acceptance of his execution. In fact, strong public protests broke out in several countries around the world—including Iraq, Pakistan and India. Street celebrations were reported in Baghdad's Shia Sadr City slums and other predominantly Shia areas. Kuwait 'officially' hailed the execution as fair and just, but its increasingly radical Islamist Sunni population was silently resentful at the rulers having leaned in favour of the 35 per cent Shia population in the country. Iran called it a 'victory for the Iraqi people' but it must have been conscious of the sectarian split the death had deepened. The Hamas-led Palestinian government denounced Saddam's hanging, and Libya declared three days of official mourning.

THE HANGING OF SADDAM AND THE ISLAMIC SPLIT

In Pakistan and India, the governments condemned the hanging because of their Sunni-majority Muslim populations. In India the protest was intense and much larger than in Pakistan. The Indian government ignored the fact that the Shia of India—estimated to be equal to the Shia population of Pakistan, which is already larger than the Shia population of Iraq—did not take part in demonstrations.[44] The leftwing politicians of India showed solidarity with the protesting Muslims because of their anti-American stance, but had no realisation that they were taking sides in a sectarian issue. Outsiders saw the protests in India and Pakistan as an expression of anger against the United States. While it is true that the Shia communities in both countries have followed the Iranian line against the United States, they were unable to agree that this should be expressed by mourning the death of Saddam Hussein. In India, the longest and most intense protest took place in the state of Jammu and Kashmir because of its Muslim-majority status and because of the strong Sunni-jihadi influence there since 1989 when the anti-Shia Saudi-funded Deobandi 'freedom-fighters' came in from Pakistan. The city of Lucknow saw a very large demonstration led by Sunni clerics while the Shia, who form a sizeable part of the Muslim community in this historically Shia city, kept their reactions low-key. Some Sunni clerics openly condemned the Shia together with the United States. The death of Saddam Hussein could become a catalyst of Indian Muslims' sectarian tendency.

Because of India's secular constitution, the Sunni–Shia schism has not led to any widespread violence. Although accused of discrimination against the Muslims in general, the state is not inclined to favour either sect in their contention. Even though the Sunni clergy has been paying a lot of attention to the rising sectarian tension outside India, its writing of anti-Shia tracts has not led to violence, as in Pakistan. The reason for this is the non-existence, so far, of a strong jihadi core of militias in India, although this may change in the coming years. The biggest matter of concern is the tendency of the Indian Muslims to opt out of the political system. More and more of them have started following their religious leaders, as they shrink away from the secular political parties that engage the electorate in India. Sectarianism spreads only when the Muslims start following the clergy instead of the mainstream political parties. This is what is happening in the Middle East after the demise of Arab nationalism in the region. In Pakistan, the trend of not voting the clergy into power remains strong even after the great success of the clerical alliance MMA in the 2002 general election. In India, the religious leader has become a part of the Indian Muslims paraphernalia of withdrawal from politics. The Indian Muslim clergy had been funded by Saudi Arabia in the 1980s to produce books against Iran and Shiism, with the result that now collections of *fatwa*s exist containing edicts of apostatisation issued against the Shia by India's major Sunni seminaries.[45] Highly regarded Indian commentator on Muslim affairs, Dr Yoginder Sikand, has noted the growth of Muslim sectarianism in India:

> The All India Muslim Personal Law Board had been reduced to a conservative, largely Deobandi institution that was insensitive to the

concerns of other sects. Sectarian rivalry among the traditionalist ulama reflects a fundamental inability to come to terms with the theological 'other'. Whether it be the non-Muslim 'other' or the sectarian Muslim 'other', they are seen and defined as 'enemies' or 'deviants', threatening the faith. This also explains why the Board has been unable to solve the sectarian problem within its own ranks.[46]

THE FUTURE OF EXPATRIATE ISLAM

Jihad continues to be the passion of a section of the expatriate Muslims. It is from this community that a new sectarian Al Qaeda will draw its strength. In their hinterland, the mujahideen are produced by a complex interaction of Saudi money, *salafist* indoctrination through local hardline revivalists, and even states using non-state actors to fight their covert wars. The passion of the expatriate has its birth in the question of identity, an introversion compelled by the conditions of living in alien societies. The Muslim is differentiated from other non-Muslim expatriate communities by reason of his transnational orientation. In his own country he is habituated to feeling secure or insecure on the basis of his identification with the mythical construct of the *ummah*. This causes alienation with the nation-state that insists on a nationalism based on its self-interest. He carries abroad a dislike of his national identity and reconstructs a new identity based on the idea of the transnational *ummah*, a function not encouraged by the nation-state but easily executed out in the alien West with full citizenship rights.[47]

The 'reconstruction' of a new 'transnational' Muslim identity in the West is assisted by the policy of multiculturalism, that is, allowing 'integration' through remaining 'separate' without any obligation to imbibe Western culture. In Western Europe and the United Kingdom, the Muslims have been allowed to attain a hardline Islamic identity more in line with the influential, financially-leveraged Arab Islam than the relatively moderate Islam of South and Southeast Asia. In the case of Pakistani expatriates, some pride is experienced in becoming more distinctly Muslim than the Muslims of Pakistan. The onus of 'discovery' is then placed by the expatriate Pakistani on fellow-Muslims back home through a number of symbols, including a new style of self-grooming and dressing. The first 'discovered' identity is cast aside and a new one, 'constructed' under conditions of freedom, is embraced. The truth, however, may be that this 'construction' is under coercion from a group and may actually be a 'discovery' while growing up in an expatriate Muslim home in the West.[48]

The new 'synthetic' identity of the expatriate Muslim is puritanical and 'judgemental' of other Muslims and that tends to focus ultimately on Muslims who have been labelled heretical down the centuries. Out of the dozens of heretical communities only the Shia stand out as an emerging power in the Islamic world. The expatriate Muslim is now compelled to turn his attention to the Shia and his new identity points its animus more forcefully to the Shia and Iran than to the Judaeo–Christian stronghold of the United States. Secretly observed mosques by journalists in the United Kingdom and Canada now praise Al Qaeda and the Taliban as sectarian organisations, an aspect missed or ignored in the past.[49]

The future of expatriate Islam will depend on how the West tackles the problems of its empowerment of Muslim communities through equality of citizenship. New, stricter laws are being enacted at the cost of civil liberties to allow the state to carry out an intrusive scrutiny of the mode of life of the Muslims. Much of the intensity of the expatriate Muslim reaction springs from the individual's awareness of his rights—rights not available in indigenous Muslim societies. The success of Al Qaeda and its terrorist enterprise is integral to this civic freedom enjoyed by the expatriate Muslim communities in the West. This intensity is bound to subside under new laws at the cost of quality of life; yet the expatriate Muslim will continue to enjoy more rights than he would enjoy in a Muslim host state or in his home state. There will be a general lowering of the temperature of Muslim 'revival' because of the transformation of jihad into sectarianism through the low-level intellectual *legerdemain* offered by Zarqawi and accepted by Al Qaeda.

SECTARIANISM AFTER
AL QAEDA LEAVES PAKISTAN

A welter of analyses is coming out of the various institutions in the United States where intelligence experts are trying to interpret the actions of Al Qaeda. It is agreed on all hands that Al Qaeda is getting ready for a new offensive against Europe and the United States. This is being predicted with the understanding that Al Qaeda has actually failed to pull off a major 'action' after 9/11. The rare Pakistani journalist with access to Al Qaeda contacts in Pakistan is also reporting a greatly enhanced Al Qaeda capacity to plan and execute new terrorist acts. While some Pakistani sources report acquisition by Al Qaeda of missiles and chemical payloads that it can deliver against chosen targets, everyone is agreed on Europe being the immediate target rather than the United States, so that America is deprived of its allies across the Atlantic. It is assumed that, when targeted, Europe will generally move to the policy of distancing itself from America, ignoring the policy of stricter surveillance Europe is now applying to its expatriate Muslim communities. It is also agreed among experts that Al Qaeda's financial outreach has actually increased.

There is also an awareness of the evolution of Al Qaeda into an anti-Iran, anti-Shia organisation. It is preparing to move out of Pakistan since its target has shifted from Afghanistan to Iraq, and Iran is no longer available as a transit territory for its warriors to penetrate into Iraq and the Caucasus regions of Russia. There is also a recognition that Al Qaeda has moved closer to Saudi concerns about the rise of the Shia in the region accompanied by Iran's drive for hegemony in the Gulf. If that is the case, Al Qaeda is bound to lose some of its anti-American edge as also its involvement with the Taliban and Pakistan's jihadi organisations. If it moves out of Pakistan and Afghanistan to its new base in the Anbar province in Iraq, its training facilities will be less easily available for Pakistani terrorists. Its exit from South and North Waziristan will change the security situation in that region of Pakistan, making it possible for Islamabad to arrive at new compacts with the local centres of power there. Reports that Al Qaeda was meeting with a lot of success in its policy of seeking new bases outside Pakistan and Afghanistan may be exaggerated since the evidence in Somalia and China so far proves otherwise. But the shifting of its base from Pakistan–Afghanistan to Iraq is feasible and is quite evident. However, it is difficult to say if the desert of Anbar would be as safe for aging Osama bin Laden and Aiman al-Zawahiri as the more salubrious environment of the Pushtun tribal areas.

One important source of information from the fastness of Al Qaeda in Pakistan reports:

> Although many Arab fighters left Afghanistan and Pakistan after the US invasion of Iraq in 2003 to join hands with the Iraqi resistance, others are now following. This will further weaken the link between al-Qaeda and the Taliban after the latter's decision to strike a deal with Pakistan. When groups, parties or individuals side in any way with the state apparatus, al-Qaeda sees them as unreliable and potentially harmful to al-Qaeda's mission. This has happened with the Taliban over their deal [over raids into Afghanistan across the Durand Line] with Islamabad.[50]

Al Qaeda has also become alienated from the largest Deobandi politico-religious party in Pakistan, the JUI, whose leader has been involved in enabling the army to reach a new understanding with the Taliban.[51] Al Qaeda has similarly fallen foul of Pakistan's premier Wahhabi jihadi outfit Lashkar-e-Taiba and its leader Hafiz Said.[52]

Jihad has been a logistical achievement and Al Qaeda's terrorism has depended on Pakistan as its pivot. Osama bin Laden left his headquarters in Peshawar in the early 1990s and established himself in Sudan after pressures on the political governments in Islamabad heightened from the friendly Arab states. In Sudan he could not make much headway in his enterprise of international terrorism, and with time the Sudanese leaders became less and less determined to withstand American pressure. He returned to Afghanistan after learning that the Sudanese government was thinking of 'selling' him to the Americans. From 1996 on, Al Qaeda has operated successfully from Afghanistan, but not without a lot of logistical help from Pakistan and its jihadi militias. Most foreign terrorists passed through Pakistan's seminaries to Afghanistan to take their training, including the 19 suicide-bombers who destroyed the Trade Center towers in New York and damaged the Pentagon in Washington D.C. in 2001. Will Iraq be a good geographical point from where to strike next at the United States and Europe?

Iraq will lack many of the 'facilities' that Pakistan offered. The Pakistani people are sympathetic and the Pakistani establishment 'was' in favour of using Al Qaeda in tandem with the Taliban for achieving its strategic purposes in Afghanistan. Since Al Qaeda presided over a combination of forces committing sectarian terrorism in Pakistan—and because the Shia in Pakistan were a minority and unable to hit back—it remained safe in the training camps it had established inside Afghanistan. In Iraq it will have to locate itself in a province that is Sunni in population but around which there is a large Shia population willing to, and capable of, opposing it militarily. The Iraqi government will continue to be predominantly Shia with strong links to Iran. Al Qaeda will have as its neighbour Syria which is an ally of Iran and borders Lebanon where Hezbollah and its Shia hinterland will form a strong deterrent to Al Qaeda's Sunni warriors. Despite proximity to Jordan and Saudi Arabia, Al Qaeda in Anbar may not have the kind of favourable environment it enjoyed in Afghanistan with Pakistan's help. If the United States stays on in Iraq it will weigh in heavily on the side of the Shia. In fact, conditions may be just the opposite of what they were in Pakistan where the Saudis had financed sectarianism in the seminaries from where Al Qaeda in turn drew its recruits.

Is Iraq the magnet that draws Al Qaeda? With the weakening of Pakistani support and increasingly successful efforts by Islamabad to regain control over the tribal region where Al Qaeda is compelled to base itself, it will most likely seek to relocate. The exit of Al Qaeda from Pakistan will weaken the sectarian trend in the country. Today, in 2007, almost all the sectarian violence against the Shia is being perpetrated by Lashkar-e-Jhangvi, the only organisation left under the financial umbrella of Al Qaeda. All other outfits involved in sectarian killings on the side have either been suppressed by Islamabad or have opted out. In 2006, for the first time, Pakistan became aware that sectarianism was being driven exclusively by Al Qaeda. After the folding up of Al Qaeda camps in the tribal areas, more sectarian recruits will not be available to it in times to come. Saudi Arabia will likely divert its resources to the Anbar base and not be as deeply involved in defeating Iran in Pakistan as in the past when the Arab states were not directly threatened.

By August 2007, however, it has become clear that Al Qaeda might seek to establish its permanent base in Pakistan. This happened after its earlier plan to set up its own state in Somalia was firmly opposed by the United States and the neighbouring states of Al Qaeda. It appears that Al Qaeda's strategy in Pakistan is linked to its strategy to oust the ISAF-NATO and US forces in Afghanistan. The advantage of this strategy is that it has the popular support of the very state it is targeting. Afghanistan, once free of the protective shield of NATO, will succumb to a condominium of Al Qaeda and its ancillary Taliban, including the Pushtun tribes of Pakistan, after possibly splitting into two.[53] Such a development will make Pakistan extremely vulnerable to Al Qaeda control through the Sunni religious parties and their militias.

NOTES

1. *The Essential Rumi*, Translated from Persian by Coleman Barks with John Moyne, Penguin Books, 1995, p. 256.
2. Marshall G.S. Hodgson, *The Venture of Islam* (In Three Volumes), University of Chicago, 1974. The author explains the title of his book in the preface.
3. Melanie Phillips, *Londonistan*, Encounter Books, 2006, p. 56.
4. *Jahiliyya* means darkness in Arabic and is applied to times before Islam. Maududi in India applied it to Muslim societies living without Islamic law (Sharia) in the first half of the twentieth century. Syed Qutb in Egypt read it and gave it a violent turn by recommending that such societies be coerced through violence in modern times. In the seventeenth century, Wahhab had already applied the term to Arabian society and used violence against it.

5. Dore Gold, *Hatred's Kingdom: How Saudi Arabia Supports the New Global Terrorism*, Regnery Publishing, 2003, p. 95.

6. Rohan Gunaratna, *Inside Al Qaeda: Global Network of Terror*, Berkley Books, 2002, p. 26. The Saudi chief of intelligence Prince Turki worked closely with Osama to coordinate both the fighting and the relief efforts, while two Saudi Banks—Darul Maal al-Islami founded by Prince Turki's brother Prince Mohammad Faisal in 1981; and Dalla al-Baraka founded by King Fahd's brother-in-law in 1982—supported the anti-Soviet campaigns. These institutions allowed MAK to develop its outreach to the US through opening of offices.

7. Muntassar al-Zayyat, *The Road to Al Qaeda: The Story of Bin Laden's Right-Hand Man*; Pluto Press, 2004. An account of al-Zawahiri's career is taken from this book. Zayyat's claim that he took a PhD degree in Pakistan can't be proved, but then if the ISI wanted to favour him they could have printed a special degree from any institution. Muntassar al-Zayyat of Gama'a Islamiyya published the book in 2002 as a kind of repartee after Aiman al-Zawahiri condemned the Gama'a's decision to give up violence in the wake of the 1997 massacre of 58 Western tourists at Luxor. This was in some ways also an answer to al-Zawahiri's book *Knights under the Banner of the Prophet*, written at Tora Bora in Afghanistan in 2001, and an attempt to disclose al-Zawahiri's own deviations from views held at earlier points of time. The book is interesting in the sense that it lifts the veil from the way the Islamists in Egypt conduct themselves, the extent of their insulation from the 'free' society of Egypt (and the consequent outlandishness of their brand of Islam) and indirectly the stamp al-Zawahiri's domination of Al Qaeda left over the jihadi outfits of Pakistan.

8. Gilles Kepel, *The War for Muslim Minds: Islam and the West*, Harvard University Press, 2004, p. 85 and p. 86.

9. Peter L. Bergen, *Holy War Inc: Inside the Secret World of Osama bin Laden*, Simon & Shuster, 2001, p. 56.

10. Rohan Gunaratna, *Inside Al Qaeda*, pp. 28–29.

11. Barnett R. Rubin, *The Search for Peace in Afghanistan: From Buffer State to Failed State*, Yale University Press, 1995, p. 103.

12. Fawaz A. Gerges, *Journey of the Jihadists: Inside Muslim Militancy*, Harcourt Inc., 2006, p. 123

13. Rohan Gunaratna, 'Al Qaeda's Ideology', in *Current Trends in Islamist Ideology*, Volume One, Hudson Institute, 2005, p. 62.

14. Kathy Gannon, '*I' is for Infidel: from Holy War to Holy Terror, 18 Years inside Afghanistan*, Public Affairs, 2005, p. 78.

15. Pervez Musharraf, *In the Line of Fire: A Memoir*, Free Press, 2006, p. 261.

16. Wilson John, 'The New Face of Al Qaeda in Pakistan', *Terrorist Monitor*, 7 October 2004, in *Unmasking Terror: A Global Review of Terrorist Activities*, The Jamestown Foundation, 2006, p. 305.

17. Ibid., p. 306.

18. Suroosh Irfani, 'Pakistan's Sectarian Violence: Between the Arabist Shift and Indo-Persian Culture', in *Religious Radicalism and Security in South Asia*, Chapter 7, Asia-Pacific Center, 2004, p. 165.

19. Mariam Abou Zahab, 'Sectarian Violence in Pakistan: Local Roots and Global Connections', in *Global Terrorism: Genesis, Implications, Remedial and Counter-Measures*, Hanns Seidel Foundation and Institute of Regional Studies, 2006, p. 383.

20. Jessica Stern, *Terror in the Name of God: Why Religious Militants Kill*, Harper/Collins, 2004, p. 199.

21. Jean-Charles Brisard, *Zarqawi: The New Face of Al Qaeda*, Other Press, 2005, p. 20.

22. Ibid., p. 21.

23. Ibid., p. 33.

24. Abu Zubayda was arrested in Pakistan from Faisalabad in 2002, the home of the Wahhabi organisations and named after the late King Faisal of Saudi Arabia, after a battle with the police, in which he was wounded, before being handed over to the United States.

25. Ibid., p. 75.

26. Ibid., p. 128.

27. Yitzhak Nakash, *The Shi'is of Iraq*, Princeton, 1994, p. 285: 'Samarra is home to the shrines of Ali ibn Mohammad al Hadi, and his son Hasan al Askari, as well as the hiding site of Mohammad Al Mahdi, the tenth, eleventh and twelfth imams respectively.'

28. Raymond William Baker, *Islam without Fear*, Viva Books/Harvard, 2005. This book by a visiting scholar at Cairo's American University correctly supports the new Islamists calling themselves *wassatiyya*. The new Islamists claimed to go back to the thought of the great Egyptian Mohammad Abduh and the Iranian reformer Jamaluddin Afghani. A debate developed around this and went into the pages of *Al Ahram*. The *wassatiyya* were led by Ghazali (late) and Qaradawi. Their message was considered of moderation and anti-violence. Qaradawi thereafter became radical within the *wassatiyya* of being moderate towards Islamic societies but being anti-West at the global level.

29. Nibras Kazimi, 'A Virulent Ideology in Mutation: Zarqawi upstages Maqdisi', in *Current Trends in Islamist Ideology*, Volume 2, Hudson Institute, 2005, p. 66.

30. Nibras Kazimi, *Zarqawi's anti-Shia Legacy: Original or Borrowed?* in *Current Trends in Islamist Ideology*, Volume Four, Hudson Institute, 2006, p. 2: 'In the jihadist version of history, in 1258 the vizier Ibn Al-'Alqami—allegedly a Shia—conspired with Nassir-eddin Al-Tusi, another Shia who acted as adviser to the 'Tatar' commander Holaku, to attack Baghdad and topple the 'Abbasid Caliphate. The last caliph, Al-Musta'asim, was killed after being bundled up by the Tatars in sackcloth and trampled to death, and the city was laid to waste with hundreds of thousands of its inhabitants put to the sword or enslaved. To Zarqawi and the jihadists, America's occupation of

Baghdad in April 2003 mirrored those events many centuries ago because it also occurred through Shia collusion'.

31. Ibid., p. 67.

32. Ibid., p. 67.

33. *The Economist*, 8 June 2006.

34. Nibras Kazimi, 'Zarqawi's Anti-Shia Legacy: Original or Borrowed?', in *Current Trends in Islamist Ideology*, Volume 4, 2006, p. 53.

35. Ibid., p. 3.

36. Website Iranmania.com, quoting Iranian news agency IRNA on 25 November 2005.

37. Fawaz A. Gerges, *Journey of the Jihadists: Inside Muslim Militancy*, Harcourt Inc., 2006, p. 252.

38. The word '*majus*' (majoos) is the Arabic rendering of Magus, singular of the Biblical Magi who came from Persia to greet Jesus Christ at his birth.

39. Nibras Kazimi, p. 60.

40. Ibid., p. 63.

41. Gaith Abdul Ahad, 'The Jihad now is against the Shias, not the Americans', *The Guardian*, 13 January 2007. The reporter describes the redirection of Al Qaeda terrorism and its merger with the Sunni-Baathist reaction in Iraq.

42. *Daily Times*, 'Iran decides to wall Pak-Iran border', 2 March 2007.

43. A CAIR representative expressed this view in a discussion on C-Span TV channel on 14 December 2006.

44. Yahoo News India, 30 December 2006. 'The All India Shia Personal Law Board (AISPLB) on Saturday took a rather strong stand on the execution of former Iraq president Saddam Hussein. Terming Saddam's execution as "justified", the AISPLB added that Saddam was tried by a court of justice and punished for his heinous crimes. "Saddam should not be seen as a Muslim as he was not following true Islam," the president of AISPLB's Mumbai chapter, Sayed Mohammed Nawab, said in an official release. Nawab said that Saddam was a tyrant and many other tyrants in Islamic history were prostrated by "Saddami Muslims" who destroyed cities and killed millions of people whom they called *kafirs* (unbelievers). These people had imposed their own kind of terrorist Islam, he added. "These are the kind of Muslims behind Saddam, praising his in human acts", Nawab said'. (http://in.news.yahoo.com/061230/211/6apch.html).

45. Mohammad Manzur Numani of India wrote his first book against Iran and Imam Khomeini in 1984 titled *Irani Inqilab, Imam Khomeini aur Shiiat* (Iranian Revolution Imam Khomeini and Shiism), which was distributed all over the world by Saudi Embassies in translation. Then Numani called for edicts of apostatisation from all seminaries of India and Pakistan and printed them serially in a journal of Lucknow, India, *Al Furqan*, in 1987 and 1988. He also compiled all of them in a book issued in 1987: *Khomeini aur Shia*

kay baray mein Ulama Karam ka Mutafiqqa Faisala, (Khomeini and the Shia in the Consensual Verdict of the Ulama).

46. Yoginder Sikand, 'In Indian Islam's Belly, the Stirrings of Reform', Tehelka. com, 5 March 2005.

47. Akeel Bilgrami, 'Notes towards a Definition of Identity', in *Daedalus*, Journal of American Academy of Arts and Sciences, Fall 2006, p. 7: Bilgrami says identity is assumed in two ways, by receiving it with dislike and by receiving it with devotion.

48. Amartya Sen, *Identity and Violence: the Illusion of Destiny*, Norton, 2006. Sen pits 'discovery' of identity against 'freedom' to choose one or many identities. In his view 'discovery' is a coercive process leading to group identification and violence.

49. *The Observer*, 'Revealed: Preachers' Messages of Hate', 7 January 2007; and Tarek Fatah, 8 January 2007, through email reproducing similar reports from the *Toronto Star*, Canada.

50. Saleem Shahzad, 'Al Qaeda's Resurgence: Ready to take on the World', in Asia Time Online, 2 March 2007. Shahzad is a Pakistani journalist with a strong religious background who has emerged as a 'source' among the Pushtun contacts of Al Qaeda and has lately emerged as a leading analyst of Al Qaeda.

51. Ibid., 'Some Pakistani religious leaders have angered al-Qaeda, including the leader of the opposition in Parliament, Maulana Fazlur Rehman, who is chief of the Jamiat-i-Ulama-i-Islam, which in turn is part of a six-party religious alliance, the Muttahida Majlis-e-Amal (MMA). Rahman's closeness to the Libyan government and President Muammar Gaddafi is one reason, and al-Qaeda believes that at the behest of the Libyans, Rehman facilitated the arrest of a Libyan group that was hiding in Pakistan's North West Frontier Province, including Abu Dahda al-Barah. Mosa-i-Saiful Islam al-Khayria, a Libyan welfare organization headed by Gaddafi's son Saiful Islam, was used as a cover for the intelligence operation. The Pakistani Taliban in the North and South Waziristan tribal areas, under the influence of al-Qaeda, have already murdered the uncle of the MMA's chief minister of North West Frontier Province and sent death threats to Rehman's brother'.

52. Ibid., 'Another person to have drawn al-Qaeda's ire is Hafiz Mohammed Said. He is suspected of embezzling about US$3 million that he was given by al-Qaeda to move Arab-Afghan families to safety after the US-led invasion of Afghanistan in 2001. Abu Zubayda handed over the money to Said, and when Said did not deliver on his part of the bargain, Abu Zubayda demanded that the money be returned. Then Abu Zubayda's hideout in Faisalabad was exposed and he was arrested and delivered to the United States. Said is believed to have betrayed him'.

53. *Daily Times*, Editorial, 12 August 2007: 'If NATO is ousted from Afghanistan, Pakistan too will be overrun by a much strengthened Taliban-Al Qaeda

combine. Just as Pakistan is hinterland to the Taliban's forays into Afghanistan, Afghanistan will become hinterland to forays into Pakistan till a clerical-jihadist state is established here'.

Conclusion: Tribal Areas and Sectarian Terror in Pakistan

The holy man laughed softly and prayed aloud,
'May God cause you to change your life
in the way you know you should'.
                                                        -Rumi, *How the Unseen World Works*[1]

Terrorism in the tribal areas of Pakistan is a result of state policy. The territory was used in the covert and deniable wars against India and the Soviet Union. It was kept administratively separated from the rest of Pakistan. Because of lack of the normal outreach of the state, the region's economy gradually delinked itself from the national economy. The tribal economy, therefore, was not strictly legal. This gave rise to the tendency of accepting 'money for services' without regard to the legality of the handout. The tribal people plied smuggling as normal commerce. They even gave shelter to fugitive criminals from the settled areas of Pakistan. This last activity paved the way for the relocation of Al Qaeda inside Pakistan.

The above factors cleared the decks for the transformation of the tribal areas as a stronghold of Al Qaeda and its foreign legions. The commitment of those who served Al Qaeda was strictly contractual, on the basis of a characteristic of the tribesmen otherwise located in a society of 'low trust'. The additional important factor was the commitment of the Pakistan army to defend the state against India and the pursuit in this connection of 'strategic depth' in Afghanistan. The bringing to power of the clerical alliance Mutahidda Majlis-e-Amal (MMA) in 2002 played an important role in the consolidation of Al Qaeda in the tribal Areas.

GEOGRAPHY OF TERROR

The following brief description of the Federally Administered Tribal Areas (FATA) will suffice for the purposes of this chapter: FATA, 27,220 square kilometres in size, shares a 600 km. border with Afghanistan. With a predominantly Pashtun population of 3.17 million, according to the 1998 census, it has seven administrative agencies: Bajaur, the smallest in size, 1,290 sq km, with a population of around 595,000, the largest in FATA, borders on Afghanistan's Kunar province. Tarkani and Utmankhel are its two main tribes. Khyber Agency, 2,576 sq km in area, draws its name from the historic Khyber Pass, which links the NWFP and Afghanistan's Nangarhar province. The Afridis and the Shinwaris are the major tribes; the population is about 547,000.

Kurram Agency, 2,576 sq km in area, with a population of around 450,000 is inhabited by the Turi and Bangash tribes and borders Afghanistan's Nangarhar province in the northwest and Paktia province in the southwest. Mohmand Agency, 2,296 sq km in area, gets its name from the majority Mohmand tribe. The population is some 334,000. Bajaur Agency is to the north; the Malakand division of the NWFP to the east. Peshawar, NWFP's capital, is to the southeast and Afghanistan to the west. Orakzai, 1,538 sq km, in area, the only area in FATA that does not share a border with Afghanistan, derives its name from the majority Orakzai tribe and has a population of 225,000. Kurram Agency lies to the west, Khyber Agency to the north, Kohat district to the south and Peshawar district to the east.

South Waziristan, the largest of the agencies, 6,620 sq km in area, has a population of around 430,000. The two main Pashtun tribes are the Wazirs and Mehsuds. North Waziristan Agency and Dera Ismail Khan District are to its north and east respectively, while Balochistan is to the south and Afghanistan to the west. North Waziristan, the second largest agency, 4,707 sq km in area, has a population of about 361,000. The two main tribes are the Wazirs and Dawars. South and North Waziristan Agencies border Afghanistan's Paktika and Khost provinces.[2]

The tribal areas of Pakistan are known as '*ilaqa-ghair*' (not-included area). Since there is no way for the census officers ever to know how many people dwell in houses sealed to scrutiny by tribal laws, the figure was always a kind of 'guesstimate'. Today, the population of FATA could be more than what is officially accepted. There is free movement in and out of the region and no one can be sure about the frequent 'injections' of foreigners into the seven 'agencies' that FATA comprises.

The non-extension of the Political Parties Act into FATA is but one factor in keeping the region as a 'badland' of law and order, a kind of Bermuda Triangle of the writ of the state suited for any adventurer like Osama bin Laden armed with money and ideology to make his base there. There are draconian laws like the Frontier Crimes Regulation (FCR) that raise the hackles of anyone minimally moved by a sense of human rights. FATA is also a black hole of government revenue. Pakistan's electricity authority WAPDA has to write off its bills there and has been forced to supply free electricity to an area where it can't send its meter-checking staff.

It is true that, in 1948, the tribal jirgas of the FATA region had reached an understanding with the founder of the nation, Quaid-i-Azam Mohammed Ali Jinnah, over the retention of their 'special status'. But that did not mean that Pakistan was doomed forever to retain the region as a 'tribal museum' where no law applied. In 1947, tribal warriors had been used as 'proxy' fighters in Held Kashmir, but that policy of the state, coming to full flower in the 1980s and 1990s, was allowed to run without much long-term analysis. Today, it is the potential undoing of the state itself, as the 'irredentism' of FATA spreads into the settled areas of the NWFP.

Among the federally administered areas, the 'non-tribal' Northern Areas have the benefit of the Political Parties Act. The advent of the 'politics of the plains' has introduced a kind of pluralism there which still stands as an antidote to the state-induced sectarian conflict. Even in the Provincially Administered Tribal Areas (PATA) the functioning of political parties with their different agendas under the Constitution has allowed—as in the case of the recent ANP-dominated Swat jirga—the prevention of the terrorists of Al Qaeda from taking over directly.

FACTOR OF TALIBAN ASCENDANCY

A large part of FATA is out of Pakistan's control and the rest of it is under severe pressure. The Tehrik-e-Taliban Pakistan, presiding over an 'emirate' in South Waziristan and Bajaur, has nailed its theses of 'conditions' on the wall, well before the new government in Islamabad puts in place its mechanism of 'negotiation' with it. After a period of intense suicide-bombing well inside Pakistan which persuades the public, politicians and officialdom in favour of the Taliban/Al Qaeda jihad, there is a period of what is called 'switch-off'. When the offensive is on, people say 'it is not our war'. Cessation in suicide-bombing is equally persuasive in favour of the killers through the sensation of relief. This tactic persuades the people that it is the return to democracy in Pakistan that has stopped the terror.

The tribal areas also include the Provincially Administered Tribal Areas (PATA) with Malakand Division and its centre, Swat, under special spotlight because of the infiltration there of the Taliban. The NWFP government wanted to negotiate and capitulate to some extent by allowing the Sharia that the Taliban decreed. But each time it sat down to talk peace, the 'Taliban-plus' invaders regrouped and renewed their assault on the population. Knowing that there was not much to negotiate, the Peshawar government then began 'anticipating' what the militants would ask for. But it was never sure what the militants would be ready to 'give' in return. The warlord Fazlullah is back on the scene after a retreat in the face of the army, and would have nothing less than his hegemony re-established there.

Pakistan appears scary to outsiders because charismatic leaders like Ms Benazir Bhutto and generals like Mushtaq Beg can be killed near the capital without much willingness on Pakistan's part to analyse the phenomenon objectively. In fact, civil society in Pakistan is too busy with its own sporadic outbreaks of meaningless violence to grasp the fact that South Waziristan's warlord, Baitullah Mehsud,* was wanted by an anti-terrorism court in Rawalpindi for the assassination of Ms Bhutto. Behind Pakistan's demand for investigation of the assassination of Bhutto by the United Nations is an unspoken desire to somehow spare Al Qaeda and pin the assassination on the establishment that has ruled Pakistan for eight years by keeping the two mainstream political parties out of the country.

This is how a latest book on the subject describes the Federally Administered Tribal Areas:

> Today, seven years after 9/11, Mullah Umar and the Original Afghan Taliban Shura still live in Balochistan province. Afghan and Pakistani Taliban leaders live on further north, FATA, as do the militias Jalaluddin Haqqani and Hekmatyar. Al Qaeda has a safe haven in FATA and along with them reside a plethora of Asian and Arab terrorist groups who are now expanding their reach into Europe and the United States.[3]

INTIMIDATION AS A POLICY OF TERROR

The embedding of Al Qaeda and its foot soldiers in Pakistan may not move the Pakistani people just because it worries the world outside. But if Pakistan somehow lets the terrorists find some kind of power-sharing inside Pakistan—which is happening in some areas within the NWFP—it may be facing a crisis outside its capacity to overcome. And it is not only America and Europe which will be upset, but Pakistan's neighbours in Central Asia and neighbour towards its west, too, as happened when it was exploring 'strategic depth' in Afghanistan with the help of the Taliban. There is no running away from the 'negotiation phase', but Pakistan should know where it will end. After the negotiation phase has collapsed, Pakistan will need all the help it can get from the world outside to save itself from the brainwashed killers dynamiting schools and destroying culture.

---

* Baitullah Mehsud was killed in August 2009 when a drone hit his house in South Waziristan.

Al Qaeda's preference for killing Muslims should be understood. If it kills Americans through suicide-bombing, the Americans will not join Al Qaeda. If it kills Pakistanis through suicide-bombing, the surviving Pakistanis will become adherents of Al Qaeda. Killing Muslims becomes more useful in terms of influence and persuasion; and Islamophobia becomes a positive intra-Muslim value. Operating in non-Muslims areas of Russia, Al Qaeda's soldiers have encountered nothing but hatred. Islamophobia has two sides: in the non-Muslim world it is a prejudice that results in hatred; in the Muslim world it is actually a fear that leads to conversion.

The Islamophobia that Pakistanis feel about what was Baitullah Mehsud's emirate in South Waziristan and Bajaur persuades them to ignore the possibility that he may have killed Benazir Bhutto. According to the Federal Interior Secretary Syed Kamal Shah, the teenage bomber, Aitezaz, arrested in Dera Ismail Khan made a startling disclosure: that he was one of the five men charged by the once warlord of Waziristan, Baitullah Mehsud, to kill Benazir Bhutto on 27 December 2007, in Rawalpindi. He disclosed that the man who fired three shots at Ms Bhutto was named Bilal and it was Bilal who later triggered the vest full of explosives that he was wearing. He also named a third terrorist, Ikram, as part of the five-man team. Thus, all the three named by him conformed to the names appearing in the intercept of a phone conversation of Baitullah Mehsud already made public by the government.

No sooner was the revelation released on the TV channels than a spokesman of Baitullah Mehsud got on the phone and denied the warlord's involvement in the events. Maulvi Mohammad Umar denied his group had links with Aitezaz, and said he had not been dispatched by Mehsud to kill Ms Bhutto: 'It is just government propaganda. We have already clarified that we are not involved in the attack on Benazir'. Maulvi Umar also declared as false the army's claim that it had killed 90 of Mehsud's militants in South Waziristan: 'The army is killing innocent people in our area, and we will avenge it'.

Here is yet another revelation that sheds light on the controversy growing around Ms Bhutto's assassination. Because of the past involvement of the state intelligence agencies with the jihadi militias now carrying out executions inside Pakistan, many observers and analysts take the official vision of what happened with a pinch of salt. The CIA's 'finding' that Al Qaeda had attacked Ms Bhutto is interpreted by most analysts on the TV channels as a 'supporting' statement for President Musharraf.[4] Earlier, however, the UK and Russia had expressed more or less the same view. From the start, more credence has been given in Pakistan to the denials issued by the warlord Baitullah Mehsud than to the government's version.

Significant support to Baitullah Mehsud's denial has come from the ex-Interior Minister Mr Aftab Ahmad Khan Sherpao who told a TV channel that the CIA statement was 'unwise and before time'.[5] He said it was not right to accuse Mehsud of a deed he had not done. He, of course, spoke before the news of the arrests in D.I. Khan had reached him. Mr Sherpao was attacked twice in his hometown in Charsadda by suicide-bombers who were assumed by most people to have been sent by Baitullah Mehsud, one certainly after the Lal Masjid incident which had extracted a word of anger from Osama bin Laden himself after a long period of silence. His Uzbek lieutenant hiding in South Waziristan, Tahir Yuldashev, had repeated bin Laden's threat when he declared that Sharia would be imposed on Pakistan and the deaths of Lal Masjid avenged.

It appears that outside Pakistan more and more people are becoming convinced about the complicity of Al Qaeda in the assassination of Ms Bhutto. Although an investigation into her death was done by the UN through a Security Council resolution, the result of the investigation was inconclusive.

FATA THE 'LOST TERRITORY'

The state of Pakistan 'perhaps' finally reacted to the loss of its territory to Al Qaeda with the military operation launched in Khyber Agency on 28 June 2008. One says 'perhaps' because the 'political enclave' may decide to 'break away' and renege on the commitment made to the army that it will stand behind the operation. In 2007, when the army got involved in the Lal Masjid Operation the political party in power got divided over it, and Al Qaeda was able to isolate the commando group involved in storming the mosque in Islamabad and subject it a suicide-bomber attack with no one in Pakistan mourning for the martyred commandos.

The problem now facing Pakistan is that once a state tolerates the loss of its territory, getting it back is possible only with an invasion of the said territory. The 'invasion' itself then begins to entail its own consequences, one being the hostile reaction of the population now living under another 'pax'. Pakistan lost its territory to foreign invaders; now its army has to become an invader to get it back. By September 2008, however, military operations began to separate the Taliban from Al Qaeda although the civilian government had its 'Interior Adviser' Rehman Malik saying that the two bands of Taliban and Al Qaeda were actually one.[6]

The growing anti-Americanism among the media and the population outside FATA has inclined the Pakistan army to become more assertive vis-à-vis the United States and the NATO-ISAF forces in Afghanistan. The 'nationalist' upsurge appears divorced from the economic needs of the country.[7] Thus, another chapter has opened in America's war against terrorism, unless the new administration in Washington changes tack in 2009 and adopts a different policy to tackle Pakistan's growing tendency to avoid confronting Al Qaeda in FATA, especially Al Qaeda's Taliban-led activities across the Durand line in Afghanistan.

Dr Farrukh Saleem has outlined the extent of the lost territory around Peshawar:

Haji Mangal Bagh Afridi [the warlord of Khyber Agency] controls most of what is west of Peshawar. Dara Adam Khel, a mere 35 kilometres south of Peshawar, is controlled by Baitullah Mehsud's loyalists. Charsadda and Shabqadar, both less than 30 kilometres north of Peshawar, are controlled by Commander Umar Khalid, TTP's (Tehreek-e-Taliban Pakistan) leader in Mohmand Agency.[8]

Outside the Peshawar region, there is more lost territory, and the operation will not be complete unless this 'hinterland' is won back too. Dr Saleem writes: 'South Waziristan now belongs to Baitullah Mehsud. Hafiz Gul Bahadur is the Taliban supreme commander in North Waziristan...Commander Umar Khalid is the boss in Mohmand. That's some 20,000 sq km of physical Pakistan terrain'. The tribal areas are bound to get whatever is left of Pakistan into trouble with the rest of the world. Almost three 'theoretical models' of invasion have become applicable to the situation.

'Loss of territory' or 'loss of effective control' of the tribal areas lays Pakistan bare to invasion because of cross-border infiltration of Al Qaeda and its warlords into Afghanistan. There is the first aspect of 'loss of sovereignty'. J.S. Mill, whose theorising has contributed to international law, forbids invasion of a sovereign state aimed at making it internally benign. All internal change, he thought, should be 'self-determined'. But this ban becomes weak if a 'community' wants out of the sovereign system. In Pakistan's case, the lost territory is becoming home to a growing community wishing to opt out of the benign state.

A CASE FOR INTERVENTION

The next aspect is that of intervention after evidence of threat from a state to a sovereign territory outside becomes available. This evidence is being carefully gathered and saved as a part of future case-making against Pakistan. The third aspect is that of pre-emptive invasion, based on the observation that Pakistan, by reason of its loss of control, poses a future threat to the region. One is not talking here of law but of practice.

One can see a regional consensus developing against Pakistan, counting within it states like India, Iran, Afghanistan, Uzbekistan, Russia, and even friendly Turkey. Out of these, Russia will react to Chechen terrorists being trained and sent into Dagestan; Uzbekistan will react to IMU's terrorists being trained and sent to Tashkent.

China will possibly keep quiet but tacitly support a reprisal attack because of the training its Uighurs receive in Waziristan.

Paramilitary forces, whose personnel warlord Mangal Bagh used to take for ransom freely, moved on 28 June 2008 into the Khyber Agency in the neighbourhood of Peshawar and destroyed the warlord's house and made his 'hundred-thousand strong' army flee from its strong-hold. What started three years ago and swelled into a near autonomous state is finally being challenged by the state of Pakistan. It will be adjudged to be a late operation by historians and blame will be apportioned to the rulers of the day.

Warlord Mangal Bagh fled to Tirah, the high altitude valley that Pakistan was ever proud of calling a tribal no-man's land. He became the ruler of Khyber after killing those who resisted him. He got his income by imposing heavy fines on the local inhabitants for petty neglect of pieties and began recruiting his army. The syndrome that surfaced in Khyber is the same as that which appeared in South Waziristan and Swat: intimidation followed by 'empowerment' of those abandoned by the state of Pakistan as soldiers and suicide-bombers of Islam.

When his 'government' became too big for Khyber's capacity to generate revenues to pay for it, Mangal Bagh descended on Peshawar, cherry-picking rich parties in borderline Hayatabad for extortion, then threatening the rich of Peshawar into paying him big cash. The snowballing of his business of death gave him the charisma he needed. As he killed innocent people in the Agency, people owing allegiance to his 'Islamic order' increased by the day in the NWFP and in other parts of the country. He began courting the TV channels when he saw that the rest of Pakistan too was ready for the plucking.

A hundred years ago a water-carrier, Batcha Saqao, arose in Afghanistan, holding aloft the banner of Islam, and actually toppled the throne in Kabul to establish his rule there. The only difference today is that in Pakistan, 20 years of jihad, allowed by the state itself, has softened it for adventurers. The sacrifice made by Pakistan for jihad was not spiritual but political: an unwise abdication from its internal sovereignty. Jihad brought Al Qaeda to Pakistan as the generals sought 'strategic depth' in Afghanistan.

HISTORICAL ROOTS OF TRIBAL JIHAD

The warlords of the tribal areas gain sustenance from the umbrella control of Al Qaeda which can supplement the income of anyone who has exhausted his capacity to live off the retreating authority of the state and the helplessness of the citizens the state has abandoned. There are other more lethal 'losses' to consider, however. What all these Al Qaeda warlords—who call themselves the Taliban—know may not be a part of our consciousness. They know that they have conquered the minds of the rest of Pakistan and its political elite through their methods of intimidation. Ayesha Jalal traces the jihad in the tribal areas to an earlier jihad in history and feels the Taliban identifying themselves with earlier 'martyrs':

> The geographic focal point of the jihad of 1826 to 1831 [waged by Sayyid Ahmad Shaheed and Shah Ismail Shaheed] on the northwest frontier of the subcontinent corresponds to the nerve centre of the current confrontation between Islamic radicals and the West. The jihad movement directed primarily against the Sikhs was transmuted in the course of the war into a conflict pitting Muslim against Muslim. This feature of intrafaith conflict in a jihad as armed struggle has not diminished its appeal for contemporary militants, who evidence many of the same failings that undermined Sayyid Ahmad's high ideals. The martyrdom of those who fell at Balakot continues to weave its spell, making it imperative to investigate the myth in its making.[9]

In April 2008, the local Al Qaeda warlord and accused killer of Benazir Bhutto, Baitullah Mehsud of Wana, convened a conference of the Tehrik-e-Taliban Pakistan (TTP) in Orakzai Agency near the tomb of Haji Turangzai to proclaim that his emirate had come to stay. He was himself not there for fear of being killed by an American drone but his deputy representing Bajaur was there, as were warriors from all other tribal areas including Malakand in the NWFP. Haji Turangzai actually stands at the axis of change in the spirituality of the tribal areas and his war against the British Raj fits him for homage by those who are fighting the global hegemony of America and punishing with suicide-bombing such American allies as Pakistan.

Fazl Wahid Haji Sahib of Turangzai (1842–1937) carried forward the legacy of the teachings of Mujaddid Alf-e-Sani and Shah Waliullah. Turangzai is supposed to have gone to Deoband in India's Saharanpur to learn the Quran where he saw the most militant of all clerics, Maulana Mahmudul Hasan, preparing a group of pupils to go to Hejaz in Saudi Arabia. He insisted on going on *haj* with Maulana Mahmudul Hasan and seemed to have repeated the experience of Shah Waliullah himself when he came under the Wahhabi influence of Haji Imdadullah in Makkah.[10]

Baitullah Mehsud suspended all peace talks with the army in June 2008 and declared that he would attack Sindh and Punjab. The politicians cringed. They would have to decide whether to support the government in this action or hang on to the reprieve they won earlier in the year by dismissing the war in the tribal areas as 'not our war' and by focusing on the lawyers' movement where they even swore to lay down their lives for the sake of democracy in Pakistan. In a way, leaders are leaders today because they live under the 'pax' of Al Qaeda.

THE FALLING OUT WITH THE US

On the other hand, in August 2008 the US began to tire of Pakistan's acceptance of the pax of Al Qaeda in FATA and the CIA sent its first commando team into South Waziristan attacking a house in Angur Adda on 3 September 2008, killing a couple of Arab terrorists along with the 'collateral damage' of people the 'militants' were probably using as shields. This led to the great falling out between the Pakistan Army and the United States. It also sent the Pakistani politicians scurrying to the side of the GHQ to prevent being seen defending the American action whose basis was described by an American scholar:

With the United States now full swing in its 2008 presidential and congressional election campaign and Pakistan's elected government still trying to find its legs, there is a danger of drift and uncertainty at the political level.... Prior to the heliborne assault, there have been other actions blurring the issue of Pakistan's territorial sovereignty—strikes against hit-and-run fighters retreating from Afghanistan, and pre-planned Predator missile attacks attempting to kill Al Qaeda leaders where they would gather.... But the issue of putting American boots on the ground in Pakistan—a more indelible red line—needs to be dealt with very carefully and not be driven by momentary needs.... That said, the new elected leadership in Pakistan should understand that there is a limit to American commanders willingness to take lethal punishment from guerrilla forces just outside their reach and stand by helplessly. Any government which promises one thing and does another, or fiddles indecisively or cynically while American blood is being shed for the betterment of a neighbouring country, and while taking good money paid for Pakistan's assistance to boot, would do well to weigh the opportunity costs.[11]

What has followed the split between the Pakistan army on the one hand, and the NATO-ISAF command and its backers in Washington on the other, has tilted Pakistan's national politics into its familiar internecine pattern. London's International Institute for Strategic Studies (IISS) may have inadvertently fuelled the fires of antagonism with its latest annual report that says, 'Zardari's major challenge will be to gain the trust of the army and build a consensus among the political establishment against terrorism and extremism'.[12] Already the opposition politicians were carefully wording their criticism in such a way that showed the PPP ploughing a separate furrow from the army. PML(N)'s leader of the opposition in the National Assembly Chaudhry Nisar Ali Khan was gradually zeroing in on the subject.

Mr Khan said on 18 September:

The US media is reporting that some agreements between the US and the Musharraf-led government had allowed incursions into the Tribal Areas. We hope that Asif Ali Zardari would give a clear policy to cope with the situation at our borders. We demand that being the powerful civilian president, he announces to scrap such agreements.

Thinking he was drawing close to the Army line and isolating the PPP, he added:

> The statement of [US army chief] Michael Mullen that US drones would continue to launch aerial strikes is not acceptable to us. We will neither accept an air-strike nor a ground offensive inside our territory.[13]

If this was not enough politics-as-usual, Brigadier (Retd) Shaukat Qadir, who once headed a think-tank under President Musharraf, wrote:

> When COAS Gen. Kayani recently met Gen. Mullen, it seemed as if Mullen understood Pakistan's position and agreed not to permit strikes across the Durand Line. However, there is a *fairly reliable* rumour afloat that newly elected President Zardari has given carte blanche to the Bush administration to attack Pakistani territory at will.[14]

BLOWBACK FROM 'STRATEGIC DEPTH'

Pakistan's policy of permanent rivalry with India and covert war in Kashmir was framed in the defining phrase 'strategic depth' by the army high command to take care of the often-levelled charge that nuclear Pakistan lacked territorial depth while facing nuclear India in war. This 'depth' was pursued during the Afghan jihad and was actually put in practice after the birth of the Taliban in 1994 and their capture of Kabul in 1996. A covert war was followed by a covert strategy of not fighting the Taliban when their warriors and leadership escaped into Pakistan after the 2001 American air attack on Afghanistan. Bruce Riedel explains the lineaments of this policy in 2000 when President Clinton came to Pakistan asking it to help capture Al Qaeda leaders in Afghanistan:

> Clinton raised the Afghan problem directly in his meeting with Musharraf pressing him to use Pakistan's leverage over the Taliban to persuade them to stop supporting terrorism and to arrest bin Laden and bring him to justice. I was with the president and was struck by

the forcefulness of his message. Musharraf was equally direct and clear: he would do no such thing. Musharraf explained that Afghanistan was of vital interest to Pakistan. It gave Pakistan *strategic depth* in its struggle with India. With an unfriendly Afghanistan, Pakistan would have been wedged between two hostile neighbours and its army left to struggle on two fronts, which would have put it at a disadvantage against a stronger India. Therefore Pakistan had to maintain close ties with the Taliban and could not try to put pressure on them on America's behalf. Doing so would also be unwise, he noted, because Al Qaeda had the capability to cause serious unrest among Pakistan's own Pashtun tribes in the border region. Strategically, Musharraf stressed, Pakistan needed a quiet border with Afghanistan so that it could focus its resources, especially its army, on the Indian frontier.[15]

The doctrine of 'strategic depth' thus changed the nature of the Afghan exodus inside Pakistan. It also led to the strengthening of the madrassa system and inclined it to jihad, another way of claiming to share the sovereignty of the state or arrogating it. In Pakistan, the state has been leeched of its 'monopoly of violence' by the madrassa with a stranglehold on the people no matter what opinion they hold about Al Qaeda and suicide-bombing. For instance, it would be useless to poll the citizens in Islamabad when 80 madrassas hold power over them and scores more have sprung up since the state's face-off with Lal Masjid in 2007. Karachi has 3,500 madrassas housing mostly Pashtun seminarians from Afghanistan and the tribal areas (FATA) of Pakistan.

Another distortion that sets Pakistan apart is the 'lost territory' in FATA and the Provincially Administered Tribal Areas (PATA). The population living under Al Qaeda here were, at first, unsure of who they supported, but after the failure of the state to protect them, they have generally swung in favour of Al Qaeda. Whereas in the tribal areas there is no difference between Al Qaeda and Osama bin Laden, in the rest of the country bin Laden is set apart as the symbol of Islam's struggle against the US.

Al Qaeda was 'facilitated' on the basis of the agreed military 'doctrine' pronounced by General Pervez Musharraf in his address to the nation on 20 September 2001 after he had decided to join

America's global 'war against terror'. His speech was lynch-pinned to this reference to India:

> What do the Indians want? They do not have common borders with Afghanistan anywhere. It is totally isolated from Afghanistan. In my view it is so surprising that the Indians want to ensure that if and when the government in Afghanistan changes, it shall be an anti-Pakistan government…. I would like to tell India: *lay off.*

It is based on this 'foundational' speech that the policy on the war against terrorism was fashioned. It committed Pakistan to retain the 'proxy' of the Taliban acquired during Pakistan's pursuit of 'strategic depth' in Afghanistan against India. Al Qaeda came in as a part of the bargain. After the 2002 election, the MMA was brought to power to underpin this policy. When the MMA brought an Islamizing legislation call the Hasba Bill to the NWFP Assembly, it inserted in its first draft a reference to the Taliban 'guests' and replicated the idea of the moral squad that had hounded the citizens in Kabul. It is during the MMA's tenure in Balochistan and the NWFP that Al Qaeda became entrenched in Pakistan. The madrassas all over Pakistan, which became the backbone of Al Qaeda and its foot soldiers, were not—or could not be—purged.

KURRAM BURNS WITH SECTARIAN VIOLENCE

On 6 September 2008, at least 30 people were killed and 70 wounded by a teen-age suicide-bomber at the Zangli checkpost 20 km from Peshawar on the road to Kohat. Seven policemen present at the checkpost were among the killed. Peshawar is now vulnerable to the Taliban because the MMA government allowed some very important cities like Kohat, Hangu and Darra Adam Khel to be dominated by the Taliban and Al Qaeda.

Last time we went looking for the Afghan refugees in the camps in order to repatriate them, none were found there. We didn't have far to look. They are all ensconced around the road going from

Peshawar to Kohat and onwards to Hangu and Kurram Agency. These settled areas are now our strategic soft underbelly. And it is growling! Our defeat is being nurtured in the society being allowed to grow in these districts.

Pakistan is seriously mistaken if it thinks its policy of ignoring the sectarian violence in the Kurram Agency will not entail serious consequences. Its policy seems to be that of moving against the Al Qaeda–Taliban combine as it threatens and takes over the Sunni population of the tribal areas of Pakistan. If it is the Shia suffering violence, it is not supposed to be of concern in the war against terrorism. It is quite possible that the Kurram massacres are actually a good diversion for America's war in Afghanistan! The sectarian trouble in the Kurram Agency is now one and a half years old and a total of nearly 1,500 people have died so far. And the killing continues at the time of writing.

Interior Adviser Rehman Malik blundered when he served a 72-hour ultimatum to the sectarians of Kurram. That nothing happened after 72 hours tells us that Pakistan is at present not interested in addressing the sectarian aspects of the Al Qaeda–Taliban phenomenon. Because of a consistent lack of policy or because of a policy of benign neglect, the latest news is that the Shia of Kurram are being reinforced by Hazara warriors from Bamiyan in Afghanistan, a development that cannot take place without a certain decision made in Tehran.

Yet a retired Intelligence Bureau (IB) chief came on TV in September 2008 to declare that Iran was the least antagonistic state in the neighbourhood of Pakistan. The dominant view in Pakistan is that the US and India are the only enemies to tackle. The state of Pakistan remains split over the two factions of the sectarian war. The ones that kill the Shia and are aligned with Al Qaeda are the ones the state once nurtured for its own asymmetrical war projects. The Shia, always reluctant to help in the covert war, and at times nudged aside by Saudi Arabia through its 'on the take' officials, have been assigned the part of 'enemy' element.

There is also evidence that the state is unaware of the role some of its representatives are playing. It has Shias in its paramilitary forces. Every time Al Qaeda catches hold of our paramilitaries they release the Sunnis on the basis of some swap deal but behead the Shias. Names are the big give-away these days. If you have a Shia name, don't go to the tribal areas and some cities of the NWFP. As far as some sections of the state are concerned—exemplified by those who backed the clerics of the Lal Masjid in Islamabad in 2007—the Shia are the enemy and so is Iran. The Sipah-e-Sahaba that captured the Iranian diplomats in Mazar-e-Sharif in 1998 and allowed them to be exterminated is about to be revived once again in Pakistan.

Ghettoisation comes before massacre. Get the Shia bundled together in one area and then go for them. This ghettoisation is complete in Quetta, and the Shia can be targeted easily. This is happening in a number of cities in the NWFP as well, as if the Shia were being offered on a platter to the Shia-killers. Yet ghettoisation is spurred by the victim's own fear of being alone. This is happening now increasingly in D.I. Khan, a settled district of the NWFP but directly in the path of the Taliban of South Waziristan. The Shia of next door in Bhakkar are scared because they are influential in the city and can be targeted.

Kurram has half a million people, with 40 per cent Shia, the dominant community with the wherewithal to fight back, but not after the state has abandoned them. The state is not only indifferent it may be opposed to them. In the Northern Areas where the Shia are in a majority the state has clashed with them and at times let them be culled by Sunni warriors from outside. If the Northern Areas becomes a province it will be a Shia province. After Iran, Pakistan has the largest Shia population in the world.

The massacres in Kurram Agency have seen regular trickles of Shia migration. Over the years, cities like Thal, Hangu and Kohat have developed significant pockets of Shia population. All this area is also the target of the Afghan refugees who have leaked out of the Afghan refugee camps and don't plan on going home because becoming a part of the Al Qaeda fighting machine is more lucrative. They take the identity of Taliban and do a lot of Shia-killing on the side. An informally named ghetto, Shiagarh, is an obvious target, located just ten miles from Kohat going towards the city of Hangu.

This is the area where Hangu's sectarian war takes place. The Shia of Kurram Agency or Hangu travelling to Peshawar through Darra Adam Khel are intercepted by the Taliban and beheaded, while Shias at times block the Kohat–Hangu road and kidnap Sunnis to exchange for the kidnapped Shias in Darra Adam Khel. Recently, the Taliban came as far as Peshawar to put down a Shia leader, knowing that the Shia fleeing from Kurram have also landed with their friends in Peshawar. In Kohat, such notorious anti-Shia persons as an ex-MNA and lawyer who serves Al Qaeda openly in the courts of law, and was present at Lal Masjid when it fought its last battle in 2007, actually orders the administration to act against the local Shia population.

Not going to Kurram and not helping the Shia in getting food and medicine—bought by the Parachinar shopkeepers—to the besieged population of the agency, is going to cost Pakistan more than most Sunni officers in the government think. And if the state revives the many offshoots of Sipah-e-Sahaba in order to restart its war with India, then the Shia will die like flies. In a way, the Shia will be asked to be the burnt offering at the altar of a revisionist state's obsession with India. But what the state must recognise is that the Shia are too many and will not be exterminated. The state will finally have to pay for this policy dearly in the context of its regional alignments.

The sectarian cauldron is not on the boil in 2008 as it was in the years following 2001. But it can be stoked again into intense temperatures because of the presence of Al Qaeda inside the tribal areas and the unleashed power of the madrassa in Pakistan. The joining of the jihadi militias with the Taliban and Al Qaeda has rendered the fight against sectarianism complicated as well as difficult.

NOTES

1. *The Essential Rumi*, Penguin Books, 1999, p. 162.

2. International Crisis Group Working Paper, Asia Report No. 125, Working Paper, 11 December 2006.

3. Ahmed Rashid, *Descent into Chaos: How the War against Islamic Extremism is being Lost in Pakistan, Afghanistan and Central Asia*; Allen Lane, 2008, p. 401. Ahmed Rashid is fair when he says Musharraf didn't let go of his policy of backing the Taliban and through them domination of Afghanistan because he thought the Americans would cut and run soon enough, leaving Pakistan holding the bag. Rumsfeld was proving him right all the time (p. 335).

4. *New York Times*, 19 January 2008: 'The Central Intelligence Agency has concluded that the assassins of Benazir Bhutto, the former Pakistani prime minister, were directed by Baitullah Mehsud, a Pakistani militant leader in hiding, and that some of them had ties to Al Qaeda'.

5. *Daily Times*, 'New Discoveries on the Security Front', Editorial, 22 January 2008.

6. *Daily Times*, 'Al Qaeda: a three-in-one challenge', Editorial, 3 September 2008.

7. *Daily Times*, 'Careful while reacting to US policy', Editorial, 19 September 2008: 'Those who recommend that Pakistan should stop logistical support to the 70 thousand odd NATO-ISAF forces in Afghanistan—"without fuel they can't last a day"—should also know that this "reimbursable logistics and fuel supply arrangement", which has accounted for a significant fraction of the $11 billion of "military assistance" to Pakistan for the last nine years, is also needed by us to fight the real "land invasion" of foreign terrorists. Commentators who angrily suggest abandonment of the War against Terror should take a close look at the alternatives available to Pakistan in case we quit the international coalition'.

8. *The News*, 29 June 2008.

9. Ayesha Jalal, *Partisans of Allah: Jihad in South Asia*,; Sang-e-Meel Publications, 2008, p. 16.

10. Sana Haroon, *Frontier of Faith: Islam in the Indo-Afghan Borderland*; Hurst & Company, London, 2007, p. 159.

11. Rodney W. Jones, 'American boot, Pakistani soil: solution?' *The Friday Times*, 12–18 September 2008. Jones is President, Policy Architects International, Reston, VA, USA.

12. *Daily Times*, quoting IISS: 'Zardari could face threat from the army', 19 September 2008.

13. *Daily Times*, 19 September 2008.

14. *The Friday Times*, 'Fighting a Hydra', September 2008, pp. 12–18. The author also opines: 'Despite the knowledge that such operations might, in the long run, be counter-productive, the Pakistan army is compelled to

undertake high profile, visible operations, claiming exaggerated successes in the hope that this might prevent more US incursions, the consequences of which are much worse'.

15. Bruce Riedel, *The Search for Al Qaeda: Its Leadership, Ideology, and Future*, Vanguard Books, 2009, p. 73.

Bibliography

Aase, Tor H., 'The Theological Construction of Conflict: Gilgit, Northern Pakistan', in *Muslim Diversity: Local Islam in Global Diversity*, Curzon Press, 1998.

Abbas, Hassan, *Pakistan's Drift into Extremism: Allah, the Army, and America's War on Terror*, M.E. Sharpe, 2005.

Abbasi, Mahmud A., *Badshah Begum Awadh, Nawabaan Awadh aur Badshah Begum ki Mahallati Mazhabi Zindagi*, Maktaba Mahmud, (n.d.).

Addleton, Jonathan S., *Undermining the Centre: The Gulf Migration and Pakistan*, Oxford University Press, 1992.

Ahmed, Akbar S., *Islam under Siege: Living dangerously in Post-Honour World*; Polity Press, 2003.

Ajami, Fouad, *The Dream Palace of the Arabs: A Generation's Odyssey*, Vintage Books, 1998.

Ali, Saleem H., *Islamic Education Conflict and Conformity in Pakistan's Madrassahs*, Oxford University Press, 2009.

Amin, Shahid M., *Pakistan's Foreign Policy: An Appraisal*, Oxford University Press, 2004.

Appiah, Kwame A., 'The Politics of Identity', *Daedalus*, Fall 2006.

AREU Case Study Series, 'Afghans in Quetta: Settlements, Livelihoods, Support Networks, and Cross-Border Linkages', Collective for Social Science Research, Funded by the European Commission and Stichting Vluchteling, January 2006.

Aziz, Khursheed K., *Religion, Land and Politics in Pakistan: a Study of Piri-Muridi in Pakistan*, Vanguard Books, 1998.

Aziz, Khursheed K., *Religion, Land and Politics in Pakistan: A Study of Piri-Muridi*, Vanguard Books, 2002.

Baker, William, *Islam without Fear*, Viva Books/Harvard, 2005.

Barks, Coleman, *The Essential Rumi*, Translated from Persian, Penguin Books, 1995.

Baxter, Craig (ed.), *Diaries of Field Marshal Mohammad Ayub Khan 1966–1972*, Oxford University Press, 2007.

Behera, Navnita C., *Demystifying Kashmir*, Brookings Institution Press, 2006.

Bergen, Peter L., *Holy War Inc: Inside the Secret World of Osama bin Laden*, Simon & Shuster, 2001.

Bilgrami, Akeel, 'Notes towards a Definition of Identity', *Daedalus*, Fall 2006.

Bose, Sugata, *A Hundred Horizons: The Indian Ocean in the Age of Global Empire*, Harvard University Press, 2006.

Bradley, John R., *Saudi Arabia Exposed: Inside a Kingdom in Crisis*, Palgrave Macmillan, 2005.

Brisard, Jean-Charles, *Zarqawi: The New Face of Al Qaeda*, Other Press, 2005.

Cook, Michael, *Commanding Right and Forbidding Wrong in Islamic Thought*, Cambridge University Press, 1990.

Cooley, John K., *Unholy Wars: Afghanistan, America, and International Terrorism*, Pluto Press, 1999.

Corera, Gordon, *Shopping for Bombs: Nuclear Proliferation, Global Security and the Rise and Fall of the A.Q. Khan Network*, Oxford University Press, 2006.

Crossette, Barbara, 'Who Killed Zia?' *World Policy Journal*, Fall 2005.

Cummins, David, *The Wahhabi Mission and Saudi Arabia*, I.B. Tauris, 2006.

Dalrymple, William, 'Inside Madrassas', in *The New York Review of Books*, 1 December 2005.

Dar, Bashir A., *Shah Waliullah and his Political Thought*, M. Ikram Chaghatai (ed.), Sang-e-Meel Publications, 2005, pp. 19–50.

Davidson, Christopher M., *The United Arab Emirates: A Study in Survival*, Lynne Rienner Publishers, 2005.

Delong-Bas, Natana J., *Wahhabi Islam: From Revival and Reform to Global Jihad*, Oxford University Press, 2004.

Enayat, Hamid, *Modern Islamic Political Thought*, Islamic Book Trust, 2001.

Epstein, Edward, 'Who killed Zia?', *Vanity Fair*, September 1989.

Fadl, Khaled M. Abou El, *The Great Theft: Wrestling Islam from the Extremists*, Harper/San Francisco, 2005.

Fadl, Khaled M. Abou El, *The Conference of the Books: The Search for Beauty in Islam*; University Press of America, 2003.

Faridi, Maulana Nasim A., *Nadir Maktubat Shah Waliullah* (Rare Letters of Shah Waliullah), Idara Saqafat Islamiya (Institute of Islamic Culture), 1994.

Fukuyama, Francis, *America at the Crossroads: Democracy, Power, and the Neoconservative Legacy*, Yale University Press, 2006.

Gannon, Kathy, '*I*' is for Infidel: from Holy War to Holy Terror, 18 Years inside Afghanistan, Public Affairs, 2005.

Gellner, Ernest, *Post-Modernism, Reason and Religion*, Routledge, 1992.

Gerges, Fawaz A., *Journey of the Jihadists: Inside Muslim Militancy*, Harcourt Inc., 2006.

Gold, Dore, *Hatred's Kingdom: How Saudi Arabia Supports the New Global Terrorism*, Regnery Publishing, 2003.

Gunaratna, Rohan, 'Al Qaeda's Ideology', in *Current Trends in Islamist Ideology*, Vol. 1, Hudson Institute, 2005.

Gunaratna, Rohan, *Inside Al Qaeda: Global Network of Terror*, Berkley Books, 2003.

Haider, Syed A., *Islami Nazriati Konsal: Irtaqai Safar aur Karkardagi* (Council of Islamic Ideology: Evolution and Activity), Dost Publications, 2006.

Hiro, Dilip, *War without End: The Rise of Islamist Terrorism and Global Response*, Routledge, 2002.

Hodgson, Marshall G.S., *The Venture of Islam* (In Three Volumes), University of Chicago, 1974.

Hollinger, David A., 'From Identity to Solidarity', *Daedalus*, Fall 2006.

Hoodbhoy, Pervez, *Islam and Science: Coexistence and Conflict*, Zed Books, 1991.

Howard, I.K.A., *Great Shii Works: Al-Kafi of Al-Kulayni*, Al Serat Vol. 2, Mohammadi Trust of Great Britain and Northern Ireland, 1976.

Hussain, Akbar A.G., *Aga Khani Musalman kaisay*, (How can the followers of Aga Khan be Muslims?), Ismaili Namazi Committee, 1996.

International Crisis Group, Brussels, 'The State of Sectarianism in Pakistan', Asia Report No. 95, 18 April 2005.

International Crisis Group, 'Karachi's Madrasas and Violent Extremism', Report No. 130, 29 March 2007.

International Crisis Group, 'Discord in Pakistan's Northern Areas', Report No. 131, 2 April 2007.

International Crisis Group, 'The Shiite Question in Saudi Arabia', *Middle East Report* 45, 19 September 2005.

International Institute of Strategic Studies, 'Nuclear Black Markets: Pakistan, A.Q. Khan and the Rise of Proliferation Networks', 2007.

Irfani, Suroosh, 'Pakistan's Sectarian Violence: Between the Arabist Shift and Indo-Persian Culture' in *Religious Radicalism and Security in South Asia*, Robert Wirsing and Mohan Malik (eds.), Asia-Pacific Center for Security Studies, 2004.

Burke, Jason, *Al Qaeda: Casting a Shadow of Terror*, I.B. Tauris, 2003.

John, Wilson, 'The New Face of Al Qaeda in Pakistan', *Terrorist Monitor*, 7 October 2004, in *Unmasking Terror: A Global Review of Terrorist Activities*, The Jamestown Foundation, 2006.

Kaplan, Robert D., 'The Lawless Frontier', *The Atlantic*, September 2000.

Kazimi, Nibras, 'Zarqawi's anti-Shia Legacy: Original or Borrowed?' in *Current Trends in Islamist Ideology*, Vol. 4, Hudson Institute, 2006.

Kazimi, Nibras, 'A Virulent Ideology in Mutation: Zarqawi upstages Maqdisi', in *Current Trends in Islamist Ideology*, Vol. 2, Hudson Institute, 2005.

Kennedy, Hugh, *The Armies of the Caliphs: Military and Society in the Early Islamic State*, Routledge, 2001.

Kepel, Gilles, *The War for Muslim Minds: Islam and the West*, Harvard University Press, 2004.

Khan, F.M., *The History of Gilgit, Baltistan and Chitral: A Short History of Two Millennia*, Ejaz Literary Agents, 2002.

Khan, Shaharyar M., *The Begums of Bhopal: A Dynasty of Women Rulers*, I.B. Tauris, 2005.

Kumar, Krishna, *Prejudice and Pride: School Histories of the Freedom Struggle in India and Pakistan*, Viking Press, 2001.

Madelung, Wilfred, *Succession to Mohammad*, Cambridge University Press, 1996.

Manger, Leif (ed.), *Muslim Diversity: Local Islam in Global Diversity*, Curzon Press, 1998.

Marr, Phebe, 'Iraq's new Political Map', Special Report 179, United States Institute of Peace, January 2007.

McMillan, Joseph, *Saudi Arabia and Iraq: Oil, Religion and an Enduring Rivalry*, Special Report, United States Institute of Peace, January 2006.

Melville, Charles (ed.), *Safavid Persia*, I.B. Tauris, 1996.

Merchant, Liaquat H., *Jinnah: A Judicial Verdict*, East-West Publishing Company, 1990.

Mir, Amir, *The True Face of Jehadis: Inside Pakistan's Network of Terror*, Roli Books, 2006.

Mirza, Humayun, *From Plassey to Pakistan: Family History of Pakistan's First President Iskander Mirza*, University of America Press, 1999.

Mirza, Kaukab A., *The Great Imam: Muslim Scientist and Philosopher Jaafar ibn Mohammad as-Sadiq*, Translated by Kaukab Ali Mirza, Iftikhar Book Depot, 1999.

Moin, Baqer, *Khomeini: Life of the Ayatollah*, I.B. Tauris, 1999.

Mujeeb, M., *Indian Muslims*, George Allen & Unwin, 1967.

Musharraf, Pervez, *In the Line of Fire: A Memoir*, Free Press, 2006.

Muztar, A.D., 'Shah Waliullah: A Saint Scholar of India', in *Shah Waliullah, His Religious and Political Thought* (1979), M. Ikram Chaghatai (ed.), Sang-e-Meel Publications, 2005, pp. 86–163.

Nakash, Yitzhak, *The Shii of Iraq*, Princeton Paperbacks, 1995.

Nakash, Yitzhak, *Reaching for Power: The Shia in the Modern World*, Princeton University Press, 2006.

Nasr, Vali R., 'International Politics, Domestic Imperatives, and Identity Mobilisation: Sectarianism in Pakistan, 1979—1998', *Comparative Politics*, Vol. 32, No 2, January 2000.

Nasr, Vali R., *The Shia Revival*, Norton, 2006.

Nayyar, A. H. and Ahmed Salim, *The Subtle Subversion: A report on Curricula and Textbooks in Pakistan*, SDPI (Sustainable Policy Development Institute), 2003, updated 2006.

Numani, Mohammad M., *Khumaini aur Shia kay barah mein Ulama Karam ka Mutafiqqa Faisala* (Consensual Resolution of the Clerical Leaders about Khomeini and Shiism), *Al-Furqan*, 1988.

Pennell, T.L., *The Wild Tribes of the Afghan Frontier*, (1909), ABI Publishing House, 1998.

Pinault, David, *Horse of Karbala: Muslim Devotional Life in India*, Palgrave, 2001.

Phillips, Melanie, *Londonistan*, Encounter Books, 2006.

Qureshi, Hakeem A., *The 1971 Indo-Pak War: A Soldier's Narrative*, Oxford University Press, 2002.

Rabbani, Ikram, *A Comprehensive Book of Pakistan Studies*, The Caravan Book House, 1992.

Rabi, Ibrahim A. (ed.), *The Blackwell Companion to Contemporary Islamic Thought*, Blackwell Publishing, 2006.

Rahnema, Ali, *An Islamic Utopian: A Political Biography of Ali Shariati*, I.B. Tauris, 1998.

Raman, B., 'Massacres of Shias in Iraq and Pakistan: the Background', *South Asia Analysis Group*, Paper 941, 2006.

Rana, Mohammad A., *A to Z of Jihadi Organizations in Pakistan*, Mashal, 2004.

Rizvi, Saiyid A.A., *Muslim Revivalist Movements in Northern India in the Sixteenth and Seventeenth Centuries*, Agra University, 1965.

Rizvi, Saiyid A.A, *Shah Waliullah and his Times*, Ma'rifat Publishing House, 1980.

Rubin, Barnet, *The Search for Peace in Afghanistan: from Buffer State to Failed State*, Yale University Press, 1999.

Sayeed Khalid B., *Pakistan: the Formative Phase 1857–1948*, Oxford University Press, 1968.

Schimmel, Annemarie, *Islam in the Indian Subcontinent*, Leiden, 1980.

Sen, Amartya, *Identity and Violence: the Illusion of Destiny*, W.W. Norton, 2006.

Shayegan, Daryush, *Cultural Schizophrenia: Islamic Societies Confronting the West*, Saqi Books, 1992.

Sick Gary G. and Lawrence G. Potter, *The Persian Gulf and the Millennium: Essays in Politics, Economy, Security and Religion*, St Martin's Press, 1997.

Standish John F., *Persia and the Gulf: Retrospect and Prospect*, St Martin's Press, 1998.

Stern, Jessica, *Terror in the Name of God: Why Religious Militants Kill*, Harper/Collins, 2004.

Taheri, Amir, *The spirit of Allah: Khomeini and the Islamic Revolution*, Adler & Adler Publishers, 1985.

Takbeer, Karachi, *Saaniha Bahawalpur main chand A'la Fauji Afsar Mulawwis hein* (Some High-Ranking Army Officers are involved in the Bahawalpur Tragedy), 20 August 1992.

Takeyh, Ray, *Hidden Iran: Paradox and Power in the Islamic Republic*, Times Books, 2006.

Takim, Liakat A., 'From Bida to Sunna of Ali in the Shii Adhan', *Journal of American Oriental Society*, 120.2, 2002.

Tarjumanul Quran, 'The Stunt of Joint Electorates', Editorial, *Journal of Jamaat-e-Islami*, Pakistan, July 2000,

The Friday Times, Lahore, 'Is the Two-Nation Theory still alive?', 1 September 2000.

The Iraq Study Group Report: *The Way Forward—A New Approach*, Vintage Books, 2006.

Turner, Colin, *Islam without Allah? The Rise of Religious Externalism in Safavid Iran*, Curzon Press, 2000.

Vassiliev, Alexei, *The History of Saudi Arabia*, Saqi Books, 1997.

Walker, Martin, 'The Revenge of the Shia', *The Wilson Quarterly*, Autumn 2006.

Wilkinson, John C., *Arabia's Frontiers: The Story of Britain's Boundary-Drawing in the Desert*, I.B. Tauris, 1991.

Yamani, Mai, *Cradle of Islam: The Hijaz and the Quest for an Arabian Identity*, I.B. Tauris, 2004.

Zahab, Mariam A., 'The Sunni–Shia Conflict in Jhang' in *Lived Islam in South Asia*, Social Science Press, 2004.

Zaman, Mohammad Q., 'Sectarianism in Pakistan: The Radicalisation of Shi'i and Sunni Identities' *Modern Asian Studies* 32.3, Cambridge University Press, 1998.

Zaman, Mohammad Q., *The Ulama in Contemporary Islam*, Princeton University Press, 2002.

Zayyat, Muntassar al-, *The Road to Al Qaeda: The Story of Bin Laden's Right-Hand Man*; Pluto Press, 2004.

Index